CW00646769

THE *ALICE* COMPANION

Charles Lutwidge Dodgson (Lewis Carroll), unknown photographer.
Courtesy of the National Portrait Gallery, London.

The *Alice* Companion

A Guide to Lewis Carroll's *Alice* Books

Jo Elwyn Jones and J. Francis Gladstone

Foreword by Roy Porter

First published 1998 by
MACMILLAN PRESS LTD
Houndmills, Basingstoke, Hampshire RG21 6XS
and London
Companies and representatives
throughout the world

ISBN 0–333–67349–2

A catalogue record for this book is available
from the British Library.

This book is printed on paper suitable for recycling and
made from fully managed and sustained forest sources.

10 9 8 7 6 5 4 3 2 1
07 06 05 04 03 02 01 00 99 98

Printed and bound in Great Britain by
T.J. International Ltd, Padstow, Cornwall

Contents

Acknowledgements

We wish to thank in particular the Dean and Chapter of Christ Church for their assistance at Carroll's college and home and for permission to reproduce the photograph used on the cover of the book. The London Library is still a haven of the values of courtesy and thoroughness which Carroll espoused, a holding ground for much that was great about the Victorians. The interest of working there is compounded by the Carrollian logic of some of its cataloguing.

We are grateful to Alice's grand-daughter, Mary Jean St Clair, whom Alice met in Hampshire as an infant, for allowing us to use the photograph of her grandmother, Carroll's favourite child-model, used on the cover of the *Companion*. The photograph of Carroll himself is published by courtesy of the National Portrait Gallery, London.

Andrew Best and George Spence have given great help with the text. Michael Wace, doyen of Carroll editors and a lifelong publisher at Macmillan, has brought expertise and patience to some of our more idiosyncratic ideas on Carroll. Patrick Griffin, Ike Williams, James Marquand, Elwyn and William Gladstone, Tony Colwell and Felicia Kaplan have reminded us that the values of friendship and encouragement which Carroll depended on are alive and well in the age of word processors. Permission to make brief quotations from Walter de la Mare is granted by The Society of Authors as literary representatives of his estate. Permission to quote from T. S. Eliot's 'Burnt Norton' from *Four Quartets* is granted by the author's estate and Faber and Faber as publishers.

Acknowledgements for Illustrations

(Numbers refer to page numbers in The *'Alice' Companion*.)

Carroll, Lewis, *Alice's Adventures Underground*. (Zincographed plates from the original line drawings drawn for Alice Liddell by Carroll in 1864); 72, 85, 145, 182, 247 and 285.

Grandville, J. J. A Wasp from *Scènes de la vie privée et publique des animaux*, Paris, 1842; 294.

Acknowledgements

Rackham, Arthur, from Lewis Carroll's *Alice's Adventures in Wonderland*, William Heinemann, London, 1907; 127.

Rimmer, Alfred, from *Pleasant Spots Around Oxford*, Cassell, Petter and Galpin, London, 1860; 17, 78, 114, 124, 151, 172, 184, 191, 194 and 295.

Tenniel, John, from *Alice's Adventures in Wonderland*, Macmillan, London, 1865. (Tenniel's 1864–5 drawings on wood were engraved by the Dalziel Brothers from Tenniel's original drawings and electrotyped for the first edition of *Alice* authorized by Carroll); 21, 36, 77, 89, 92, 97, 112, 118, 165, 180, 183, 205, 216, 231, 241 and 263.

Tenniel, John, from *Alice Through the Looking Glass*, Macmillan, London, 1871; 27, 81, 100, 122, 133, 146, 168, 169, 170, 179, 189, 198, 209, 210, 213, 218, 223, 245, 271, 274, 277, 280 and 283.

(See also 'Illustrators* of *Alice*').

Foreword

What Lewis Carroll would have made of an *Alice* companion invites a tea-party of altercation. Indeed, how would he have reacted to a book with the name 'Gladstone' adorning the title-page, since his feelings about the Grand Old Man (see below *sub* Gladstone*) were far from charitable? Charles Lutwidge Dodgson was fiercely protective of his literary disguise, hence his later horror at the prospect of being 'outed' in a dictionary of pseudonyms. Yet he was not absolutely so. On rare occasions he did let the mask drop, and before a trusted audience (typically those young girls he loved to mesmerize with his tales as he photographed them) he was willing, for instance, to disclose that it was none other than he who was the Dodo* in the Pool of Tears.

Perhaps it was not too hard for sharp-eared and -witted contemporaries to divine that that harmless, flightless and extinct old bird was none other than Dodgson, the stammering don. And if *one* of the cast of the Alice books was indeed identified, why not all the rest of the *dramatis personae*? Ever since *Alice in Wonderland* appeared in 1865, there have been as many identity parades of his characters as there have been namings of Jack the Ripper or disclosures of the original Sherlock Holmes.

In *The Red King's Dream* (1995) – Jo Elwyn Jones and Francis Gladstone offered their own golden key* – presenting the Alice fantasies as a surrealistic metamorphosis of the already utterly absurd politics of Oxford University (which stretched, of course, to Oxonians and others far beyond the city of dreaming spires). The authors acknowledged, however, that though their code-breaker seemed to chime with Carroll's crotchets, divining the mysteries of his mind was bound to be a matter of ifs and buts. Hence it is only right and proper that the authorial duo should present, here in their *Alice* companion, copious evidence, from firm facts to the slithiest of suppositions, which might serve as skeleton keys for the reader eager to pick those cryptic works, revealing what is to be Found There.

Some *Alice* aficionados may here take umbrage, holding to the purist view that the *Alice* secrets, like all the best confidences, are best kept: if *Alice* means actually something, won't it spoil all the fun? If that is your disposition, burn this book at once, lest you, like Alice, succumb to the temptation of obeying the 'Drink Me!' label.

But would this most enigmatic of Victorians truly have wanted readers to pore over his stories without taking up the challenges he threw down in every name, logical paradox and lexical spoof in this knowing maze of nonsense? After all, the young girls he truly adored were those who got involved with his rhyming riddles and were intrigued by his jokes and anagrams, games and gadgets. Carroll did not want to be found out – hence the charade of anonymity – but he required that his admirers should at least engage with his persona. Once a child-friend ceased to be responsive to the seduction of her wits (who might blame her?), she would be dropped without further ado. In view of this, surely Carroll would savour the thought that, precisely a century after his death, indefatigable Carrollians are still labouring to penetrate the enigmatic smile of that clerical cat from Cheshire who, if he came back today, would be viewed either as a paedophile or as a potentially outstanding child-therapist.

This book prompts a broader question: would Carroll have welcomed a companion? Albeit aloof, austere and set in his ways, he unquestionably enjoyed companionship – of the right kind; afternoons rowing on the river with his muses, and even the decorous donnish exchanges punctiliously performed in Christ Church's leathery combination room. Maybe – and here perhaps lies the explanation why, after 1863, the company of the Liddell* ones was denied to him by their mother – he even sought the companionship in matrimony of one of his principal muses.

What is for sure is that, had this present *Companion* appeared before his eyes, thanks to the miracles of Carrollian reverse time-travelling, it would have become further grist for his mockery mill. In their various ways the verse of Isaac Watts and William Wordsworth, the science of Huxley* and Darwin* and the theology of High, Low and Broad Church* were delectably transmogrified into the wonderland bestiary through the looking-glass. In like manner, would not this A-to-Z guide to the maggots of his mind have been turned into provender for parody? But that, as Jo Elwyn Jones and Francis Gladstone would be the first to recognize, is part of the appeal of that man born a dodo who might so easily have ended up the hero of a college pantomime called 'The Importance of Being Edgar' (see Carroll*).

Roy Porter
Professor of History of Medicine
The Wellcome Institute for the
History of Medicine, London

Authors' Introduction

Alice has stood the test of well over a hundred years and been translated into most languages. It is hard to enter a bookshop anywhere in the world and not find a paperback copy in some edition or another. There are few more popular books. *The* Alice *Companion* is written as a companion to *Alice's Adventures in Wonderland* (1865), *Through the Looking-Glass and What Alice Found There* (1871) and the precursor and slightly shorter version of *Wonderland* which was handwritten and later published as a facsimile, *Alice's Adventures Under Ground* (1864).

No companion to *Alice* can be complete, for the books have been subject to multifarious interpretation. The amount of relevant material is compounded by the way in which the life of the author, Charles Lutwidge Dodgson (1832–98), alias Lewis Carroll, and his subject and muse, Alice Pleasance Liddell (later Hargreaves, 1852–1934) play into the text. Recent decades have seen many biographies of Carroll. Since Martin Gardner's *The Annotated Alice* (1960), there has been less textual criticism except at an academic level. We wanted to remind readers of *Alice* itself, of the sheer virtuosity of the two stories and of the way in which Carroll's and Alice's real lives played in to the jokes, whimsy and adventures of this self-confident Victorian girl. More deeply considered, the continuing impact of *Alice* has to be in the way it enables adults to comprehend the incomprehensible, arbitrary, irrational and verbally obtuse aspects of real life. The Surrealist movement is generally charted as a twentieth-century movement. Carroll was one of its precursors.

Because we felt this, we wrote *The Red King's Dream* (1995) which suggested that the vibrancy of the characters and creatures in the *Alice* stories was informed by Carroll's observations of certain great Victorians he knew and knew of. He also poked fun at some of these individuals in satirical pamphlets, and made derisory remarks about others in his private diaries. A number were known to Alice Liddell, including John Ruskin, Alfred Lord Tennyson and Henry Acland, a pioneer of public sanitation and Professor of Medicine at Oxford. Tim Farmiloe, Publishing Director at Macmillan, had enough faith in our observations to ask us to prepare this companion.

This book is arranged alphabetically. Cross-references are marked thus: Guildford*, the * denoting an article about that city. Where there might be confusion – for example does 'Child-Friends' come under 'F' or 'C'? – the letter of the alphabet where the article is to be found carries the *. Thus Child*-Friends is to be found under 'C'. What errors we have made, we regret.

Aspects of Carroll's life and writing beyond *Alice* stray into the text where we think they are revealing to *Alice*. Essentially this book does not deal with *The Hunting of the Snark*, *Sylvie and Bruno* and its companion, nor with much other poetic, satirical and mathematical writing.

Under Ground, *Wonderland* and *Looking-Glass* are shorthand for the three texts. *Alice* is shorter shorthand. 'Dodgson' is 'Carroll' throughout our text, except for two articles of a biographical nature. 'Dodgson' under 'D' has material on Carroll's family, a brief chronology of his life and some notes on how his multi-facetted personality was seen by those who met him at first hand. 'Dodgson' is also covered in what follows, a short essay on his life, which argues that it is the uniqueness of his writing that matters. Carroll, we suggest, was odd, but he was of a certain breed of Victorian Englishman. Analysis of his oddities goes only part way to an analysis of his genius. It is *Alice* that matters, tried out on various children, thought about in smoky railway carriages, painstakingly written out into the night at Croft and Christ Church.

Charles Lutwidge Dodgson, 1832–98
A Biographical Sketch

On a hot summer Sunday in July 1838, as on every other Sunday in the year, a mother and four, perhaps five, of her children would have made their way from the small and featureless country parsonage at Daresbury, to the sandstone church, where their father would celebrate matins, pray for the newly crowned Queen and preach at length while gentry and country folk alike tried to suppress their shuffling and yawns. Outside, pigeons would have cooed. The children in the curate's pew would have done their best not to fidget while their father spoke. The eldest boy, Charles, in his dark jacket and stiff collar, might have shown himself to be particularly attentive. Although the world of the industrial revolution seemed a long way off from the yew tree-shaded–church, after matins the curate might have set off, perhaps taking his son with him, a mile's journey to the canal connecting Warrington with Birmingham. Here he used to take a service for the itinerant Irish labourers who were working there. If the young Carroll did not go with his black-suited father on such an occasion, they must have taken numerous walks together around those fields.

If Carroll was a normally inquisitive child, and there is no reason to believe differently, he would have asked his father questions about the new Queen, or why blackbirds nested in particularly dense hedgerows or why buttercups reflected yellow when you held them up to your chin; about the meaning of long words like 'transubstantiation', perhaps about prime numbers and the tricks for knowing whether three was a factor of a particular number. Gradually, as Carroll grew from five to seven and eight, he developed a love for word games, railway games, conjuring tricks and toy theatres. He was expected to read the Bible a good deal and he did so, assiduously. He was expected to be kind to others, good mannered at table, to clean his nails, to say his prayers, to be aware of his sins and ask forgiveness of them, to realize that life on earth was transitory and fleeting and that, as a baptized child and a member of the Church of England, what awaited him, if he did not sin, was the privilege of life among the angels.

The family grew in number and moved to Croft in Yorkshire when Carroll was 11, a place that was both close to the railway and deep in the English countryside, although the big skies and open, arable fields of Yorkshire were very different from the oak-lined hedges of the Cheshire dairyland around Daresbury. What was exceptional about Carroll was that he retained in later life a deep nostalgia for childhood and the lyric sense that developed the landscapes of *Alice*. In the fundamentally anti-intellectual world of an English boarding school, particularly that where *Tom Brown's Schooldays* was set, Rugby School, as later at Carroll's Oxford, scholarly boys and young men like Carroll, the 'saps', were dominated by the 'bloods', the sporting boys who were generally careless about religion. The saps were dominated, bullied, sometimes beaten, but they were not generally obliterated. Slightly soft looking and walking, according to Alice Liddell, with a poker-like gait, Carroll was tall, quiet and dead-pan and never, as far as we can see, without friends. Christ Church, when Carroll was an undergraduate in the 1850s, turned out many, many young clergy, and Carroll's religious – perhaps sanctimonious – posture made him as much part of a mainstream group of men as those who stopped in Oxford only to dally on the route to running their country estates.

After graduating brilliantly, Carroll was honoured with tenure by his college in the form of a Studentship. As a teacher he may have been something of a stuttering mouse faced with fat cat undergraduates who mocked him. No one knows quite what went on in his small classes and tutorials, but the universities and schools of England were full of gentle, scholarly teacher-types with little grasp of how to convey interest in their subject or how to discipline undergraduates. If a tutorial was rough, there was the leather-padded comfort of the Senior Common Room to retire to and Carroll there found a number of friends who shared his pleasure in gently mocking – the obscurity of the language was half the pleasure – the new, Liberal Dean of the college. Christ Church dons seem to have taken equally seriously questions of Cathedral procedure, Common Room food, the letters columns of *The Times*, the conversion of certain clergy to Rome and the cost of train tickets to the Lake District.

These dons were almost all ordained. They were provided with servants. They grumbled, sometimes inwardly, and they accepted that many of their kind had specific scholarly interests and were often silent. They were men whose life was centred on islands of their minds and who would just occasionally break out of monastic silences with the strangest of jokes. They were not rich but they considered themselves gentlemen and they were sensitive to social propriety. They walked a lot, read a lot, attended many services in church, cathedral and chapel. They cultivated friendship unless they were the very remote kind of don.

That Carroll's mother died one day before his nineteenth birthday was quite normal for a Victorian; that his father died at the age of 68 – he was as old as the century – leaving Carroll to organize a house for all the sisters was also quite normal. Other dons had this kind of background; other dons had wayward brothers, like Carroll's brother Wilfred. Other dons had spinster sisters who were a bit of an embarrassment if they came to visit Oxford. Other bachelor dons were taken on by families, as Carroll appeared to be by the Liddells* and the Aclands,* and as he was by the MacDonalds,* the Terrys* and, later, the Cecils* to amuse their children. It was all quite normal.

Where Carroll took this further was the particular way in which he latched on to Alice Liddell. She responded. He made her an icon, first in child photographs that are far more than mere recordings of a particular Victorian child, for they express something universal about the magic of childhood; then in the two *Alice* books. Here he expressed in its most eloquent form the view that he must have shared with his father but never quite expressed before, that the adult world was strange, arbitrary, irrational, conceited, full of half meanings or transparent meanings, a view that the world was askew and full of the oddest people. This true but original view found fullest expression in his *Alice* stories.

Alice Liddell was clearly an exceptional child; lithe, nimble in conversation, adept as a model, able to enjoy Carroll's complex jokes and able fully to reciprocate a relationship with an uncle-like figure. *Alice*, which she inspired, was much more exceptional and, once published, Carroll's sense developed that he – most charming of men when he chose to be so, devoted friend, meticulous present-giver and rememberer of birthdays – should now begin to isolate himself. He developed a reputation for crustiness and his fame made him a curiosity. He became self-conscious about it. Yet, in many ways, *Alice* did not change him. Carroll always remained a don who wrote. He could have gone on doing *Alices*, but he chose not to imitate his success, and to strike out in other directions, each of which he considered entirely original. As a don he could eventually afford to give up teaching but he remained a member of Christ Church, his behaviour coloured by its customs. As he grew silver-haired and slightly stooped he was increasingly seen as old-fashioned, snobbish and standoffish where Liberals were concerned; fastidious about matters of religious observance. When he was not being cold he could still be very funny in a gentle way.

Carroll's type of English bachelor became less common after 1871 when dons were allowed to marry. Still the breed, although it became rare, continued. Such true bachelors inhabited the common rooms of the universities, certainly until the 1950s. They could also be found in the classical and mathematical departments of public schools, perhaps in the sub-editing offices of *The Times*, in certain publishing houses, and certainly in the Church. It is fashionable in a period when such bachelors as Carroll seem no longer to exist, to speculate, even assume, that there was always some underlying lewdness in the personalities of such men. Possibly that is so, and certainly Carroll's fascination for little girls is cause for continued scrutiny.

What should not be forgotten are their virtues, their fastidious sense of intellectual truth, their sense of humour, their love of word-games, nonsense and crossword puzzles, and the value they placed on platonic friendship, particularly friendship based on what E. M. Forster (1879–1970) called 'true chivalry', where generations can show affection for each other, with humanity and without sex.

Acland, Dr (later Sir) Henry Wentworth (1815–1900) Acland was
Professor of Medicine at Oxford and the Liddells' family doctor. He and his
wife were close friends of Alice's father, H. G. Liddell,* and Acland looked
after Alice when she was ill.

The Aclands were urbane and well-connected. It was through them that
Carroll met the sculptor, Alexander Munro (1825–71). In turn, Munro
invited him to London,* so broadening his contacts in the world of publishers,
literary figures and illustrators. The Aclands did not always accede to Carroll's
desire for new social contacts, however. Mrs Acland turned him down flat
when he asked her for an introduction to the Duchess of Marlborough, whose
children he hoped to photograph. Before he became established in London
circles, Carroll visited the Aclands, although irregularly.

Mavis Batey, who has written about Carroll in Oxford* and who has lived
at Christ Church,* has argued that Carroll first told sections of *Wonderland*
to the Acland children, notably the episode of the Mad Tea-Party*, which
he did not tell to Alice Liddell and her sisters.

Acland's crucial contribution to the University of Oxford* was in proposing
and fighting for the modern, glass-roofed Natural History Museum,* a new
university centre for science* teaching. Carroll opposed it on grounds of cost.

Acland, with his wife working as a nurse, performed pioneering work by
feeding cholera victims during the dreadful outbreaks at Oxford in 1854. We
take the view that the figure of the White Rabbit* in *Wonderland* is partly
inspired by Acland, bewhiskered, often running late, smartly dressed and
delving down into the depths of his laboratory. Both Acland and Liddell were

concerned with going *Under Ground* – the original title of *Wonderland* – to inspect the leaking sewers which, they were rightly convinced, were contaminating drinking water and were the cause of cholera in the slums around the University Press. No social reformer, Carroll had that particular Christian/ Victorian/Conservative view that the lot of the masses was to do with God's arrangement of society. In 1864 he wrote the *Examination Statute*, a satire (see Alphabet Poems*) about Oxford figures, in which 'A is for Acland, who'd physic the masses ...'

On another occasion, Acland asked Carroll to photograph the skeleton of a tunny fish which he had donated to the Museum. The tunny fish had been brought back from Madeira when Acland took Alice's father there to cure the bronchial illness which threatened to kill him. Alongside the tunny fish – it is still there – Acland and Liddell composed a long Latin inscription about its history. Carroll, with justification, for the inscription is pompous, composed an alternative which was circulated in Oxford. In this it is not the tuna which is huge and over-blown, but Acland and Liddell.

Acrostic   An acrostic is a poem or puzzle in which the first letter of each line, read downwards, spells out a phrase, name or sentence, in this case Alice Liddell's full name.

> **A** boat, beneath a sunny sky,
> **L**ingering onward dreamily
> **I**n an evening of July—
>
> **C**hildren three that nestle near,
> **E**ager eye and willing ear,
> **P**leased a simple tale to hear
>
> **L**ong has paled that sunny sky:
> **E**choes fade and memories die:
> **A**utumn frosts have slain July.
>
> **S**till she haunts me, phantomwise,
> **A**lice moving under skies
> **N**ever seen by waking eyes.
>
> **C**hildren yet, the tale to hear,
> **E**ager eye and willing ear,
> **L**ovingly shall nestle near.

In a Wonderland they lie,
Dreaming as the days go by,
Dreaming as the summers die:

Ever drifting down the stream—
Lingering in the golden gleam—
Life, what is it but a dream?

This sentimental acrostic poem about Alice was added to the otherwise unsentimental *Looking-Glass*. Carroll also composed, sometimes when sleeplessness troubled him, double acrostics, the last – or the middle – letter of each line of verse composing a word as well. Carroll enticed and charmed his 'child-friends'*, often when he was trying to make their acquaintance, by writing letters to them containing acrostic verses. (See also Games.*)

After-time   When Carroll had reached the end of *Under Ground*, he added a note about the future, in his view the 'after-time', after Alice had woken up. His musing suggests that he was confident about the durability of his tale.

> Then she thought, (in a dream within a dream, as it were,) how this same little Alice would, in the after-time, be herself a grown woman: and how she would keep, through her riper years, the simple and loving heart of her childhood: and how she would gather around her other little children, and make *their* eyes bright and eager with many a wonderful tale, perhaps even with these very adventures of the little Alice of long-ago...

Age, Alice's   The real Alice and the fictional Alice were of rather different ages. In *Looking-Glass* Alice was seven and a half. She told the White Queen she was seven and a half 'exactly', which the White Queen mispronounced 'exactually'. Because the *Looking-Glass* is supposed to happen on 4 November, the night before Guy Fawkes' bonfires are lit in Britain; and because Alice's birthday was 4 May, that would set the second story on 4 November 1859. Martin Gardner* surmised that Alice was seven in *Wonderland*. That is something of a leap of faith as the only evidence of dates in the book is that the Mad Tea-Party* took place on 4 May. No year is given. However, seven was the age at which most children began to fully appreciate Carroll's puzzles and stories.

In reality Alice Liddell* was about seven when the fragments of the stories were first told to her and her sisters on walks, river trips and during photographic sessions. She was ten when Carroll told the story in full on a July river expedition and was urged – by Alice herself, she says – to write it down. She was 12 when the handwritten and hand-illustrated *Under Ground* (see *Alice's Adventures Under Ground**) was presented to her by Carroll. She was 13 when this was published in an expanded form as *Wonderland* at the end of 1865. She was 19 at the time of the publication of *Looking-Glass*.

Later Carroll realized that *Alice* was too sophisticated for small children and so produced the simpler *Nursery Alice* in 1890. He gradually came to realize that the appeal of his stories was wide and he wrote in the foreword to the *Nursery Alice* that the stories could actually be enjoyed:

> ...by Children, aged from Fifteen to Twenty-five: yet again by Children, aged from Twenty-five to Thirty-five: and even by ... Children of a 'certain' age, whose tale of years must be left untold, and buried in respectful silence.

Aged Aged Man, The   This was the hero of the poem that the White Knight* recited to Alice after he fell head first off his horse. This, he claimed, improved his ability to make inventions.

> "Is it very long?" Alice asked, for she had heard a good deal of poetry that day.
> "It's long," said the Knight, "but it's very, *very* beautiful. Everybody that hears me sing it—either it brings the *tears* into their eyes, or else—"
> "Or else what?" said Alice, for the Knight had made a sudden pause.

Or else it doesn't, explained the Knight. Well, it did not. There was nothing moving about the Aged Man's behaviour. He claimed he hunted for haddocks' eyes and dug for buttered rolls and sounded like a cadging old countryman...

> Whose hair was whiter than the snow,
> Whose face was very like a crow ...

Carroll developed the poem from a spoof he had written when he was 24 for the comic magazine, *The Train*. Martin Gardner* has traced it to a parody – 'travesty' was the word he used – by Carroll of William Wordsworth's aged leech-gatherer in *Resolution and Independence*. And, just as the aged man changed the title of the poem he said he was going to recite four times from *Haddocks' Eyes* to *Ways And Means* to *A-sitting On A Gate* to *The Aged Aged Man*, so Gardner showed that Carroll poked fun in this poem at a grown up love song by the Irish poet, Thomas Moore, entitled *My Heart and Lute*. The words of the song were about grown up love, and these Alice did not understand. On occasion Carroll signed letters to child*-friends as being from 'an aged aged' man.

A third source for Carroll's parody – for the White Knight's song is clearly no love song – may be the intricate inventions* described in prose in

Samuel Smiles'* best-selling *Lives of the Engineers* (1861–2). The Knight's last verse broke away from a formal line-length of 8 lines for each verse, and ended in a frantic 19-line crescendo. When the effect had subsided, the White Knight revealed to Alice that she was about to become Queen. (See also Tennyson.*)

Albums, Carroll's Photographic Albums, generally small in size, were the form in which Carroll collected most of his own and other people's photographs. Alas, at the auction at Oxford of his chattels after his death, 33 albums were sold and dispersed, his relatives failing to consider them of interest. (See Sale of Carroll's effects.*)

The albums are modest items such as would be bought from a stationer, often in imitation leather. The prints are small and sometimes roughly cropped by hand. The top edges of a number of prints have been cut to form an arch, probably by Carroll. The title of the print is usually in his handwriting or that of the sitter. There is often an index of titles as well. Photography* brought Carroll and Alice together.

Since the sale of Carroll's effects, some but not all of the albums have surfaced. In the 1930s, the American collector, Morris Parrish, had bought some Carroll albums. In 1948–9 the German emigré and pioneering historian of early photography, Helmut Gernsheim,* came across an unidentified Carroll album in London. From this time onwards, Carroll's reputation as a photographer was re-established. Since then, occasionally, albums given away by Carroll, not of the original 33, surface in British auctions. One appeared at Phillips in 1994, sold by a family who were direct descendants of Ella Bickersteth (née Monier-Williams, 1859–1954).

Important collections of Carroll's photographs, many in album form, are in the Harry Ransom Humanities Research Center in Austin, Texas (The Gernsheim Collection) and Princeton University (The Parrish Collection). Two volumes of portraits are in Christ Church, one in the National Portrait Gallery. Another album of great fascination is that given by Carroll to Alice containing views, child photographs of Alice and her sisters and a number of adults, many mutual acquaintances of Carroll's and Alice's.

Alice Pleasance Liddell, later Hargreaves (1852–1934): see Liddell, Alice.*

Alice's Adventures Under Ground   This is the first title given to what, in expanded form, became *Alice's Adventures in Wonderland* illustrated by Tenniel. Carroll and others have stated that the stories which made *Under Ground*, starting with Alice sitting on the river bank, were told on what Alice later called a 'blazing summer afternoon' and Carroll later described as a 'golden afternoon'.* This was 4 July 1862 and the bank described is clearly a reference to Port Meadow, near the little village of Godstow, upstream of Oxford (see Thames*).

The stories took a time to gestate as did the idea that Carroll should write them down. Between then and the autumn of 1864 Carroll struggled with the layout and illustrations for *Under Ground*, seeking the help of various friends, some of whom, if not all, felt that the stories merited publishing. Thus the process of developing *Wonderland* as a professional publication was already in train while *Under Ground* was still being completed for Alice Liddell.* Carroll reported finishing the illustrations at his family home at Croft* on 13 September 1864 and the vellum-bound manuscript was sent to the Deanery two and a half months later, on Saturday 26 November. There it is said to have occupied pride of place – Carroll now was out of favour – on a hall table. When Alice was married in 1880 and went to live with her husband, Reggie Hargreaves,* at Cuffnells in south Hampshire, the book went too and sat again, according to Alice's grand-daughter, Mary Jean St Clair, among the impedimenta of a country house hallway; visitors book, postal scales, riding crops and umbrellas.

Alice had been married in 1880. In 1885 (see Zincography*) Carroll borrowed the manuscript in order to make a facsimile of it for publication. It was duly returned to Alice and remained with her until after the First World War when she found her fortunes pinched. Her husband, Reggie Hargreaves, had died in 1926 and his investments had not prospered in the Depression. To offset the cost of running Cuffnells, she and her remaining son, her youngest, Caryl, decided to sell the manuscript. Sotheby's were consulted to organize the sale.

At this point a number of outraged commentators wrote to *The Times* deploring the possibility that the manuscript might leave England. An offer to buy the book on behalf of Christ Church* for £5000 was made. Alice did not budge. The Pierpont Morgan Library in New York wanted the manuscript as did several private collectors. In the manoeuvring, it was reported that the flamboyant and commercially brilliant American book dealer, A. S. W. Rosenbach (1876–1952) offered to purchase the manuscript for £10,000 before the auction and then pass it on at cost to the British Museum. He said he would also donate 200 guineas to the purchase price. However, if there was such an offer, Alice rejected it. She and her advisers took the view that the price might go higher in the glare of publicity Rosenbach had lit up. They were right. On 3 April 1928, Rosenbach acquired the manuscript for £15,400. The British Museum dropped out of the bidding at £12,500. Rosenbach took the manuscript back to America with him to offer it to the highest bidder he could find. Rosenbach's price was the highest paid to that date for a literary manuscript.

Rosenbach, in turn, sold the book for double what he paid for it to Eldridge R. Johnson, the multi-millionaire founder of Victor Talking-Machine Company which became the RCA-Victor Corporation. So attached was Johnson to this treasure that he took it around with him in a safe, even on his yacht.

Alice was present at the Sotheby's Sale. She was present, too, aged 80, when the manuscript was displayed at Columbia University (see Dream-Child*) in New York on the centennial of Carroll's birth in 1932. She died in 1934.

Eldridge Johnson died in 1944 and the manuscript came back on the market in 1948. A consortium of American bibliophiles was organized by Luther H. Evans, Librarian of Congress. This included Dr Rosenbach whose biographer said that he had by now had 'a million dollars of publicity' from the purchase. The Dodgson family had had nothing. Only one of Carroll's siblings, his sister Louisa, who never married, was alive in 1928, but Alice Jane Donkin who married his brother, Wilfred, was still alive as were eight of her nine children. So were his two Collingwood* nephews and his other sister-in-law, Isabel Mary Dodgson, wife of Skeffington, who had three living children. None of these benefited. (For Carroll's family, see Dodgson.*)

In a gesture of American solidarity, the Americans presented the manuscript to the British people in recognition of Britain's courage in facing Hitler before America came into the war. The Archbishop of Canterbury, Dr Fisher – Carroll would have been flattered by this – accepted the manuscript on behalf of the British Museum, describing the gift as 'an unsullied and innocent act in a distracted and sinful world'. The manuscript now resides in the British Library.

Aloof Lewis Carroll, faced with a brush-off from people who were both his social superiors *and* his employers, decided to remain 'aloof'. The fact was that although he felt himself the initiator of the distancing, he had no alternative. Mrs Liddell* had brushed him off for reasons that fascinate fans of Carroll, the more for remaining obscure even to Alice. Later in his life he refused all the Liddells' invitations except one; and this was to meet a Princess of the Blood, the Duchess of Albany, after dinner and at her express command.

Alphabet Poems   In 1841 the first issue of *Punch*, Carroll was then nine, included a child's alphabet, written as for the eyes of the young Queen Victoria,* beginning: 'A is for Aristocracy'. In *Examination Statute* (1864), Carroll followed suit with a satirical Oxford alphabet. He claimed that the Liberal reformers were misdirecting University funds with 'Z' for Zeal. Carroll's grievance was that the reformers were trying to protect science* students from the rigours of the Oxford classical Latin and Greek syllabus. Carroll appeared in the alphabet, not under 'D' for Dodo,* but under 'I', the first person singular pronoun, whose occupation was not mathematician but 'rhymer erratic'.

His alphabet poem was dated 2 February 4681 (i.e. 1864). It singled out 'A': for Acland,* 'J': for Jowett* and 'L': for Liddell,* all Liberals and University reformers. 'U': was University 'factiously splitting', 'X': the expenditure which had run out of control due to the need to build facilities for science. (See also Oxford University.*)

The pamphleteer had the poem printed, distributed throughout the University and posted on Common Room notice boards. Carroll cared passionately about such issues. To some of Carroll's critics, his long-outdated University squibs are only of passing interest. They are seen as stilted satires on long-forgotten issues. Another view is that the University of Oxford was pivotal in British life and that Carroll agonized over its transition towards materialism and science. The battles in which he participated appear to concern only the University. The University was seen to much of the Establishment as a litmus paper for the moral state of Britain. Carroll participated with the informed, reactionary perspective apparent in all his squibs. (See also Games* for 'Alphabet Games'.)

American Telegrams   This is a satire against Dean Liddell and the Canons of Christ Church* written and circulated by Carroll in early 1865, the year that *Wonderland* was published. Dean Liddell,* 'President of the Northerners', was accused of complicity with 'General Butler', code-name for the butler of Christ Church, who overcharged in battels (college bills). Carroll's unsigned attack on Liddell exemplified the distrust of the existing administration felt by the Senior Common Room.

The 'President' in the *Telegrams* was also accused of succumbing to 'the roar of Canons', that is, siding with the Canons in whom so much power resided, against the college tutors, who wanted better pay and conditions. Carroll and his colleague, T. J. Prout* were two who dared to stand up to this roar. Finally they called the Dean's bluff and Prout was known as 'the Man who slew the Canons'.

American Telegrams came to light in 1968 in Christ Church when the history of these internecine struggles was being prepared for a college centennial (see Bill and Mason in the Select Bibliography). We think that the same satire is visible in *Alice* in the Mouse's tale,* shown by the preoccupation of the mouse which tells the tale with the letters 'C' and 'D', for Canons and Dean. (See also Bread-and-Butter* Row.)

Anagrams   Two of Carroll's best known anagrams are from W. E. Gladstone's* name. One is 'Wilt tear down all images?', a satire on Carroll's dislike of Gladstone's church policies. His other reflected the view of a patronizing Tory: 'Wild Agitator! Means well!' We believe that there may be, within the text of *Alice*, a few cases where names and titles of books are hidden, for example '"It was the *best* butter," the March Hare meekly replied ...' when the Hatter told him that butter 'wouldn't suit the works' of the pocket watch. 'It was the best butter' contains the letters of Charles Kingsley's book title, *The Water-Babies*, except for an 'a' which must be used twice. The joke depends on the circumstantial evidence that the Hatter is a parody of Charles Kingsley.* If this is right, then the 'imperfect anagram' may not be so far-fetched.

A similar use of anagram may appear in relation to the Gryphon,* partly a parody of John Ruskin.* Carroll records the shriek of the Gryphon, which Alice remembered long after she woke from her dream, as: 'Hjckrrh!' All the letters 'Hjkr' are to be found in the names: John (Jh) and Ruskin (Rk) which leaves the letters 'Chr' unaccounted for. Ruskin's pet-name to his child-friends was 'St Chrysostom'. It meant 'St John-the-Golden-Mouthed' and children who knew it used it when they wrote to him. The first three letters of 'Chrysostom' release the consonants (Chr) into the Gryphon's cry.

Our critics find this argument strained. It may attribute to Carroll a cleverness he did not intend. However, if we are right in our contention that what gives the edge to the fantasy characters in *Alice* are human foibles based on real people whom Carroll and Alice Liddell encountered, this line of cryptographic* research should not be abandoned. (See also Jowett* for comment on more satirical word games depending on sound.)

Anatomy   Comparative anatomy was *the* subject over which mid-century natural historians argued. Most of the displays at the new Natural History Museum* in Oxford, which Alice and Carroll visited together, were arranged to demonstrate anatomical gradations in the plant and animal kingdoms. *Alice* is laced with remarks about her body changing shape, being distorted, being incorrectly put together. Comparing Alice and the Red Queen in the

Garden of Live Flowers, the Rose said of the shape of the Red Queen to Alice: "'Well, she has the same awkward shape as you ... but she's redder — and her petals are shorter, I think.'"

One of the nastiest instances of this was in the *Looking-Glass* sequence which Carroll suppressed. An old Wasp* dismissed Alice just before she became a Queen, saying that her mouth was too small, her jaws were too short and ...

> "Then your eyes—they're too much in front, no doubt. One would have done as well as two, if you *must* have them so close— ".

(See also Science.*)

Annotated Alice, The   See Gardner*, Martin.

Anonymity   Carroll assiduously courted anonymity, so Dodgson did not admit to the existence of Carroll. Most Victorians, and many in this book, were flattered to be approached by 'Spy' whose mild mannered cartoons, published in the long-running *Vanity Fair* give a satirical record of eminent Victorian and Edwardian figures. When 'Spy', Leslie Ward (1851–1922) approached Carroll to be allowed to make a cartoon of him, Carroll 'begged to be excused'. He said, 'Nothing would be more unpleasant to me than to have my face known to strangers'.

However, Carroll did reveal his identity from time to time, and could even be gallant about his pen-name to child*-friends. One of these was Mary Marshal (dates unknown), to whom he explained in April 1870, that Lewis Carroll was 'writing another book about Alice'. In the person of C. L. Dodgson,* he informed her that Lewis Carroll thanked her for the bookmark she had sent him, her gift having been addressed to 'Lewis Carroll' at Christ Church.* He stayed in the role of Dodgson to thank her, saying that Lewis Carroll 'was very unwilling to take' the present, but that C. L. Dodgson 'persuaded him to take it at last'. Having wrong-footed Carroll for being ungrateful for a gift from a child, he wrong-footed Mr Dodgson in the role of Carroll:

> Mr Carroll says I ought to have seen you safe to your journey's end, and that *he* would have behaved better if he had been in my place!

(See also Lewis Carroll* and Falconer Madan.*)

Antipodes   When Alice fell *Under Ground* – 'Down, down, down. Would the fall *never* come to an end?' – she wondered if she was heading for Australia or New Zealand. In *Wonderland* the first slip of the tongue that Alice made was to name the Antipodes 'The Antipathies'. In both this and *Under Ground* she thought she was falling through the earth and mused:

> "How funny it'll seem to come out among the people who walk with their heads downwards!"

Thinking ahead to her arrival in the Antipodes, she blamed herself for not knowing the difference between an Australian and a New Zealander:

> "Please , Ma'am, is this New Zealand or Australia?" [and continued] "... What an ignorant little girl she'll think me for asking! No, it'll never do to ask: perhaps I shall see it written up somewhere."

Two of Carroll's acquaintances did not enjoy their sojourns in Australia. One was the Pre-Raphaelite sculptor, Thomas Woolner, the other the novelist, Henry Kingsley.* Each came back, having failed to make their fortune. Their experiences may have prejudiced him, hence his antipathy for Australia.

Arithmetic   Finding herself in the hall with the glass table in *Wonderland*, Alice tried out her multiplication tables to see how alert she was after her fall. She gave herself a task that was not easy for a child of seven. She tried to multiply four by five, by six and by seven. Her answer came out all wrong:

> "Let me see: four times five is twelve, and four times six is thirteen, and four times seven is—oh dear! I shall never get to twenty at that rate!"

Edward Wakeling* in *Lewis Carroll's Games and Puzzles* has suggested why she would never get to 20 in the arithmetic series on which she had launched out.

Alice has trouble with her arithmetic in *Looking-Glass* as well, but the puzzles were not so complex. The Red Queen* was testing Alice's sums to see if she was ready to become a Queen. She demanded that Alice add: 'one and one and one and one and one and one and one and one and one and one'. The ones add up to the roman numeral X (ten), but Alice missed it because the

Queen spoke so quickly that she was forced to reply: 'I don't know! I lost count.'

Carroll was a solemn, old-fashioned mathematics lecturer. His lectures were shunned by undergraduates. Yet he managed again and again to be funny without showing he was serious, when he looked at his field of expertise through *Looking-Glass* eyes. (See also Questions.*)

Arnold, Ethel (1862–1908) and Julia (1866–1930)   Ethel and Julia were the nieces of Matthew Arnold, the poet, and the grandchildren of Thomas Arnold (1795–1842), the reforming headmaster of Rugby School. The Arnold children were friends of the young Liddells and they were the first subjects to pose for Carroll when he moved his photographic studio to the roof above his rooms at Christ Church.* He photographed them in the bridesmaids' dresses they wore for their older sister's wedding. She was Mary Augusta who became the well-known writer, Mrs Humphrey Ward. She was famous at the period of the struggle for votes for women. Mary led the women's branch of the Anti-Suffrage Movement in a momentarily effective rear-guard action. Like all the Arnold girls, she was clever, and from the evidence more companionable than the Liddells.*

Hoping that *Alice* would eventually be staged professionally, on 7 December 1874 Carroll went to an evening performance of the scene of The Mad Tea-Party at the Arnolds' home, which was 'very creditably done' with a cast of four. These included two professional child actors, Maud and Beatrice Fearon. Julia, with Huxley powers of concentration, played the Hatter.* Ethel Arnold played the March Hare.*

Carroll dedicated his word game, *Doublets*, to Julia and Ethel in 1879. Julia became the mother of Aldous Huxley* and Julian Huxley, whose son was Francis Huxley. Both Aldous and Francis Huxley wrote about Carroll. (See also Games* and Queen's English.*)

Auden, W. H. (1907–73)   Auden and Carroll are the greatest writers to have had connections with Christ Church as undergraduates and later in life. Their portraits are among the few in the Hall that are not of major benefactors, statesmen or Deans of the House. The college protected these difficult and brilliant men. It provided Carroll with a life-long home and Auden, from 1972 with a 'grace and favour' cottage by the Meadows which he occupied in the last year of his life. The Meadows were where Carroll walked daily, either in solitude or with children.

Auden admired *Alice*. He wrote a review about Carroll in the *New York Times* in 1962. Auden considered that the theme of language was so omnipresent in the stories that it had the dimensions of a character in *Alice*.

In *Alice*, 'words have a life and a will of their own'. Auden considered Alice 'an adequate symbol for what every human being should try to be like', combining as she does with such self-sufficiency the attributes of adulthood and childhood, logic and imaginative response. In the 'Afterword' to the modern edition of George MacDonald's* children's story, *The Golden Key*, Auden praised MacDonald for the gift of being able to create:

> ... an atmosphere of goodness about which there is nothing phoney or moralistic. Nothing is rarer in literature.

Carroll, surely, shared this gift in writing *Alice*.

BOAT-HOUSE, ABINGDON

17

B is for ...

Balthus (1908–)   Like Carroll, this most mysterious modern painter refuses to reveal much about his life. His real name is Balthazar Klossowski de Rola and he was born in Paris. His first London retrospective was held at the Tate Gallery in 1968.

Balthus' painting explores topics in the space we dream we occupy in sleep or in day dreams. Enigmatic card games played by very young girls with the expression of sleep-walkers haunt his pictures. Young girls of the age Carroll preferred obsessed Balthus too, whose finest naturalistic drawings are chalk drawings of abandoned-looking child*-friends. In describing Balthus' reiterated depiction of young girls waking, sometimes to caress a white cat, the critic John Russell, in his introduction to the Tate Gallery exhibition catalogue, emphasized many parallels with Carroll's *Alice*:

> No English person is likely to get far in this exhibition without thinking of Tenniel's Alice, curled up in her armchair with the black kitten and a ball of worsted, and standing for a stage in life and for certain attitudes within it to which Balthus was to turn to uniquely good advantage. As she sits half-curled in the chair, she wonders which will prove the more rewarding as playmates: the children, or the grown ups?

Russell pointed out that Balthus' 'thraldom' with the theme of *Alice* was 'as complete as anything in this century's painting'. Carroll created the space. Modernists like Balthus have colonized it. (See also Illustrators* of *Alice*.)

Bats (and Belfry) On rare occasions, bats still flit through the Christ Church* quadrangles as the light fades. In the nineteenth century they must have been much commoner in Oxford* than they are in the polluted twentieth century. To amuse child visitors, Carroll designed a mechanical flying bat, 'of gauze and wire worked by a piece of twisted elastic'. He designed this toy to stay in flight for over 30 seconds. When shot out from the window into the quadrangle it delighted child*-friends, but served as a hazard to college servants carrying trays of food across the Quad.

Martin Gardner* in his *Annotated Alice* noted that Carroll's mathematical colleague, Professor Bartholomew Price, was nicknamed 'The Bat' and that the *Wonderland* song 'Twinkle, twinkle, little Bat!/ How I wonder what you're at!' was written to show that this professor's meaning was not always crystal clear. The Hatter's song about the bat parodies 'Twinkle, twinkle, little star!' from Jane Taylor's *Rhymes for the Nursery*, 1806.

The belfry in which the Christ Church bats might have roosted did not exist until after *Alice*, but is pertinent because it shows how acerbic he could be towards the Dean. It also shows how right he could be on matters of architectural taste. Carroll compared the design, one of Liddell's grandest projects for the college – the other was the hideous Meadow Buildings – to a 'gigantic copy of a Greek Lexicon'. Liddell's other *magnum opus* was Liddell and Scott's *A Greek-English Lexicon*. Carroll accused the Dean of building the belfry for self-aggrandizement. Carroll's squib on the belfry was published just after *Looking-Glass* appeared. Luckily the architectural climax of the design the Dean wanted, the huge campanile, which would have destroyed for ever the character of old Christ Church, was not built. As it is, the squat tower that was built, more like a box than a lexicon, compares weakly with the lines of Tom Quadrangle and Wren's Tom Tower.

Bible, The Holy Ethel Arnold* recalled:

> Carroll's sense of humour, exquisite as it was, failed absolutely when any allusion to the Bible, however innocuous, was involved. The patriarchs, the prophets, major and minor, were as sacrosanct in his eyes as any of the great figures of the New Testament; and a disrespectful allusion to Noah or even Nebuchadnezzar would have shocked him deeply.

There are no bishops in the chess game in *Looking-Glass*. However Carroll cannot have liked his own bishop, Samuel Wilberforce,* known as 'Soapy Sam' for the difficulty people had in tying down his arguments. Wilberforce sacked Carroll's great friend, H. P. Liddon* from Cuddesdon Theological College.* The Ugly Duchess'* pronouncements on morals bear resemblance to his effusive style.

Bibliographies   Because of the diversity of Carroll's interests – writing, photography and mathematics – tracing publications related to him can be difficult. Language barriers reinforce this difficulty. Although some of the best French work on Carroll has appeared in English, much English work has not been translated into French. Almost no Italian, Japanese or German work has been translated into English. A further difficulty is that some publications, notably American, are designed in limited editions and are exceptionally difficult to find. *Jabberwocky*, the journal of the English Lewis Carroll Society is also not easy to access.

The standard bibliography includes Sidney Herbert Williams, *A Bibliography of the Writings of Lewis Carroll* (1924), which was updated by Sidney Herbert Williams and Falconer Madan,* as *A Handbook of the Literature of the Rev C. L. Dodgson (Lewis Carroll)* (1931). There is also S. H. Williams, Falconer Madan and Roger Lancelyn Green's*: *The Lewis Carroll Handbook* (1962), and S. H. Williams, Falconer Madan, Roger Lancelyn Green and Denis Crutch's *The Lewis Carroll Handbook* (1979). In addition, the catalogues of the centenary (1932) exhibitions at Columbia University and in London are useful for information about rarer items.

Since the 1960s, Edward Guiliano has produced *Lewis Carroll: An Annotated International Bibliography, 1960–77* (1981). This is well organized and casts a wide international net. The Norton Critical Edition of *Alice* (1971) edited by Donald Gray; and Peter Heath's *The Philosopher's Alice* (1974) also have useful bibliographies.

More recently, Rachael Fordyce's *Lewis Carroll: A Reference Guide* (1992) has been published. This is a *critical* bibliography of Carroll's work, containing 970 entries and 18,000 index entries. Alas this, too, is hard to find in England. So is *Semiotics and Linguistics in Alice's Worlds* (1994) which she co-edited, and which includes a selection of critical works. (See Punctuation.*) In this same publication is a European bibliography *Some More Writings on Carroll* by the Urbino-based Maurizio del Ninno. The French scholar, Jean Gattégno* produced his *Bibliographie* in 1990. The catalogues of the book departments of auction houses are also useful hunting grounds for rare items, notably Sotheby's, Christie's and Phillips' in London and Swann in New York.

Bill the Lizard   A little bill – 'The Rabbit Sends in a Little Bill' is the title of Chapter 4 of *Wonderland*. Bill came down the chimney after Alice drank the unlabelled potion:

> She went on growing and growing, and very soon had to kneel down on the floor: in another minute there was not even room for this...

To squeeze herself into this painful position, Alice put 'one arm out of the window, and one foot up the chimney'. Meanwhile Bill the Lizard, a slithery, stupefied reptile, came down the chimney in an attempt to remove Alice. Alice gave it a sharp kick and Bill flew up in the air. The rescue of Bill was then organized. The White Rabbit* suggested giving it brandy. In *Under Ground* Carroll shows two guinea pigs administering the brandy, although this is not in the text, nor in Tenniel's* later illustration.

'Bill the Lizard' has components of a pun on the name of a politician who was, to many Tories and Liberals, a slippery customer – Benjamin Disraeli* (1804–81), Tory Prime Minister of Britain. The joke echoes the contemporary *Punch* stereotype of Disraeli as a wily snake winding its way up the Tory greasy pole. That the slippery lizard slopped ink about with the end of its tail at the trial may allude to Carroll's dislike of Disraeli's populist novels, *Coningsby* (1844) and *Sybil* (1845). See also Natural History Museum* for the hint that the chimney that Bill comes down is parodied; the chimney being part of an elaborate building that presented the university with not a little bill, but a large one.

Biographers Carroll's biographers have written from a number of perspectives. He is a difficult subject because his great literary work, *Alice* (and, outside the scope of this book, *The Hunting of the Snark* and *Sylvie and Bruno*) only occupied small parts of a varied life that he compartmentalized and hid from view. Among the important works are the following, with publication dates and publishers given in the Select Bibliography.

Collingwood,* Stuart Dodgson, *The Life and Letters of Lewis Carroll (Rev. C. L. Dodgson)*. This is a formal and sentimental record by Carroll's nephew, written in the year of Carroll's death, the only source of some important information and diary* entries.

Reed, (Herbert) Langford, *The Life of Lewis Carroll*. This was written in 1932 without access to Carroll's diaries or letters but is in some ways the stronger for that; it concentrates on the literary aspects of Carroll's writing. Reed saw Carroll as an important contributor to the European comic and satirical tradition.

Lennon, Florence Becker, *Victoria Through the Looking Glass: The Life of Lewis Carroll*, was published in America in 1945 and in England in 1947 as *Lewis Carroll*. This biography was the first to address the quirks in Carroll's character and provides some psychological insights, but is now dated. It made use of the first selection of Carroll's letters to be published, Evelyn Hatch's* *Selection of the Letters from Lewis Carroll to his Child-Friends* (1933).

Green,* Roger Lancelyn, *The Story of Lewis Carroll*. This was written in 1949 for 'young readers' and was characteristic of the uncritical school to which Collingwood's biography belonged, but contained material then new, for Green had seen and was to edit Carroll's diaries.

Taylor, Alexander L., *The White Knight*. This was first published in 1952. In it, contemporary Oxford* controversies were explored, in response to Shane Leslie's* suggestions that church figures were parodied in Alice.

Hudson, Derek, *Lewis Carroll*. This straightforward and lucid biography was published in 1954. A second edition was *Lewis Carroll – an Illustrated Biography*. Hudson was the first biographer, apart from Roger Lancelyn Green (mentioned above) with access to Carroll's diaries. Making no claims to 'interpret' Carroll, this book has aged better than any that preceded it.

Pudney, John, *Lewis Carroll and his World* (1976). This is brief and researched what was then new material relating to Carroll.

Clark, Anne, *Lewis Carroll, A Biography* (1979). Clear-headed and thorough, probably the best primer for someone newly-interested in Carroll's life. She has also written *The Real Alice*, one of two lives of Alice Liddell.*

Cohen,* Morton N., *Lewis Carroll: a Biography*, published in 1995. Cohen has published much on Carroll and his work of many years on Carroll's *Letters** gives him an extensive knowledge of Carroll's many social contacts. Unless, as is unlikely, some major new source on Carroll should come to light, Cohen's life will be hard to displace as the standard one. Cohen is strongly attached to his subject, calling him 'Charles'. The biography discounts what we consider to be of great importance to Carroll, the Oxford controversies of the day which were either religious or to do with the curriculum. It is, however, full of insights into Carroll's moods and the psychological and religious issues that tortured him.

de la Mare,* Walter, *Lewis Carroll*, first published as an essay in 1930 and then in book form in 1932, the strongest argument for *Alice* as very great literature to that date.

Gattégno*, Jean, *Lewis Carroll – Fragments of a Looking-Glass*, published in English in 1976, originally *Lewis Carroll: Une Vie d'Alice à Zénon d'Elée*, published in Paris in 1974. The work is set out as an 'A to Z', 'A' being for Alice, 'Z' for Zeno's paradox. Gattégno considered that Alice, the child, and Zeno, the logician, are to be viewed as a unity. The book is fond, gallic and witty – either charming or chauvinist depending on the reader – amused rather than hung-up on the quirks of Carroll's attachment to young girls.

Greenacre, Phyllis, *Swift and Carroll: a Psychoanalytic study of Two Lives*. Written by the pioneering student of these hang-ups, this book was, in 1955, fresher than it appears today.

The key issue of interest in Carroll's life is his relationship with Alice. Whether the future will see major advances in understanding Victorian child love remains to be seen. (See also Child*-Friends.)

Birthdays and Un-birthdays   Carroll was meticulous in giving books he admired to his child-friends on their birthdays. On the other hand anyone who gave Carroll a birthday present, whether they were a member of his own family or an adult friend, risked rebuff. Humpty Dumpty* in *Looking-Glass* preferred 'Un-birthday' to 'Birthday' presents because there are 364 more chances of getting the Un-birthday one. What Carroll preferred as his 'birthday present' was simple. It was a letter from a favoured child-friend. One he treasured was from 'a Charity Child'. Carroll kept even the envelopes for they bore his name and address in their childish handwriting and reminded him that their writers loved him. (See also *Alice's Adventures Under Ground**, Anonymity*and Catherine Sinclair.*)

Björk, Christina (1938–)   Christina Björk is the author of a carefully researched Swedish book for children about *Alice*'s Oxford world, *The Story of Alice in her Oxford Wonderland* which has been published in English translation. The story is told as to children and the book introduces *Alice* to European children in a way that is closer to Carroll than the now pervasive and gung-ho Disney books, toys and film.

Blacking The Gryphon made puns about 'Soles', 'Eels' and 'Whiting'*
under the sea, in contrast to the Soles, Heels and Blacking needed to shine
shoes in Alice's world, where children have feet, not fins or fish tails. All these
jokes have an obsessive quality in keeping with Carroll's real-life fastidiousness
about boots and shoes and cleaning.

Alice did not clean her own shoes. The servants* blacked them for her,
as they did for Carroll. Carroll always wore black shoes, even when he wore
white flannels to take the girls rowing on the Thames* and made jokes such
as those about whiting shoes under the sea. (See also Fish and Fishy Jokes,*
Gryphon* and Soles.*)

Books Carroll Read as a Child At the age of six or seven – Alice's
age* in *Wonderland* – Carroll owned a tiny linen bag which he filled with
'hand-written texts and pious sentiments' which he had collected. He
learned these by rote along with lessons from his 'home-made' prayer book,
prelude to jollier rectory writings and drawings when he grew older. From
an early age, he imposed on himself high religious standards. What changed
between the seven year old sobriety and the construction of *Alice* was the
lack of moralizing in the latter.

Among the books Carroll read at his mother's knee were *The Juvenile Sunday
Library*, Baker's *Scripture Characters*, Hannah More's *Cheap Repository* and *The
Shepherd of Salisbury Plain* and novels and tract books by Maria Edgeworth,
including *The Early Lessons* and her still-popular *Flat Iron for a Farthing*. By
the age of seven, too, he had read John Bunyan's *Pilgrim's Progress*. He
enjoyed 'how-to' books, such as *The Parent's Cabinet of Amusement and
Instruction* and at the age of eight he had a taste of technological invention
at a major exhibition in Warrington, not far from the rectory at Daresbury,*
where he saw a display of 323 'curiosities', 250 'natural history specimens'
and 42 'pieces of philosophical apparatus' and had his profile painted in
silhouette, prelude to a lasting passion for portraiture, layout and typography.

As for the historical texts he had to read in the schoolroom, he never lost
his sense of fun about them. One of these was Magnall's *Historical and
Miscellaneous Questions for the Use of Young People with a Selection of British and
General Biography*.

What queen poisoned herself to avoid the insults of the Roman conqueror?
Boadicea, queen of the Iceni, in Britain. What two Saxon generals
assisted in subduing England? Hengist, and Horsa. They were brothers.
What was the Saxon Heptarchy? The union and mutual agreement of
seven Saxon princes, to divide England into seven different parts, and each

take a share. Who was the first Christian king in Britain? Ethelbert, fifth king of Kent.

Magnall went through many editions and the edition we read has 445 pages of questions and answers on French kings, Roman emperors, British history, astronomy and 'Common Subjects'. The 'Common Subjects' in Chapter 25 include: What is pewter? Whence comes lode-stone? What is rhubarb? Where do nutmegs grow?

Jokes about schoolroom history and geography* keep surfacing in *Alice*. Even if Miss Prickett (see Governesses*) did not make the Liddell* girls read Magnall, they would have toiled through similar texts to those Carroll read as a boy and a young man. It was not his kind of subject; hence his sympathy by the Pool of Tears with Alice's struggle with a whole tract of nursery history which did nothing at all to help her get dry.

Boredom   If dull lessons were the dullest part of Alice's life, having 'nothing to do' was even worse. Alice was 'tired of sitting by her sister on the bank' at the very start of her *Wonderland* adventure. Thus 'she was considering, in her own mind ... whether the pleasure of making a daisy-chain would be worth the trouble of getting up and picking the daisies', when the White Rabbit ran by, and so began Carroll's tale. Alice had plenty to do for the next 11 chapters, but her sociological problems did not go away. With marriage as their mothers' only goal for them, education of girls like the Liddell sisters took a secondary place.

Bough   A Rose and a Daisy met Alice in the Garden of Live Flowers.* They explained to her that they were not afraid to be alone in the garden because there was 'a tree in the middle'. Alice, whose out-door companions were a governess and sometimes a don, questioned the 'Live Flowers' further about being in public without a chaperon. What protection could a tree offer a flower?

"But what could it do, if any danger came?" Alice asked.

In two puns which the French translator, Jacques Papy, described as one of *les jeux de mots des plus mauvais*, 'the worst imaginable puns', the Live Flowers explained that a tree could be a watch-dog:

"It could bark," said the Rose.
"It says Bough-wough!" cried a Daisy. "That's why its branches are called boughs!"

Bowman, Isa (1874–1958)   A former child actress, Isa Bowman wrote as elaborate an account of the experience of having Carroll as an 'uncle' as any of his child*-friends. It was entitled *The Story of Lewis Carroll* and was originally published in time for Christmas 1899, 23 months after his death. It was republished as *Lewis Carroll as I Knew Him* by Dover (1972). Although Isa did not meet Carroll until 1886, her relationship with him, her descriptions of the games* he devised for her, the letters, the visits to Oxford,* the summer visits to Eastbourne,* give an insight into his relationship with Alice.

In Isa's memoir, she recalled that he often addressed her stagily as 'my own darling'. She described his mock scoldings which Alice Liddell* earlier reported, his letters containing mathematical games that made no sense and his odd calculations to do with kisses* and kittens. She also described how he called himself the 'Aged Aged Man',* as in the White Knight's* poem, and how talk between them focused on etiquette, parties and invitations. Of staying at Eastbourne, she wrote, (and she must have been 15 at the time):

> To begin with, we used to get up very early indeed. Our bedroom doors faced each other at the top of the staircase. When I came out of mine, I always knew if I might go into his room or not by his signal. If, when I came into the passage, I found that a newspaper had been put under the door, then I knew I might go in at once; but if there was no newspaper, then I had to wait until it appeared. ... Then we used to go downstairs to breakfast, after which we always read a chapter out of the Bible. So that I should remember it, I always had to tell it to him afterwards as a story of my own.

Isa Bowman says that he visited the dentist frequently and took child-friends to do the same; that his eyes were a clear blue, his handshake firm and that:

> he was afflicted with what I believe is known as 'Housemaid's knee' and this made his movements singularly jerky and abrupt. (See also gait.*)

With regard to his stammer,* she said that every day he would read aloud a scene from Shakespeare, but that this never removed the impediment entirely. Carroll helped Isa and her sisters with their careers in the theatre. By Christmas 1888, he had seen that Isa's brother, Charlie, had been cast as the White Rabbit,* with a subsidiary role as the Unicorn,* in the revived London stage version of *Alice*. Her little sister, Empsie, played the Dormouse* as well as an Oyster* which danced a hornpipe in Act I.

Carroll set up his favourite, Isa, in the principal role of Alice in the revival. She had 215 speeches, some of them extensions of the existing text written for her by Carroll. She performed her part twice a day, and even

Carroll admitted it was a gruelling routine. For voice lessons, Carroll supplied Isa with none other than Ellen Terry.*

Boys Boys were of much less interest to Carroll than girls. References to Harry Liddell in Carroll's diaries diminish after Carroll became well acquainted with Alice. Unlike so many children's books and in contrast, notably, to Charles Kingsley's *The Water-Babies*, Carroll's central child character was female, as were the great majority of the companions he sought to photograph, correspond with and take on holiday to Eastbourne.* Greville MacDonald's* long-remembered affection for Carroll, however, belies the idea that he was only interested in girls, as does his interest in the Tennyson* boys, at least for as long as their mother could tolerate Carroll. A boy, the 'Beamish Boy' is the small, undaunted hero who slays the Jabberwock* in a poem whose tones, unlike most of those parodied in *Alice*, are not light and whimsical, but dark and militant.

It was after consultation with mothers – not fathers – that Carroll removed the David and Goliath-like illustration of the boy and Jabberwock from the frontispiece of *Looking-Glass* and replaced it with one of that most unheroic of male figures, the White Knight.*

Bread and Butter This was at issue in the Mad Tea-Party* because there was none. In real life the 'Bread-and-Butter Row' took place when the undergraduates took the lead from Carroll and his disgruntled colleagues on the High Table at Christ Church* to complain in the columns of *The Times* that they were being short-changed in their diet by Dean Liddell* and the profiteering steward. (See also *American Telegrams.*)

Dean Liddell, in his reforms of Christ Church, refused to alter the contracting system in the kitchens whereby the Butler and Manciple could profit – profiteer according to some – from supplies. This obstinacy and centralizing of power around himself and the Canons was the bane of Carroll's life and he and a don called Prout* led the way in Senior Common Room protests against many of the Dean's actions. The Dean's response was generally not to reply. However when aristocratic undergraduates, rather than graduates, brought the issue into the columns of *The Times*, the Dean had to retreat. An echo of it is visible in the Hatter's* confusion at the trial with his bread and butter and teacup. The issue became known as 'The Bread-and-Butter Row'. The old sub-contracting system was changed. In addition the Senior Common Room's management was put into the hands of its members and for several years Carroll was its curator, meticulously ordering wine,* blotting paper and that accessory to letter writing without which no Victorian desk was complete, mourning stationery.

Broad Church *The Oxford English Dictionary* defined a Broad Churchman as one who:

> takes its doctrines in a broad or liberal sense, and holds that the church should be comprehensive and tolerant so as to admit of more or less variety of opinion in matters of dogma and ritual.

The idea that the Church of England should be 'broad' and tolerant was developed within Oxford in the early 1860s as *Wonderland* was being written and in reaction to the ultra-High Church Oxford Movement which was founded in 1833, a year after Carroll's birth and to which Carroll's father, Archdeacon Dodgson* subscribed.

For Carroll's generation of tutors, this debate was really the crucial debate of the time, taking up more time in thought, contemplation and common room chat than any other. The Church of England had long been divided into 'high' and 'low', low church supporters having much in common with the non-conformists. By the time Carroll was an undergraduate in the early 1850s, the debate over whether the true English church should be high had become heated. Some, such as (later Cardinal) Newman,* had become so high that they left the Church of England altogether and converted to Rome. Others, such as Canon Pusey,* felt that Oxford's primary purpose was the training of clergy for what was the true Catholic Church, Rome being seen as having strayed from the true faith. Into this debate – that sometimes approached hysteria, 'high' church dons accusing others of 'infecting' undergraduates with their ideas – Arthur Penrhyn Stanley* (later Dean

Stanley), Liddell's* ally among the Canons, introduced the idea of moving beyond factionalism. Writing in the Liberal *Edinburgh Review*, he claimed that the Anglican Church was 'by the very conditions of its being, not High, not Low, but Broad'.

The Anglican church should have its own belief, Stanley said, but it should be tolerant of others. As a result of pressure exerted by himself, Benjamin Jowett,* H. G. Liddell and others, Oxford began to show itself to be broad. Through Acts of Parliament it gradually widened the social and religious intake of its undergraduates and developed as a modern university rather than a dogmatically controlled theological college. The establishment of both Keble College and Cuddesdon Theological College were attempts by the High Church to keep its footing. However, with the decline of the Pusey era – Canon Pusey died in 1882 – Oxford became much broader and, in general, agnostic.

All this, however, was after *Alice*. During the writing of the books, the debate was at its height. Carroll's views about the theatre suggest he may have been broad in some ways. The High Church believed in eternal damnation – and it meant eternal hell fire for all time – for non-believers in the Church of England; and held this to include the damnation of children and particularly unbaptized children. We believe that satires on the High Church/Broad Church pervade *Alice*, particularly *Looking-Glass* which was published after the death of Carroll's High Church father. The authors have claimed, basing their arguments on work done by Ronald Knox* and Shane Leslie,* that the frenetic atmosphere that pervades *Alice* mirrors the apparent illogic of much of the High Church versus Broad Church debate.

C is for ...

Cambridge   Lewis Carroll never found it necessary to visit the 'other' university. By the 1860s and 1870s, Cambridge appeared from the distance to have become a hot-bed of free-thinkers, Broad Church* Anglicans and Christian Socialists.* These included Charles Kingsley,* Leslie Stephen and members of the Tennyson* circle.

Two Cambridge men whom Carroll admired enough to write to at length when he felt they were in the wrong were F. D. Maurice* and Alfred, Lord Tennyson. Alexander Macmillan,* Carroll's publisher, received his commercial impetus by publishing the latest works of Broad Church Cambridge theologians. The rich clergymen, the Hare brothers gave him his backing. There is one allusion to a Cambridge undergraduate in Carroll's verse. This was to the narcissistic middle-class lad in Carroll's poem, *Hiawatha's Photographing*, shown as a fop who read Ruskin.*

Cameron, Julia Margaret (1815–79)   A Victorian photographer, Julia Cameron was a friend and neighbour of the Tennysons* on the Isle of Wight.* Carroll, 17 years her junior, met her there in 1864. For a time they were friendly, although Carroll was not one of her lunch guests. Cameron was effusive and well-connected in literary circles. Each summer she gathered together a large contingent of friends, relations and their children at Dimbola Lodge, the house she made at Freshwater Bay by converting two fishermen's cottages. She erected her photographic studio in a glass house barely large enough to contain her equipment, her models and the fancy dress and props she used to photograph them with. The house (see also Sites*) was a quarter of a mile from the staid Plumblys Hotel at Freshwater Bay where Carroll stayed. Benjamin Jowett,* the young, unhappy, Ellen Terry,* and the poet and retired civil servant, Sir Henry Taylor (1800–86) were among Cameron's most distinguished guests. As was often the case with the famous, Carroll was both fascinated by and derisory of Cameron. On one occasion he wrote, 'Went to the Photographic Exhibition which was very scanty and poor. I did *not* admire Mrs. Cameron's large heads taken out of focus'.

It is possible that there are elements of the shawl-draped Mrs Cameron in the *Looking-Glass* portrait of the untidy White Queen, whose flying hair and dress Alice is expected to pin back in place. (See Virginia Woolf.*) Cameron became familiar with the Liddells* when Carroll was no longer socially acceptable to them. She photographed Alice Liddell and her sisters when they passed their summers at a rented house between royal Osborne, where the Queen stayed, and her own Bohemian Freshwater. She photographed Alice with garlanded hair, dressed as a depressed Pomona, the goddess of harvest; and as a forgiving Cordelia, King Lear's youngest daughter. Thus Alice was photographed by two of the greatest British photographers of this period. If Cameron 'stole' Alice, Carroll may have caused her irritation by more literally stealing two of her models, Ellen Terry and Henry Taylor. He met both in Cameron's circle on the Isle of Wight and in London. For the bitchy account by a child*-friend turned gossipy writer see also Una Taylor* whose *Guests and Memories* (1924) described Carroll's eventual unpopularity in the *environs* of Dimbola Lodge.

Carpenter

> "'O, Oysters,' said the Carpenter,
>   'You've had a pleasant run!
> Shall we be trotting home again?'
>   But answer came there none—
> And this was scarcely odd, because
>   They'd eaten every one."

Carroll ended his *Looking-Glass* ballad with a disastrous disappearance which provoked the fair-minded Alice to question Tweedledum and Tweedledee after they had recited it to her. At first Alice believed that one of the pair, the Walrus,* had deceived the Oysters* less than the Carpenter.* Tweedledum* and Tweedledee* persuaded her that this was not the case. She concluded: 'Well! They were *both* very unpleasant characters—.'

Martin Gardner* noted that Carroll gave Tenniel* the choice of a Butterfly, a Baronet or a Carpenter to be the Walrus' mate when he sent him the chapter to illustrate, and it was the Carpenter Tenniel selected. There is a garbled quotation from John Ruskin's* *Modern Painters* in the ballad. In *Modern Painters* there is a section entitled 'Many Things', a piece of prose which included references to 'cats and monkeys and kings'. Carroll's parody is the resonant 'Cabbages and Kings', suggesting that the ballad was a *Punch*-style spoof about two leading Oxford aesthetes, John Ruskin (1819–1900) and Walter Pater*(1839–94). 'Walrus' compresses the 'Wal' of 'Walter' with 'Rus' of 'Ruskin'. At the time this was written, around 1869, Ruskin was – or had on an occasional basis been – employed by Mrs Liddell* to teach Alice to draw, thus retaining an intimacy with the teenage Alice that was denied to Carroll.

Carroll, Lewis as a Pseudonym   Dodgson invented this when he was aged 24 and contributing for *The Comic Times*. He offered the editor, Mr Edmund Yates (n.d.), four alternative pseudonyms. They were:

Edgar Cuthwellis (an anagram* of 'Charles Lutwidge').
Edgar U. C. Westhill (ditto).
Louis Carroll (derived from Lutwidge = Ludovic = Louis, and Charles, from the Latin name for Charles, Carolus).
Lewis Carroll (ditto).

Would *Alice* have had the same magic if written by Edgar U. C. Westhill? For the choice of Lewis Carroll, we must thank Mr Yates.

Caterpillar   The blue, hookah-smoking Caterpillar Alice met in *Under Ground* and *Wonderland* refused to accept what Alice knew to be inevitable: that it would metamorphose into a butterfly. She knew this because she was interested in natural history and had visited the Natural History Museum* in Oxford. The Caterpillar pretended to know best, but she knew better.

   Among the literary eccentrics who tried to remain anonymous, Carroll had his equal in Edward Fitzgerald (1809–83) the aristocratic, Irish and hookah-smoking poet who had been educated at Cambridge,* lived deep in the Suffolk countryside and was a close friend of the Tennysons. He translated *The Rubáiyát of Omar Khayyam* anonymously. The manuscript had been discovered in the Bodleian Library in 1856 by Fitzgerald's Persian teacher. The translation attracted little attention until Dante Gabriel Rossetti* picked up a copy for a penny in the box of remainders at Quaritch's book shop in London. In his hands it soon found a cult following.

   Rossetti became fascinated with the poem's sybaritic philosophy, so close to his own. The 'Rubáiyát' was as much in the air as *The Origin of Species* when Carroll was writing *Alice*. We think that the drugged Caterpillar is a reference to the Victorian fascination with Hindu, Persian and Arab tales and, in particular with the Persian poet and mathematician Omar, conversing on his mushroom with little Alice beside him in the Wilderness.

Carroll may also have had Fitzgerald in mind when he wrote the *Looking-Glass*. A late quatrain of the Rubáiyát reads:

> 'Tis all a Chequer-board of Nights and Days
> Where Destiny with Men for Pieces plays:
> Hither and thither moves, and mates, and slays,
> And one by one back in the Closet lays.

Thus Carroll:

> "I declare it's marked out just like a large chess-board!" Alice said at last. "There ought to be some men moving about somewhere—and so there are!"

'How I *wish* I was one of them!' Alice continued. And, of course, she was.

Cecil   Cecil is the family name of the third Marquess of Salisbury (1830–1903) who was Prime Minister in four administrations. Salisbury was a Christ Church* undergraduate two years older than Carroll. They did not know each other then. In 1870, when *Wonderland* was famous, Salisbury was Chancellor of the University and Carroll – imagining that *Wonderland* 'had a great deal to do with my gracious reception' – was given permission to photograph the Salisbury children. Thereafter he enjoyed visits to Hatfield

House, the home of the Salisburys, and developed a fond relationship with them, as well as a sympathy for Salisbury's Tory paternalism.

Lord Salisbury led the Tory party in five general elections after 1885. The Salisburyites concentrated their electoral endeavours on the reform of constituency boundaries into equal electoral districts, and the courtship of urban voters, especially in the North, where Carroll's family origins lay. By turning large towns into single-member constituencies, middle-class northern seats like north Leeds, and southern ones like Eastbourne where Carroll spent his summers, began to fall to Salisburyite candidates. In all this, Carroll, as a University constituent, took an active part, attending Parliamentary debates and checking off results in a partisan way in his diaries.

Lord David Cecil (1902–86), grandson of the third Marquess and Professor of English at Oxford, wrote a literary reminiscence of Carroll, who read to his father as a child, in *The Library Looking-Glass* (1975). In this he chose as his favourite passage from *Alice* the dialogue between the White Knight* and Alice about the White Knight's over-loaded horse, armour and baggage. Like de la Mare* and Langford Reed* a generation before him, he admired Carroll, but particularly as a nonsense writer, saying that, 'As music is the quintessential art ... so is nonsense humour the quintessential kind of humour'. (See also Critics.*)

Celibacy   Celibacy was required of Christ Church Students and Fellows of Oxford (and Cambridge) colleges until 1871 when an Act of Parliament changed the rule. For example, both Carroll's and Alice's fathers had to resign their studentships on marriage. However, when he was elevated to Dean of Christ Church, Liddell was allowed to marry. Canons also could marry, as could those with special appointments such as Henry W. Acland,* Professor of Medicine.

In the 120 years since this change, the requirement for Fellows to be ordained has also been abandoned and the number of bachelor dons in Christ Church declined to almost none. So Christ Church lost for ever its monastic-collegiate character, a place where a group of ordained bachelors lived, ate, taught, worshipped and – last but far from least – gossiped and conspired.

Chataway, Annie Gertrude (1866–1951)   Child*-friend who left an affectionate account of Carroll, Gertrude Chataway was one of 15 children. Her father was the Reverend James Chataway (1827–1907), who took lodgings for his family next to Carroll's in Sandown on the Isle of Wight,* where they met in 1875 when Carroll was aged 43. Gertrude Chataway gave two descriptions of Carroll, the first to Collingwood,* the second in *The*

Hampshire Chronicle. She described seeing Carroll on the lodging of his balcony sniffing the sea air. To Collingwood she said:

> He would come onto his balcony, which joined ours, sniffing the sea–air with his head thrown back, and would walk right down the steps on to the beach with his chin in air, drinking in the fresh breezes as if he could never have enough.

As was usual in these cases, acquaintance was struck up, the parents were involved, photographs were shown, visits exchanged, more photographs shown, more acquaintances made with more parents of more little girls.

Carroll drew the small-boned Gertrude in the jersey, cap and rolled-up trousers of a fisher lad and photographed her sitting on a table in the same garb. Both are shown in Morton Cohen's* edition of the *Letters*.* They give a sense of transexuality, a boyish girl in boyish clothes, that appealed to Carroll. (See also the last part of Dodgson* for first-hand accounts of Carroll.)

Cheshire Cat, The   This creature made its appearance in Chapter VI of *Wonderland* in the kitchen sitting by the Duchess, and then again when the baby changed into a pig and ran off into the woods. The Cat appeared on the bough of a tree, vanishing in one of Tenniel's notable illustrations, into a smile where once a Cat had been.

> The Cat only grinned when it saw Alice. It looked good-natured, she thought: still it had *very* long claws and a great many teeth, so she felt it ought to be treated with respect.

The Cheshire Cat's long claws and teeth and insider's knowledge of the royal court, suggest that the Cat may have been inspired by the real-life figure of Canon (later Dean) Stanley* (1815–81), Dean Liddell's* closest Broad Church* ally in the Oxford University Reform Movement. Carroll's contact with Stanley came through his friendship with Stanley's down-trodden secretary, Augustus J. C. Hare (1834–1903), a journalist and Oxford gossip. Hare later became one of those Victorian travel writers whose journeys are mostly enjoyable ambles in pleasant watering places such as Nice.

Stanley was the butt of several of Carroll's Oxford squibs. Like Carroll he came from Cheshire but, in Stanley's case, from the aristocratic Cheshire family of the Earl of Derby, who owned several country houses. Stanley had the cunning of a cat in pushing through reforms that Oxford Conservatives like Carroll saw as the thin end of a wedge of undesirable changes in the constitution of the University.

Alice asked the Cat which way she ought to go, to which the Cat replied with tolerance (Broad Church tolerance, it might be said), "That depends a good deal on where you want to get to". The Cat, in its few scenes, either placed itself in a tree looking down on the ordinary mortal Alice, or hovering in the sky at the Croquet* Match.

"That depends a good deal on where you want to get to," said the Cat.

Stanley, somewhat of a forgotten figure today, prided himself on being able to see both sides of the theological argument, as the Cat did when it suggested Alice should either visit the Hare or the Hatter. Stanley, whose Broad Church views appealed to the Queen, was appointed Dean of Westminster in 1863. He had a sense of humour and subtlety in negotiation that his ally, Liddell, lacked. In Carroll's photograph of him, the humour does not convey itself, but the cleverness does.

Chess   Alice saw the *Looking-Glass* landscape as a vast chessboard, and
Carroll claimed in a preliminary diagram in the *Looking-Glass* story, that it
was a game that the White Pawn* (Alice) was going to 'play, and win in eleven
moves'. Chess and mirror-imaging determined the possible moves that
Alice, the White Pawn, could make. Of the 32 chess pieces he might have
written into the story, Carroll concentrated on eight, two white pawns, Alice
and Lily, a Red and a White King* and Queen* and the White Knight,* all
of which have major roles in the story. The Red Knight, the Castles and the
Bishops are played down in order to simplify the game for a child of seven
and a half, as Alice was in the story. A Queen was the most powerful piece
on a chessboard. Alice was queened after moving forward to the Eighth
Square.

Already, during Carroll's lifetime, there was much speculation as to how
serious was the chess puzzle laid out at the beginning of *Looking-Glass*. Do
the chess moves in *Alice* have meaning or are they random? In response to
the debate on this issue, Carroll wrote a new foreword to *Looking-Glass* in
1896 saying that:

> Anyone who takes the trouble to set the pieces and play the moves as
> directed, will find it strictly in accordance with the laws of the game.

Possibly they were random moves and this was a nonsense chess game.
Falconer Madan,* who worked on the bibliography* of Carroll, was sceptical
of finding any meaning to the chess 'problem' Carroll set in the story. John
Fisher,* however, in *The Magic of Lewis Carroll* (1973) was not so sure. He
pointed out that the auction catalogue of Carroll's effects contained three books
about chess, all of which were published at least 15 years before Carroll wrote
his *Looking-Glass* story.

The Reverend Ivor Llewellyn Davies, Fisher claimed, 'attempted to
rationalize' Carroll's moves, but this seemed to be more for the benefit of
those with a serious knowledge of chess than child readers of *Alice*. In the
1970s, there was a flurry of articles on the subject in *Jabberwocky*. Llewellyn
Davis then suggested that Alice's chess game derives from a variety of chess
with a 'Marked Pawn' that was described in one of the books Carroll owned
on the subject.

Carroll himself explained in 1896 that the moves he wrote for the White
Pawn, Alice, were moves as they might have been seen from the White Pawn's
point of view. This was ingeniously in keeping with the tight focus Carroll
kept on his heroine's point of view as she travelled over the landscape of
her dream.

Child-Friend   This is the term Carroll used to describe his relationships with (mainly) little girls. Evelyn M. Hatch,* who posed undressed for Carroll's camera in 1879, and later edited *A Selection from the Letters of Lewis Carroll to His Child-Friends* (1933), evidently admired him, and gave credibility to the term 'child-friend'. There was no question in her mind that Carroll's friendships were innocent. With the Liddells,* there was almost always a chaperon, but that was not the case with many child-friends, particularly later in Carroll's life when girls of eight and nine would stay with him at Eastbourne.*

The key questions to arise from this behaviour are whether Carroll's adoration of these young girls was sexually perverted, whether it was sexually perverted in a way that was harmful to the children, and whether, by extension, the art that derived from the relationships, *Alice* and the photographs, is tainted.

There seems to be no evidence that it was so. Some mothers would not give consent to him to be with their daughters, or gave very limited consent. Some of the children found his presence cloying. Eyebrows were raised on some, and possibly many, occasions about his obsessive regard for pretty girl children. In 1893 his sister Mary (Collingwood*) protested about a girl guest at Eastbourne and Carroll wrote back accusing her of listening to gossip. In general most of these children, as letters and memoirs testify, delighted in the presence of a pious man who had great clerical rectitude and could see exceptionally into their young minds.

On the question of whether Carroll's love of these children was sexually-charged, this was a subject which Victorians generally avoided. While the remarks above would suggest there was a world of difference between Carroll's child-loving and the paedophilia of men of his generation who exploited child prostitutes or purchased photographs of naked and suggestively posed children, certain modern scholars take the view that there was a great deal of sexual charge in the kind of friendships that Carroll enjoyed *and* in the photographs by which he described these relationships visually. In particular, the American scholar, James Kincaid (1937–, see also Critics*) sees the whole relationship with the child – ours as well as the Victorians – as a sexual relationship. Whether this approach becomes widely accepted and a distaste develops for the kind of photographs of clad, half-clad, or on rare occasions naked girl children that Carroll took is a subject beyond the scope of this article. Perhaps the fairest way to treat Carroll is not to blame him, but to ask ourselves how far his photography makes us face complex questions about our own sexuality in its relationship to children.

Carroll was meticulous in obtaining the consent of his child-friends' parents when he escorted them to the theatre or took them on holiday and on other excursions. His favourite child-friends were often, as in the case of the Cecils,* the Arnolds* and the Butlers, a bevy of sisters whose parents Carroll looked up to. From this group, as with Alice Liddell,* Julia Arnold and Violet Butler, he would mark off individual members for special attention.

It was part of the probity he maintained as a lonely gentleman that the term, 'child-friend', which he used in letters and in conversation, implies that these special friends were sexless. This was a convenient euphemism, for they were girls of his favourite ages to whom Carroll was attracted *because* they were girls. There is intense emotional concentration in his letters to them.

Virginia Woolf,* in a review of the 1930s Nonesuch Edition of Carroll's works, a review reprinted in *Aspects of Alice*, noted that while for most adults, childhood fades slowly away, with Carroll 'it lodged in him whole and entire. He could not disperse it'. Sixty years later, Morton N. Cohen* considered this same theme, which Woolf was the first to approach, in a chapter of his 1995 biography of Carroll, entitled 'The Pursuit of Innocents'.

It was said of Carroll that his love for his child-friends usually ended when he had to raise his hat to them.

Contemporary *Alice* critics* have not failed to pursue the question of platonic love as represented in one form by the relationship Carroll claimed to have with child-friends. Robert Duprée, a scholar based at the University of Dallas, Texas in a 1982 article entitled 'She's all my Fancy painted Him', proposed that Carroll's children's story should be interpreted as part of the Pre-Raphaelite revival of the tradition of courtly love. He argued that Alice Liddell, Carroll's principal child-friend, was to his muse what Laura was to Petrarch's and Beatrice was to Dante's. Alice, by this interpretation, was a most special child-friend – Carroll's audience, heroine, story-teller and leading lady, and besides, the conversationalist with whom he most liked to engage.

> The ritual courtship he enacted over and over again was not the product of an obsession, or even a compensation for a lost fulfilment. It was a way of life that he discovered through Alice, a kind of purificatory rite that led him, like Dante and Petrarch, to a sense of some higher reality.

Albert Camus (1913–60) also saw the higher reality with which Carroll endowed his affection for chosen child-friends as a return to:

> ... the soft resonance, the muffled mystery of a lost paradise, the paradise of childhood, as fresh as Baudelaire's '*vert paradis*'.

Such literary interpretations appear to accord well with the Anglican theocratic universe which Carroll inhabited as a child and as an adult.

Christ Church Known as 'the House', Christ Church was Carroll's Oxford college and his home from the time he first arrived as an undergraduate in 1851 until his death in January 1898. This article is organized into a general introduction, followed by sections on the Library and the Cathedral, tenure in Victorian Christ Church, Carroll's rooms, Christ Church Meadows, and finally Christ Church and royalty.

INTRODUCTION Christ Church is entered under Tom Tower built in 1681 by Christopher Wren. The gateway under this high clock tower leads into Tom Quad, the largest of the Oxford quads, low, understated and sober, built of pale – in some lights honey-coloured – stone. All around the quadrangle runs a raised walkway, originally intended by Cardinal Wolsey (c. 1475–1530) as a cloister. On two sides are Canons' and some tutors' residences. On one side is the Dining Hall, below which is the Senior Common Room where Carroll was Curator with a special interest in wine.* Opposite Tom Tower are the Cathedral and Deanery, Alice's home.

The proportions of the quadrangle are such that within it there is always comparative quiet – away from the traffic outside – well-kept lawns and the 'great pool', known as 'Mercury' from its statue, from which water flows. The circular driveway is, and always was, kept free of vehicles, although the Dean's carriage would have been an exception. This central part of Christ Church still suggests a monastic establishment. A visitor in Carroll's day, seeing black figures in clerical gaiters and mortar-boards crossing the space of Tom Quad, perhaps a child or two, like Alice or the children of one of the Canons, and one or two scouts (the undergraduates' servants), would take this to be a place given to quiet study, to religion, and, to a small degree, to family life. The terriers, blood hounds, fox hounds, pointers and retrievers kept by the wealthier undergraduates were generally not visible in Tom.

Beyond the Deanery side of Tom is Peckwater Quadrangle, the eighteenth-century quadrangle where Carroll lived in his first year as a young undergraduate. One side is taken up by the Library, the other three by undergraduate accommodation. Peckwater was notorious for being dominated by the hunting-set and by college 'rowdies' rather than by 'reading men' such as Carroll. It was in Peckwater in 1870 that the most notorious of all Christ Church pranks occurred, when undergraduates, in response to Liddell's sacking of a porter who used to smuggle undergraduates – and sometimes women – in and out after hours, climbed into the Library, took out the valuable collection of busts, and started a bonfire around them, causing a national scandal.

When Carroll arrived at Christ Church, undergraduates were divided into four classes. The Noblemen wore gold tasselled mortar-boards, were not obliged to take examinations and when in College, would sit at High Table with the Dean. All but a few did little work, preferring to keep dogs, organize cock-fights, hold gambling parties and hunt. To their chagrin they had to attend services in the cathedral and be counted by – and humiliate if they could – humbler undergraduates, known as 'prickers-in'. Carroll was for a time a 'pricker-in'.

Below the Noblemen came the Gentlemen Commoners like Liddell,* Gladstone* and Ruskin.* They were more serious students and were required to take examinations. Then came the Commoners, of whom Carroll was one, as were many of those who progressed from Christ Church to country livings in the Church of England. These livings, like Carroll's father's, were often in the gift of Christ Church. The lowest of the low were the Servitors, who paid their way by serving at table and performing other college duties.

The loudest of the undergraduates, the 'rowdies', treated Oxford as a rite of passage – or right of passage – on their way to a life running landed estates. Only criminal acts could remove them from the college and, because the Dean judged what was criminal, this seldom happened, even when a kettle filled with gunpowder was attached to his front door. Happily the kettle was removed and a possibly fatal explosion prevented.

Dean Liddell, unlike Benjamin Jowett* of Balliol, who wished to expand the social reach of the new intake of the university, felt he could improve the existing crowd, particularly as sports like rowing became more central to college life. He welcomed aristocrats to Christ Church, seeing their unlawfulness as part of a pattern of behaviour expected of the ruling class. Even after the great Library riot, Liddell seemed more upset by the fact that these events were reported in *The Times*, than by the events themselves.

CHRIST CHURCH LIBRARY   The library at Christ Church was where Carroll was given his first paid work in the college. A building fronted with Corinthian columns, it dwarfs the already grandiose three sides of Peckwater Quadrangle. The lower floors of the library are now filled with modern books and serve as an undergraduate reference library. Beyond, and up the circular stairs, is the great panelled upper library which houses the college's famous antiquarian collection, now deserted except by a few specialist scholars. All is intact as in Carroll's day, when he was paid as a very young don to catalogue books in a small room hidden behind ornate panelling. His little office has almost the only view possible over the spacious Deanery garden.* While he would have seen the Liddell children pass through Tom Quad, here he could gaze on them uninterruptedly. It was from here that, in his first attempt at photography, he called down to young 'Harry' Liddell, Alice's handsome eldest brother, to entice him to Southey's rooms to have his picture taken.

This high view over the flat planes of the Deanery garden with the Cathedral beyond and the garden's old, slightly crumbling walls is the most poignantly and perfectly preserved of all the places of interest that still exist in the development of Carroll's friendship with Alice and her sisters. Some of the coal smoke grime that Nathaniel Hawthorne noted as so predominant on Oxford stone is gone; the plants in the beds are more modern hybrids; the rest is little changed by 150 years.

CHRIST CHURCH CATHEDRAL   At the centre of Christ Church is the Cathedral which is both college chapel and Cathedral of Oxford. Hence the term 'The House', or 'Houseman' for an undergraduate or graduate of the college: Christ Church is the House of God, never 'Christ Church *College*'.

Christ Church was founded by Cardinal Wolsey at the time of the dissolution of the monasteries as a college surrounding the ancient, mainly romanesque, cathedral of St Frideswide.* After the execution of Wolsey and the hiatus this caused, the college was re-established by Henry VIII in 1546 and ever since then its Dean has been Dean of the Diocese of Oxford as well as head of the college.

The high, narrow cathedral has its central part enclosed in a square of romanesque arches. The stone is pale and reflective of the light which comes slanting down from above, for the windows are high. The dark wood of the choir and of the Canons' and Students' stalls is elaborately carved. Carroll worshipped in the Cathedral daily. That must have given him a sense of the privilege of being alive and it must have sharpened his aesthetic sense. Cathedral services were the regular and sacred punctuation of Carroll's daily life and he resisted any change. When Dean Liddell suggested that the early morning service should begin later, Carroll strenuously objected. The idea was practical. Carroll wanted no change to Cathedral conventions.

During Carroll's time, the way that revenues were shared between Cathedral and College were under University and Parliamentary review. When Canon Pusey feared that the Canons might lose control of Cathedral discipline, he expressed abhorrence at the idea that Christ Church might become a 'mere college'. Carroll generally took Pusey's side. The existence of the Cathedral within Christ Church gave the college, and its devoted Students like Carroll, their sense of having a unique place in English life.

TENURE AT VICTORIAN CHRIST CHURCH   Students, similar to fellows in other colleges, were graduates elected to life tenure, which they kept so long as they did not get married. Some were resident, some were not. Gladstone, for example, was a Student although he did not reside in the college after he had taken his degree. In December 1852, when he was 20, Carroll heard from his father that he had been recommended for a studentship by Dr Pusey*.

His 'good conduct' and brilliance in examinations were noted. This was a remarkable achievement for someone so young.

Although Carroll tended to agree with his father's friend and his mentor, Canon Pusey, he seldom agreed with Dean Liddell. When Liddell was appointed Dean of Christ Church, certain changes in the privileges and powers of Students were made. Carroll was a Student of the Old Foundation, because his appointment pre-dated Liddell's and he seems to have felt prickly about all changes in the ancient tradition. Crucial to the understanding of this and to seeing Carroll as a political animal is a book written by E. G. W. Bill, ex-archivist of Christ Church, and J. F. A. Mason, former tutor in history and Librarian. They were the authors of *Christ Church and Reform, 1850–67* (1970). This describes relations between the Liddell regime and the Christ Church Students while Carroll was writing *Alice*. Although Carroll was a small player on this Oxford college stage, given the importance of Oxford in nineteenth-century Britain and Christ Church in nineteenth-century Oxford, the stage seemed far from small. Carroll felt these issues, such as syllabus reform, the decline of classical teaching and the rise of science, were crucial, not just in his own fortunes, but to the ethos of his country. For better or worse, he was right. Cambridge and Oxford set the tone for the establishment of Great Britain. Mason and Bill's dense monograph was the first to draw attention to the schisms that broke out in the decade from 1857 to 1867 between the tutors, the Christ Church Canons and Dean Liddell over the status of college tutors granted tenure before 1857.

These members of the 'Old Foundation' included Kitchin,* Liddon,* Prout,* Ranken* and Southey* in Carroll's immediate circle. The controversy rumbled on all through the time that Carroll was writing *Alice*. The references to 'C' and 'D' in the Mouse's tale/tail,* appear to us to refer to the initial letters of those most closely involved in suppressing the Old Foundation, the Canons and Dean. What was really at stake was the passing of an old order. Before Liddell, no one meddled with the Christ Church constitution because that was how life was lived. Students took up residence, did some teaching, were mutually ignored by the undergraduates who spent much time hunting, worshipped God with differing degrees of cynicism, ate, drank, plotted and lived their comfortable Oxford lives. Liddell clearly saw that the University and its colleges must train undergraduates for other than the priesthood. None of this was to the liking of Carroll and his colleagues of the Old Foundation. For them a quiet life, a life with an eighteenth rather than a nineteenth-century rhythm was preferable. The Mouse had a sad tale and a long tale. It was angry with the C and D.

CARROLL'S ROOMS AT CHRIST CHURCH   The rooms at Christ Church occupied by Carroll have been carefully researched, particularly by Edward Wakeling.* In his first year as an undergraduate, Carroll had rooms in the traditionally aristocratic Peckwater Quadrangle, overlooking the Library. Then he moved to the cloister where he remained for eight years in an ancient set of rooms. It was on the sofa here that *Alice* evolved, that some photographs were taken, and many developed, for Alice a thrilling moment. In 1862 Carroll moved to a more airy set in Tom Quad, on Staircase 7. In 1868 Lord Bute was forced to give up rooms above, one of the most spacious sets in the college. Edward Wakeling has described this in detail in *Jabberwocky* (summer 1983) and suggested that the move was possible because of the 1867 Christ Church Reform Act, disallowing aristocrats to keep a residence in the college which they hardly used.

Carroll occupied, by Wakeling's reconstruction,

A first floor with a large sitting room, tower rooms at the corners, a view of the Archdeacon's garden, a small bedroom off the sitting room, and a small dining room and scullery parallel to each other. On the floor above were the main bedroom, bathroom and toilet and a small dark room. This floor gave access to the roof and the photographic studio. In 1884 an Asbestos fire was fitted in the upper bedroom, greatly adding to Carroll's comfort. By March 1887 Carroll had four of these fires, 'and no coals at all.'

This was his home for life, thought by some to be the best set of rooms in Oxford. Christ Church being the creation of Cardinal Wolsey, the last English cardinal before those of Carroll's time, Manning* and Newman,* the flat Cardinal's hat with its dangling tassels was – and is still – the emblem of the college. It is carved in a particularly attractive way below the windows of Carroll's extensive set of rooms in the college, on the St Aldate's Street side. If Carroll was amused by the irony of High Church dons living daily in the presence of this idiom, he would not have shown it. Clerical jokes of all kinds were beyond the pale. (See also Bats and Belfry,* Bread and Butter,* Christ Church* Meadows below, Deanery* and Sites of interest.*)

CHRIST CHURCH MEADOWS   The Meadows occupy open land between the college and the river and were a daily haunt of Carroll's. They provided, and still provide, one of the most picturesque landscapes in Britain; wild overgrown meadowland where cattle graze along the river, intersected by formal walks, in Carroll's day lined with elms, now mostly gone. In the nineteenth century the Meadows would frequently flood and sometimes freeze. In 1852 when Carroll, then 20, was first at Christ Church, the flood was so deep that boats sailed over the Meadows.

The Meadows comprise 46 acres in front of Christ Church, Corpus Christi and Merton, providing a rustic place on the doorstep of Carroll's college, in which he could walk alone, or with friends and children, notably with Alice. They crossed them when they walked towards Salter's Boat Yard from where they rented rowing boats on the Isis or Thames,* the Oxford river having two names. The Meadows were part of the original college grant from Henry VIII which Christ Church has defended over the years, partly thanks to the number of House men in parliament. Various improving schemes, including a major bypass, have been proposed and fended off.

During Carroll's time, Dean Liddell added to the Meadows' side of the buildings a large, pseudo-Gothic, residential block. It solved the acute accommodation problems of the college, but few have forgiven him since. His other 'improvement' has a great deal more charm. This is the long avenue that Dean Liddell constructed between Christ Church and the river. Few landscape photographs* by Carroll remain. One of them is in the album* he gave to Alice, a view down the Broad Walk with the black old elms arching over it and light penetrating their branches, a strong and beautiful evocation of the space where he and Alice walked.

CHRIST CHURCH AND ROYALTY   Henry VIII's favourite, Cardinal Wolsey, founded Christ Church as a college on the site of a monastery. After Wolsey's ruin, Henry VIII re-founded the college. Henry's great portrait dominates Christ Church Hall and, with his square chested stance, is reminiscent of the King of Hearts in *Wonderland*. The monarch remains the Visitor at Christ Church, equivalent to a patron. The Liddells already had a royal connection from their days at Westminster. This made 'The House' the obvious college for the Prince of Wales* to attend. This further royal association reinforced the sense of the college superiority to insiders, who liked in those days to think of it as *the* Oxford college.

In fact, Queen Victoria may not have regarded Christ Church with undiluted enthusiasm. She strongly detested the High Church faction of which Canon Pusey was the leader. Nor did her husband, Prince Albert, want his son influenced by profligate and high living undergraduates. So the Crown Prince lived outside the college and had no regular college contacts. Meanwhile, just as the Queen was sceptical of Pusey, so Carroll, Pusey's friend, was sceptical of the Queen's own brand of protestantism.

In *Wonderland* Alice threw the King and Queen to the wind, for they were only a pack of cards. In *Looking-Glass* Alice, a commoner, became Queen. Both books mock and undermine the – in the third decade of Victoria's reign – almost unassailable idea of monarchy. German fairy stories tended to allude to ghouls and hobgoblins. Here is an English book which seems to make absurd kings and queens their equivalents. It was written in a college founded by the most terrifying of all British monarchs. (See also Deanery and Deanery Garden* and Queen Victoria.*)

Church Attendance   'Oncer' was a derogatory late Victorian term applied to those who only attended church once on Sundays. In an age when sermon- and preacher-following was as obsessive as following serials in the magazine, some like W. E. Gladstone* and H. P. Liddon* were even 'thricers'. Carroll was certainly a 'twicer' on most Sundays, attending Communion and Matins. He would have attended college chapel in the Cathedral once each day, with additional visits for Evensong as well. The Dean would have been expected to have presided at Morning Service and Evensong in the Cathedral. (See also Preaching.*)

Cohen, Morton Norton (1921–)   Morton Cohen is the doyen of Anglo-American Carroll scholarship. He is Canadian, but has worked largely in the USA. His field is Victorian literary bibliography and letters. Based at the Graduate School of the City University of New York from the 1950s, Morton Cohen's publications include two literary biographies, the earliest of Rider Haggard (1960) and the latest his acclaimed biography of Lewis Carroll (1995). In addition, he published a stream of annotated publications and discoveries. It was he, for example, who identified Carroll's pen and ink sketch of Edith Liddell* under the photograph of her older sister Alice, in the British Library *Under Ground* manuscript.

   Morton Cohen came to investigate the Carroll archives for the first time when Roger Lancelyn Green,* the English editor of Carroll's diaries, found he could not track down some of the Carroll holdings that had been sent to America. Cohen recalled that the invitation to become a Carroll scholar was made over tea in 1960 in Lancelyn Green's garden in the countryside outside Liverpool, not far from Daresbury,* Cheshire, Carroll's birthplace. Cohen noted that he had:

> ... no idea that it would take five whole years and thousands of letters to libraries and collectors simply to track down Carroll's own letters ...

That was only the beginning. Many of the recipients, young girls when Carroll wrote to them, subsequently married and often went abroad. It took 19 years before his two-volume edition of Carroll's *Letters** appeared, which was followed by Carroll's correspondence with the House of Macmillan* and an edition of Carroll's friend, Henry Parry Liddon's* journal of their visit to Russia. Collector and commentator on many aspects of Carroll's life, Morton

Cohen elucidated Carroll's contacts with the maze of family responsibilities and child-friendships before during and after the publication of the *Alice* stories.

The Letters (1979), the *Russian Journal* of 1867, the commentaries on Carroll's nude studies and on the Kitchin* family have thrown light on pressures driving Carroll after the publication of *Alice*. If Cohen, doyen of Carroll studies, has a fault, it is that he is more a devotee of Carroll the man, whom he refers to as 'Charles' throughout his 1995 biography, than of the man's writings.

Morton Cohen writes children's stories and, under the pen-name, John Moreton, is the author of detective stories.

Collingwood Family Carroll's parents had 11 children. The four oldest failed to marry, as did the four youngest. In the middle Mary, Skeffington and Wilfred did marry. Mary Charlotte (1835–1911), was the only girl to marry and that did not happen until she was 34. Her husband was the Rev Charles Edward Stuart Collingwood (1831–98), for 35 years Rector of Southwick, part of the Tyneside community of Sunderland. Later she was frankly critical of Carroll over his relationship with girls.

The Collingwoods had two sons. One was a scientist and doctor of medicine, Bertram Collingwood (1871–1934). He was helped financially by Carroll when studying at Cambridge. It was due to him that the funds were raised for the Lewis Carroll Ward for Children at St Mary's Hospital in London, where Collingwood worked. Bertram's elder brother was Stuart Dodgson Collingwood (1870–1937), Carroll's nephew, godchild, and literary executor. Collingwood was, in the family tradition, a Christ Church* undergraduate. He graduated in theology in 1892 and held positions as a theological tutor in a seminary in Hertford. He became a headmaster in Ireland where he lived as a bachelor.

Carroll seems to have been fond of both brothers and to have held them in respect, saying, when they were in their twenties, that their powers of argument were 'rather unusually developed'. The last known letters Carroll wrote, nine days before he died, included one to Stuart, whose father had just died, warning him about being overcharged by the undertaker. Collingwood, who died childless in Ireland, was the last person to access the manuscripts of those of Carroll's private journals that are missing.

As Carroll's literary executor, Collingwood became 'keeper of the flame'. His biography, *Life and Letters of Lewis Carroll* (1898) published so soon after Carroll's death, gave his uncle a prominence enjoyed by few writers of children's books. It is as 'innocent' a portrait as he and Carroll wished it to be. It was as the author of *Alice* that Carroll was known and those books, everyone accepted, were written for children. Collingwood's saccharine view of Carroll, and sentimental accounts of his child-friendships set an uncritical tone for Carroll studies for several generations. (See also Biographers.*)

Collodion   The wet collodion process was invented by F. Scott Archer (1813–57) and patented in 1851 just before Carroll took up photography* in 1854. It quickly displaced the early daguerreotype and calotype techniques for it needed less exposure time – from a few seconds to a few minutes depending on available light. The wet collodion technique still necessitated deftness in the handling of chemicals and glass plates in the field or dark room, or in a portable dark tent. The equipment was heavy and exposure times were still long, requiring considerable directorial ability from the photographer. In particular, Carroll, as a photographer of children, needed to get those who posed for him in the right mood, and to keep them there while the glass plate absorbed the light from the image.

In preparing the plate, a mixture of chemicals had to be poured on to the perfectly clean glass plate in such a way as to ensure an even coating. Over this viscous covering, the photographer poured silver nitrate solution, which combined to make light-sensitive silver iodide. The process gave the fine detail of highlight and shadow that is characteristic of Carroll's best photographs. It is possible that his mastery of collodion inspired the tastes Carroll wrote about in the bottle labelled DRINK ME! which Alice tasted when she first arrived in Wonderland:

> It had a sort of mixed flavour of cherry-tart, custard, pine-apple, roast turkey, toffy [toffee] and hot buttered toast.

In processing the collodion plate, the photographer used an alcohol-drenched, ether-based solution of potassium iodide, and some potassium salts are as red as cherries. The glass plates were finished with albumen – egg white, also the ingredient of nursery 'custard'. The resulting mixture was as sticky as 'toffy', and as treacly brown as toffee because of the iodide in the mixture. When she was interviewed in 1932, Alice particularly remembered the fun and mystery of helping mix up these chemicals in Carroll's dark room.

Wet collodion photography retained its popularity until 1881, by which time dry processes, of which Carroll did not approve, took its place. Carroll claimed he gave up photography when wet collodion was supplanted.

Combe, Thomas (1797–1872)   Thomas Combe was Senior Partner in the University Press at Oxford, and the Press was, until the coming of the railway carriage works, the only industrial employer in the city. The revenues of the Press expanded greatly in mid-century with the increase in demand for Bibles,* particularly to British colonies, and continued sales of Clarendon's multi-volume history of the English Civil War. The High Church,* fox-hunting Thomas Combe prospered greatly as a result of this and the Combe household became a focal point in Oxford for the meeting of interesting artists and theologians.

Combe purchased many paintings from the Pre-Raphaelites,* especially from Holman Hunt. Carroll photographed Combe who then helped him devise the trial layouts for *Alice*. Carroll's professionalism in page layout owed a good deal to Combe's tuition. In October 1863, Combe introduced Carroll to the publisher, Alexander Macmillan.* In June 1865 Combe's Clarendon Press printed the first 2000 copies of what was intended to be the first edition of the book of *Wonderland*. Tenniel* rejected this edition with indignation on technical grounds. Carroll advised Combe that he wished to recall the entire Clarendon edition at his own expense. Carroll's arrangement with Macmillan was that he himself should pay for the printing, wood-engravings and advertising of *Alice*, Macmillan receiving fixed commissions on sales.

In spite of the fact that Tenniel obliged Carroll to turn to his rival, the printer, Richard Clay, Combe remained sympathetic to Carroll, who was High Church and pious like himself. He restored the old mill at Wolvercote as the paper mill for the press, and Carroll and Alice visited this on up-river expeditions past Port Meadow. It was here that the story of *Alice* began. (See also Oxford, city.*)

Congregation and Convocation Carroll attended these University parliaments at Oxford,* but is only known to have spoken on one occasion, on the Jowett* issue.

Conversation *Alice* contains many references to polite conversation and good manners. For example, by the Pool of Tears, when the Mouse says it does not want to hear the name *cats* again:

"I won't indeed!" said Alice, in a great hurry to change the subject of conversation. "Are you—are you fond—of—of dogs?" The Mouse did not answer so Alice went on eagerly...

And, at the Mad Tea-Party*:

"Who's making personal remarks now?" the Hatter asked triumphantly.
Alice did not quite know what to say to this: so she helped herself to some tea and bread-and-butter, and then turned to the Dormouse, and repeated her question...

To some extent Alice's adventures in both *Wonderland* and *Looking-Glass* are adventures in conversation. Alice's wits were put to the test: of making the right reply; of being firm, even rude by Deanery standards, when challenged; of finding the right opening, the right next question, the right mood in others. Etiquette was at the centre of the Liddells'* world, and, in its more bachelorish way, of Carroll's also. Knowing how to converse was perhaps the key issue. Books on etiquette could teach some of the rules of calling and calling cards, of when to send them and how to have them printed, of table manners and public manners, of dress and decorum, but at the centre of the social encounter was conversation, which had to be kept going however formal the situation, however awkward the circumstances.

The issue at stake was not just that conversation should be proper, but that the speaker should be kind, and also tactful. That was the Christian side of Victorian manners that distinguished them from the rougher world of the Regency period. Christian tact was the essence of the worlds Carroll and Alice inhabited. In the maddest way, after Alice has been introduced to the leg of mutton ('Alice—Mutton; Mutton—Alice') the Red Queen,* in 'Queen Alice', says:

> "May I give you a slice?" she said, taking up the knife and fork, and looking from one Queen to the other.
>
> "Certainly not," the Red Queen said, very decidedly: "it isn't etiquette to cut anyone you've been introduced to. Remove the joint!" And the waiters carried it off, and brought a large plum-pudding in its place.

Copyright   Under the 1842 Copyright Act, copyright subsisted for 42 years after the first publication or seven years after the author's death, whichever was the longer. The 1911 Act extended the period to 50 years after the author's death. Thus the text of *Wonderland* came out of copyright in 1907 and of *Looking-Glass* in 1948. Not surprisingly, in 1907 publishers rushed to produce new editions of Carroll's famous book and at least a dozen appeared within a few months of one another. Tenniel* did not die until 1914, so his illustrations remained in copyright until 1964.

Critics   Among the English literary critics from the inter-war period who were also writers, and who took Carroll seriously, W. H. Auden,* David Cecil,* T. S. Eliot,* William Empson,* Robert Graves,* Walter de la Mare,* Langford Reed,* Evelyn Waugh,* Edmund Wilson* and Virginia Woolf* were notable. In the post-war period, Carroll criticism in England and America has become atomized, influenced by social movements seeking endorsement in Carroll's masterwork or social historians treating Carroll's century-old vision as a convenient window into the Victorian world. The dominant strands of current Carroll scholarship, outlined below, are not mutually exclusive.

CARROLL AS A CONFLICTED CLERGYMAN   Humphrey Carpenter is the son of a bishop of Oxford, biographer of an archbishop and author of biographies of J. R. R. Tolkien and W. H. Auden as well as co-author, with Marie Pritchard, of *The Oxford Companion to Children's Literature*; and of *The Golden Age of Children's Literature* (i.e. *English* children's literature). Accepting the originality of the *Alice* books, he sees the rest of Carroll's life and work as caught up in obscurities. Seeing no possibility that satire inspired the nonsense of *Alice*, he emphasizes that Carroll was a cleric whose rationalism severely challenged his faith. (See also Evelyn Waugh.)

THE LIBERATIONIST SCHOOL OF CARROLL CRITICISM   This school continues to emphasize an inferred favourable status of women as reflected in *Alice*. For example, Nina Auerbach suggested that Carroll rejected the Victorian idealization of women and children and portrayed a girl heroine who was decisive, confident and even cruel by nature. Her qualities of curiosity and assertiveness give a truer portrait of Carroll's child*-friends than had hitherto been delineated.

In a broader vein, Juliet Dusinberre emphasized in *Alice to the Lighthouse; Children's Books and Radical Experiments in Art*, (1987) that *Alice* served to challenge not just Victorian ideals of womanhood, but also received ideas in general. Carroll, she suggested, inspired writers like Kenneth Grahame (1859–1932) and Virginia Woolf to create 'a new secular fiction'. Dusinberre suggested that Carroll's 'irreverence' in the *Alice* books was an irreverence towards 'pretension in the adult world towards children, whom Carroll understood on their own terms as no writer had done before'.

CARROLL AS A PRE-RAPHAELITE AUTHOR, PHOTOGRAPHER AND ILLUSTRATOR   U. C. Knoepflmacher of Princeton in 1982 described Carroll's relationship with Christina Rossetti, his indebtedness to William Wordsworth's verse and his admiration for and falling out with Tennyson.* He reviewed Dennis Potter's script for the film, *Dream-Child** and traced the influence of George MacDonald* and Jean Ingelow (1820–97) on Carroll's work in *Ventures into Childland: Victorians, Fairy Tales and Femininity* (1996), maintaining that Carroll was not an isolated, donnish recluse, but a gifted member of the Rossetti *milieu*, a suggestion first effectively elaborated by Jeffrey Stern and Robert Duprée. (See Child*-Friends).

SEMIOTICS AND CARROLL CRITICISM   Rachael Fordyce, Dean of Humanities at Montclair State University in New Jersey, is editor and bibliographer of works relating to children's theatre and literature. In 1988 she published a critical bibliography,* *Lewis Carroll: A Reference Guide*. (See Punctuation* in *Alice*.) She was co-editor of the papers of the 1990 conference about *Alice* and language that took place in Urbino, Italy.

ALICE AND VICTORIAN ADULT EROTIC FANTASY   Between the wars, psychoanalytic criticism of *Alice* was Freudian in emphasis. This emphasis has now shifted towards the controversial topic of child eroticism. Two *Alice* critics who have explored Carroll's love affair with the child and fascination with the child's capacity to imagine horror are the American scholars, James R. Kincaid in *Child-Loving; the Erotic Child and Victorian Literature* (1992) and Carol Mavor in *Pleasures Taken; Performances of Sexuality and Loss in Victorian Photographs* (1995).

Joyce Carol Oates (1938–) the American author, critic and literary sage teaches at Princeton and is also a Carroll critic. In 1982 she wrote a limpid and elegant contribution, *Dodgson's Golden Hours* to the *English Language Notes* compendium on Lewis Carroll (see the Select Bibliography). Her essay reviews a limited edition of *Wonderland* and of *The Hunting of the Snark* and in it she revived Robert Graves'* view that Alice was 'the prime heroine of our nation'. She also noted the importance of cannibalism in *Alice*.

> This particular reader, as a very young child, found most terrifying the conclusion of the 'Looking-Glass' feast when all that has systematically been denied becomes possible – becomes manifest. Madness is given the spin of logic. Candles rise to the ceiling, bottles take on plates and forks for limbs, the nightmare is nearly uncontrollable when Alice discovers that the guests are about to be eaten by their food ...

CARROLL AND THE DRUG EXPERIENCE   Robert Phillips (1938–) is a Carroll scholar who has published studies of W. B. Yeats, James Joyce and Dylan Thomas. He ended his collection, *Aspects of Alice* (1972), with two controversial entries written in the mid-1960s, relating *Alice* to drug* usage in Carroll's day.

Defending his decision in *Jabberwocky* the following year, Robert Phillips emphasized that the articles he had commissioned were intended to be taken seriously. One is a satire by Thomas Fensch, photographer and journalist, entitled 'Alice in Acidland'. The other is the catchy lyric, 'White Rabbit', written by Grace Slick for the Jefferson Airplane Rock Group when she was lead singer. Carroll's connections with mind-changing drugs are proposed and rejected at various times. In his defence of his decision to publish these two pieces, Phillips cited R. A. Durr's monograph, *Poetic Vision and the Psychedelic Experience* (1970). This discusses Thomas de Quincey's *Confessions of an Opium Eater*. Phillips claimed controversially that:

Carroll's intensification, expansion, and freeing of the mind, which normally would be called merely 'imaginative', fall well within Durr's definition of psychedelic elements.

THE NONSENSE SCHOOL OF CRITICISM Twentieth-century critics have emphasized that Carroll, with Edward Lear (1812–88), created the 'Nonsense' literary style as a style unique to Victorian England and one that is governed by its own strict rules. The Belgian critic, Emile Cammaerts (1878–1953) pioneered this school of criticism with *The Poetry of Nonsense* (1925). Elizabeth Sewell (1919–), Professor of Humanities in North Carolina after 1974 began her literary studies of nonsense with *The Structure of Poetry* (1951) and *The Field of Nonsense* (1952). Primarily concerned with the poetry of Rimbaud and Mallarmé, she informed us that her first two books were 'laced with references to Carroll, since I was pursuing Method, or thinking, and so, I was convinced, was Carroll'. In essays dedicated to T. S. Eliot and Michael Polyani, she noted that scenes in *Alice* describe trials which mirror real-life trials unanticipated by Carroll such as the Dreyfus Trial, the Reichstag Fire Trial, Stalinist show trials in Moscow and the US McCarthy hearings. She believed that the analytical interpretation of Carroll's nonsense has been too frequently neglected in favour of psychoanalytic, erotic or social contextual approaches to his work, concluding:

> We do not need to be reminded, in this day and age, that we of the West have been walking ever since the time of Descartes, further and further into a world constructed upon the outlook of mathematics, logic, analysis. Carroll's message is that this leads into a world of game-playing, nonsense and nightmare.

As Sewell noted in 1952 in *The Field of Nonsense*, 'There is nothing more inexorable than a game'.

CARROLL AS SATIRIST We are biased towards a view which emphasizes that *Alice* was in part a satire on human affairs based on Carroll's observations of individuals he photographed or communicated with in the Victorian world that he inhabited. (See also William Empson* and Shane Leslie.*)

Croft, North Yorkshire Carroll's father was appointed Rector there in 1843 when Carroll was 11 and it continued to be the family home until the death of his father in 1868. A small village on the edge of the River Tees, Croft is set in prosperous, rolling farm-land ten miles south of Darlington. The National School where Carroll gave a magic lantern show to his family and local children still stands.

The three-storey Georgian rectory overlooks the church and churchyard and they, sheltered by lime trees, overlook the rippling river. The church, St Peter's, is of russet-coloured sandstone and so ancient that everything built after 1500 is described in the local guidebook as 'modern'. It has been argued that various emblems in the church influenced Carroll and that one of the gargoyles there was his model for the Cheshire Cat*. Certainly the church is furnished with some strange objects, such as the Milbank family pew, raised up like a little Renaissance stage on pillars, reminiscent of the high throne on which the King and Queen of Hearts sit at the trial of the Knave.

More important, the airy rooms at Croft and the Rectory's secluded garden were places where an imaginative boy could develop ideas for games, fantasies and puzzles. *The Rectory Magazine* was produced at Croft with Carroll as chief editor and major contributor. In the soft northern light of Croft, Carroll took many of his best early photographs, interior and exterior, mainly of his sedate-looking sisters in their hooped skirts.

The grave of Carroll's parents is by the north-east corner of the church. There is a plaque commemorating Carroll on the left just inside the door. (See also Sites of interest.*)

Croquet   A French import based on the old game of *paille-maille*, croquet was called pall-mall in Elizabethan times. First played in England in around 1852 when Carroll came to Christ Church,* it soon became popular. Mrs Liddell's* approach to exercise for her girls suggests that they would have participated in what became, until eclipsed by tennis, the most popular of all country-house summer lawn games.

Carroll, perhaps to make a mockery of the game – as indeed he did in *Alice* – devised sets of new rules for croquet. He also proposed alternative rules for tennis and billiards. 'Croquet Castles: A new game invented by the Rev. C. L. Dodgson' was published in the form of a four page pamphlet in 1863 and an amended version in 1866. The Liddell children found the new variant on a game they enjoyed taxing. The croquet match is a spoof at the centre of *Wonderland*, a large set piece in the narrative which has echoes of grand parties and games on the Deanery* lawn. As for Carroll's revision of the rules, this echoes other occasions where the semi-serious pamphlets written anonymously or by C. L. Dodgson, for example on proportional representation, overlap with nonsense in the *Alice* texts. (See also Parliamentary Representation.*)

Cryptography   Cryptography held a life-long interest for Carroll, both in its formal sense, that of devising specific ciphers and, in its informal sense, in the codes, word games, puns, double meanings, looking-glass illusions, disguises, hidden jokes and puzzles that run through *Alice*. As spies searching for spies helped to define the real world in the era of the Cold War, so Alice, puzzled but self-confident, helps us define the world's puzzles in a more philosophical, more imaginative way. The connection is not entirely spurious.

Carroll may or may not have started an interest in codes and ciphers at Christ Church. One definitely continued after him, at least up to the generation of those like Professor Hugh Trevor-Roper (now Lord Dacre, 1914–) who were recruited into the World War II secret services, and probably beyond this generation to the present. It is the view of the American mathematician, Francine Abeles who is editing an edition of his mathematical papers that, whilst he thought of himself as a 'dilettante of cryptography', Carroll 'constructed the first cipher system based on mathematical principles'.

Cuddesdon Theological College (now Ripon Theological College) The college was opened in 1854 when Carroll was beginning to prepare himself for ordination. Henry Parry Liddon* (1829–90), Carroll's theological adviser and travelling companion in Russia, became Vice-Principal but was dismissed, being thought, unjustly, by the Bishop to veer to Rome. Carroll walked through the lanes to Cuddesdon to see Liddon and was ordained Deacon there. In the library is Carroll's moving studio photograph of Liddon, uncaptioned and unrecognized.

Built on a ridge six miles south of Oxford*, the college is near the site of what was the Bishop of Oxford's Palace. The Palace later burned. Such was the ferment in the young Carroll's Oxford caused by conversions to Rome that the purpose of the College was to prevent Oxfordshire parish churches 'being sown broadcast' with Romanized young clergy. John Henry Newman* (1801–90) set up his small retreat in the village of Littlemore half way between Cuddesdon and Oxford and it was not unknown for dons to hide in the bushes to try to catch potential converts from Cuddesdon or the University visiting.

D is for ...

Dali, Salvador (1904–89)   Like other illustrators* of *Alice*, Dali created a series of *Alice* prints and was, like Alfred Jarry, Franz Kafka,* Vladimir Nabokov* and the painter Balthus,* an inheritor of the surreal view of life that Carroll espoused. Dali shared Carroll's obsession with childhood fantasy. A 1950 painting is entitled: 'Dali at the Age of Six When He Believed Himself to be a Young Girl Lifting the Skin of the Water to Observe a Dog Sleeping in the Shadow of the Sea'. Earlier, Dali had painted 'Myself at the Age of Ten when I was the Grasshopper Child' in 1933.

Dali's series of *Alice* lithographs were published in a folio edition by Random House (1982). In each of the original coloured lithographs, Alice is seen as a different tiny figure in line, turning her skipping rope in the corner of the plate. One has to search to find her. Dali used the minute skipping figure of Alice emblematically, as Whistler used the butterfly mark on many of his plates.

Dance   Ordained men like Carroll were generally not allowed to dance by their bishops, although they might attend dances and balls. As far as is known, Carroll did not dance and he wrote to a child*-friend, Gaynor Simpson (1862–1954), in 1873 saying that he never danced unless allowed to do it in his own particular way and that this was similar to the way of a 'Hippopotamus ... at the Zoological Gardens'. Similarly, Alice had to deal with not one clumsy creature but the two, Gryphon* and Mock Turtle.* Like Carroll's parody of himself, these two lacked any grace in their quadrille*, the dance of choice when *Alice* was being composed.

In the eighteenth century the quadrille had been part of the repertoire of French ballet. In the nineteenth it became popular in English ballrooms, drawing rooms and at school dances. It involved four people in a square, hence 'quad', and within the dance were separate figures which translate from French approximately as the 'pantalon', the 'summer', the 'chicken', the 'pastoral' and the 'finale'.

The group of four could be multiplied to eight, twelve, sixteen or twenty. The dance required a good deal of skill and practice and Alice Donkin, who was proposed to by Carroll's brother at a very young age, knew that Ruskin* danced it clumsily although with great pleasure when he taught the girls at Winnington Hall in Cheshire. We think that there is a possibility that Carroll knew this and that the portrait of the Gryphon is in part a parody of Ruskin. Alice would probably have learned or have been learning the intricate steps of the quadrille when *Under Ground* was composed: hence the cogency of the joke about the clumsiness of her partners. The theme also crops up in Alice's encounter with the Red Queen.*

> "Speak in French when you can't think of the English for a thing—turn out your toes as you walk—and remember who you are!"

Such were the instructions given by the Red Queen as she took leave of Alice on the Second Square of the Chess* Game. Cartwheels might have been out of the question, but not 'turning out your toes as you walk'. Alice's dance training – one of those extras on the school bill discussed by the Mock Turtle – would have made her more adept at holding her pose either in the *tableaux vivants* (see Games*) which she executed for her mother's guests or when posing in front of Carroll's camera. For these it was necessary to stay stock still for at least 30 seconds and often more. In one photograph, 'Open Your Mouth and Close Your Eyes', she successfully held a stretched pose on the tips of her toes and appeared about to bite at a cherry as well. (See also Collodion* and Photography.*)

Carroll did occasionally attend ballet performances. On his first visit he did not like what he called 'the studied ugliness of the attitudes'. Then, on the evening of 21 April 1857, at the start of a four-day visit to the London theatres, Carroll bought tickets for the relatively cheap 'pit' of the Haymarket. He saw first the opera, 'The Daughter of the Regiment' with an Italian cast, then the ballet which followed. On this occasion he approved.

Daresbury, Cheshire   This is the small sandstone-and-brick village where Carroll was born in 1832, and where his father was curate, the living being in the gift of Christ Church.* The Lewis Carroll Birthday Trust owns an acre of land on the site where Carroll lived as a child. A plaque marking the site of the parsonage was laid by the Trust in 1974, and there are plans to extend the memorial on this historic acre. The 1831 census gave the population as 143. Consisting only of a handful of houses, Daresbury is today within a few hundred yards of the M56 motorway and within a few miles of the largest concentration of chemical factories in England. However, sheltered from the main roads by lime trees, the village still has some of the sense of rural idyll which Carroll absorbed.

The parsonage which was Carroll's home was, to judge from a photograph taken before it burned down in the 1880s, a small house for a family of nine Dodgson* children. The parsonage stood apart from the village and the church, which was restored in the usual High Church* way and so lacks the rural simplicity of the pre-Victorian church. A local poem described the Daresbury countryside thus:

> The whip cracks on the *plou* [Cheshire for plough]
> team's flank
> The thresher's flail beats duller
> The road of day has warmed a bank
> Of cloud to primrose colour.
>
> The dairy girls cry home the kine
> The kine in answer lowing
> And rough-haired louts with sleepy shouts
> Keep crows whence seed is growing
>
> The creeking wain brushed through the lane
> Hangs straw on hedges narrow
> And smoothly cleaves the soughing plough
> And harshly grinds the harrow

Few people remember the scene of their childhood with quite the attachment that Carroll did. He recalled in the poem 'Faces in the Fire', written when he was 27, not the people who worked the fields and hedgerows, but the place:

> An island farm – mid seas of corn
> Swayed by the wandering breath of morn –
> The happy spot where I was born ...

The family moved away when Carroll's father was promoted to a better living at Croft.*

de la Mare, Walter (1873–1956)   English poet and children's writer, Walter de la Mare's verse and stories link dreams and reality with good-tempered ghosts and fairies. His children's stories and poems included *Songs of Childhood* (1902), *The Three Mulla Mulgars* (1910) and *Peacock Pie* (1913). He also wrote a perceptive literary essay, *Lewis Carroll* (1930 and 1932) published by Faber for the centennial of Carroll's birth. His last anthology had a title that would have appealed to Carroll, *Come Hither: a collection of rhymes and poems for the young of all ages* (1944).

Walter de la Mare's insights into *Alice* are those of one story-teller assessing the work of another. He placed the *Alice* books in the top rank of world literature and was the first major critic to do this. He judged that the structural framework of *Alice* was a particularly ingenious literary creation. Dipping into any section of the *Alice* books, he noted, the reader becomes absorbed in questions to which Carroll, in the person of Alice, devised almost perfect answers. De la Mare grasped what many adults sense but few articulate, 'the timelessness, the placelessness' of *Alice*. This he put on the level of Blake's *Songs of Innocence* and 'medieval descriptions of paradise'.

De la Mare's book deserves re-reading not least for the picture of Alice-as-heroine which it paints. It is symptomatic of the lack of attention, in recent times, that has been paid to the literary critics that de la Mare's appreciation of *Alice* is not mentioned, for example, in Anne Clark's biography of Carroll. As his book is hard to find, a useful source is the excerpted passage in Robert Phillips' (1938–) *Aspects of Alice* (1971). (See also Biographers* and Critics.*)

Deafness   Carroll was deaf in his right ear. His deafness was caused by an 'Infantile Fever', according to one of the few scraps of writing in his mother's hand that survive. Carroll's mother is a shadowy figure, beleaguered by children and, presumably, their illnesses. His hardness of hearing was made worse later by mumps, but reports about Carroll's deafness are few. Morton Cohen* cites a late report by a curate from Eastbourne* who said that Carroll attended the parish church (Christ Church) because the services were said more slowly than elsewhere.

Deanery and Deanery Garden   Christ Church* was Alice Liddell's* home for 25 years, from the time that she was three, in 1855, until she moved away after marrying Reggie Hargreaves* in the summer of 1880. The spacious house, running along the north-east side of Tom Quad at Christ Church, was only a hundred yards from Carroll's rooms in the north-west corner. The Liddells did much to brighten the Deanery to make it suitable for a young family and to remove the fusty atmosphere left by the previous incumbent. A large new staircase, suitable for entertaining royalty and nicknamed 'The Lexicon', paid for with the proceeds from Liddell and Scott's Greek *Lexicon*, was installed. One of the major assets of the house was the view over the large, private Deanery garden.

The garden was one focus of the *Alice* stories. It is large and enclosed and has, in the manner of the best English urban gardens, a feeling that it is a secret place. Specifically the Deanery garden is enclosed by the Cathedral, the Deanery and the Library. Carroll was Assistant Librarian and the view from the window of his small office gave him a view that no one else in the college had. The high-walled garden* was the setting for Carroll's earliest photographs* of Alice, before he began to take interior photographs. They were taken in the strong daylight essential for photographic exposure. This garden was the scene of croquet, see-saw and other games Carroll watched or played with the Liddells, or elaborated on in the quiet of his rooms for Alice to play later.

The Deanery garden was the scene of the Liddell's grandest summertime receptions. It is not surprising that the Queen's croquet* lawn in *Wonderland* has the feeling of this garden.

Carroll's 1863 photograph of the garden appears in Alice's album (see Albums*), all blacks and greys, with a knotted hawthorn in the foreground and the peeling, grime-encrusted stone of Christ Church Library in the background. It has a sense of mystery about it. Carroll took few landscape photographs. The few moody studies in natural light that he did compose portray this garden and the Broad Walk in the Meadows at Christ Church. It is interesting that the only prints we know of these dream-like views of landscape were those he gave to Alice.

Death in *Alice* Tweedledum* and Tweedledee* warned Alice that if the Red King* woke, she might be snuffed out like a candle. Death hovered over *Alice* too, when she rowed with the Sheep in the dark waters by the Mill. Alice herself sounded murderous when, at the very beginning of *Looking-Glass*, Carroll described a game his heroine once played:

> And once she had really frightened her old nurse by shouting suddenly in her ear, "Nurse! Do let's pretend that I'm a hungry hyaena, and you're a bone!"

If Alice's Nanny had been a bone, she would have been dead.

Thoughts about dying mark the opening of *Looking-Glass*. Carroll prefaced the first edition with his poem 'Child of the pure unclouded brow':

> Come, hearken then, ere voice of dread,
>   With bitter tidings laden,
> Shall summon to unwelcome bed
>   A melancholy maiden!
> We are but older children, dear,
> Who fret to find our bedtime near.

Carroll's equation runs: 'Dying is like being sent to bed. We, like children at bedtime, must sleep before a new day dawns'. /

The author acknowledged the loss of Alice's companionship and equated it with a grown-up dread of death. Psychologically-inclined commentators have suggested that Carroll referred here not to death, but to loss of virginity. A reading of Carroll's diary* recorded the Liddell children's shocked state when he took them out for a walk to distract them after the death of their new baby brother at the Deanery in 1863. Such real-life events suggest a more straightforward interpretation.

Deportment of Alice Straight backs for little girls when they were standing and when they were sitting, were expected by mid-Victorian mothers by whom lessons in dance* were approved. In Carroll's portrait photographs, on the other hand, much of Alice's charm is that she is sometimes casually posed, as in the profile of her sitting sideways in a hard chair. In Tenniel's* pictures in *Alice*, she invariably carries herself well, as did Alice Liddell. Regardless of how boring a tea party might be, or a family meal – Alice herself said tea parties had not come into fashion – she would have been disciplined never to slouch at table. Alice was a child from a world where 'sitting up' was seen as important to growing girls as 'fresh air' in the lungs and hard bread in the diet.

Depression Morton Cohen* in his 1995 biography of Carroll, cited a passage by Carroll in the 'Preface' to the *Nursery Alice* where a world-weary Carroll spoke of:

the solemn mockery, and the gaudy glitter, and the hopeless misery, of Life.

Carroll's *angst*, Morton Cohen suggested, may have been part of the 'deep sadness' of a man doomed to watch as child*-friends pass him by, as Alice had.

Diaries, Carroll's These were kept in 13 notebooks of varying thickness, all of them quarto volumes. They were used as a source of information by Stuart Dodgson Collingwood* for his *Life and Letters* (1898), the authorized biography of Carroll. They were then not seen again by anyone who was not a member of the family for many years. They are the single most important research document available to Carroll scholars.

By 1930, four of the volumes had disappeared: the remaining volumes were in the care of Menella Dodgson* (Carroll's niece, the daughter of his brother Wilfred) who, together with her brother, Charles, and sister, Violet, thought they would attempt to edit them with a view to publication; but no publisher was found. Some years later they contacted Roger Lancelyn Green,* by then author of a children's book and several essays about Carroll, to edit the diaries for publication. With a fellowship from Liverpool University, Green completed the task in May 1953. Green considered that the 'lost' diaries had simply been lost by accident. Helmut Gernsheim* was convinced that they were destroyed by Collingwood.

Carroll began to keep a diary in 1854, and had completed the 13 volumes by December 1897, when the record ends. His first diary for 1854 is missing. The diary he wrote covering the last three months of 1855 and those from May 1858 to April 1862 are also missing. 1858 to 1862 were the years of Carroll's intense interest in Alice Liddell,* as were the later parts of 1862 and 1863. Gernsheim's theory of wilful destruction by concerned second-generation family members remains a theory, as does the final fate of the missing diaries.

Dodgson family editing in the diaries needs to be cautiously interpreted. For example, Karoline Leach in 1996, while researching in the diaries in the Guildford* archive, claimed to have made a discovery that Carroll's nieces wished to suppress all mention of Carroll's relationship with the 14-year-old Lorina Liddell* (later Mrs Skene), Alice's older sister. The whiff of a scandal concerned the girl's age. She went out at least 15 times with Carroll with her younger sisters, and was of an age when it was considered impossible to go out unchaperoned. This led to the suggestion that it was Lorina with whom Carroll was in love. Two English newspapers gave considerable coverage to the suggestion, an indication of the interest Carroll-related items still stir up today.

With his usual precision, Carroll started each entry with the month, followed by a colon, followed by the day of the month, followed by a full stop. He always put the day of the week in brackets, thus:

Feb: 8. (Sun). Went to Chapel in surplice for the first time since 14th of October 1855. I read the second lesson in the afternoon. Harry [Liddell] ran up to me afterwards to tell me, 'You've got your white gown on, and you read in the church'.

Most of Carroll's diary entries were from one to fifteen lines long. The entries became less frequent towards the end of his life, so that there are, for example, slightly over 60 entries for 1896, that is to say little more than one a week. The most frequently mentioned person in the diaries was his brother Wilfred, who has 55 entries in the published diaries.

Places mentioned often are Croft,* the Olympic and other London theatres and the Royal Academy. Eastbourne* has 58 entries, more than any other place indexed in Green's 1953 version of the diaries, emphasizing the importance to Carroll of this summer resort, where he met many of his child*-friends. Green admitted leaving out such entries, 'I have often omitted long accounts of how he saw children on the shore at Eastbourne, but failed to cultivate their friendship'. Beyond this, he claimed to have omitted only what he considered trivial, such as entries relating to forgotten people, train times, notes of which sisters were at Guildford and so on. In fact he sanitized the diaries by this means, particularly by removing Carroll's long, anguished prayers.*

To rectify these omissions, Edward Wakeling* is re-editing the diaries, publishing them in full for the Lewis Carroll Society.* He says that family sensitivities were still delicate in the early 1950s and entries were removed in particular which relate to Carroll's obsession with little girls. One of these is a list of over 104 children in alphabetical order of Christian name, little girls whom Carroll hoped would be his sitters at a time he was afraid of losing Alice Liddell's friendship. The text of Carroll's diary is often as ponderous as a statement by a Dodo.* It seems likely, nevertheless, that it may have been Carroll's fondness for Alice and her sisters which caused his reluctant executors to resort to censorship. Morton Cohen* persuaded the Trustees of the Carroll Estate to deposit the remaining diaries with the British Library, where they are available on microfilm.

Diet Carroll was sparing, rather than fastidious, about eating. He did not enjoy dinner parties or feasts at High Table in Christ Church. Indeed, he did not enjoy lunch. Violet Dodgson, his niece, said that when lunch-time arrived at The Chestnuts, Guildford,* he would either go out for a long walk or sit at table nursing a small glass of sherry and a dry biscuit. He noted, 'luncheon, as you know, is not one of *my* meals'. Carroll claimed he eschewed dinner parties because they had too many courses. He considered tea 'that unwholesome drug', hence perhaps the way it tinkled at the Mad Tea-Party. Jokes about food, rich dishes and meagre dishes, keep surfacing in *Alice*: oysters,* whiting,* bread and butter,* pea soup,* mock turtle soup,* tea and treacle.

For at least one child friend, the attraction of a visit to Carroll at Christ Church* was the meringues to which dons had access after big dinners in Christ Church Hall. However the day-to-day realities were not so enticing. Cauliflower, in particular, was a vegetable served by the Manciple to undergraduates and dons in Christ Church Hall with a regularity and lack of taste which bothered Carroll. He repeatedly urged the Christ Church kitchens to cook the vegetable they served so frequently, to a less watery consistency. He grew intemperate on the subject in his correspondence.

Carroll did not comment in his diaries* on what he ate. Yet food and meal jokes abound in *Alice*. They include the hot tureen of mock turtle soup, the talking joint of mutton at the end of Alice's *Looking-Glass* adventures, the vanishing oysters of Tweedledum* and Tweedledee's* ballad, the goose of which Father William* ate the bones and the beak, and a Bread-and-Butter-fly. (See also Fish and Fishy Jokes* and *Looking-Glass* Insects.*)

Dinah   The *Looking-Glass* story opened with one of the kittens of Alice's cat, Dinah, unravelling a ball of wool. One of the kittens was white and the other was black. It ended with Alice asking the black kitten the key metaphysical question: who dreamed it?

As Anne Clark pointed out in her biography of Carroll, the real cat at the Deanery was Dinah who, together with her brother, was given a cold bath by the Liddell children. The brother later died after eating poison. Dinah's name originated in the heroine of a favourite London Music Hall ballad about a Cockney milkman, Wilkins, pronounced in the accent of Samuel Weller Sr, 'Villikens', whose visits Dinah naturally liked. Villikens in the ballad, first composed by John Gay, courted his Dinah, daughter of a rich London merchant. She married him and lived happily ever after. The Liddell sisters sang this song. Though they loved Dinah and her kittens, and she and they appear in *Alice*, no Villikens is known to have been admitted among the cats at the Deanery.*

Disney, Walter ('Walt') Elias (1901–66)   Born in Chicago, Disney died in Los Angeles, head of one of the greatest film businesses in the world. No other single popularizer spread Carroll's *Alice* stories so far and wide. Whilst the Disney version is not regarded as essential to *Alice*, everyone agrees that the Disney version helps to sustain the fame of Carroll's story.

Brian Sibley in an article called 'A Californian Yankee at the Court of Queen Alice' (*Jabberwocky*, 1973) reported that Disney had hoped to make a cartoon film of *Alice* as early as 1931. After one false start, for which Aldous Huxley (see Queen's English*) was approached, Disney took the plunge. The now well-known film was released in 1951 'becoming one of the worst box office disasters' of the year. An earlier Disney *Alice*, in which the part of Alice was acted and other characters were played by animated cartoon creatures, is described by Christopher Finch. Disney had been interested in *Alice* earlier, in Kansas City, before moving to California. In 1923, Walt Disney, aged 21, wearing natty plus-fours and a jaunty bow tie, launched his new film series, which he called, *Alice's Wonderland*. Its semi-success carried his company, equipment and cast to a vacant lot on Hollywood Boulevard.

Alice, the central character in Disney's *Wonderland* series, was a live girl of seven years old, who had had an amateur modelling career in Kansas. This first film Alice was Virginia Davis; he then recast the lead twice over the next four years with Dawn O'Day and Margie Gay, as each grew too old for the part.

Disney's 'Laugh-O-Gram Alice' episodes included 'Alice's Fishy Story' and 'Alice Gets in Dutch'. In them, the live Alice meets proto-Disney cartoon characters, cats, rabbits, dogs and ducks. Sixty episodes were completed by 1927. Margie Gay, Disney's third Alice, wore a juvenile cow-girl costume and toted a ukulele, as Carroll's Alice Liddell* and her sisters had at Christ Church. When Disney dropped Margie Gay, he went on working with animated cats, rabbits, ducks and mice that she had met in the Laugh-O-Grams. So started the cartoon adventures of *Oswald the Lucky Rabbit* and by 1928, Mickey Mouse in *Plain Crazy* and *Steamboat Bill*. Thus, in his formative years, 1923–7, the young Disney explored Carroll's live and animal characters. So *Alice* took Disney to Hollywood, rather than the other way round. (See also Films* of *Alice*).

Disraeli, Benjamin, MP (1804–81)   Tory statesman, Chancellor of the Exchequer and Prime Minister (1868, 1874–80), Disraeli was Jewish by birth. He converted to Christianity and the Anglican Church, but was distrusted at first by High Church clergymen of Carroll's generation throughout the crises of the Oxford Movement and Church and University Reform.* Although astute and talented, Disraeli did not go to university. He had decided opinions about the subject, and they sometimes coincided with Carroll's. When Gladstone,* Liddell* and others tried to push through the first stage of an Oxford University Reform Bill in 1854, and create more professorships on the German model, Disraeli mocked the idea in Parliament, saying: 'Give me Oxford, free and independent, with all its anomalies and imperfections'.

Though unpopular with High Church dons, when Disraeli visited Christ Church* in 1853, Carroll must have seen him acclaimed by the undergraduates as he took an Honorary Degree. This was the gift of Disraeli's political mentor, Lord Derby (1799–1869), Chancellor of the University of the day. Disraeli appeared in *Looking-Glass* as John Tenniel's* Man In the Paper Suit in the railway carriage.* This is a character, like the monkey by the Pool of Tears, of which there is no mention in the text. Tenniel had drawn Disraeli in *Punch* from the 1850s and even portrayed him in a Government White Paper suit.

Disraeli knew the Oxford gossip. At the Deanery on a royal occasion, it was Disraeli who made public in John Ruskin's* presence, the story of

Ruskin surprised by Dean and Mrs Liddell* at a surreptitious *soirée* with Alice and her sisters.

Dodgson, Charles Lutwidge (1832–98)   Author of *Alice*, known throughout this book by his pseudonym, Lewis Carroll,* Dodgson was the son of Archdeacon Charles Dodgson (1800–68) and Frances Jane Lutwidge (1803–51). Carroll's parents shared the same grandfather, an Irish Protestant bishop. Carroll's father was educated at Christ Church* and, when he decided to marry, became a curate at Daresbury* in Cheshire where Carroll was born. In 1843 the curate was promoted to be Rector of Croft* in the north of Yorkshire. While Croft Rectory remained the family home, Carroll's father held additional clerical appointments, as Canon of Ripon and then Archdeacon of Richmond. There is a short biographical essay about Carroll after the Authors' Introduction.

THE DODGSON FAMILY   Charles and Frances Dodgson had 11 children. Frances Jane and Elizabeth Lucy were four and two respectively when Carroll was born at the beginning of 1832, the year that saw the passing of the Great Reform Bill, one measure that confirmed that eighteenth-century England had disappeared for ever and that a modern, more widely franchised and educated world was arriving. At intervals of two or three years came two more girls, and Carroll's first brother, Skeffington, was born in 1836. In 1837 Victoria* came to the throne. In 1838 the third Dodgson boy, Wilfred, was born, followed by three more girls and finally Edwin, the youngest of the 11. Little is known about Carroll's mother. She died just before Carroll's nineteenth birthday when her eldest child was 23 and her youngest five. Her bachelor brother, Skeffington Lutwidge,* was a witty and sophisticated uncle, who also provided the bonus of living in London. (See also Collingwood.*)

Carroll's father, Charles Dodgson, took first class degrees at Christ Church in both classics and mathematics. His decision to marry compelled him to give up his position at Christ Church as a Student. He did write a handful of papers on clerical subjects later in life, defending various High Church* positions, but the living at Daresbury can hardly have challenged his academic abilities. Edward Bouverie Pusey,* one of the most reactionary of High Church canons at Christ Church, was his contemporary and friend. Dodgson, in spite of the same first class degrees that W. E. Gladstone* had received from Christ Church a year or two earlier, failed to make a mark in the fast changing world of the nineteenth century. Carroll, his son, on the other, was always on the move and always making fun and satire of his times.

From what little is known of old Dodgson, he seems to have been a retiring figure. He imparted to his son a sense of scholarship and a sense of the fun of word games,* puzzles and riddles. Carroll was to live a life where there was time to remember the birthdays* of many friends, to take the trouble to find a German grammar for someone who was badly in need of it. When he was good mannered, which was not always, he was very good mannered indeed; when he took the trouble to amuse people with jokes, he could be very funny indeed. His love of games, conjuring and the composition of little magazines developed young and he was clearly a precocious child, if not noticeably a brilliant one. The Dodgson home – kind, stable and Christian – nurtured his values as a social individual and a religious man. Although he read some novels as a young man, he lived in a home where there would probably have been some distrust of such books,* for much English literature was not considered improving. Perhaps that is why he never really saw himself as a writer – strange for a man who must now be on almost everyone's list of great English writers.

BRIEF CHRONOLOGY OF CARROLL'S LIFE

1832   Born in Daresbury, Cheshire, son of an Oxford* educated rural clergyman, christened Charles Lutwidge Dodgson. Third child.

1843   Growing family, eventually 11, moved to Croft in Yorkshire.

1844–9   At school. Richmond in Yorkshire and Rugby as a boarder. Excelled in maths, loved word games, pantomime, amateur theatricals. Invented the pseudonym, Lewis Carroll.

1851   Undergraduate at Christ Church, Oxford. Mother died.

1854–62   Stayed on at Christ Church as Student, ordained Deacon but not priest, taught maths, took up photography,* wrote nonsense satire which he published in small magazines. Realized his passion for theatre with frequent visits, met Alice and other children of the new Dean of Christ Church. Told the *Alice* stories orally on various occasions, notably to keep the children in the right mood when photographing them and on expeditions (see Golden Afternoon*) on the river Thames.*

1863   Alice's mother appeared to prevent Carroll's frequent visits and burnt all his letters to Alice, to her regret. As a result, Carroll held himself 'aloof'.*

1864   In spite of Alice's mother's actions, Carroll gave Alice a vellum bound copy of *Alice's Adventures Under Ground** – hand-written and illustrated by himself. Alice's mother gave it pride of place in the Deanery.*

1865 *Under Ground* expanded to become *Alice's Adventures in Wonderland*, illustrated by *Punch* cartoonist John Tenniel,* published by Macmillan.*

1865–8 Continued to write stories, poems and satire, made new girl 'child*-friends', photographed them, and had a developing range of theatrical and literary acquaintances.

1868 Father died. Carroll found a house for his six spinster sisters in Guildford.*

1871 *Through the Looking-Glass and What Alice Found There* published. Somewhat reluctantly illustrated by Tenniel.

1870s & 1880s Prolific and international success of two *Alice* books. Wrote three mathematical books as well as *The Hunting of the Snark*, *Sylvie and Bruno* and many other sketches and increasingly bitter satirical pieces.

1877 Started a pattern of spending summers in Eastbourne,* writing and taking photographs, frequently seen with child-friends, many of whom came to stay, some of whom he met on the beach.

1880 Gave up photography saying he did not like new dry plate process, but real reasons unclear.

1881 Reduced his mathematics teaching load in order to have more time to write.

1886 Original manuscript of *Alice's Adventures Under Ground* published in facsimile (see Zincography*).

1892 Further reduced Oxford duties in order to write, but continued to reside at Christ Church.

1898 Died at Guildford on 14 January. Buried there (see also Sites*). Much correspondence destroyed. Most photographs auctioned.

1899 Biography published by literary executor and nephew, S. D. Collingwood*.

1932 *Alice* books continued to sell. Revival of interest in author on centenary. Notably, Langford Reed* and Walter de la Mare* argued that *Alice* had a place among the great works of English literature.

1940s to present Rediscovery of Carroll as a photographer, publication of his diaries.* Beginning of a steady flow of books about him. The English and some Americans wrote biographies; American academics became particularly interested in the psychological aspects of Carroll's relationship with fictional and real young girls; the French and the Italians remained more interested in the literary values and linguistic structure of *Alice*. Walt Disney's *Alice* and *Alice* products impinge on younger generations, to the regret of some.

1998   Centennial of Carroll's death at Guildford. *Alice* continues in print all over the world.

SOME NOTES ON FIRST-HAND ACCOUNTS OF CARROLL   Carroll was a multi-faceted and elusive personality. Perhaps because of this combination of fame and elusiveness, he attracted a large number of brief reminiscences by dons, child-friends and others. Any reader trying to piece him together will find a return to these mainly brief, often biased, but generally entertaining sources a worthwhile exercise.

Many, many little girls wrote reminiscences of him when they grew up and many of these are mentioned in the footnotes to Morton Cohen's* edition of Carroll's *Letters*. Others are mentioned in Lancelyn Green's* edition of the *Diaries* which also contains interviews with Dodgson relatives living after the Second World War. Another source is Cohen's *Lewis Carroll: Interviews and Recollections*. Others are to be found in interviews transcribed in Collingwood's and Derek Hudson's biographies* (see the Select Bibliography). For other sources see in the Select Bibliography, Bowman;* Furniss; MacDonald, Greville;* Kingsley, Henry;* Taylor, Una; Terry, Dame Ellen.* For Alice's charming account of him, see Liddell, Alice Pleasance.*)

The many accounts that we have read reflect varying facets of Carroll. For a dark view of Carroll, we find the memoir of W. W. Tuckwell (1829–1919) persuasive. Tuckwell was a Fellow of New College and biographer of Chaucer and Spencer. He was a Christian Socialist* and enthusiast for the allotment system and other community projects which he implemented in the North of England, on neither count endearing himself to Carroll. Tuckwell considered Carroll disruptive. The following is from his *Reminiscences of Oxford* (1907):

> Except to little girls, [Lewis Carroll] was not an alluring personage. Austere, shy, precise, absorbed in mathematical reverie, watchfully tenacious of his dignity, stiffly conservative in political, theological, social theory, his life mapped out in squares like Alice's landscape, he struck discords in the frank harmonious *camaraderie* of College life.

For a child's view, Ethel Arnold's* (1866–1930) late, affectionate old lady's account of her first meeting with Carroll in Oxford in 1872 is evocative:

> It was a typical Oxford afternoon in late autumn – damp, foggy, cheerless; the grey towers of the distant colleges across the 'Parks'... looked greyer

than usual in the dim autumnal light. A number of little girls, bursting with youthful spirits, and all agog for mischief, danced along one of the paths, a staid governess bringing up the rear. Presently one of their number spied a tall black clerical figure in the distance, swinging along towards the little group with a characteristic briskness, almost jerkiness, of step. – 'Here comes Mr. Dodgson,' she cried. 'Let's make a barrier across the path so that he cannot pass'.

Lewis Carroll charged with his umbrella, the children clung to him, and he took two of them by the hand, one of them Ethel. They remained friends for life.

Alice Raikes (later Wilson Fox, 1862–1945) wrote to *The Times* giving an account of her first meeting as a child with Carroll on 24 June 1871 in the garden at Onslow Square. She was asked by Carroll, as a form of reality-testing of the second *Alice* book, to imagine herself in front of a looking-glass with an orange in her right hand. She recalled him asking, if she were able to go through the looking-glass, whether the orange would still be in the same hand. She remembered his laugh when she assented. 'Well done, little Alice! The best answer I've had yet'.

Not all child-friends were enthusiastic and stimulated by their encounters, however. Isa Bowman recalled that once, and only once, Carroll turned away very angrily when she drew a caricature of him, and then embraced her in his anger, frightening her even more. There were a few little girls who could not stand his puzzles, or even ran away when sent to stay with him in Eastbourne by their mothers.

Florence Ruth Gamlen, later Waterhouse (1882–1964) was an Oxford child-friend who described Carroll at 60 as:

> … a very upright old man with nearly white hair, wearing the long, old-fashioned clerical coat and the turn-down collar and white tie so often worn by old dons in Orders at that time.

She described the embarrassment to which her parents, otherwise good conversationalists, were subjected when invited by Carroll to dinner; and how Carroll dropped her 'like a hot potato', as her father had warned would happen, when she did not prove clever enough for his games.*

From a quite different perspective, the views of Harry Furniss (1854–1925), the illustrator, are of interest. Like John Tenniel, Furniss drew for *Punch*. He also illustrated both *Sylvie and Bruno* and *Sylvie and Bruno Concluded* and he gave a rare, detailed account of a working relationship with Carroll. Unlike Tenniel, he did not allow the exasperation of work with Carroll to overcome him. His patience came from his admiration for *Alice*. Carroll said of Furniss' wife that she was the most privileged woman in the world because she was allowed to read *Sylvie and Bruno* in manuscript. So secretive was Carroll that he cut his whole manuscript into strips, jumbled it and asked Furniss to reassemble it with a code that was sent separately. Furniss went on strike.

Carroll demanded that Furniss should take the likeness of Sylvie from many different photographic models, but in fact Furniss had already decided to use his own infant children as models, as Sir John Everett Millais, the painter (1829–96) often did. Although Carroll was so demanding, he rewarded Furniss well and offered him a share of royalties. Furniss said in his memoir, *Confessions of a Caricaturist* (1902):

> Lewis Carroll was as unlike any other man as his books were unlike any other author's books ... Carroll was a wit, a gentleman, a bore and an egotist – and, like Hans Andersen, a spoilt child. It is recorded of Andersen that he actually shed tears, even in late life, should the cake at tea be handed to anyone before he chose the largest slice. Carroll was not selfish, but a liberal-handed philanthropist, but his egotism was all but second childhood.
>
> To meet him and to work for him was to me a great treat. I put up with his eccentricities – real ones, not sham like mine. – I put up with a good deal of boredom, for he was a bore at times, and I worked over seven years with his illustrations, in which the actual working hours would not have occupied me more than seven weeks. I treated him as a problem, and I solved him, and had he lived I would probably have still worked with him. He remunerated me liberally for my work ... his gratitude was overwhelming.

Dodgson, Pronunciation of the Name   Carroll said the family name must always be spelled D-O-D-G-S-O-N and always *pronounced* D-O-D-S-O-N. However, Carroll often pronounced it with a stammer, as 'Do-Do-Dod'son, hence his choice of the Dodo* for one of his best self-portraits in *Alice*. (See Anonymity.*)

Dodo   Unmasking the identity of the Dodo is one of the few revelations about hidden characters in *Alice* authenticated by the author. 'The Duck from the Dodo, 9 June 1887' was the dedication Carroll wrote in the front of a copy of *Alice's Adventures Under Ground** when he had published the facsimile. Carroll – the Dodo's – signed dedication was to his friend, Canon Robinson Duckworth* (1834–1911), by then Chaplain-in-Ordinary to Queen Victoria.* Though it was unusual for Carroll to break his anonymity,* Duckworth had been the other adult member of the party which rowed up the river on Friday 4 July 1862 and Carroll was happy to reveal his source in this private instance.

The Dodo was a flightless bird which once flourished on the island of Mauritius but became extinct in the seventeenth century. When the Natural History Museum* opened in Oxford,* the skeleton and claws of a Dodo which belonged to the University was removed from Canon Pusey's* carriage house where it had been stored for some years. They were put on display near a painting by John Savory, showing the bird in its quaint plumage. Visitors still view what is left of it. Readers of *Alice*, however, see no claw on Tenniel's* Dodo. In its place they see the author, Carroll's hand, emerging from a sleeve where the claw would have been.

Dormouse Dormice resemble very small squirrels. They are nocturnal and live in overgrown hedges and patches of ancient woodland where they hibernate. They are still found in Herefordshire and Gloucestershire where coppicing is practised but are sadly extinct in Carroll's boyhood haunts in the north of England. In Alice's day they were popular as pets – and are as passive as a pet can be. A dormouse sleeps curled up with its nose tucked between its paws and stumpy tail. Poor Dormouse! It is perhaps the most sympathetic of all the creatures with a speaking part in Alice. The Dormouse slept through much of the banter of the Hare* and Hatter,* seemed to be their friend, yet they tried to force it into the teapot.

Martin Gardner* suggested that Dante Gabriel Rossetti's* favourite wombat inspired the Dormouse in *Alice*. It is also possible that the Broad Church* F. D. Maurice* may have provided Carroll with his model. The High Church

Canons of Christ Church who controlled Maurice's Chair at London University removed the Broad Church Maurice from office for doubting the doctrine of Eternal Punishment, a theological view with which Carroll was himself sympathetic. If Maurice was indeed part of the inspiration of the Dormouse in *Alice*, the Mad Tea-Party* can be interpreted as a parody of the Christian Socialist* movement of which Maurice was founder. Christian Socialist campaigns on behalf of underprivileged working men were disapproved of by Carroll in diary entries recorded before he wrote *Alice*.

Dream-Child 'Dream-Child' is a 90-minute film* directed by Gavin Millar and based on Dennis Potter's theme that Alice Hargreaves' (i.e. Alice Liddell's*) true love was Charles Lutwidge Dodgson.* This fact she realizes in the plot of the film, when she arrives in New York in 1932 as an old lady for the celebration of the centennial of Carroll's birth. The film takes the aged Alice on a journey through New York, where at first she refuses to speak to the journalists who besiege her. She breaks down her guard for a young hack journalist who sees financial opportunity in the interviews he believes she would grant him. He falls in love with her companion to whom she is imperious.

Alice's 'Carrollian days' are shown in flashback to the Deanery and the river Isis. *Wonderland* is depicted with the old Alice Hargreaves, played by Maggie Smith, meeting life-size Wonderland puppets, created by Jim Henson. Carroll is played by Ian Holm, who comes across as a 50-year-old voyeur, not as a don of 28. In a river-bank scene, Reggie Hargreaves,* Alice's intended, watches. Carroll's stutter prevents him from completing a poem. The adolescent Alice's pity for him begins, in this scene, to pinpoint the love between them that her youth had prevented her from understanding.

Dennis Potter's theme, that Carroll and Alice longed for a territory of love on which neither could really venture, was partially confirmed in Alice Liddell's own memories by her claim in old age that she had been haunted all her life by *Alice*. (See also Alice Liddell's* first-hand account of Carroll.)

Dream, The Red King's One of the strangest conundrums in the *Alice* books is the following:

> "He's dreaming now," said Tweedledee: "and what do you think he's dreaming about?"
>
> Alice said, "Nobody can guess that."
>
> "Why, about *you*!" Tweedledee exclaimed, clapping his hands triumphantly. "And if he left off dreaming about you, where do you suppose you'd be?"

"Where I am now, of course," said Alice.

"Not you!" Tweedledee retorted contemptuously. "You'd be nowhere. Why, you're only a sort of thing in his dream!"

"If that there King was to wake," added Tweedledum, "you'd go out—bang!—just like a candle!"

Alice worried that the noise the two quarrelsome boys were making would rouse the King; they implied she could never wake him however hard she tried for she was not real.

"I *am* real!" said Alice, and began to cry.

If *Alice* was a dream, then who was dreaming? The question must have been serious, for Alice's failure to answer it reduced her to tears.* At the end of the book, Alice said to Dinah, remembering the Looking-Glass puzzle:

> "Now, Kitty, let's consider who it was that dreamed it all. This is a serious question, my dear, and you should *not* go on licking your paw like that— as if Dinah hadn't washed you this morning! You see, Kitty, it *must* have been either me or the Red King. He was part of my dream, of course— but then I was part of his dream, too! *Was* it the Red King, Kitty? You were his wife, my dear, so you ought to know..."*

Kitty has no answer, so the question is permanently begged of every reader of *Alice*. At the very end of the story, Carroll took the matter further. He turned to the reader and asked:

> "Which do *you* think it was?"

Which do *you* think it was?

In our previous book, *The Red King's Dream*, we argued that the dream in *Alice* is set at two different levels, a childish one and an adult one – Alice's level and the Red King's. To end, as Carroll did, on a question for which neither Alice nor the reader has an answer, any more than a kitten has, is a reminder that the reader is in the hands of a metaphysical master.

Dress, Alice's *Alice*, in the course of her adventures *Under Ground*, was drawn by Carroll himself. His drawings – perhaps 'illustrations' for he could never really draw – portray his child heroine in a soft, clinging tunic. In fact Alice and her sisters wore fashionable fitted children's dresses with soft trims – Greek *appliqué* patterns or *broderie anglaise* – different from Carroll's preferred 'slight disorder in the dress'.

Carroll purchased Arthur Hughes' painting, 'Lady with the Lilacs'. The young girl is nymph-like in a long-sleeved, soft, clinging muslin smock gathered at her waist. She leans dreamily against a bank of lilacs, in a pose Carroll attempted in his *Under Ground* Alice, modelled, according to Anne Clark, Alice Liddell's biographer, on Carroll's drawings and photographs of Alice's younger sister, Edith.

Tenniel's* Alice, with her bar shoes, waisted dress and long hair, bears little resemblance to Alice Liddell or to Carroll's own drawings of his nymph-like heroine. This Alice pre-existed Carroll's story as a cartoon character in *Punch** and surfaced eight times or more from 1860 to 1864 before Carroll's *Wonderland* commission. Whereas Alice Liddell was dark and short-haired, Tenniel's Alice had long fair hair. The cautious Carroll may have wished to defer to Tenniel, already the lead illustrator of *Punch*, rather than redesign Tenniel's Alice costume according to his own preferences. Only when he produced the facsimile *Under Ground* Alice in the 1880s did readers learn about Carroll's idea of Alice's dress.

Lou Taylor, costume historian at the University of Brighton, observes that Tenniel's Alice is dressed in the conventional 'at home' clothes of a middle-class girl of the 1860s. One cartoon he drew for *Punch* in 1860 shows the proto-Alice seated in a chair wearing the full skirt, pale stockings, flat shoes and band over her loose hair like Alice in the later stories. Lou Taylor suggests the following fabrics for such a dress:

> ... poplin, fine alpaca or piqué, all washable. It could have been white or pale pink or blue. The full skirt has four deep tucks, typical of the period when women's skirts were at their fullest and worn over crinoline cages.

Of Alice's skirt, Carroll begged Tenniel, 'Don't give Alice so much crinoline'. Over her skirt, Tenniel's Alice wore a boilable pinafore-overall with short, wide-capped and frilled sleeves made of white cotton and buttoned to her dress at the waist. The pinafore in *Looking-Glass* had a bow, and was more decorative than practical, and the stockings were striped. Her shoes were flat, squared off at the tip of the toe and strapped across the foot to hold them on. They would have been made of fine leather or black cotton or silk.

In the railway carriage, and when she was 'queened', Tenniel's Queen Alice ceased to be a Pre-Raphaelite nymph. She wore – with no maid to dress her – 'a very up-to date, bustle-backed "polonaise" dress similar', according to Lou Taylor, 'to the smartest Parisian styles of the period'.

Carroll did not like little girls who sat for him in his studio to wear black stockings when he photographed them, preferring: 'dark brown, or any dark colour'. Alice in *Wonderland* wore plain white or pale stockings. In *Looking-Glass* these are more theatrical, with horizontal stripes.

Drugs   That drugs provide stage props in *Alice* is noticeable in the entrancement of the hookah-smoking Caterpillar.* It sits on a mushroom which Alice nibbles, and listens to her reciting 'Old Father William' 'all wrong'. Carroll knew a number of people who smoked opium or took laudanum. Both were prescribed for medicinal purposes at the time he wrote *Alice*. Oscar Rejlander, his photography* teacher, was a serious drug-taker. So were Dante Gabriel Rossetti* and his wife, Lizzie Siddal. Another was Henry Kingsley,* Charles Kingsley's* younger brother, sent to the Australian gold-fields as an undergraduate before taking his degree for founding an Oxford society for opium-eating. He had claimed to be interested in Eastern mysticism as an undergraduate friend of Carroll's.

> When you take something that tastes like cherry tarts [i.e. the cake marked 'Eat Me'], custard, pineapple, roast turkey and toast at the same time and it makes you grow and shrink – baby, that's tripping out!

So wrote Thomas Frensch in *Alice in Acidland* in, predictably, 1968. 'White Rabbit', written by the American rock singer, Grace Slick, even suggested that the Dormouse was on drugs rather than treacle. (See also Critics.*)

Carroll's knowledge of mind-altering drugs is an under-explored subject, lately opened up again by Michael Carmichael in *The London Miscellany* in an article entitled 'Wonderland Revisited'. A medico-technical Victorian book about mind-bending drugs was among the medical books in Carroll's library* at Christ Church when he died. This was Anstie's *Stimulants and Narcotics*. It is not known how many other books he owned on narcotics, for the bulk of his medical books were given to Bertram Collingwood,* his nephew. Robert Phillips was criticized for publishing two papers on this topic in *Aspects of Alice*.

Duchess, Ugly   Ducal visits to the Deanery were not uncommon and royal visits were frequent. As part of their normal social round, Alice's parents, who had relatives who were earls, dined with the Duke and Duchess of Marlborough. Tenniel's* Duchess is thought to have been modelled on a portrait of Margaret, Duchess of Carinthia who, in turn, is thought to be the ugliest woman ever portrayed. John Ruskin* emphasized that the medieval love of beauty was directly linked to the medieval fascination with the grotesque. Alice beside the grotesque Duchess on the Queen's Croquet ground is possibly a parody of this kind of, then fashionable, aesthetic value.

The characters of T. H. Huxley* and Bishop Wilberforce,* bitter enemies after their debate on evolution in the Natural History Museum* at Oxford, may be reflected by different moods shown by the Ugly Duchess. Her speech-ifying, the moral of this and moral of that, sound like Wilberforce. Her far from beautiful looks have within them traces of the gaunt face of Huxley, whom Carroll photographed. There is also a sense that her kitchen is a kind of boiling pot of evolution and that her baby who turns into a pig is also one of Carroll's mockeries of evolution. (See also William Empson.*)

Duckworth, Robinson (1834–1911)   Duckworth was a Fellow of Trinity between 1862 and 1864 when he sometimes chaperoned the Liddell girls when Carroll took them on picnics. It was he who pulled stroke to Carroll's bow when they rowed to Nuneham and Godstow. In his memoir of the expedition, Duckworth recalled 'turning round and saying, "Dodgson, is this an extempore romance of yours?"' Duckworth, Prince Leopold's tutor at Oxford, seemed accident-prone as a chaperon. A biography, *Queen Victoria: a portrait* (1991) by Giles St Aubyn noted that one of her daughters fell head-over heels in love with him when he was Royal Chaplain at Windsor.

Carroll gave an impression of Duckworth's urbane manner and beautiful singing voice in *Under Ground*, a reference he subsequently suppressed in *Wonderland*, when the Dodo* moved 'that the meeting adjourn, for the immediate adoption of more energetic remedies'.

"Speak English!" said the Duck, "I don't know the meaning of half those long words, and what's more, I don't believe you do either!" And the Duck quacked a comfortable laugh to itself.

(See also History.*)

DOVECOTE, STANTON HARCOURT

E is for ...

Eastbourne, Sussex   Eastbourne became part of Carroll's life when he was already famous after writing the two *Alice* books. Creature of habit that he was, Eastbourne became his summering place for 21 years from 1877, aged 45, until the last summer of his life, 1897. In *Time to Spare in Victorian England*, John Lowerson and John Myerscough described the attraction of the town:

> This middle class resort had all the key attractions of a seaside holiday. Natural beauty up to Beachy Head, solid boarding houses, bathing machines, a good crowd on the lawn, young ladies promenading in groups.

Brighton, patronized by the Prince Regent, had been *the* fashionable resort in the early nineteenth century. By the 1870s it had become too full of 'trippers'. Eastbourne was able to describe itself as more 'select'.

Carroll first saw Eastbourne in 1870 when looking for a place to take his sister Louisa, 'whose strength needs recruiting', but they settled on Margate. When he did come to Eastbourne, it was regularly to 7 Lushington Road. He rented 'a nice little first floor sitting room with a balcony, and a bedroom adjoining'. His landlords were the Dyers. Mr Dyer worked at the Post Office. Lushington Road, built in Regency style, was a grandiose street with a view of the Downs. The whiff of sea air was always present. The Grand Parade and pier were only a quarter of a mile distant. To the spare bedroom of Carroll's quarters came numerous child-friends when their mothers gave Carroll permission to take them for a week to the seaside.

When he was without companions, Carroll found the perfect pool into which to cast his net on the beach at Eastbourne. His diary entries from his first visit there in the summer of 1877 provide a detailed record of children encountered. Prettiest and brightest that summer was Dolly Blakemore, who was with her parents on the pier. Although her family were members of what he snootily called the 'Commercial Classes', Dolly was five and filled with life and zest. He also met one Bakewell, three Bells, one Burton, one Christie, five Dymes, two Gordons, two Smiths, five Waddy sisters, one Whicher and one Woodruffe. The four Hull sisters he met on 20 August were given their own entry in his diary and became child-friends. He later sent them acrostics*, riddles* and avuncular advice, as he had the little Liddells* and Terrys.* (Also see Sisters.*)

Contrary to the view that Carroll only kept company with child-friends while they were young, older friends, including Gertrude Chataway,* came to stay with him there when they were grown up.

When at Eastbourne, Carroll worshipped at Christ Church, which has no connection to the college, most of the town belonging to the Duke of Devonshire rather than to the Dean and Canons of Christ Church,* Oxford. In the last summer of his life, Carroll gave children's sermons there, one of which was:

> ... to illustrate temptations to which children are exposed, and to teach them how they may be avoided and conquered.

The addresses were delivered with deep feeling; at times the speaker was scarcely able to control his emotions, especially when speaking of the love and compassion of the Good Shepherd. (See also Child*-Friends and Preaching.*)

Eggs, Good and Bad Eggs appear in *Alice* on several occasions, in tree-top nests, on walls or balancing on their long axes on the shelves of the Sheep's magic shop. Not many of these eggs were good and each belonged to somebody. Disappearing eggs were props for professional party conjurors, and the *Oxford English Dictionary* defines *a bad egg* as 'a person or thing that comes to no good', dating the expression to 1853.

Henry Luke Paget (1852–1937) was a Christ Church* don who became Bishop of Chester. In 1932, he wrote a letter to *The Times* recalling that in the bad old days at the House while *Alice* was being written, undergraduates were allowed to serve themselves two boiled eggs at the Buttery in Hall 'because one was invariably bad'. Paget's note carried with it an echo of the 'Bread-and-Butter* Row' at Christ Church, shadowed also in the eating habits of the Hatter* during the Trial.

Alice seems to have been aware of the risk of being sold a bad egg. In the Sheep's shop she wondered what to buy, decided on eggs, did not ask the cost, because that would be ill-bred and instead asked: 'How do you sell them?' The Sheep explained that they cost fivepence farthing (five and a quarter pence) for one; or twopence for two and anyone who bought a pair must eat both. Alice paid the high price and bought a single egg, reducing the odds of having a bad egg by half and found that the one that she bought turned into Humpty Dumpty.* 'They mightn't be at all nice, you know.' As in Christ Church Hall, so in *Alice*.

Eliot, Thomas Stearns (1888–1963)   As *Alice* began to be taken seriously as literature, the number of writers the book influenced grew. Several poets and writers of the inter-war years, including W. H. Auden,* Walter de la Mare,* Robert Graves* and James Joyce incorporated themes derived from Carroll in their works. Dame Helen Gardner (1908–1986) showed that

T. S. Eliot echoed Alice's arrival in *Wonderland* to create the mood of the opening of the first of the *Four Quartets* published in 1935. 'Burnt Norton' was written in a conversational and lyrical mode, and confronted problems of art, history and morality. The poem mused on the theme of time* and lamented how little reality mankind could contemplate.

T. S. Eliot patterned the opening of his poem on Alice's arrival in *Wonderland*. He echoed the moment when Alice lost sight of the White Rabbit* which had led her there. Finding herself trapped without a guide, she listened, alarmed, to footfalls echoing:

> Down a passage which we did not take
> Towards a door we never opened
> Into the rose-garden.

T. S. Eliot, poet, playwright and publisher, was Anglo-Catholic in religion, royalist in politics and classical in his literary tastes. He described himself as an 'aged eagle' because of his beaked nose. Though serious from a very young age, and in spite of a Dodo*-like solemnity, he was known, like Carroll, for his propensity for practical jokes.

Elopement This was a dangerous topic for a young clergyman to grapple with, but a real possibility in Victorian times. Carroll's brother, Wilfred, arrived at Christ Church as an undergraduate in 1856 aged 17 or 18. He fell in love with Alice Jane Donkin, who was 11 when Wilfred was 24 and, having no Studentship to protect (the holder of a Studentship, like Carroll, had to be a bachelor) determined to marry her.

In that year, 1862, Carroll created a composite photograph (reprinted by Helmut Gernsheim* and Morton Cohen*). He photographed Alice in her nightdress, which is covered by a cape, escaping from her house. Then he photographed the exterior of the house with a rope ladder descending from the first-floor bedroom window. The finished composite shows a slender, nightdress–clad girl outside an upper floor window about to climb down the escape ladder. The composition is called *The Elopement*.

What, we wonder, was Carroll thinking? Was he thinking that an *11*-year old really might elope? He claimed in part of his diary, suppressed by Roger Lancelyn Green* but reported by Anne Clark, to be troubled by Wilfred's relationship with Alice Donkin, the child who was the model for *The Elopement*. The little girl really was Wilfred's intended and Wilfred finally married her; Anne Clark's biography of Carroll showed that Carroll was so anguished about his and Wilfred's respective Alices that he found it necessary to make an appointment to mull the problem over with his uncle, Skeffington Lutwidge.*

Carroll's construct, *The Elopement*, is an illustration of the quandary in which he found himself when he gave the Deanery manuscript to Alice Liddell. He had written the *Under Ground* story to show how much he cared for its heroine. The photomontage of Alice Donkin's elopement was a dream sequence, like Alice's adventures. Wilfred was, by implication, in the offing to receive the runaway. Carroll fantasized about a step young Alice Donkin might have taken. In the fullness of time, Wilfred's Alice took it. Carroll's did not.

'Elsie' 'Elsie' was a rustic sounding nickname given by the Dormouse,* who presumably lived in the countryside, to the classically-named person known to have been Lorina Charlotte Liddell,* Alice's older sister. The initials 'L'* and 'C' when spoken out loud in sequence, produce the girl's name in the tale. Lorina Charlotte Liddell was the Dean's eldest daughter. She was born in 1849, was three years older than Alice Pleasance, and was named after her mother. Charlotte was also the name of her paternal grandmother, Charlotte Lyon, an ancestress of the present Queen Mother, who is thus distantly related to Alice Liddell.*

Martin Gardner* noticed a second pun in the tale. It was on the name Liddell. The Dormouse began its report on the drawing lessons down the Treacle Well with: 'Once upon a time there were three little ["Liddell"] sisters'. The pun on 'Liddell' (which rhymes with 'fiddle') echoes throughout *Alice*, though it has seldom been annotated. It surfaced again at the end of the first verse of the dedicatory poem Carroll wrote, 'All in the Golden Afternoon'. There are three mathematically-placed 'Liddell' puns in the poem, one for each of the three sisters in their birth order. The image is of Ina, Alice and Edith guiding the boat. Two have an oar and one is at the tiller:

> For both our oars, with little [Liddell] skill,
> By little [Liddell] arms are plied,
> While little [Liddell] hands make vain pretence
> Our wanderings to guide.

(See also 'Lacie'* and 'Tillie'.*)

Empson, Sir William (1906–84)   Cambridge literary critic and oriental scholar, William Empson taught English Literature in Japan, China and Sheffield. He taught in Japan before moving to Peking, then left Peking when the Japanese invaded China. Like George Orwell, he worked during the Second World War in the BBC, in Empson's case in the Far Eastern Section. This was an unusual background for a poet and a Milton and Coleridge scholar but Empson's reputation has always been that of a polymath. That reputation was sustained by his densely written critical essays which include *Seven Types of Ambiguity* (1930), *The Structure of Complex Words* (1951) and *Using Biography* (1984).

By 1935, as he travelled from Japan to become a life-long friend of China, his interest was captured by some of the contributions to the centennial of Carroll's birth. In *Some Versions of the Pastoral*, his essay about *Alice*, 'The Child as Swain' opens with the following peroration:

> It must seem a curious thing that there has been so little serious criticism of the 'Alices', and that so many critics, with so militant and eager an air of good taste, have explained that they would not think of attempting it. Even Mr de la Mare's book, which made many good points, is queerly evasive in tone. There seems to be a feeling that real criticism would involve psycho-analysis, and that results would be so improper as to destroy the atmosphere of the books altogether.

Empson's model for *Alice* was a pastoral stereotype, a 'swain'. He claimed that *Alice* was written in the tradition of pastoral poetry. Alice was like the countryman, an innocent: here the swain is a child. The argument put forward was that Carroll had been innovative to transfer the pastoral tradition to an expression of 'child-sentiment' by which 'the child as the underdog speaks up for itself'.

He suggested that *Alice* was laced with contemporary ideas. Alice and the animals, the monkey and the Dodo* were Darwinian creatures. The salt water of the Pool of Tears was analogous to the salty fluid from which all life derived. The Caucus Race was a parody alternative to the contentious doctrine of Evolution* by Natural Selection. He also saw Tenniel's* railway carriage as a parody of Victorian ideas of progress and self-improvement. Cambridge critics, like Empson at this period, looked long and hard at the interface between science* and literature and moved away from the more genteel Georgian critics such as de la Mare* in order to explore it.

Empson regretted the extent to which Alice's encounters with the ideas of Charles Darwin, Michael Faraday and Alfred, Lord Tennyson* had been brushed under the carpet by *Alice* annotators. He felt that the suggestion that Carroll parodied Victorian icons like Cardinal Newman* and the verse of the Poets Laureate* – Southey, Wordsworth and Tennyson – should be more fully explored. As Alice pulled the table cloth and banquet on to the floor at the party for her Coronation, Empson concluded:

> The guests are inanimate and the crawling self-stultifying machinery of luxury has taken on a hideous life of its own. It is the High Table of Christ Church that we must think of here ...

Lancelyn Green* and Morton Cohen* were each dismissive about Empson as a commentator. Cohen cannot even bring himself to mention the name of this great critic. To some to suggest that there is meaning in *Alice* is to spoil the childish fun. To others, the idea that there is meaning, which Empson pioneered, explains the books' lasting value and fascination for adults; the qualities which make Carroll a satirist on a par with Swift or Voltaire. Jonathan Miller* made it the starting point for his film of *Alice*. Empson's essay was the most serious attempt of its day to build contextual meaning into *Alice* criticism. It has been reprinted in *Alice in Wonderland: A Norton Critical Edition* (1971) and in Robert Phillips' *Aspects of Alice* (1972).

English as Spoken in *Alice*   See Queen's English.*

Evidence   There is evidence and Evidence just as there are knaves and Knaves. 'Alice's Evidence' was the title of the last chapter of *Wonderland*. The trial was presided over by two judges, the King and the Queen of Hearts, and observed by an all-animal jury. There was no Counsel and the participants fell into logical trap after logical trap. Alice denounced these proceedings, saying: 'I don't believe there's an atom of meaning in it'. But the King disagreed. He claimed the poem the White Rabbit* read was 'the most important piece of evidence we've heard yet'. The evidence presented by the White Rabbit ended:

> Don't let him know she liked them best,
>> For this must ever be
> A secret, kept from all the rest,
>> Between yourself and me.

Martin Gardner* speculated that the poem was about a man who loved Alice:

> Did Carroll introduce the poem into his story because the song behind it tells of an unrequited love of a man for a girl named Alice?

This would lead to the view that Alice ended the proceedings to cover up the fact that the Knave was guilty in a trial at a court where justice never could have been done. (See also Kafka.*)

Evolution, The Theory of   In the form formally proposed by Charles Darwin in 1859, this theory caused, in the words of William Empson* 'a pervading bad smell' in clerical circles in Oxford.* It is the view of Empson – and we agree – that jokes about evolution bubble up to the surface of 'Alice' in various places. The jokes start with monkeys and primordial fluid in the Pool of Tears and continue with the mention of the adaptation of parts of the body as Alice gets larger and smaller and her body parts are seen as incorrectly assembled when compared with other creatures. (See also Anatomy* and Science.*)

Alice experienced a problem of communication with the Fawn (a lower with a higher animal) and the book is scattered with jokes about domestication of plants and animals, mimicry and the expression of human emotion – all important themes explored by Darwin. (See also Huxley,* Natural History Museum,* Thistle* and Wilberforce.*)

F is for ...

Faces

"Oh! *please* don't make such faces, my dear!"

This is what Alice begged the Red King at the beginning of the *Looking-Glass* story. To Alice, there was a proper facial expression for each occasion, and wearing it was like keeping yourself tidy, or having the servants clean your boots – a matter of protocol.

The Rose in the Garden of Live Flowers* in *Looking-Glass* commented on Alice's face:

"Said I to myself, 'Her face has got *some* sense in it, though it is not a clever one!' Still you're the right colour, and that goes a long way."

Alice, besides being pretty, was practised at holding the required facial expression for Carroll's camera. She used this skill when taking part in the Liddells' *tableaux vivants* (see Games*) for the benefit of Deanery* guests. She was able, from a young age, to freeze with the appropriate expression for a particular role; a valuable talent for a child who moved, when called upon, in royal circles.

Fainting in Coils

This was was the Mock Turtle's* term for oil-painting and was the part of the art syllabus at the School Under The Sea in *Wonderland*. Stretching is a joke about sketching, which Alice did under the tuition of John Ruskin,* becoming a competent amateur; it is also a joke about stretching canvasses. There are also comments on uglification,* undoubtedly a satire on Ruskin's *Modern Painters*.

Falling   Many children have fantasies about leaping down stairs or even further – and *Wonderland* starts with this happening to Alice. As she fell:

> "Well!" thought Alice to herself, "after such a fall as this, I shall think nothing of tumbling down stairs! How brave they'll think me at home! Why, I wouldn't say anything about it, even if I fell off the top of the house!"

To which Carroll added in parenthesis, striking a macabre note at the very beginning of the story: '(Which was very likely true.)'.

For 'House', read Christ Church.* If Alice fell off the house, she would not be there to tell the story. These elements are point and counterpoint of the *Alice* narrative, the everyday fantasy or experience of the child counterpointed by the solemn grown-up world of the narrator.

Alice had had a serious fall from her pony. She had, no doubt, leapt down the Lexicon Staircase at the Deanery* where she grew up, several steps at a time and had not been caught, or had dared her sisters to do so and, when they had had a tumble, she 'wouldn't say anything about it'.

Fan   Alice picked up a fan and a pair of gloves which the White Rabbit* dropped when she arrived in *Wonderland*. She fanned herself with it, 'as the hall was very hot', in the manner in which she was no doubt learning from her mother. Fans were still a crucial accessory to courtly behaviour and remained so throughout Alice's youth.

Fans and kid gloves were also important conjuror's props which Carroll learned to use competently as a boy, together with thimbles, rabbits, standing-up eggs and top-hats. (See John Fisher* for more on Carroll and magic and games.)

Father William   Alice, at the time she met the Caterpillar, had difficulty remembering things:

> "Can't remember *what* things?" said the Caterpillar.
>
> "Well, I've tried to say 'How doth the little busy bee', but it all came different!" Alice replied in a very melancholy voice.
>
> "Repeat '*You are old, Father William*'," said the Caterpillar.
>
> Alice folded her hands, and began:—
>
> > "You are old, Father William," the young man said,
> >   "And your hair has become very white;
> > And yet you incessantly stand on your head—
> >   Do you think, at your age, it is right?"

Alice's poem parodied a similar verse by Robert Southey (1774–1843):

'You are old, father William,' the young man cried,
  'The few locks which are left you are grey;
You are hale, father William, a hearty old man,
  Now tell me the reason, I pray?'

The 'message' of the poem was child-like. Southey's old man was cheerful because:

  In the days of my youth I remembered my God!
  And He hath not forgotten my age.

We have argued that Carroll's portly, white-haired Father William referred to a well-known cynic: that Carroll had placed in Alice's mouth a skit about the Oxford reformer and Broad Church theologian, Dr Benjamin Jowett,* whom he parodied cruelly in University pamphlets. The references to his standing on his head and turning backward somersaults repeat Carroll's view that Jowett was turning Oxford on its head. 'Suet' and 'do it' appear to be rhymes on Jowett or 'Juet'.

The poem is one of the formal set-pieces in *Alice*. In the *Under Ground* and *Wonderland* versions, Carroll worked out four large illustrations to the verses. These are more anarchic than Tenniel's. In Tenniel's illustrations, the young man is a neat country bumpkin in a smock, and the Old Man is a rotund and jocular John Bull. Carroll's earlier sketches for the same scenes show a young man with his hair on end looking like a drawing Carroll made of himself as a mad student with his hair in a gale. Tenniel softened Carroll's robust intentions in the verse.

Carroll campaigned openly to stop Jowett from teaching at Oxford and wrote a large number of protest verses in his effort to fell him. He failed, with the rest of High Church Oxford, from Dr Pusey* and Bishop Wilberforce* down to the humblest curate and deacon. The final triumph of Jowett over the High Church* faction is marked by the Old Man's shout to the young one: 'Be off, or I'll kick you down stairs!'

Films of *Alice* Although many attempts have been made to film *Alice*, generally with the two stories combined, few have succeeded either as independent works of art or in enlightening Carroll's texts. Although in some ways 'filmic' (see punctuation*), the structure of Alice is so episodic that it does not translate into the narrative demands of the 90-minute motion picture. Illustrators* can, on occasion, give a new view of *Alice*, enabling us to see the text in a different light to Tenniel,* but the demands of film tend to come up against the arcane nature of Carroll's humour. As far as we can see, and we have seen only a handful of the films of *Alice*, most of these productions are rightly forgotten.

The American, David Schaefer, of the Lewis Carroll Society of North America,* has done detailed research into *Alice* films and filmography, and made a collection of them. He has noted that films were already being shown as 'chasers' to the main film of the evening at the time of Carroll's death, for the Lumières' Cinematograph was opened at the Polytechnic in London in 1896. With his passion for invention and visual trickery, it is hard to believe that Lewis Carroll did not see at least one film before he died. David Schaefer's essay on *Alice* films until 1973 was published in *Lewis Carroll Observed* (see Edward Guiliano in the Select Bibliography).

Walt Disney's* *Alice* is different from Carroll's. She is blue-eyed, bobby-soxed, simpering, pre-feminist and suburbanly pubescent and she is, through the marketing of dolls, Disney books and videotape, *the* image of *Alice* for millions of children. For all that, the Disney film is moving, if not quite emotionally, then certainly as a remarkable piece of action and animation.

Our favourite is Jonathan Miller's* version, perhaps because Miller was influenced by William Empson* and his view that *Alice* contained parodies of real Victorians as seen by a small child. Intrigued by the idea that Carroll was a satirist, Miller cast well-known actors and personalities in well-known roles. Michael Redgrave was the Caterpillar,* dusting an old archaeological model in the Sir John Soane Museum, and Peter Cook was the most brilliant Mad Hatter* there has ever been.

Perhaps the problem with films of *Alice* is that the standard narrative treatment of Hollywood and London studios produced something too plodding and too literal. There is still room for a great *Alice* for the cinema, perhaps with a kind of disregard for the norms of time and space that has best been shown on television in the *Monty Python* genre, rather than in more staid film comedy.

As an example of the importance of *Alice* as a popular icon, one of the first productions shown at the glamorous new Strand Theatre in New York in 1915 was a six-reeler, a version of *Wonderland* that was an hour long. David Schaefer considered the film 'charming'. We have not seen it. It ran for no less than six years.

The best known early *Alice* film is the 1933 version produced by Paramount. The director was Norman Z. McLeod (1898–1964) who had previously directed in the mad-cap comic tradition of the Marx Brothers. Alice was aged 12 in the film. She was played by Charlotte Henry, who never succeeded in her subsequent Hollywood career. The script was by the distinguished Joseph L. Mankiewicz. In the end the film is, in our judgement, flat, the images dominating the imagination rather than, as *Alice* does, allowing it to roam.

Fireworks   At the height of their friendship, Alice Liddell and Carroll watched the great firework party for the wedding of the Prince of Wales in Oxford. In *Looking-Glass*, as the fictional Alice woke from her dream, she wrenched the table cloth and royal china and glass to the ground, and in Tenniel's* illustration, a firework display burst across the sky. This fictional 5th of November was Guy Fawkes Day, presaged in the opening chapter of the story.

As with the fictional Alice's lack of fear of heights (see Falling*), Alice Liddell relished the Oxford municipal fireworks. Her enthusiasm seems to have distressed Carroll. Known disputes between Alice and Carroll are rare. In old age, she recalled her childish puzzlement at his anger at her passionate enthusiasm for the display they watched together. This is how Alice Liddell recalled the incident:

> One particular [illumination] took my fancy, in which the words 'May they be happy' appeared in large letters of fire. My enthusiasm prompted Mr Dodgson to draw a caricature of it next day for me, in which underneath those words appeared two hands holding very formidable birches with the words "Certainly not".

(See also Alice Liddell's* first-hand recollection of Carroll.)

Fish and Fishy Jokes   There are Fish Footmen in *Alice*; there is a Mock Turtle;* there is a lobster,* a conger eel, a whiting* and a snail;* there are soles* and crabs and there are sharks. No respectable Victorian dinner was served without a fish course and, as the century advanced, so did the elaboration of Victorian gastronomic decoration, as can be seen in contemporary editions of Mrs Beeton's *Household Management*. Here lobsters appear as centrepieces, wonderfully pink, looking out of their little eyes and almost waving their whiskers.

'Fishy' means 'suspicious', on the grounds that bad fish smells bad: it was an everyday schoolroom and undergraduate adjective. It is not surprising that there are a number of fishy jokes in *Alice*. It is, after all, a fishy book, suspiciously full of half-hidden things that don't quite surface.

> "Oh, as to the whiting," said the Mock Turtle, "they—you've seen them, of course?"
>
> "Yes," said Alice, "I've often seen them at dinn—' she checked herself hastily.
>
> "I don't know where Dinn may be," said the Mock Turtle, "but if you've seen them so often, of course you know what they're like."
>
> "I believe so," Alice replied thoughtfully. "They have their tails in their mouths;—and they're all over crumbs."

Forty two

When is a whiting a whiting, and when is it a character in a book? Right up to the time that the Leg of Mutton acquired a face and a smile and two legs, the fishy question of what can eat what is never far from the surface in *Alice*. See Soup,* in particular Mock Turtle soup, dark imitator of the greatest fishy delicacy of all, true Turtle Soup.

Fisher, John (1945–)   Fisher was author of *The Magic of Lewis Carroll* (1973), one of the liveliest of the numerous anthologies of Lewis Carroll's dispersed and assorted mathematical games, puzzles, conundrums and word-games. To these, Fisher added a well-explained set of conjuring tricks and origami ideas linked editorially to games played in *Alice*. He pointed out that the Viennese conjuror, Herr Döbler (1801–64), came to England in 1842 and – it seems from the *Diaries* – again in 1863 when Carroll saw him perform. The influence of Victorian dumb show and conjuring, the cutting into two of volunteer bodies on stage, white rabbits pulled out of the air alive and kicking, fans up sleeves, ever-full ink bottles and card tricks always fascinated Carroll. Like many of his contemporaries, he took a great interest in spiritual and psychical* phenomena and no doubt saw these stagy shows as real-life counterparts.

Forgetfulness   In his 1890 pamphlet, which Evelyn M. Hatch republished in *A Selection from the Letters of Lewis Carroll to his Child-Friends* (1933), 'Eight or Nine Wise Words about Letter-Writing', Carroll included a wise suggestion on how to avoid forgetfulness. It was the following:

> When you take your letters to the Post, *carry them in your hand*. If you put them in your pocket you will take a long country walk (I speak from experience), passing the Post-Office *twice*, going and returning, and, when you get home, will find them *still* in your pocket.

Much of the charm of the early part of *Wonderland* depends on Alice's forgetting who she is and what she knows, jokes even more touching to a child reading the story in an age when so much learning was done by rote.

Forty-two   Edward Wakeling* has argued with ingenuity that the number 42 was, like the day of the week, Tuesday, of particular interest to Carroll. For example, he shows in *Lewis Carroll's Games and Puzzles* that the total age of the two Queens in *Alice*, on the day Alice joins them as a Queen, can be calculated to be 74,088 days, for each is 101 years, 5 months and 1 day old. That number is 42 to the power of 3, 42 x 42 x 42, a royal triple, one of many hidden references to this number in Carroll's works.

Open references to this number include the forty-two illustrations in *Wonderland*, and the forty-two Baker's Boxes in *Snark*. Hidden references to the number forty-two have provided a motif for the journal *Jabberwocky* since 1977, including the ingenious suggestion by George Spence that Carroll related his interest in this number to Mendeleyev's discovery of the regularities of atomic weights on which he based his systematic Periodic Table of the Elements.

Frideswide, St   Alias the 'Fair Daughter Friswith', *c.* 700AD. Legend, as recalled by the Oxford bibliographer, Falconer Madan,* has it that St Frideswide, patron saint of Oxford,* ran away from her suitor, Algar, and hid in a pigsty with her handmaidens. Meanwhile Algar besieged the city until blinded by a flash of lightning. Glad to be saved from that sexual threat, the pious Frideswide started a nunnery on the site of the present Cathedral of Christ Church.* The flash of lightning is commemorated in the *Frideswide* window of the Cathedral.

Friendship   Between Carroll and adult men and women, friendship is an elusive subject. Carroll stammered, walked in an odd way, had a reputation as a recluse, and loved the company of little girls, or solitude, to the point that it is hard to know whether he ever had adult friends. Clearly, he could be excellent Common Room company, but that does not mean that he really had friends. When he mixed with such lions as the Tennysons* or Julia Margaret Cameron,* Carroll could be spiky: either they looked upon him as potentially amusing but in no way their social equal and thereby hurt him; or they saw him as a strange animal, capable only of unequal love with child*-friends. Often he was either piqued by adults or indifferent to them.

Henry Parry Liddon* appears to have been a life-long friend, travelling companion and religious confessor. Carroll called him 'my dear old friend' when he heard the news of his death in 1890. However there is no mention of him in Carroll's diary for five years before that. A glance through the index to Carroll's published diaries and letters suggests that the people he reported on or corresponded with, tended to be part of his life for a time, but then dropped out of it completely.

His sisters and brothers are an exception to this rule, but with none of them was he intimate. Besides Liddon, the exceptions were Vere Bayne and the MacDonalds,* but he sought none of them out after 1882. His relationship with Ellen Terry* spanned many years but was always one of admiration and amusement – intermingled now and again with shock – rather than intimacy.

G is for ...

Gait

He always carried himself upright, almost more than upright, as if he had swallowed a poker.

So wrote Alice Liddell* in old age of Carroll. Haigha, the Messenger in *Looking-Glass*, also walked oddly:

[He] kept skipping up and down, and wriggling like an eel, as he came along, with his great hands spread out on each side.

Haigha was, of course, the March Hare: only he was not a hare in his movements, but a human making a silly imitation of a hare. A long tradition of making fun of clever Englishmen with funny walks came to a head in John Cleese's development of a Ministry of that name.

Games

Fragments of Victorian children's indoor amusements which diverted the Liddell children at the Deanery – including alphabet and card games, a child-learner's view of chess* and croquet, charades, recitation and dance* – pepper the dialogue and action of *Alice*. There follow some variants of games the Liddell sisters played, and which Carroll sometimes transformed for their amusement.

ALPHABET GAMES   The Red Queen* in *Looking-Glass* quizzed Alice about her knowledge of the alphabet. The White Queen, who mispronounced words in an unqueenly way, suggested to Alice that the two of them should 'often say it over together, dear!' She then revealed one of her 'secrets' – that she was nearly illiterate: 'I can read words of one letter! Isn't *that* grand?' The

White Queen had almost learnt the alphabet. What she might not be able to do was to read words of 'more than one letter'. (See also Questions.*)

Carroll liked children to think about letters and words. In 1877, in a letter to 'Aggie' (Agnes) Hull (later Keith, 1867–1936) and her three sisters, he sent two alphabet games. He asked the sisters to identify a word made of the first seven and the ninth letter of the alphabet. He gave no answer, but 'big-faced' may have been the word intended. Carroll also sent his love to whichever Hull sister's name 'ended in a consonant'. Three sisters were called Alice, Eveline, Jessie and Agnes. His love was entirely for Agnes, the sister with the sibilant 's' at the end of her name.

An alphabet game was played by the Dormouse* in *Alice* at the Mad Tea-Party. The Dormouse described a drawing lesson during which 'Elsie',* 'Lacie'* and 'Tillie',* names which are a play on the names of the Liddell* sisters, drew 'all manner of things ...', everything ...

> "that begins with an M, such as mousetraps, and the moon, and memory, and muchness—you know you say things are 'much of a muchness'—did you ever see such a thing as a drawing of a muchness?"

Alice herself led a Looking-Glass Alphabet Game on the letter 'H', although she had not yet met Ronald *Hargreaves*, her future husband. The game was based on the children's spelling game: 'I love my love with a ...' which is played with all the letters of the alphabet. Her subject was the Anglo-Saxon Messenger, Haigha.

> "I love my love with an H," Alice couldn't help beginning, "because he is Happy. I hate him with an H because he is Hideous. I fed him with—with—Ham-sandwiches and Hay ..."

Carroll's fun in *Alice* with the letters of the alphabet marks the playful side of his adult interest in cryptography.*

'ANIMAL, VEGETABLE AND MINERAL' In this game, the players try to reach the answer by attempting to classify a hidden subject. In the Queen's Croquet Ground, the Ugly Duchess* became confused about how to classify 'mustard'. She went off on a tangent, classing together flamingoes and mustard, for 'both bite'. She then drew a moral: 'birds of a feather flock together'. Alice corrected her:

> "Only mustard isn't a bird," Alice remarked.
>
> "Right, as usual," said the Duchess: "what a clear way you have of putting things!"
>
> "It's a mineral, I *think*," said Alice.
>
> "Of course it is," said the Duchess, who seemed ready to agree to everything that Alice said: "there's a large mustard-mine near here. And the moral of that is—'The more there is of mine, the less there is of yours.'"

"Oh, I know!" exclaimed Alice, who had not attended to this last remark, "it's a vegetable..."

Mines, minerals and morals: all are mocked in *Alice*.

CARDS IN *ALICE*   A glance at Cassell's *Book of Indoor Amusements, Card Games and Fireside Fun* published in 1881 – when the 'Alice' books were in the nursery – shows card games, card tricks and card magic that Victorian children and adults played. But Alice finally lost patience with the game:

"Who cares for *you*?" said Alice (she had grown to her full size by this time). "You're nothing but a pack of cards!"

She met a King, a Queen and a Knave of Hearts. She saw three card rose-gardeners, the Two, Five and Seven of Spades. The ten club cards were royal guards and served in Carroll's illustrations as croquet hoops. The ten courtiers were the diamonds. Ten numbered hearts were royal children – cut out by Tenniel – two of whom are seen kissing each other in the foreground of Carroll's Croquet-ground sketch.

THE CAUCUS RACE   This was both anarchic and democratic, but a *Wonderland* children's game. The race was devised by a Dodo,* a bird that Darwin showed had lost in the struggle for survival, and the rule was a simple one; no one could win it and all present received a prize.

HEADS, BODIES AND LEGS   Animal and human figures and some of their body parts are changeable or interchangeable in *Alice*, rather as they are in the game of that name that involves each player drawing a head, folding it over, passing it to the next person who adds a body and so on until all are unwrapped and absurd figures appear, the last step being to give them a name. Tenniel's* Dodo has human hands and a cane. The Caterpillar was not dressed but held, with human hands, a hookah at which it puffed.

TABLEAUX VIVANTS   were played like charades, but had the additional advantage that, to quote again the ever-popular book of indoor games published by Cassell: 'in their representation no conversational power is required'. Alice Liddell seems to have had good conversational skills as a child, part of her charm in Carroll's eyes, but she was trained to be adept from a very young age at 'looking, rather than speaking, her thoughts'.

In order to perform a *tableau*, all the players freeze simultaneously into a final attitude at a given signal – and hold their position for three or four minutes, while the audience guesses by question and answer – directed to the producer of the scene – what their silent *tableau* portrays. Such performances gave Alice and her sisters training in staying still for photographic exposures. Though it was not noted which of the sisters played Beauty, the Liddell girls performed a fancy dress *tableau vivant* of *The Sleeping Beauty* when Queen Victoria* dined at the Deanery.* Another pose is captured in one of Carroll's photographs* – a *tableau vivant* showing Alice in profile, head held back, about to bite at a cherry held by Lorina. The answer to the charade was: 'Open your mouth and close your eyes'. The Prince of Wales* liked the cherry tableau so well when Carroll showed it to him on 12 December 1860, that it was one of the twelve Dodgson prints the Prince stuck in his personal album.*

Poses, recitations, cards in *Wonderland* and chess pieces throughout the *Looking-Glass* were tangible, familiar game images that Carroll used. They allowed Alice to enter the landscape of her dream, travel over it and then, after she had woken, leave it safely behind her.

Garden of Live Flowers   Lewis Carroll's 'Live Flowers' were garden flowers growing in a *Looking-Glass* flower bed, but they behaved like girls pertly upstaging one another in the wings during the performance of an amateur play. In the Garden of Live Flowers, Alice met: a Tiger-lily, which seems to us to be the leading lady among the flowers (see Ellen Terry*); a Rose which thinks a rose is the only thing in the world to be; and a modest Violet. Commentators have suggested the Rose and Violet may be name jokes about Rhoda and Violet, Alice's younger sisters, estranged from him at this favourite age by the breakdown of his friendship with the Liddell family after 1863. The children were 11 and 6 at the time *Looking-Glass* was published. Then there are an excitable Larkspur and some pink-tipped daisies.

Martin Gardner* noted that the flowers Carroll chose closely match those in Maud's garden in Tennyson's* *Maud*. This is how the relevant verse runs:

> She is coming, my dove, my dear;
> She is coming, my life, my fate;
> The red rose cries 'She is near, she is near;'
> And the white rose weeps, 'She is late;'
> The larkspur listens, 'I hear, I hear;'
> And the lily whispers, 'I wait'.

In *Maud*, the pink-edged white daisy turns pink when stepped on by the delicate feet of Maud, watched in secret tripping about her garden by an entranced, poetic lover. The London critics had gone for Tennyson for this but he claimed he knew this happens, and it does. Tennyson, a Lincolnshire man, prided himself on his knowledge of gardening and country matters. Carroll's odd personal relationship with Tennyson did not in any case survive the year 1870, as Morton Cohen* recorded in his biography.

Carroll's evident willingness to mock Tennyson while at the same time sending him a vellum presentation copy of the second *Alice* story, drew the line as far as theological jokes were concerned. Carroll refrained from including Tennyson's Passion Flower and Lily in the list of rebellious flowers he cast in the second *Alice* story. He may have considered Christ's passion and Christ's lilies too sensitive a reference. He did, however, include in the *Looking-Glass* garden a willow-tree, which served as chaperon to the flowers.

The floral fantasies in Tennyson's *Maud* were loved by some of Carroll's child-friends, whose performances in drawing-room recitals by the piano Carroll may have been mocked in 'The Garden of Live Flowers'. Julia Margaret Cameron* in particular posed young women, including the Liddell sisters, grown older and more willowy, as a posy of live roses, or as Pomona or Flora, among other Tennysonian fantasies.

The nineteenth century was a century of flowers, of the import of thousands of new species from far flung corners of the world. No writers but the nonsense writers Carroll and Lear had the temerity to mock the Victorian female retreat – exemplified in Tennyson's *Maud* – into the language of flowers.

Gardens in the Landscape of *Alice* In *Wonderland,* Alice tried to enter a garden full of flowers, but she was the wrong size. The Queen's Croquet Match took place in a garden and in *Looking-Glass* Alice found herself in the 'Garden of Live Flowers'.* Both stories are set in a tamed, but beautiful, countryside. Walter de la Mare* compared it to a medieval Italian landscape. The woodlands were never so deep as to contain the terrors of

Little Red Riding Hood; and there were hills, not mountains, from which the landscape looked like a chessboard. Though much covered in polythene today, the market gardening and orchard land around the Vale of Evesham to the north-west of Oxford still looks like the countryside of mid-century Oxford. It was a countryside of lanes enclosed by high hedgerows of hawthorn and wild rose, of water meadows scattered with yellow, purple and white wild flowers, of old churches and abbeys, of bridges over streams where minnows flickered and boys fished, of the, in summer, idly flowing Thames with cows grazing and drinking at the water mark. (See Riddles.*)

The wood round the Hare's* house, the lawn where the Mad Tea-Party was held, the wood where Alice met the Fawn, the 'deep waters' on which she tried to row the old Sheep, all bear strong resemblance to the Oxfordshire that Carroll and Alice Liddell* experienced by boat or on foot on their walks or looked at from the train to Oxford; or, in Alice's case, when out riding her pony with her father.

Gardner, Martin (1914–)   Gardner is best known for his popular books on mathematics and science, in particular for his 'Mathematical Games' column in *Scientific American*, which had a cult following for 25 years after 1960. He is also the author of *The Annotated Alice*, *More Annotated Alice* and *The Annotated Snark*. They reproduce the text, and in the case of *The Annotated Alice*, the original illustrations of the book, with admirably informative notes on the background and references in the text alongside.

In 1996, he published *The Universe in a Handkerchief*, which surveys Carroll's word-play, mathematical recreations and the articles and pamphlets he wrote to explain them. He has also written introductions to the Dover editions of *The Nursery Alice*, *Alice's Adventures Under Ground* and Carroll's late, least lovable work, *Sylvie and Bruno*.

Gathorne-Hardy, Gathorne (1814–1906)   Tory MP for Oxford and later first Earl of Cranbrook. In 1865 Gathorne-Hardy beat W. E. Gladstone* (1809–98), four times Liberal Prime Minister, in the election for parliament for Oxford, the University having its own two MPs. A third candidate was William Heathcote.

There were three candidates at the election which ousted Gladstone from the traditionally Liberal seat of Oxford University. The *Looking-Glass* plum-cake was also magically split into three parts by Alice's knife during the *Looking-Glass* battle. To the delight of Carroll and other High Church Tory dons, the Tories won, giving Oxford two Tory representatives. When Carroll went to the House of Commons to hear Gladstone and Disraeli* (1804–81), twice Prime Minister, it was to Gathorne-Hardy that he applied for tickets.

Besides canvassing for him, Carroll met him on several occasions and photographed him.

Martin Gardner cited 'as being widely believed in England' in Carroll's time, the idea that the Lion and Unicorn which fought for the Crown referred to the well-known antagonism between Gladstone and Disraeli. We have argued that the severe facial expression and hurt pride of Tenniel's* Unicorn seemed more like Gladstone than Disraeli. Carroll's *Looking-Glass* Lion in that case was a British lion, a Tory one, and furthermore, one which was the victor of the swing to the Tories at Oxford elections after 1864.

A letter spoofing a petulant Liberal reaction to another unexpected Tory victory at the earlier by-election in Woodstock was published by Carroll under the misleading pseudonym, 'A Liberal of the Liberals' in the *Oxford University Herald* in November in 1868.

Gattégno, Jean (1935–95) *Alice* found a fond readership in France from the time that it was first translated (see Translations*) in 1869. The idea of the old professor and the spritely young girl appealed, as did the whimsy and nonsense. Carroll was a Tory. By a cross-Channel metamorphosis, he became, between the wars, something of an icon of the French Left. Louis Aragon (1879–1982) and André Breton paid homage to *Alice* in their pre-war Surrealist* Manifesto and Antonin Artaud, Brassai, Albert Camus and Claude Roy followed. (See Child*-Friends.) Then Carroll found one of his greatest fans in Jean Gattégno, professor at the University of Paris, whose numerous writings on *Alice* established the books in the French academic curriculum.

While Anglo-Saxon biographers* and critics* have concentrated, during the last three decades, on the details of Carroll's life and relations with young girls, Gattégno, refreshingly, concentrated on Carroll's charm, on his delight in children and his application of logic to a children's book. His book – whose title in its translation is *Lewis Carroll: Fragments of a Looking Glass* – is arranged as an A to Z, starting with Alice and ending with Zeno's Paradox. The book is a distillation of Carroll, a portrait achieved through an analysis of 26 aspects of his brilliance. Gattégno also edited and added a chronology, bibliography and notes to the leather-bound Gallimard edition of Carroll's *Oeuvres*, a collector's item which has further helped to establish Carroll's Gallic reputation. Hélène Cixous has followed in Gattégno's footsteps in the University of Paris and the *Alice* books have become the subject of linguistic and philosophical study in other French universities. French bookshops, like Italian, today contain a number of different translations of *Alice*.

Gentleman   Being assumed a gentleman was essential to Carroll in his self-conscious passage through society. As a gentleman, he was able to enter almost any drawing room; as a gentleman he could command a certain respect from ticket-collectors, porters, footmen and other servants. What constitutes a gentleman in England is complicated. In Victorian times it was not a matter of accent, for regional accents penetrated all layers of society (see also Queen's English*). It was the later age of Jeeves that produced the so-called 'upper-class' accent. Archdeacon Grantly in Trollope's *Last Chronicle of Barset* (1867) was described as:

> ... the battered Perpetual Curate of Hogglestock, a graduate of Oxford it is true, but a man bearing ... the scars of harshest poverty.

Yet he claimed:

> 'We stand,' said [the Archdeacon], 'on the only perfect level on which such men can meet each other. We are both gentlemen.'

At Christ Church* throughout Carroll's tenure, things were less simple. Until such distinctions were abolished, Aristocrats, also known as 'Tufts' because of the gold tassels they wore on their mortar boards, stood above Gentlemen Commoners, who stood above Commoners, who were waited on by Servitors. Carroll as an undergraduate was a Commoner, one of several facts about him that rankled with Mrs Liddell.* To college servants later in the century, undergraduates, however they behaved, were always 'young gentlemen'. To dons, they were simply 'men' – thus 'rowing men' or 'reading men' like the virtuous and assiduous young Carroll.

Geography   This was a most important part of the Victorian home curriculum. Boys learned classical Latin, but girls' lessons emphasized modern languages, history and geography. At the time of *Alice* there was considerable excitement in the laying of the first transatlantic cable on the Atlantic sea-bed, which pushed to the limit the resources of the Survey Service of the British and American Navies and the Royal Geographical Society's map-making skills. The Mock Turtle* was interested in Seaography.

At the beginning of the list of names Alice had to learn in her schoolroom were the Antipodes,* which she called the Antipathies. It is possible that Carroll, having suffered from the same kind of rote-learning, was antipathetic to the whole process. His alternative was to amuse little girls with jokes and riddles,* with tests of logic and meaning, rather than to expect them to learn each of the capitals of Europe. This is one of a number of ways in which *Alice* undermines the values of the nursery schoolroom. Alice's adventures with a clergyman storyteller involved an exciting exercise in spiritual geography, one where she could fly though space and cross boundaries mysteriously. (See also Governesses* and Lessons.*)

Geology   Alice fell down and down and thought she was falling through the centre of the earth. Explaining to a little child that the earth was an oblate spheroid with a centre was a challenge to Carroll. Then when he took Alice Liddell* and other child*-friends to the new Natural History Museum* in Oxford,* they were participating in a hymn to geology. John Ruskin* had arranged for each pillar to be of a different marble and everywhere round the museum were cases of fossils and geological specimens. The layout of the specimens and the patterns in which they were organized were themselves a delight, an Aristotelian hymn to what was about to become a scientific body of thought led by determined reductionists like Thomas Henry Huxley.*

The story was told by William Gaunt in his book, *Oxford* (1965) that Dean Gaisford, Dean Liddell's predecessor, thought he had seen the end of science.*

'Thank God! We shall have no more of this Geology!' exclaimed Dean Gaisford when Dr Buckland, whose discoveries seemed to question the accepted story of the Creation, went to Italy.

William Gaunt noted that another Oxford don thought his barometer looked nicer hung on its side. Carroll, unlike them, was fascinated by instruments and measuring devices. Nevertheless, palaeontology was enough of a comedy to him for him to put an extinct animal, the Dodo,* as a living creature, indeed as himself, among the living. It took Darwin, with his Edinburgh and Cambridge* attitudes to field science, to crack the nut. The comedy was over. Archaic ecclesiastical Oxford was shattered by beliefs about evolution* which rested on newly-presented raw data about extinction and geological transformation.

Germanizing   A term applied to the theological tendencies of opponents of the Oxford Movement. They were otherwise described as Broad Church.* Julius Hare* (1795–1855), Charles Kingsley* and Benjamin Jowett* were Germanizers. So was Albert, the Prince Consort. Carroll was most definitely not.

Gernsheim, Helmut (1913–95)   Historian and collector of Victorian photographs, born in Germany, Gernsheim came to England as a refugee before the Second World War. With his wife, Alison, he established himself as a leading figure in photographic history, particularly of the pioneering Victorian age. By chance backed by scholarship, he rediscovered Carroll as a photographer while working on Julia Margaret Cameron's* life. This happened when a London dealer offered him an unnamed album of what seemed to be Victorian photographs. Gernsheim thought they might be Carroll's. Intrigued, he consulted Carroll's unpublished diaries* with the help of Carroll's niece, Menella Dodgson, and published the first study of Carroll's studio photographs, *Lewis Carroll: Photographer*. Thirty-three albums were auctioned on Carroll's death. Gernsheim speculated that those albums numbered XI and higher were 'filled with the usual *carte-de-visite* and cabinet photographs'. Of these 33 albums, Gernsheim traced 12. Gernsheim's collection was purchased by the University of Texas where it is now held.

His book, *Lewis Carroll: Photographer* (1969) contains 64 plates which show the range of Carroll's photographic talent and a careful – though incomplete – description of Carroll's sitters; a subject updated by Edward Wakeling* for publication in 1998. (See also Albums.*)

Gladstone, William Ewart, MP (1809–98)   Liberal statesman who, in his long political career, was Liberal Chancellor of the Exchequer and several times Liberal Prime Minister. He was also a university and Christ Church reformer. As an Honorary Student on the Old Foundation at Christ Church,* Gladstone was a highly-placed supporter of the reforms of Henry George Liddell,* Alice's father. Thus Gladstone supported Liddell against Carroll and many of his Tory contemporaries at Christ Church.

Alice Liddell* as a child met Gladstone at Oxford* and in Llandudno, when he visited the Liddells' summer house, Pen Morfa.* Recalling in old age the time when Liddell was so ill he had to go to Madeira to convalesce, Gladstone emphasized that the Dean's loss at the height of the reform campaign, which was long overdue, would have been a national disaster.

Carroll was not so sure. At the time of the 1865 Oxford Election (see Gathorne-Hardy*) he opposed Gladstone's Liberal candidacy, and wrote squibs against him and his supporters including Liddell. Suggestions were put forward at the time of the earliest reviews of *Alice* that Carroll had parodied Gladstone as the Hatter*. There is little about the behaviour, facial expression or rhetoric of the Hatter to endorse this, but it does show that from the earliest reception of *Alice*, the text and Tenniel's* illustrations* gave rise to the idea that Carroll was partly parodying real people. We believe that there is considerable likeness between the Unicorn* and Gladstone and that the Lion, symbol of Britain, may be partly a parody of his opponent in the Oxford election, the Tory Gathorne-Hardy. Gladstone's impatience with Alice has a ring of reality about it, and the *Looking-Glass* cake is cut into three. The election was a three-way fight, with two seats being awarded. Gladstone failed to win one of them. Others have suggested the Lion is Gladstone, and the Unicorn Disraeli. The most important point is that elements of many real people beside Carroll himself may be scattered through *Alice*: Carroll's humour was most cogent when he and Alice knew or knew of and could recognize, albeit through a veil of secrecy, the subject of the jokes and parodies.

Carroll wrote squibs and anagrams* against Gladstone and his followers. Morton Cohen* noted his parody throughout the political satire, *The Dynamics of a Part-icle* (1865), more pointedly in the following passage, a mock-geometrical proof:

> To work the following problem algebraically, it is best to let the circle be ... referred to its two tangents, i.e. first to WEG [Gladstone], WH [William Heathcote, the other candidate in the three-way contest], and afterwards to WH, GH [Gathorne-Hardy]. When this is effected, it will be found most convenient to project WEG to infinity [i.e. get rid of him – fighting talk, for he was nationally admired].

Carroll devised the best of several anagrams that were published on Gladstone's full name and pasted his portrait into one of the albums* held at the University of Texas.

Whilst sharing Gladstone's High Church religious views, Carroll hated his politics, in particular the idea of Irish Home Rule and his support for university reform, two crucial platforms of Gladstone's political life. Carroll believed that both would be 'a gigantic catastrophe'.

Gnat, The   As Carroll developed the Mouse's Tale* into the wavy, typeset shape of a Mouse's Tail, which grew smaller and smaller as the end of the tale was reached, so it was with the Gnat's almost inaudible remarks to Alice. Carroll ordered the type of the passages spoken by the Gnat to be set at about half the size of the type of the rest of the book, to reflect the tiny, high-pitched buzz of the Gnat. (See also Punctuation.*)

Alice met the Gnat in the railway carriage. She could barely hear what it was saying. She told it that the stream of jokes it suggested to her were 'very bad ones'. The pleading tone of the Gnat's conversation led William Empson* to suggest that this character may be a self-portrait by Carroll – a self-demeaning one – showing himself with a child*-friend bored by his tedious word-play. The Gnat followed Alice off the train into the woods and grew larger, until it was 'about the size of a chicken'. Fanning her with its wings on the edge of the wood where things have no names, the Gnat, one of several creatures in *Alice* to embrace mortality in front of her eyes, gave her a lesson about Looking-Glass Insects* and left with tears rolling down its cheeks, sighing itself out of existence.

Golden Afternoon   Myth has it that the first *Alice* story was told to Alice, her two sisters and Robinson Duckworth* on a single river expedition on 4 July 1862.

> All in the golden afternoon
> Full leisurely we glide;

Carroll's entry from the 1862 diary gave a sense of his interest-filled Oxford summer days, a row up river, tea on the bank, return to Christ Church* after eight, then a session with his photograph albums.* The entries are often practical: details of his plans for the journey, censored in the edited diaries, by foot, train and river and once a sign of irritation at having to tell *Alice* his 'interminable' tale.

Twenty-five years later there was a change. He began to establish the myth that *Under Ground* was the spontaneous creation of a single afternoon. In prefatory remarks, he wrote:

> Many a day had we rowed together on that quiet stream—the three little maidens and I—and many a fairy tale had been extemporised for their benefit... yet none of these tales got written down: they lived and died like summer midges, each in its golden afternoon until there came a day when, as it chanced, one of my little listeners petitioned that the tale might be written out for her....
>
> Full many a year has slipped away, since that 'golden afternoon' that gave thee birth, but I can call it up almost as clearly as if it were yesterday— the cloudless blue above, the watery mirror below... the three eager faces, hungry for news of fairy-land.

Since then, an assumption about the 'golden afternoon' has influenced many Carroll studies. The idea, as developed by Carroll, was perpetuated immediately after his death by Stuart Collingwood.* Writers of the 1930s, to whom Carroll's diaries and letters were not available, accepted it; so did Roger Lancelyn Green,* to whom they were. Alice Liddell* said that the stories that made up *Under Ground* coalesced on a particular summer afternoon on the river, but that many others, and possibly the same ones, were told earlier.

The argument over the 'Golden Afternoon' is germane because it separates those (see Critics* and Biographers*) who believe that *Alice* was no more than whimsical nonsense, plucked from the summer air by an − admittedly very clever − story teller; and those who believe that the cogency of the nonsense in real life situations and the ability of the characters to stay alive through five generations imply that the stories must have been built up more carefully. For all his apparent spontaneity, Carroll was joking about real situations and people whom he and Alice both knew, or knew of. Some episodes in the stories could be interchanged for others. In other words the narrative is not tight and Alice is the only character to appear regularly. However, each story has a distinct beginning, one where Alice enters an imaginary world, perhaps in a dream state in which time, space and her size go awry. It is the other world, behind a mirror, where reality is back to front. Each has well-balanced changes of mood, and a very distinct and brilliantly conceived metaphysical end. Each story, examined closely, is a tract about the nature of reality and language. It would have taken a genius indeed to come up with *Under Ground* on a single 'golden afternoon'. Not everyone, however, wishes to face this. To many the idea of artistic guile in the construction of the narrative spoils the fun.

On a more mundane note, arguments have been put forward that the meteorological records showed that it rained and was not 'golden' on that afternoon. These have been challenged, as Oxford afternoons can often be both showery and golden, perhaps only proving that investigation of this kind is ultimately futile. What matters is the power of Carroll's imagination, not the weather on a particular day when he was with Alice.

Governesses   In 1850, just before Alice was born, there were 21,000 single women working in England in private homes as governesses and the number continued to rise. Alice, from the age of six to ten when Carroll knew her, spent longer with her governess, Miss Mary Prickett (later Foster) than anyone else except her sisters. Her governess was solely responsible for her education and the *Alice* books are full of references to the rote-learning by which she taught.

A governess might either be the daughter of gentlefolk who had not the means to provide a marriage settlement, so making marriage unlikely, and could not afford to keep her, or she might come from a middle-class family which would welcome the contact with the upper classes. No other career was open to such women. Carroll himself, who felt that the Tennysons exploited their sons' tutors, on one occasion acknowledged that tutors and governesses were 'down-trodden'. He even urged the parents of one child*-friend to help her seek work in the Post Office, so worried was he by the indignities to which this class of teacher was subject.

The parents' expectations of their governess were considerable, and the wages of about £70 to £100 a year were meagre, even compared with those of male tutors who were hired to educate boys at home. In the few respectable clothes they could afford, governesses were housed, literally and metaphorically, on a half-landing between the servants' quarters, the downstairs of a house, and its upstairs. They stood on an even narrower emotional half-landing. The children they cared for might show them affection but they could no more return it than an Oxford don could break the laws of celibacy. This was particularly painful in cases where mothers were distant figures – Mrs Lorina Liddell* probably was not – for governesses were dismissed if they became too familiar, or worse, if they began to have 'followers', the word used for suitors.

John Ruskin,* Charlotte Bronte and Mrs Charlotte M. Yonge* were among those authors who reprimanded employers of governesses where lessons in respect needed to be learned. In trying to understand Mrs Liddell's relations with Carroll, it may be that she looked on him as an extra tutor who came free; a useful, educative, part-time companion for her children. By this token he would have looked on her as a friend while she cast him as a harmless male equivalent to a governess, rather than as Alice saw him, logician and mathematician, and, worst of all, a potential suitor.

Mary Prickett (1833–1913) was Alice's governess when Carroll knew her. In the Deanery she was known as 'Pricks'. She was Carroll's age and a spinster. To his chagrin, he was spotted so frequently in her company that he was thought to be 'dancing attendance' on her. Rhoda, the Rose in the Garden of Live Flowers,* described the Red Queen* as one of the thorny kind. This may be a joke on her nickname, 'Pricks'. Roger Lancelyn Green* wrote that the Red Queen was said by Carroll late in his life to be characterized by 'the concentrated essence of all governesses'.

Mary Prickett was the daughter of the Butler at Trinity. Her father held office in Carroll's father's day, long before the 'Bread-and-Butter* Row' brought an end to the power and well-lined pockets of butlers. 'Pricks' described her father as a gentleman, which made her a lady, and thus suitable to be a governess. That she was socially ambitious and shrewd is suggested by the fact that she was married in 1871, when Alice was 19, to Charles Foster, a leading Oxford wine merchant, adviser on the running of public functions and owner of the respectable Mitre Hotel.

When 'Pricks' was Alice's governess, her family's house was close to Folly Bridge, which is where St Aldate's Street crosses the Thames and below which Carroll rented boats from Salter's Boat Yard. She was employed by Mrs Liddell as a governess from 1856. Carroll felt a certain discomfort when the children were in her company and not in his. According to Caryl Hargreaves, Alice's one surviving son, Miss Prickett never took to the determined Alice. He wrote: 'Alice was not her favourite among the three sisters'. Pricks not only taught the girls from a slender armoury of rote-learned knowledge. She also organized their regime of meals and outings, of dressing and re-dressing. She is unlikely to have been amused by the number of schoolroom jokes in *Alice*. (See also Antipodes,* Books Carroll read as a child,* Boredom,* Geography,* Grief,* History,* and Recitation.*)

Grandville, J. J. (also written 'Gran'ville') (1803–47)   Grandville was the pen-name of Isidore-Adolphe Gérard, who charmed Parisians in the 1840s with his *Fleurs Animées* and his prodigiously vain insects and monkeys. These illustrations were engraved for *La Caricature*. His fables depicting men with animal heads in human clothing, his cosmogonies, phantasmagoria, zoomorphs* and phytomorphoses heralded the birth of the Surrealist* Movement. In the 1930s, Marie Mespoulet traced ways in which John Tenniel,* with Carroll the original illustrator* of *Alice*, was indebted to Grandville for the visual whimsy in *Alice*, which she believed to have been anglicized by Tenniel to suit Carroll's story.

Graves, Robert von Ranke (1895–1985)   Robert Graves' poem, 'Alice' (1925) was written when he was Professor of English Literature in Egypt after the period of his life covered by his semi-fictional memoir, *Goodbye to All That* (1929). Like other World War I veterans, Graves returned to the childhood roots that *Alice* represented. His poem proposed that Alice's fantasy marked a new way of looking, and that Carroll's adult characters were people in their own right, not representations of others, as his Cambridge contemporaries Empson* and Leslie* proposed. Graves celebrated Alice's journey through the Looking-Glass and her return to earth loaded with dreams, flowers and laughter as a rejection of the rigidity of 'Victoria's* Golden Rule'. He called Alice a 'national hero'.

Green, Roger Gilbert Lancelyn (1918–87)   Educated in Liverpool and Oxford, Green was Deputy Librarian of Merton College, Oxford, until 1950, when he was appointed a research fellow in English Literature at his native Liverpool University. Here he edited the Carroll diaries* and stayed for most of his working life, living in Poulton Hall in the nearby Wirral, an ancestral home with walled gardens and woodland that is itself something of a 'Wonderland' in an otherwise rural and suburbanized world across the Mersey.

For several years, the Greens put on an elaborate performance of *Through the Looking-Glass* in their garden. The family performed on a chessboard laid out on the lawn. Alice would pass through the mirror and the audience would watch her adventures on a turntable turned by the local Boy Scouts and their fathers.

Roger Lancelyn Green was a prolific author, producing several books a year between 1945 and 1979, some of them plays and poems, many on the subject of myths and fairy tales. He edited the *Kipling Journal*, wrote about James Barrie, Andrew Lang, Shakespeare's tales and King Arthur with an ebullient yet scholarly delight. Having established himself in the world of children's literature he became, by a series of connections, trusted by those of Carroll's descendants who were the guardians of the Carroll diaries.*

The editing of the diaries required meticulous research into for example, many long-forgotten acquaintances of Carroll's, long-forgotten plays he had seen and other related matters. In 1962 Lancelyn Green revised the standard Carroll bibliography* of Williams and Madan. It was as a result of work done by Morton N. Cohen* with the assistance of Roger Lancelyn Green that the two remarkable annotated volumes of *The Letters of Lewis Carroll* were published in 1979.

Greenacre, Phyllis, Dr (1894–)   That the male characters in both *Alice* books are weak was one of Phyllis Greenacre's psychoanalytical comments on *Alice*. Dr Greenacre was Professor of Clinical Psychiatry at Cornell University Medical School and author of *Swift and Carroll* published in 1955. She wrote:

> Mr W. Rabbit is a scared and fussy little person [worrying] whether the Duchess will be cross with him. There follow successively 'Pat', the cowardly handyman, and ineffective Bill the Lizard; the peremptory but indolent Caterpillar with his oversized hookah ... the mad March Hare and the equally Mad Hatter, the somnolent Dormouse, the Five, Seven and Two of Spades, who are clumsy gardeners and fall on their faces; the timid King of Hearts ...

'In contrast,' she noted, the women characters in both *Alice* books were 'belligerent and noisy'. Dr Greenacre wrote in her book, *The Character of Dodgson as revealed in the Writings of Carroll*, quoted in the Norton Critical edition of *Alice* of 1971:

> [Dodgson's] effeminacy was sufficiently obvious that some of his less sympathetic students once wrote a parody of his parodies and signed it 'Louisa Caroline'. He disliked garish colours, preferred pinks and greys ... [but see Red*] He is said to have requested one of the little girls not to visit him in a red dress.

The sharp-eyed psychoanalyst makes inferences drawn from themes of decapitation and body extension in *Alice* and emphasizes, with regard to Carroll's imaginative writing after the *Alice* books:

Had not the aggressive and sexual drives been so firmly checked in him, it is probable that he would have fulfilled many times over the promise of intellectual genius which was early noted.

Later commentators on Carroll's contribution to literature and mathematics shared her view. The idea that Carroll was creatively blocked must be kept in perspective, however. After all, he put his frustrations sufficiently aside to write two of the greatest short books in the English language and one of its greatest long comic poems.

Grief　This was the term used by the Mock Turtle* to describe Greek lessons at The School Under the Sea. The pun on the name of the lesson* implies that Greek is less enjoyable than Latin ('Laughing'). Because Alice's father, Dean Liddell,* was a famous Greek scholar, his daughters in particular, if they spotted the pun, would have enjoyed Carroll's joke.

Gryphon　'If you don't know what a Gryphon is, look at the picture': thus Carroll said to Alice, or rather to his readers, when the Ugly Duchess* took Alice to meet the Mock Turtle and they came upon the Gryphon asleep in the sun. If you do know what a Gryphon is, a beast with the head and wings of an eagle and the hind-quarters of a lion, you will not be surprised by Tenniel's* illustration. It was based on a heraldic Gryphon, but this one was unusual in being totally supine, as though it had crash-landed, an unheraldic thing for a Gryphon to do. Carroll's Gryphon in *Under Ground* is an altogether more eccentric creature, with a cry which was spelt: 'Hjckrrh!'

Carroll amused Alice when she was a child by helping her to cut out the tiny embossed heraldic seals from the envelopes received at the Deanery, which she kept in a scrap-book; it is now in Christ Church Library. Gryphons, none of them supine, feature among them.

Carroll knew the works of John Ruskin* and photographed him in his studio. Alice Liddell was Ruskin's student at Oxford. Ruskin lauded the artistic superiority of carved Lombardic gryphons in medieval Verona. The authors have argued that Carroll had Ruskin's teaching in mind when he created the at first lazy – then violently dancing – Gryphon. Certainly he peppered the talk in the Gryphon's fast-paced scenes with Ruskinian views about Beauty and Uglification.* (See also Anagrams.*)

Guildford   English city in Surrey. The death of Carroll's father in June 1868 made it necessary for the bereaved Dodgson* family to leave Croft* Rectory in Yorkshire. Carroll became head of the family on his father's death and thus responsible for finding a new home. Why, when the family had so many northern connections, a local home was not sought is not clear, unless it was to do with proximity to Oxford* and the London* theatre. There is also a sense in his diaries* that he found life at Croft, where his father was the Rector, or at Ripon, where he was a Canon, dull.

Carroll started house-hunting seven weeks after his father died, and headed for Guildford. He liked the fine view from 'The Chestnuts' and the proximity to London. He settled on a new and hitherto unoccupied house for his sisters. It resembles a Georgian rectory and faces north with a view over the River Wey and, incidentally, the burial ground where Carroll is buried. It was near the Parish church of St Mary's where the vicar was an ex-Fellow of Wadham College, Oxford.

Carroll quickly effected an introduction through a local vicar who was a Christ Church connection, and explored the possibility of his younger brother, Wilfred, becoming a curate at St Mary's – but nothing came of this. He walked extensively around Guildford. 'The Chestnuts', which still stands, became the home of Carroll and the unmarried Dodgson sisters. Among the families that moved to the Guildford area at this time were George Frederick Watts and the Leonard Huxleys. Carroll's child-friend, Julia, wife to Leonard and mother of Aldous Huxley (see Queen's English*) became a head-mistress there. Carroll died at 'The Chestnuts' on 14 January 1898.

Today the Guildford Muniment Room houses a significant collection of Carroll material, including material collected by Derek Hudson, the biographer.* At the heart of the collection is Dodgson family material which has been deposited by various members of the family on occasions since October 1965. Of particular note in the family collection is Item D: *Friends of C. L. Dodgson, including their reminiscences* which has first-hand accounts of Carroll not found elsewhere. A detailed catalogue of holdings is available. (See also Sites.*)

THE THAMES, NEAR GODSTOW

H is for ...

Hands ... and Gloves   Like the conjuror he was, Carroll was fastidious about his hands, wearing grey or black cotton gloves all the year round, and buying them in bundles of half a dozen at a time. This could cause problems as there was a very specific type of 'thread' glove that he liked. On one occasion, in Eastbourne,* he visited 14 shops without being able to find what he needed. Carroll worried about his hands. He worried too about those of his characters. While the characters which were not human were called 'it' in the *Alice* narrative, many of these creatures have a pair of human hands.

Hare, The March   During the spring mating season, the hare's behaviour is unusually wild. Hence the expression 'as mad as a March hare'. Hares are now scarce in southern England due to intensive farming, but were prolific in Carroll's day. One of Charles Kingsley's* poems attacked a landlord for protecting hares as game, while the hares ate his tenants' food crops.

The role of the Hare at the Mad Tea-Party* was that of a crony to the more dominant Hatter.* We believe that the Mad Tea-Party is a parody of unequal sharing, the danger inherent in the doctrine of Christian Socialism,* from Carroll's logical perspective. Everyone moved round at the Party, but the only one who gained anything was the Hatter. The character of the Hare may be a parody of Julius Charles Hare (1795–1855), a Germanizing* Archdeacon of Lewes, and supporter of Charles Kingsley's earlier Christian Socialist ideals.

The Hare brothers were members of the Broad Church* clergy trained in Cambridge.* It was Julius and his brother Augustus (1792–1834) who, in 1843, helped Alexander Macmillan* and his brother to buy the Cambridge bookshop where the Macmillan publishing business began. The Hares were responsible for introducing a more 'German' element into the Church of England. Prince Albert and Queen Victoria* approved. While their book *Guesses at the Truth by Two Brothers* may sound eccentric to 1990s eyes, it sold solidly throughout the mid–century.

Julius Hare became rector of Herstmonceux, the richest living of any in England, which was in the gift of his family. He was notably eccentric: he would, for example, go out for long walks over the downs just as his guests arrived for a meal and there was no telling when he would return. Time,* and the conventions relating to it, meant nothing to him. His morning service might continue in winter until the early dusk. His first biographer was A. J. C. Hare (1834–1903), a relation, who lived in Christ Church* during the time that Carroll was writing *Looking-Glass*. Cambridge theologians, such as the Hares and Charles Kingsley were the butt of the ire of High Church Oxford. Mouse, plural mice, German '*maus*', as in Dormouse, may be a joke on the name F. D. Maurice,* another Macmillan author and Christian Socialist.

Hare may be Hare. So may another crony of Charles Kingsley – a model for the Hatter – his brother, Henry Kingsley,* who Carroll photographed and who was 'as mad as a March hare', bounding round the countryside near his brother's parish in Hampshire. (See also Drugs* in *Alice*). In *Looking-Glass*, the March Hare reappeared as Haigha, keeper of the King's ham sandwiches and hay, which it kept in a pouch round its neck. It rolled its eyes 'wildly from side to side' and wriggled like an eel, its great hands 'spread out like fans'. Hatta and Haigha, the Anglo-Saxon messengers, handed round white and brown bread during the fight between the Lion and the Unicorn,* as unkempt in appearance and manner as the Germanizing royal courtiers, Charles Kingsley and the Hare brothers.

Hargreaves, Reginald (1852–1926)   Alice married Hargreaves in 1880. In the view of her biographer, Anne Clark, in *The Real Alice* (1981) her match with Hargreaves only became a possibility when her parents steered her away from a relationship with Prince Leopold. Alice actually does become royal in her own way in *Looking-Glass* – see Queens* and Questions.*

Reggie Hargreaves had no title, although he was a gentleman and a rich one. He was educated at Eton College and Christ Church.* He married Alice when they were both 28. Carroll must have known of him as an undergraduate for he took a remarkable six years to finish his degree. Carroll's diary* suggests that he felt some embarrassment when he met Hargreaves at the time of his engagement to Alice.

Physically Reggie Hargreaves was everything that Carroll was not – tall, with the easy gait of an athlete. He was bearded and had a face that did not so much express authority as the complete confidence that his was the best of all possible worlds. The letter Reginald Hargreaves wrote to his friend, A. W. Ridley, announcing his engagement is revealing: the Junior Carlton Club notepaper, the intention to take Alice sailing for the Cowes Regatta off the Isle of Wight, the nickname he used for Ridley ('Ribsy'), the reference to London as 'town' and the use of the phrase 'bye the bye' establish his background.

Reginald Hargreaves never had to work for his living. He lived the life of a wealthy country gentleman: a large house in Hampshire, fishing, shooting and cricket. It may be sentimental to think that Alice was as intellectually alert as Carroll's heroine in *Wonderland*. One book she left behind was the fat, leather-bound, visitors book from the Hargreaves' house, Cuffnells, now in Christ Church library. With its pages of repetitive signatures of guests, many known to her since Deanery* days, many from the landed aristocracy, it reflects the life of a comfortable and confident age, which vanished with the First World War.

Hatch Family   The Hatch's were an Oxford family, with close connections to Carroll. Edwin Hatch (1835–89), the father, was a Reader in Ecclesiastical History at Christ Church* and wrote the Victorian hymn, *Breathe on me, Breath of God*. He and his wife, Bessie (1839–91) were known to Carroll and through them he may have rubbed shoulders with the poet, Algernon Charles Swinburne (1837–1909), the painter, Edward Burne-Jones (1833–98), and the critic, Walter Pater* whose idea of 'Art for Art's Sake' was antithetical to Carroll's moralizing view of art and society.

Carroll was fond of the Hatch children, in particular Beatrice (1866–1947) and Evelyn (1871–1951). Although a number of the letters had been published before, Evelyn Hatch's *A Selection from the Letters of Lewis Carroll to His Child-Friends*, published in 1933, gave the first comprehensive view of Carroll's love for his child*-friends.

Carroll's pattern of acquaintance with the Hatch girls was not unusual. He first saw the children and Mrs Hatch at a theatrical party at the house of a clergyman in 1871, struck up an acquaintance, gave copies of *Alice* to the children and then was given permission to photograph them. They are the best known, and rather coy subjects of his few remaining nude child photographs.* Carroll's friendship with the Hatch girls was long-lasting and belies the idea that he gave up such friendships when girls became young women. Notably he paid the fees of Ethel Hatch when her father died at the age of 54. She was an art student under Hubert von Herkomer* who painted portraits of both Carroll and Dean Liddell.* In the introduction to her book, Evelyn said that, when Carroll was seen in company on his daily Oxford walks, he was always joking, further evidence that he was not the lonely, dour man that some have portrayed. (See also Dodgson, C. L.,* – the section dealing with first-hand accounts of Carroll; and Sisters.*)

Hatter, The Mad   The 'Mad Hatter' with a capital 'M' has become proverbial since *Alice* was published, though in the original story, it was the Tea-Party he attempted to dominate that was 'Mad'.

Census records suggest there were 100 tailors in mid-century Oxford* and that hatters were equally numerous. Correspondence in *The Times* in 1932 suggested that an Oxford furniture dealer, Theophilus Carter, was an Oxford model for the Mad Hatter: he was an eccentric who is said to have designed an automatic tip-up bed for late risers at a Paris industrial exhibition. (There have, however, been alternative identifications, one being W. E. Gladstone.*)

Carroll himself wore a mortar-board for college duties, a top hat on other occasions and a straw boater for picnics and boating in summer. In Oxford, undergraduates wore hats most of the time. Part of Carroll's duties as a Proctor, one of the University police, was to catch up with hat-less undergraduates roaming the backstreets. In college, hats were stolen either as a prank or in retribution, college chapel being a particular time for confusion and theft. Ethel Arnold* in her reminiscence of Carroll, said that his love for his child-friends usually ended when he had to raise his hat to them.

Heresy So fierce were doctrinal battles between the High Church and the more liberal Broad Church* faction that a charge of heresy was levelled by the Bishop of Oxford, Samuel Wilberforce,* against Benjamin Jowett* and other authors of the innocuously entitled *Essays and Reviews*. Wilberforce's faction said that 'it was provable by law'; meaning religious law, that Jowett had 'denied the supernatural inspiration of Holy Scripture'. While tolerance of all other religious doctrines and points of view had never been the norm in British history, this was an extreme position for a Bishop to take up in the mid-nineteenth century, evoking the sixteenth-century inquisitions at the time of 'Bloody Mary'.

In the end, Wilberforce met an enemy stronger than himself. The Lord Chancellor, Lord Westbury, successfully argued against the legality of the jurisdiction of the religious Court of Arches and described Wilberforce's arguments against Jowett as 'so oily and saponaceous that no one could grasp them'. Thereafter, Wilberforce was nicknamed 'Soapy Sam'. The passion of these arguments underlies both action and rhetoric in *Alice*. Carroll, and those of like mind, wanted to silence Jowett because – although he was acknowledged as a great educator – he was 'infecting' generations of Oxford undergraduates with his heretical views.

Herkomer, Sir Hubert von (1849–1914) A prolific portraitist, his work included portraits of many Oxford professors and heads of colleges. Dean Liddell was painted by him, and Carroll was painted by him posthumously. Both portraits hang in Christ Church* Hall.

High Church See Broad Church*.

Hillman, Ellis Simon (1928–96) Founder (1969) and Honorary President of the Lewis Carroll Society, local government councillor, collector of Carrolliana, and of strange facts about London. Like Acland* and Liddell* in Oxford in Carroll's day, Ellis Hillman had a particular interest in underground London and the city of sewers, pipes, cables and tunnels that exists under the capital.

Taking the view that real people and events inspired characters and events in *Alice*, Hillman, like William Empson,* was intrigued by titbits of the history of science and technology that can be discerned below the surface of *Alice*. He suggested, among other contributions, that George Hudson (1800–71) might have inspired Carroll's Humpty Dumpty* and that Charles Babbage (1792–1871), pioneer of the calculating machine, might have inspired the Hatter.

Without disagreeing that the Hatter's behaviour echoes that of the quarrelsome Babbage, we are intrigued by the first three letters in Babbage's name and link him with the wailing Baby in the Duchess' Kitchen. For years, Babbage complained to the royal court for its failure to recompense him for his invention, the prototype of all modern computers which, as Carroll discovered, he never really completed. When Carroll called on Babbage on 27 January 1867 and looked over his workshop, he found, as Babbage's detractors maintained, that his ingenious calculators were not 'to be had'. (See also Inventions.*)

History and History Lessons   After being told off by the Gryphon for not knowing what 'Uglification' was:

> Alice did not feel encouraged to ask any more questions about it, so she turned to the Mock Turtle, and said, "What else had you to learn?"
>
> "Well, there was Mystery," the Mock Turtle replied, counting off the subjects on his flappers,—"Mystery, ancient and modern, with Seaography..."

For Mystery, read 'history'. *Wonderland* is peppered with anti-schoolroom jokes: there are more about geography than history, but history figures boldly. It is a clever way to a little girl's heart for a don to poke fun at familiar school subjects.

In the mid-nineteenth century much of what was taught – in whatever subject – had to be learned by rote. It is unlikely that Alice's governess,* Miss Prickett, had much more understanding than a 7-year-old of the importance of the Norman Conquest of Britain in 1066. The Mouse, in front of the company assembled round the Pool of Tears, gives a taste of such teachers:

> "'Edwin and Morcar, the earls of Mercia and Northumbria, declared for him; and even Stigand, the patriotic archbishop of Canterbury, found it advisable—'"
>
> "Found *what*?" said the Duck.
>
> "Found *it*", the Mouse replied rather crossly: "of course you know what 'it' means."
>
> "I know what 'it' means well enough, when *I* find a thing," said the Duck: "it's generally a frog or a worm. The question is, what did the archbishop find?"
>
> The Mouse did not notice this question, but hurriedly went on, "'—found it advisable to go with Edgar Atheling to meet William and offer him the crown...'"

(See also Robinson Duckworth.*)

House   Fury met a mouse in 'The House', the insiders' name for Christ Church,* alias 'the House of God'. (See also The Mouse's Tail/Tale.*)

Hull, Agnes Georgina (1867–1936)   Child-friend of Carroll's, Agnes was ten when Carroll met her in Eastbourne in August 1877. She was four years younger than her eldest sister, Alice. In 1879, Alice Hull sat an entrance exam for Oxford; she was of the first generation of girl candidates to be admitted to Oxford or Cambridge as result of competitive examinations. She was a year older than her sister Evey, and four years older than her sister, Jessie. The Hull sisters occupied a special place in Carroll's affections, rather as the Liddells had done, and at a similar time in their lives. In 1877, he wrote a jingle for Jessie in which she was supposed to fill in the gap. It ended:

> When the grave college Don, full of love inexpressi –
> ble, puts it all by, and is forced to confess he
> Can think but of Agnes and Evey and – – –

The answer is 'Jessie'. He also composed anagrams,* alphabet games* and alphabet poems* for the Hulls, all of which suggest that he was particularly fond of them, especially the second sister, Aggie. Among these anagrams were: 'dearest' to read 'east-red' and the word 'love' to read 'evol' (short for evolution)'. 'Vin-log' was the way he wrote 'loving' and he referred to his love for Agnes with the pun: 'My Agg own ie!', i.e. 'My own Aggie'.

He then pretended that Agnes was a Gnome who lived in Hyde Park. This was 'Mr Gnome Emory', anagram for 'Memory Gone'. Carroll fantasized that he had engaged the Gnome to teach him how to forget his distracting affection for the Hulls after the summer holidays in Eastbourne were over. However it ended in tears* as usual. One day, Carroll noted flatly in his diary: 'Agnes lost her book of riddles'. These he had composed and written out for her. Agnes Hull, like so many child*-friends, had not the stamina to work out the answers and did not like the gift. (See also Depression,* Terry,* Ellen.)

Humpty Dumpty   It – or he? – is the egg which is the hero of the traditional English nursery rhyme, 'Humpty Dumpty sat on the Wall'. Alice's encounter with this great talking egg began after she bought what might turn out to be a good or a bad egg,* synonymous with a good or a bad character, in the *Looking-Glass* shop. Personal questions passed between Alice and Humpty Dumpty. Alice concluded that Humpty Dumpty was neither good nor bad but 'unsatisfactory', like the proverbial Curate's Egg. She dismissed him:

> "Of all the unsatisfactory—" (she repeated this aloud, as it was a great comfort to have such a long word to say) "of all the unsatisfactory people I *ever* met—"

Both the Caterpillar and Rose made comments on the shape of Alice's body and the strange (to them) human symmetry of her face.* (See also Wasp.*) Humpty Dumpty disparaged Alice in the same way, and added a disquisition based on chop logic and long words, including the words in *Jabberwocky*.*

The shape of an oblate spheroid fascinated Carroll, and provided a 'cannibalistic' joke. Such a joke is almost subliminal to a child reader – children eat *boiled* eggs and crack or cut through the egg shell before opening them – hence Alice's worry about the broad smile on Humpty Dumpty's face. As Alice shook his hand, she remarked:

> "If he smiled much more, the ends of his mouth might meet behind, and then I don't known what would happen to his head! I'm afraid it would come off!"

Humpty Dumpty explained a number of portmanteau words to Alice from the *Jabberwocky* poem. Among them was Brillig:

> "Brillig means four o'clock in the afternoon – the time when you begin *broiling* things for dinner."

The implication is that the egg itself, which acts as translator, may be cooked.

Ellis Hillman* suggested in *Jabberwocky* in 1972 that the royal-favour-seeking Humpty Dumpty was a hidden portrait of George Hudson (1800–71), the Railway King whose bankruptcy matched Humpty Dumpty's fall. When, in 1849, Hudson's companies failed it had a major effect on the London Stock Market. From then until 1865, when he was committed to prison for a brief spell for contempt of court, Hudson ignored the moneys he owed to his creditors, and went on being applauded with much solemnity at municipal banquets. Perhaps Hudson is reflected in the character of Humpty Dumpty, with his inflated views, know-all attitude and sly refusal to acknowledge dangers that were right in front of his eyes.

Huxley, Francis (1924–)   Francis Huxley is great-grandson of T. H. Huxley* and author of *The Raven and the Writing Desk* (1976). This is the kind of book Carroll would have loved to take on a train because it was constructed like a pure diversion with no particular beginning, middle or end. It has a chapter between VIII and IX called 'Intermission: The absurd' which starts:

> C. L. Dodgson's grave is in Guildford cemetery. It is marked by a white cross bearing his name, and common sense might hold that it should also mark the end of our enquiry. But there are two good reasons for not ending here. The first is to be found in *A New Theory of Parallels*, where Dodgson raised what in this context is an eschatological problem. His words, already quoted, are worth repeating...
>
> When we come to the limit, what then? What do we come to? There must be either Something, or Nothing...That there should be neither of these is absurd.

For Walter de la Mare,* *Alice* was a landscape; for Huxley, whose uncle, Aldous Huxley (see Queen's English*) claimed to speak in a precise Oxford cadence of Carroll's day, *Alice* was a puzzle.

Huxley, Thomas Henry (1825–95)   Biologist, educationalist, materialist, and proponent of Darwin's views on evolution, Huxley was a lecturer at the Government School of Mines when Carroll photographed him in Oxford. Could there be a joke about the tussle between Sir Richard Owen, the anti-Darwinian, and Huxley for control of the Government School of Mines in the Duchess' answer in the game* in *Wonderland* of 'Animal, Vegetable and Mineral': 'The more there is of mine, the less there is of yours'?

Huxley was empire building for the new biology when he came to Oxford in 1860 to debate evolution with Bishop Wilberforce,* Bishop of Oxford. Wilberforce made the mistake of insulting Huxley. He asked

Huxley whether he believed himself to have been related to an ape on his mother's or father's side. With that, Wilberforce lost the advantage: it was not the rhetoric of a gentleman. The Ugly Duchess,* in face, manner and the tendency of her baby to evolve in a retrograde direction appears to parody Huxley. The kitchen of the Duchess' house is full of smells and 'stinks', the derogatory word for chemistry.

Carroll's photograph shows Huxley looking rather worried, his big head on a rather slight body, placed in the middle of a room with a paper backdrop behind him. He carries his top hat in one hand and wears a frock coat and collar that does not quite fit. As with his photographs of Tennyson,* Carroll managed to catch what other photographers missed, the frailty and humanity of a notable intellectual at a turning point in his life.

Carroll gave his photograph of T. H. Huxley to Alice in the album* he presented to her. Not far from this, in a similar pose, he placed his photograph of Bishop Wilberforce. (See also William Empson,* Evolution* and Science.*)

THE MARLBOROUGH COLUMN

I and J are for ...

Illustrators of *Alice*   Alice Liddell recalled that Carroll took his drawing as seriously as his photography.* He went on trying to improve his figure drawing until the end of his life. When writing the manuscript of *Alice's** *Adventures Under Ground*,* Carroll prepared the whole book for Alice, page layout, text and illustrations. These have their own strong character, particularly displaying Alice's discomfort. (See also Dress.*)

When the idea of publication was put forward, Carroll was not considered competent to illustrate the book himself, even though he had been the first illustrator of *Alice*. He had tried to improve his style with tutors and had powerful visual ideas, as was clear to members of the MacDonald* family. He may have drawn partly on Edward Lear's ideas for his own line drawings, particularly for Father William*, but he had little of Lear's facility. He eventually chose Tenniel* who brought professionalism to the project, although Tenniel missed the frenetic feeling which Carroll caught. Carroll resented this.

The sequence of four illustrations of the ballad of *Father William* demonstrates that Carroll's line drawings are odder but flatter. Tenniel's are more jocular and more competent. There is no doubt that the *Alice* texts flowered in Tenniel's hands and that their greatness owes a lot to him. There are at least three accounts of what is known of Tenniel's relationship with Carroll:

> Edward Hodnett, *Image and Text; Studies in the illustration of English literature* (Scolar Press, 1982);

Rodney Engen, *Sir John Tenniel, Alice's White Knight*, a biography of
Tenniel (Scolar Press, 1991);

Michael Hancher, *The Tenniel Illustrations to the 'Alice' Books* (Macmillan,
1986), which analyses Tenniel's *Alice* sources.

What made *Alice* a particular challenge to illustrators in his own day was
the knowledge that Carroll had strong feelings about page layout* and the
content of the illustrations. He was not a writer who wrote a text and left
the rest to others. The strength of his feelings about detail drove Tenniel to
refuse to work with him again – and to warn other illustrators to stay well
clear of him.

In the twentieth century, illustrators of *Alice* have taken many liberties with
Carroll's concepts. The ending of the copyright of *Wonderland* in 1907
meant that there was a rush by publishers to cash in on its popularity.
(*Looking-Glass*, because of changes in the law, remained in copyright until
1948, 50 years after Carroll's death.) In 1972, Graham Ovenden, himself an
illustrator of *Alice*, compiled a catalogue, with John Davis as commentator,
The Illustrators of Alice in Wonderland and Through the Looking-Glass. This listed
90 of the illustrators of English language editions of *Wonderland*.

A further 21 illustrators were cited by Ovenden as illustrators of the
Looking-Glass story, and 33 more for editions where both *Alice* stories were
published in one volume. In France, *Visages d'Alice* (1983) – catalogue of an
exhibition at the Pompidou Centre, Paris – was compiled by Jean Verame.
(See also Translators* of *Alice*.)

The illustrator of *Alice* has to decide whether to retain a Victorian, English
image of Alice, and whether to (as Ralph Steadman did with conspicuous
success – see below) include the image of Carroll himself among the
characters. The American illustrator, Willy Pogany, whose edition was
published in 1929, drew a 1920s *Alice* with boyishly parted hair, a short check
skirt and plain button shoes, the sort of pre-prep look of the privately
educated American girl. Max Ernst, in his *Lewis Carroll's Wunderhorn*
(Stuttgart, 1970) engraved plates in which she appears as a late Victorian
German child with short, frilled sleeves, a low cut dress and a long skirt.

Besides the question of dress, illustrators of *Alice* have to choose how
grotesque the characters should be. Scale is another problem: how large or
small should Alice be in relation to those around her? What follows are notes
on the illustrative ideas of Rackham, Laurençin, Mespoulet, Peake, Steadman,
Blake and Moser.

ARTHUR RACKHAM (1867–1939) Arthur Rackham's *Wonderland* was
published in 1907. Tinted in browns and rusty reds, Rackham's dimly-lit
full-page illustrations have a disturbing way of penetrating Carroll's text

without dominating it. Rackham excelled at depicting a world where gnarled trees and swirling vegetation bear down on supernatural characters. He brought this landscape to the task of illustrating *Alice*. Rackham's landscape is a 'Wonderland', not the English countryside portrayed by Tenniel, and is closer perhaps to the German or Scandanavian children's book tradition than to the English. The difficulty with Rackham's *Alice* watercolour and line illustrations is that they are always Rackham, defying Carroll's text rather than interpreting it.

MARIE LAURENÇIN (1883–1956)   Laurençin illustrated *Alice* in a series of lithographs for the Black Sun Press edition of *Alice's Adventures in Wonderland* (1930). She emphasized the lyricism of Carroll's work. Alice, in Laurençin's plates, is a serene dream-child, with the fragility and abstraction of a Sèvres porcelain shepherdess. Laurençin's *Alice* thus lacks the occasional horror of Carroll's and Tenniel's originals. Her coloured lithographs, in black, blue, red and green line, are celebratory and pastoral. This Alice wears a tartan skirt and floats over green grass and blue water, her hand laid trustingly in her sister's lap.

Laurençin's dream-child with a long ribbon twined through her hair is little known to Anglo-Saxon commentators, though recognized as the work of an artist of major importance by Japanese art-lovers. Contemporary with Laurençin, was Marie Mespoulet.

MARIE MESPOULET (active in 1930s)   While professor of French literature at Columbia University, she wrote a book about illustrators of *Alice* called *Creators of Wonderland*. It was dedicated to E. O'Keefe and was published, like Laurençin's Black Sun edition of *Alice*, close to the centennial of Carroll's birth.

On Christmas Eve, 1938, before the fall of France, she sent a copy of her book to Miss da Costa Greene at the Pierpoint Morgan Library in New York. It was published by the Rydall Press, Santa Fé, New Mexico. With this gift, which she presented as 'an elegant thimble'; she sent the following note:

> I have read about everything you have done to honour the art and thought of France. May I, in return, beg of you to accept this little book, which intertwines English and French fantasies?

Mespoulet proposed, and sustained her argument with skill:

> Have not Alice's mid-Victorian animals, and with them all of the Wonderland and Looking-Glass books, a flavour of an earlier generation? Do they not, however strikingly and delightfully English, partly belong to mid-nineteenth century Europe?

By Europe, Mespoulet meant France, and by France, she meant the graphic art of J. J. Grandville,* one of the most original graphic artists of his day. *Charivari* was Thackeray's source for the English *Punch*.* Grandville's vignettes, proposed Mespoulet, inspired many of Tenniel's compositions for *Alice* – for example the scene where Alice lends her thimble to the Dodo,* a scene based on Grandville's Guillemot's Wedding. Other masquerading animals, including Tenniel's Mock Turtle* also overlap with Grandville's zoomorphs*.

Before and after the Second World War, two of the most mysterious illustrators to be inspired by *Alice* were Balthus* and Mervyn Peake.

MERVYN PEAKE (1911–68)   Peake made his (Stockholm, 1946) *Alice* period-less in her dress. His *Alice* shared the charm and innocence of Laurençin's. In contrast, his characters have a comic sense about them that caught the ironic spirit of Carroll's drawing, which eluded Tenniel. His picture of the bespectacled and snooty Sheep is particularly effective. His Hatter* has a strange insouciance.

RALPH STEADMAN (1936–)   Steadman completed a full set of black line illustrations for *Wonderland* in 1967 and *Looking-Glass* in 1977, and is one of Carroll's most passionate twentieth-century exponents. In 1977, he illustrated *The Wasp* in a Yellow Wig* in colour after its first publication. His work is disliked by some Anglo-American commentators on *Alice*. Although Steadman is one of the outstanding cartoonists and illustrators to re-interpret Tenniel's plates, his inclusion of the figure of Carroll in many of his most elaborate illustrations, as in the chessboard scene in *Looking-Glass*, distressed traditionalist lovers of Carroll's work (though not the authors) as did his accolade to Carroll's genius: 'My only regret is that I didn't write the story'.

More grotesque in his approach, they are so grotesque they lose sight of the foolish fallibility of Carroll's characters.

Steadman noted in 1972 that his instinct had been to follow Carroll's technique of portraying characters he knew personally when he devised the adult characters in *Alice*, an interpretation he shared with William Empson* and Shane Leslie:*

> The animals [I drew for *Alice*] remind me of people I know, rather as Lewis Carroll apparently created them around friends and associates.

Steadman gave a political edge to Carroll's *Alice* and updated its relevance to his day. His *Jabberwocky*,* for example, updated Tenniel's by having a Union Jack clamped on to its tongue and atomic bomb mushroom clouds steaming from its ears. A vulnerable-looking modern boy in pyjamas tries to resist it. The impact is that of a twentieth-century political cartoonist unwilling to draw a veil over dire totalitarian challenges, rather than a children's book illustrator. Steadman was awarded the Black Humour Award in France in 1986.

PETER BLAKE (1932–)   Blake designed a series of coloured screen prints for *Alice* starting in 1970. A painter rather than book illustrator in the accepted sense, his extraordinary pictures inspired by Carroll's text (not Tenniel's line illustrations) created flesh tones for Alice that give the impression of a Victorian studio photograph that has been tinted. Such tones, with their claustrophobic Victorian glow, Carroll commissioned for several photographs of child*-friends, with parental permission.

Peter Blake's *Alice* is a truly 1970s little girl of seven. She is an untidy modern child caught unaware in a noisy primary school playground, an urban, not a pastoral child.

Elsewhere Blake re-interpreted pictures of Old Masters set in a contempory location, sometimes in California. His art has a cunning effect of forcing the viewer to look freshly at old images. Blake's Hatter in prison has attached to his foot a Victorian ball and chain. Yet his shoes are contemporary, as is his red enamel prison-issue tea mug. Each of Blake's screen prints has a caption copied from *Alice*, bearing Blake's signature and the date. It is Blake's Hatter and yet it makes the viewer rethink Carroll's and Tenniel's.

BARRY MOSER (1940–)   Moser made 95 wood engravings for the distinguished Pennyroyal Press *Alice* (1981), which is built up from a series of major wood engravings, the central character being his own daughter at Alice's age. The plates are epic, sympathetic to the text, and disturbing, while still evoking the humanity inherent in Carroll's characters.

In his introduction to this American *Alice* James Kincaid (see Critics*) noted:

> The Red King may be dreaming Alice, but Carroll has the power to dream not only the Red King, but also his special 'dream Alice', even if the dreaming jokes squint self-protectively, and even if he is dreaming 'as the summers die'.

In the Pennyroyal edition, Humpty Dumpty is cast as Richard Nixon. (See also Salvador Dali.*)

Impenetrability
The infallibility of the Pope was a source of jibes in *Punch* during the writing of *Alice*. It was the view of Ronald Knox* that Carroll's 'impenetrability', the most complicated word Humpty* Dumpty had to explain to Alice, was a joke against the doctrine of 'Papal Infallibility'. Humpty Dumpty gave the following definition, or rather what he claimed was the definition:

> "... we've had enough of that subject, and it would be just as well if you'd mention what you mean to do next, as I suppose you don't mean to stop here all the rest of your life."

Of course this is not a definition at all, just as to Carroll the exact meaning of infallibility, endlessly argued over, was without a definition, but a subject to be debated.

Later in their dialogue Humpty Dumpty told Alice that words were workmen whom he paid on a piece-work basis. The more meanings they had, the more he paid them. Carroll's dry comment on this industry of theological obfuscation was that:

> (Alice didn't venture to ask what he paid them with; and so you see I can't tell *you*).

The remark is in parentheses, as if the writer was expressing his scepticism, for once speaking through Alice's dream. (See also Shane Leslie.*)

'... Innocent and Right in the Sight of God'   Seeing himself as such was the first of two tests that Carroll set himself when inviting child*-friends and young women to stay with him in his lodgings in Eastbourne.*

The second test was that parents should give '*full* approval', although Carroll failed to differentiate between 'approval' and '*full* approval'. How many eyebrows were raised in the four decades from the 1860s to the 1890s, when Carroll changed from being a man in his 30s to one in his 60s, will never be known. Gossip about Carroll and his habits remained gossip and was lost.

An 1893 letter by Carroll from Lushington Road, Eastbourne, to his younger sister, Mary, suggests, however, that she was more than willing to reflect a rumbling and long sense of outrage at his behaviour. After fumbling into his reply to her allegations with words about her husband's health and the weather, Carroll wrote accusing her and her husband of having lived their lives protected from a world he knew about only too well, in which malicious gossip circulated. He claimed his behaviour could be counted on to be: 'entirely innocent and right, in the sight of God ...', punctuation which makes Carroll's defence ambiguous, to say the least.

Insects, Looking-Glass   In Chapter III of the Looking-Glass story, the Gnat told Alice about three Looking-Glass insects. They were based on a horse-fly, a dragon-fly and a butterfly – insects that might be seen on river expeditions. Looking-Glass insects, it turned out, had rather unusual names.

The Gnat told Alice about a swinging, 'bright and sticky' Rocking-horse-fly which lived on 'sap and sawdust'.

Then it described the Snap-dragon-fly, its head on fire with brandy, which sustained itself on frumenty (a pudding eaten in the nursery made of wheat boiled in milk) and mince pie.

Then the Bread-and-butter*-fly alarmed Alice by crawling along the ground towards her, and refusing to go away. It lived on weak tea and cream. (See also Diet.*)

The description led to Alice's lucid explanation of insect nomenclature before she entered the Wood where Things have No Name:

> "What's the use of their having names," the Gnat said, "if they won't answer to them?"
>
> "No use to *them*," said Alice; "but it's useful to people that name them, I suppose ..."

Wonderland mocks evolution.* In *Looking-Glass* Carroll mocked the intensity of Victorian taxonomy where insects, with their thousands of similar species, provided considerable challenges. He and Alice would have seen the cases of these in the Museum of Natural History*. Insects were also a feature of the dung-strewn towpath of the Thames, which on hot days would have been alive with different species of butterflies, wasps and dragon-flies.

Inventions   As the White* Knight led Alice towards the Eighth Square of the Chess Board, he sang a song about an Aged* Aged Man and pretended he had written it. The Aged Aged Man was a skit on the mid-Victorian enthusiasm for patents on food, drink, cosmetics, pieces of carriage and parts of bridges; the sort of inventions that had been acclaimed at the Great Exhibition of 1851 and others like it. Carroll had first been to a small version of such an exhibition as a boy of eight in 1840. This was the *Warrington Trade Exhibition.*

Most of the Aged Aged Man's inventions were nonsense items. One was not and recalled something that Carroll had seen as a child on a trip to North Wales. This was Isambard Kingdom Brunel's (1806–59) invention of an annealing process for steel which was used in building the Menai Strait Bridge. The Aged Aged Man states:

> ... for I had just
> Completed my design
> To keep the Menai Bridge from rust
> By boiling it in wine.

Carroll had a fascination with new devices, notably his camera and, in 1867, a calculating machine that would add to one million. He bought an odd electric pen and then, in May 1888, a Hammond Type-Writer, the keys of which, because of a spring-loaded device, did not have to be hit with consistency to give a good impression on paper. He then devised 'a simple dodge' for this machine that enabled it to justify, not just the left-hand margin, but both left and right. When he bought a phonograph in 1890 he predicted that it would, like the camera, become a popular item. The list of devices he collected that has been compiled meticulously by Morton Cohen,* includes travelling inkpots, a machine for turning music over, Ferrometers and Bob the flying bat.* They sound not unlike the Aged Aged Man's own catalogue. Perhaps this is not surprising: Carroll described himself by that very name to some of his child*-friends.

Jabberwocky   Carroll's *Looking-Glass* poem about the Jabberwock had an immediate appeal to boy readers. Although he liked Tenniel's* illustration, Carroll worried about its violence: his intention was to use it as a frontispiece. Nervous about the effect of the image of a boy raising a sword to kill the Jabberwock, he submitted it to 'about thirty of his married lady friends'

recorded Collingwood.* The survey produced an unfavourable result and a new picture of the White* Knight in his armour was then used as the frontispiece.

Roger Lancelyn Green* noted that *Jabberwocky* burlesqued *The Shepherd of the Giant Mountains* by La Motte Fouqué, pen-name of Baron Friedrich Heinrich Karl (1777–1843). A translation of the poem was known to Carroll for it was made by his cousin, Menella Smedley. *Jabberwocky* was originally composed by Carroll when staying with these cousins at Whitby. In 1855, aged 23, he gave his first English translation of its nonsense 'Anglo-Saxon' words in a contribution (published under the title 'Stanza of Anglo-Saxon Poetry') to the comic journal, *Mischmasch*.

By 1871, Carroll had developed the fragment into a full length nonsense ballad for the *Looking-Glass* story. Alice read out this very same stanza aloud to herself in Looking-Glass writing at the beginning of the story. (See also Recitation.*) In the *Mischmasch* version, the word 'the' was written 'ye' throughout, and Carroll's mock Anglo-Saxon characters were peppered with mock Anglo-Saxon commas, semi-colons, colons and full stops. (See also Punctuation.*) The 1855 stanza read:

> 'Twas brillig, and ye slythy toves
>   Did gyre and gymble in ye wabe:
> All mimsy were ye borogoves;
>   And ye mome raths outgrabe.

Alice 'couldn't make it out at all'. Or could she? 'Take care of the sense, and the sounds will take care of themselves', the Duchess* told her when she discussed 'morals' in *Wonderland*. *Jabberwocky* is strange for a reverse reason. By taking care of the sounds, the sense seems to take care of itself. The poem seems to the reader to make alliterative sense. Although the 'difficult' words have no meaning in common usage, it is to some the greatest nonsense poem ever written in the English language.

There is no one with common sense in *Jabberwocky* – for common sense *Alice* is a reader rather than a participant. It has a strong story and a strong mood. The 'beamish boy' was surrounded by horrific creatures in an environment of 'borogoves' and 'raths'. Confronted with the threat of the Jabberwock and the Bandersnatch, he responded with the prowess and the modesty of a Tennysonian 'perfect, gentle knight'. Armed with his 'vorpal' sword, boy beat monster, indeed decapitated it, a voice in the wings commenting with an encouraging 'Callooh! Callay!' He galloped away leaving the borogoves mimsy. A metaphorical sun set on his victory.

After reading and thinking about the poem, Alice found herself in The Garden of Live Flowers.* As in a dream, the subject matter reappeared when she met Humpty Dumpty* and talked about the nonsense words in the poem in detail.

There are 28 words in *Jabberwocky* that defy obvious explanation. In 1971, John Hanna, in a survey of Carroll's schoolboy Latin verse in the journal, *Jabberwocky* suggested meanings for a number of these nonsense words which are different from those Carroll gave in *Mischmasch* and *Looking-Glass* and can be attributed to Cleveland dialect words. Croft,* Carroll's second childhood home, is on the edge of the Cleveland Hills. Dialect words were in common use in rural Cheshire and north-west Yorkshire during Carroll's boyhood: words which he would not hear at home could be heard at the church door, on local farms and in the lanes. They must have been a source of fun and interest to Carroll and his sisters, as they were to numerous clergymen and their families, who sent glossaries, the work of a lifetime, to the compilers of the word-lists published by the English Dialect Society after the 1870s. (See also Queen's* English).

Martin Gardner* researched the nonsense words in *Jabberwoocky* for *The Annotated Alice*. What follows are some notes of our own which are to be read alongside Hanna's and Gardner's work.

Some of these words are 'portmanteau' words. Alice had never, for example, come across the word 'Slithy':

> "Well," [said Humpty Dumpty] '*slithy*' means 'lithe and slimy'. 'Lithe' is the same as 'active.' You see, it's like a portmanteau—there are two meanings packed up in one word."

Carroll returned to this explanation in 1876 in the 'Preface' to *The Hunting of the Snark* and later still in 1888 in a letter to schoolgirl fans in Boston:

> Take the words 'fuming' and 'furious'. Make up your mind that you will say both words, but leave it unsettled which you will say first. Now open your mouth and speak. If your thoughts incline ever so little towards 'fuming', you will say 'fuming-furious'; if they turn, by even a hair's breadth, towards 'furious', you will say 'furious-fuming'; but if you have the rarest of gifts, a perfectly balanced mind, you will say 'frumious'.

However, not all strange words in *Jabberwocky* are portmanteau words. Others are anachronisms. All introduce problems of meaning. For some, even if Carroll suggested an explanation, he changed it with apology at a later date.

In alphabetical order, the new words were:

BANDERSNATCH   A Bandersnatch was a fast-moving invisible monster that was never caught. Carroll gave no explanation for the word, nor did Martin Gardner in his *Alice* annotations. In the *Oxford English Dictionary*, 'bandicoot' is given as 'a large Indian rat ... as big as a cat and very destructive'. There is a possibility that Raj-Hindi could have contributed to Carroll's portmanteau thinking. This would suggest that the Bandersnatch is likely be a four-legged mammal, a terrifying, invisible rat-cat, that could 'snatch'.

BEAMISH BOY   Martin Gardner noted that the word 'beamish' meant 'shining brightly, radiant' in the sixteenth century when it was in use. Few boys crossed Alice's path in the course of her *Looking-Glass* journey and none to whom this positive adjective could be applied. The Tweedle* brothers were bullies and could not bear to fight seriously; they were not beamish at all.

BOROGOVES   In *Mischmasch* (1855) these were:

> ... an extinct kind of Parrot. They had no wings, beaks turned up, and made their nests under sun-dials: lived on veal.

For the *Looking-Glass* version of the stanza, this predecessor of the Dodo* had evolved into a nonsense wading bird and lived in a mangrove swamp. Humpty Dumpty explained that they were 'thin shabby-looking' birds with 'feathers sticking out all round – something like a live mop'. Tenniel's engraving resembled the sad toucan by the Pool of Tears, hunched over its long legs, a tall, depressed, academic-looking bird.

If there is a hint of the Groves of Academe in Carroll's annotation – he was at the time of first publication in *Mischmasch* Sub-Librarian at Christ Church* – it is also clear that the borogoves followed in the wake of the creations of Edward Lear, whose ornithological lithographs of parrots, toucans and owls were made at the home of Lord Derby in Knowsley, Cheshire, where he wrote his first nonsense limericks when Carroll was a boy.

Carroll's advice about the pronunciation of the word was noted in the Introduction to *Snark*; it seemed it was commonly mispronounced. The first two syllables were pronounced 'burrow'.

> The first 'o' in 'borogoves' is pronounced like the 'o' in 'worry' [that is to say like 'u' in 'up']. Such is Human Perversity.

BRILLIG   Humpty Dumpty told Alice he understood the *Jabberwocky* poem even though it contained 'plenty of hard words'. The first one he explained was 'brillig' in the first line of the poem. (It had been explained in *Mischmasch* by Carroll, rather than Humpty Dumpty.) Humpty Dumpty explained that it:

> "... means four o'clock in the afternoon—the time when you begin *broiling* things for dinner'.

Having learned from her misadventures whilst talking to the Mouse,* the Pigeon and the Mock Turtle* not to mention dinner, lunch or tea, Alice quickly changed the subject. Aware perhaps of the indelicate fact that eggs* may be cooked at that time of day: 'That'll do very well', she said.

BURBLE   In December 1877, Carroll sent Maud Standen an 'explanation' for this 'Jabberwocky' word. He had refused to discuss it earlier. He implied – but he could have been teasing – that it might be a triple portmanteau word made up as follows:

... as to 'burble': if you take the three verbs, 'bleat', 'murmur' and 'warble', and select the bits I have underlined, it certainly makes 'burble'; though I'm afraid I can't distinctly remember having made it in that way.

Martin Gardner suggested it was a composite of 'bubble' and 'burst'. It appears, given these two valid alternatives, that there were several ways to pack one of Carroll's portmanteaus.

CALLOOH! CALLAY!   Martin Gardner connected the cry 'Callooh!' with the call of an arctic duck. It may be a portmanteau word, an amalgam of two sporting cries, the first being the fox-hunter's sighting call: 'View! Halloo!'.

Alice was also familiar with the sportsmen's cheer: 'Hip! Hip! Hooray!'.

The portmanteau of college sportsmen and Oxfordshire fox-hunters could produce the harmonious Jabberwocky whoop, 'Callooh! Callay!' Undergraduates in hunting pink would have been familiar to the Liddell* girls as they passed through the Christ Church quads. The boat races marked the height of the Oxford summer season. Beside the Liddells, a number of Carroll's acquaintances hunted, notably Thomas Combe*, the University printer, and Bishop Wilberforce*, to whom Carroll made his deacon's vows.

CHORTLE   This word is admitted to the *Oxford English Dictionary* as: 'a word coined by the author of *Through the Looking-Glass*: app. the fusion of *chuckle* and *snort*'.

The suffix 'ort' enfolded in a chuckle gives a good imitation of what it feels like to laugh.

FRABJOUS   Martin Gardner and the *Oxford English Dictionary* did not discuss this composite expression, but if it is treated as a portmanteau word, 'joyous' and 'fabulous' seem to fit. Mrs Gaskell (1810–65) set her novels in the parishes round Daresbury where she and Carroll grew up. She used the now forgotten prefix 'frab' and 'frabble' as a Cheshire dialect word meaning 'worrying'. (The Wasp,* in 'The Wasp in a Wig' – the chapter Carroll omitted from the final version of *Looking-Glass* – also used the Yorkshire dialect expression, Worrity! Worrity! in the same sense – See also John Hanna's suggestions above.)

FRUMIOUS   This was a word which described a Bandersnatch and a pair of biting jaws. It turned out to be a portmanteau word unpacked by Carroll with a flourish. Frumious, he finally explained (see above), was a portmanteau of 'furious' and 'fuming'.

GALUMPHING   Carroll used this portmanteau again in *Snark*. The *Oxford English Dictionary* says 'perhaps a fusion of *gallop* and *triumph*: to march on exultantly with irregular bounding movements' – (the very motion of the Anglo-Saxon Looking-Glass messenger, Haigha).

GIMBLE   Alice learned from Humpty Dumpty that 'to gimble' was 'to make holes like a gimlet'. Carroll's explanation in 1855 in *Mischmasch* was that it meant to screw holes in anything.

GYRE   In *Mischmasch* in 1855, Carroll said that the word came from the Anglo-Saxon word for Dog – 'Gyaour' or 'Giaour'. He said that the verb meant to 'to scratch like a dog'.

By the time of the *Looking-Glass* explanation, Humpty Dumpty groped for a clue to the origin of the word, not in a portmanteau, but in his own remarkable girth. He told Alice it meant 'to go round and round like a gyroscope'. Like gimble, the word described the rotating motion of a tove.

Martin Gardner has particular insight into Carroll's geometrical interest in chiral structures. In 1953, a 'double helix' was identified in Cambridge* as fundamental to the structure of DNA, the molecule that gyres and gimbles to give all life-forms their vitality.

JABBERWOCK   Much thought has been devoted to the etymology of this word. It was for the Boston Girls' Latin School in 1888 that Carroll turned to Anglo-Saxon English and portmanteau word-play to explain the suffix: he wrote that the word 'wocer' or 'wocor' signified 'offspring' or 'fruit'.

As for the whole word:

Taking 'jabber' in its ordinary acceptation of 'excited and voluble discussion', this would give the meaning of 'the result of much excited discussion'.

John Hanna, taking as his source Cleveland dialect usage, came up with an explanation that had nothing to do with monsters. He wrote:

As for the title itself, 'Jabber' or 'Japper' is a 'billow', in its poetic [dialect] usage for 'sea'. 'Wock' or 'Wauk' is a dirge sung at a wake. This gives the meaning of the title as 'The Wee Sea-Dirge'.

Carroll wrote the poem in Whitby, where there was a local fishing community, making this a likely explanation. (Michael Wace pointed out (1997) that 'wauk' and 'walk' are variants of 'wake', the vigil of mourners over a corpse, a dialect word also widespread in Northern Scottish and Hebridean English.) Carroll's nonsense etymologies were arrived at on the basis, not only of Anglo-Saxon, but of many of the other variants that have gone into the making of the English language.

JUBJUB   In the second verse of *Jabberwocky* the beamish boy was warned by his mother to beware of three predators: the Jabberwock, the Bandersnatch and the Jubjub bird. This last, like the Bandersnatch (see above) sounds Anglo-Indian. Carroll mentioned it four or five times in *Snark*, but explained that it was too rare to illustrate. Frank L. Warrin translated this nonsense bird name into cheerful French, as 'l'Oiseau Jube' in an article for *The New Yorker* (1931).

The 'bulbul' or Persian nightingale, was well known to readers of Fitzgerald's *Omar Khayyam* and of Indian love stories (see Caterpillar*), and the call of Shakespeare's woodland birds was 'Jug! Jug!'. Perhaps this name is a portmanteau of the trilling Persian nightingale and the call of a startled English blackbird.

MANXOME   Martin Gardner suggested that the word 'manxome' referred to the Celtic language that used to be spoken on the Isle of Man, geographically close to Carroll's boyhood home of Daresbury.* Carroll stated to the mother of Gertrude Chataway in 1876 that the *Snark* poem could be located:

> on an island frequented by the Jubjub and the Bandersnatch – no doubt the very island where the Jabberwock was slain.

A Manx-speaking tax-collector on the island during the Cromwellian period in the 1650s was 'Illiam Dhone', Black William or William Christian, executed by the Royalists after the Restoration and ancestor of William Christian who led the Mutiny against Captain Bligh. Manx insurgents were the Fenians of their day, and manxome suited the Jabberwock, given Carroll and his father's Tory politics. The portmanteau which has Manx as prefix, bears the suffix '–some' – from 'fearsome'.

MIMSY   Carroll wrote in *Mischmasch* that 'mimsy' meant unhappy. He derived it from 'mimserable' which came, he said, from 'miserable'. The word 'mimsy' is in the *Oxford English Dictionary*, where it is defined as 'prim, prudish and contemptible'.

MOME   Carroll suggested in 1855 that 'mome' meant 'grave' and came from 'Solemome, Solemone and Solemn'. Here, the archaic 'Solemome' explained the word. This was not Humpty Dumpty's explanation to Alice by 1871. Though he was 'not certain about' the meaning, he thought it might be short for 'from home' – meaning that they'd 'lost their way, you know'. Humpty Dumpty's suggestion of a compression, four letters dropped and four retained, gave 'mome'. The green pigs called 'raths' had wandered far from home, like the pigs going to market in the nursery counting game.

The dictionary definition is much simpler: 'a blockhead, a fool'.

OUTGRABE   The cry of a rath ('a sort of green pig' said Humpty Dumpty), was an 'outgribing',

> "...something between bellowing and whistling, with a kind of sneeze in the middle".

Humpty Dumpty suggested that Alice could confirm his explanation by keeping her ears open:

> "...you'll hear it done, maybe—down in the wood yonder—and when you've heard it, you'll be *quite* content'.

RATHS   'Mome raths' appears at the dying fall of the refrain. Raths, Humpty Dumpty said – he was an egg – were 'a sort of green pig'. Piglets which do not reach home are made into bacon, in this case 'green bacon' – unsmoked bacon, one of the many sinister food jokes in 'Alice'. (See Fish* and fishy jokes, Oysters* and Riddles.*)

Rath-ripe is a dialect word for early ripe fruits sent to market. John Tenniel portrayed four raths to the right of a sundial. In his illustration, they snuffle about energetically, running in four compass directions, just like farmyard piglets.

For Alice's clever observation about the directions in which the raths moved see 'Wabe' below.

SLITHY   The *Oxford English Dictionary* defined 'sleathy' as an obsolete Middle English word meaning 'slovenly'. However, Humpty Dumpty's explanation was:

> "Well, '*slithy*' means 'lithe and slimy'. 'Lithe' is the same as 'active.'"

SNICKER-SNACK   'Snickersnee' was a method of knife-fighting practised by sailors from Holland. Carroll shifted the suffix to a word which rhymes with a good old English broadsword stroke, 'to hack'.

TOVES   Carroll explained in *Mischmasch* that the tove was a species of badger with smooth white hair, long hind legs and that its name rhymed with 'groves'. Its head bore stumpy staghorns. Its diet* was mainly cheese.

Humpty Dumpty agreed that they lived under sundials but saw the species as a chimera:

> "Well, '*toves*' are something like badgers—they're something like lizards —and they're something like corkscrews."

No one has given any indication that its name was other than a convenience word to help him solve the rhyming scheme of the first and last verse of his poem.

TULGEY   A portmanteau of 'thick' and 'bulgey' has been suggested. In 1877, Carroll said distinctly in a letter to Maud Standen that he couldn't explain it. Alice's reaction is relevant in general: 'Somehow it seems to fill my head with ideas—only I don't exactly know what they are!'

TUMTUM TREE   The most obvious reference is to the abbreviation of 'stomach'. Martin Gardner has:

> ... referring to the sound of a stringed instrument, especially when monotonously strummed.

(One of the *Oxford English Dictionary* definitions is 'to strum'.) There is also a related Northern dialect word describing raw wool being laid out before being spun on bushes and trees.

UFFISH   In December 1877, Carroll explained 'uffish' to Maud Standen. He said it was a triple portmanteau – (in this instance stripping out a common denominator from three sources rather than overlapping them) – suggested by:

> a state of mind when the voice is gruffish, the manner roughish, and the temper huffish.

VORPAL   The medical word 'palpate': 'to explore by touch as a method of medical examination' gives a possible origin for the suffix. The Spenserian English word, 'forepassed' – 'passed through and through' – also could have entered into its composition. Carroll left no clue.

During the Second World War, W. H. Auden,* an admirer of Carroll, used it again in the text of his *New Year Letter*. It is now in the *Oxford English Dictionary* as a word invented by Lewis Carroll and defined as 'apparently with the sense "keen, deadly"'.

WABE   In 1855 in *Mischmasch*, Carroll explained that 'wabe' was a geographical description of a wet, slithery slope. He derived it from an unquoted Anglo-Saxon word for 'swab or soak'.

The etymological jump Carroll made for 'wabe' – 'to soak' – to a word which means 'a soaking slope' is suspicious, like many of the *Mischmasch* etymologies. He claimed that 'wabe' meant: 'the side of a hill (from its being soaked by rain)'.

Here was a straightforward portmanteau word made up of 'swab' and 'wade'. By the time he wrote *Looking-Glass*, he was ready to change it to a mathematical concept of the many 'ways' a convex mound may slope. The suffix 'be', Alice observed, was at the beginning of four direction words. (These directions were the ones along which the green raths set out.) The words are: 'be-cause, be-fore, be-hind and be-yond'. Alice helped Humpty Dumpty along:

> "And '*the wabe*' is the grass-plot round a sun-dial, I suppose?" said Alice, surprised at her own ingenuity.
>
> "Of course it is. It's called '*wabe*,' you know, because it goes a long way before it, and a long way behind it—"
>
> "And a long way beyond it on each side," Alice added.

WHIFFLING   This meant smoking, drinking and exhaling in short puffs, an evocative word that Carroll merely borrowed from Middle English.

In 1872, Robert Scott, co-author with Dean Liddell of the Greek Lexicon, published a remarkable German translation of the poem in *Macmillan's Magazine* and both Hassard H. Dodgson,* Carroll's inventor uncle, and Augustus Vansittart (1881) translated *Jabberwocky* into Latin. (See in addition, Translators* of *Alice*.) The search for etymologies in *Jabberwocky* between 1855 and the present day has never stood in the way of ingenious translators of *Alice* in spite of Humpty Dumpty's guarded enquiry to Alice: 'Who's been repeating all that hard stuff to you?'

Jowett, Benjamin (1817–93)   Broad* Church don, controversialist, Master of Balliol College and translator of Plato, Jowett was the key figure in the development of a more meritocratic and tolerant Oxford.* He was certainly the Oxford figure most frequently lampooned by Carroll.

Jowett's questioning of High Church orthodoxies, particularly the doctrine of Eternal Damnation (which awaited all those who were not admitted members of the Church of England) made him a reviled figure to the more conservative clergy. Oxford produced large numbers of country clergy who still had a vote in various aspects of University affairs. Many of these (and Carroll's father was typical) were High Church.

Besides achieving the office of Master, Jowett was appointed to the Professorship of Greek, after Dean Liddell,* in his grand manner, had turned it down. Jowett's supporters in Oxford then started a campaign within the University to have the Professor's meagre salary increased. This was still at a token level of £40 per year established centuries earlier. However the measures that reformers such as Liddell (who opposed the increase) introduced had increased professorial duties and given them a heavy lecturing and teaching load.

The matter was referred to the University consultative bodies, Congregation* and Convocation, at which point Jowett's doctrinal adversaries used the issue to punish him for his unorthodox religious teachings. On the only recorded occasion in which he spoke out in Congregation, Carroll tried to get the two issues separated. His logic, however, did not prevail; a failure for which he reproached himself bitterly.

The prejudices against Jowett (who in protest took to sitting with the undergraduates in the Hall and the Chapel at Balliol) were diverse. Even Dean Liddell, who might have been expected to support Jowett's views on university reform, opposed him for what appeared to be parsimonious reasons. The Professor's salary was – by one of the strange financial and constitutional anomalies that characterized Oxford – paid by Christ Church,* instead of the University. Even the influential Broad Church leader Dean Stanley* could not prevail against the High Church forces lined up against Jowett. Instead what developed was an almost hysterical attempt to run Jowett out of Oxford and to try him for heresy as the editor of the innocent sounding but revisionist – by High Church standards – *Essays and Reviews* (1860).

Only when Canon Pusey* wrongly accused Jowett of lying in the correspondence columns of *The Times* did national opinion start to run strongly in Jowett's favour. In the meantime the religious Court of Arches had already dispossessed other contributors to *Essays and Reviews* of their ecclesiastical livings. It took intervention by the Lord Chancellor to challenge this court's jurisdiction to bring the hue and cry against Jowett to an end. (See also Heresy.*)

Jowett's detractors claimed that he was 'infecting' Oxford, with his liberal opinions; established in the undergraduate community, it would run down the generations. While the word 'infection' may have been inappropriate, it was undoubtedly the case that High Church influence, of the kind Carroll sympathized with, declined at this period. This decline was followed by a more general decline in religion at the University.

Jowett was short, rotund, bald and as cherubic in looks as he was fearsome in debate. He was lampooned by Carroll in *The New Method of Evaluation As Applied to π*, π being used in the calculation of the circumference of circles, Carroll's way of parodying Jowett's (considerable) girth, and (also considerable) sense of self-importance. (See also Father* William.)

K is for ...

Kafka, Franz (1883–1924)   There are striking similarities between Carroll and Kafka, the Czechoslovakian writer. Each preferred anonymity. In their stories, the reader enters a literary world that is believable, but which involves nightmarish journeys out of reality. Creatures and people metamorphose and mutate. Time switches. Walls and mirrors are penetrable. The paranoid thoughts of creatures, like Carroll's Gnat* or Kafka's beetle, are overheard by the reader. In their books the struggle for consciousness itself is crucial. Each writer saw ambiguity as an elemental force. Kafka called his own prose works: 'these testimonials to my solitude'. W. H. Auden* held him to be, with Carroll, 'the first author of our age'.

Keble, John (1792–1866)   Like his friend Newman* (1801–90), Keble was a writer of some memorable hymns. Keble was a clergyman, Professor of Poetry at Oxford, and was considered by Newman to be the 'true author' of the Oxford Movement of 1833. He was one of those who, together with Pusey* and Newman, defined the climate of religious struggle in the Oxford in the half century – Carroll's first 50 years – following 1833.

Keble College (1870) was built in memory of John Keble. Carroll's friends Liddon* and Pusey were important figures in the fund-raising. It was intended as a college – the first brick-built college in Oxford* – that would provide a haven where clergy could be trained in a safely High Church environment, away from the rest of Oxford which was seen as increasingly Broad Church and liberal.

Key, The Golden   After falling down the Rabbit Hole, Alice found a 'tiny golden key' on the glass table in *Wonderland*. In Carroll's own drawing, Alice looked anxious and rapt, gazing beyond the key; perhaps because Carroll lacked the drawing skill to show her actually looking at it.

The key-that-revealed-secrets was an idea that Carroll and his friend, George MacDonald,* had in common. In *Jabberwocky* (1976), R. B. Shaberman traced the relationship between these two children's writers from the time they met at their speech therapist's waiting room in Hastings, in 1859. Over the next 12 years each came to be regarded as among the most significant imaginative children's writers of the day. Their stories stood apart from Tom Hughes' and Charles Kingsley's* boys' stories which displayed a boyish patriotism of a kind that excluded girls.

Carroll threw away the opportunity for plot development which the finding of a Golden Key offered at the beginning of *Alice*, a break with traditional fairy tale narrative, a tradition which MacDonald burnished over the years. In MacDonald's story *The Golden Key*, the key was a magical one. Alice found her golden key before her adventures began in earnest and her dealings with it led to a good deal of frustration.

Kings of Hearts, Red and White   In both *Alice* books, the Kings have lesser parts and find less to say than their wives. Not one of them is in control of his surroundings because of the overbearing behaviour of his wife. The snoring Red King at the edge of the forest in *Looking-Glass* is positively supine. In contrast to the low level of masculinity of the Kings, their wives (see Queens* in *Alice*) talk and behave in front of Alice in a *Looking-Glass* way, like pantomime dames – men dressed as women. (See also Red King's Dream.*)

Kingsley, Charles (1819–75)   By the 1850s, Kingsley was a best-selling author. Macmillan* published his sermons, children's stories and novels. Carroll was sceptical of the 'do-goodery' in the novels and of the pagan themes explored in them. He admired Kingsley, even if he also reviled him, and wanted to photograph him, but without success. Kingsley was an energetic man: he was at one and the same time, country parson, founder-supporter of the early Christian Socialist* Movement, and tutor to the Prince of Wales* when the Prince was at Cambridge.*

Kingsley's best known children's book, *The Water-Babies*, was published by Macmillan in 1863, two years before *Wonderland*. Its format was the one that Macmillan suggested to Carroll, Carroll choosing bright red for his cover instead of Kingsley's green. While Carroll and Kingsley were both ordained and authors of famous children's stories, the similarity stops there. Kingsley had royal connections, loved manly sport and hard exercise, and wrote vividly about the conditions of the poor, whom Carroll thought of as the 'lower orders'.

Overwork drove Kingsley into deep depression,* a state from which no home comfort could rouse him. He would, on occasion, stalk out of his Hampshire parish and stride off into the countryside, not returning for days. It is our view that the Hatter* has a facial resemblance to Kingsley, and there are resemblances in his stammering, commanding speeches, to his rhetorical way of speaking. Whether the facial resemblance was of Tenniel's devising, or suggested by Carroll is unlikely ever to be known, so little evidence having come to light of the details of their collaboration on the *Alice* illustrations. The Mad Tea-Party* certainly has many ingredients of a parody of Christian Socialism in action. Everybody is supposed to share equally, but only the dominant character, the Hatter, comes out on top – as Alice noticed every time she was told to change her place.

Wonderland was set on the real Alice's birthday and Alice started at the head of the table, where her father, the Dean of Christ Church,* also sat each night in Christ Church Hall. It is hardly surprising that Alice was shocked at having to relinquish the privileged position she assumed as if by right, when she was ordered to move round the table in a peremptory way.

Carroll and Kingsley met briefly at the Macmillan offices in London, after *Alice* was published. By this time Kingsley's views on society and church affairs had moved rightwards, closer to Carroll's.

Kingsley, Henry (1830–76)   A fan of the *Alice* books from the first moment Carroll showed him the manuscript of *Alice's Adventures Under Ground,** Henry was the untidy, down-at-heel younger brother of Charles Kingsley.* Two years older than Carroll, he was educated at Worcester College, Oxford but failed to take a degree. He was sent down in disgrace for opium-smoking. After five years in Australia, the 'Antipathies' in *Wonderland*, he returned to England and made his way as a novelist and newspaper war correspondent. His first success as an author was *Ravenshoe*, which Carroll read.

Carroll, perhaps looking for an introduction to his brother, approached him on the Isle of Wight to have his photograph taken on his honeymoon. Henry Kingsley, who had known Carroll as an undergraduate, may have been instrumental in recommending Carroll's *Alice* to Alexander Macmillan* for whom he acted as talent scout. Henry Kingsley said that it was the best thing he had read since Dickens' *Martin Chuzzlewit* (1843).

Our view is that the Hatter's* Mad Tea-Party was in part a parody of Charles Kingsley and Christian Socialism.* An appendage to that argument is that the Hare* and Haigha contain elements of the character of Henry Kingsley. He was energetic, frenetic and untidy like his brother, but always the lieutenant, not the leader, in the projects they undertook together.

Kisses The number of kisses Carroll sent at the end of his letters to child*-friends varied from none to ten million, but he did not use the usual cross to represent them. Ten million was the number of kisses Carroll sent to Gertrude Chataway* – she was then aged 12, an age at which his child-friends often became expendable – at the end of a letter written on Reading Station on 13 April 1878. As he wrote the letter, Carroll checked in Bradshaw's train timetable, hoping to ascertain:

> ...whether you are [still] at home – and whether you get my letter – and whether you're still a child; or a grown-up person – and whether you're going to the sea-side next summer – and anything else (except the alphabet and the multiplication-table) that you happen to know. I send you 1.0000000 kisses.

Carroll began sending postal kisses like these at a precocious age. The earliest letter (probably 1837) that survives in his hand was to his Nanny, 'Bun'. In his letter he converted 'ss' in every word to 'tt' to create phonetic baby-talk, a prelude to his invention of false Anglo-Saxon words for *Jabberwocky*.* He sent Bun his love, ending with:

> A kitt [kiss] from little Charlie with the horn of hair. I'd like to give you a kitt but I can't'.

Kitchin, George William (1827–1912) Kitchin was Carroll's exact contemporary at Christ Church* and, like him, a clerical mathematician. Kitchin became a mathematical examiner at Christ Church in 1854. He approached Carroll, who was sympathetic to his educational aims, to teach at Christ Church when he completed his undergraduate degree.

When Kitchin married, he and his wife extended true friendship to Carroll and their daughter Alexander ('Xie') became a special child*-friend. In their home he was welcomed by both adults and children. Carroll's correspondence with the Kitchins has been edited and introduced by Morton N. Cohen in *Lewis Carroll and the Kitchins: Containing Twenty-five Letters Not Previously Published and Nineteen of His Photographs* (1980). (See also 'Xie' Kitchin.*)

Kitchin, Alexandra ('X' or 'Xie') (1864–1925) Xie succeeded Alice Liddell* as Carroll's favourite photographic model. He started taking photographs of her in costume while he was writing the late drafts of *Looking-Glass* and she was nearly seven. She was eight years younger than Alice, and a friend of Alice's younger sisters, Edith*, Violet and Rhoda. When Xie posed for Carroll, which she often did after 1870, he was experienced as a photographer. Carroll's relationship with Xie's parents and younger brothers lacked the volatility of his relationship with the Liddells. The Kitchins respected Carroll as a mathematician and writer and had none of the Liddells' feelings of doubt, fear and social superiority with regard to his affection for their daughter.

Carroll posed one of his earliest portraits of Xie, in June 1869. It was a *tableau vivant* (see Games*) entitled 'Where dreamful fancies dwell'. In it, Xie, her long hair cut in a short fringe over her brow, lies sleeping, her stumpy fingers clutching a turned-down sheet. Photographs of children asleep were popular in the days of wet collodion* photography because the long exposures made it easier to keep a child still in this pose than when awake and lively. In one of Carroll's earliest sleep-feigning tableaux, Alice Liddell, still a small child, posed with her eyes tight shut, extended on the bare ground.

Carroll praised Xie's modelling skills in a riddle.* One of his illustrators, Henry Holiday, recalled it like this:

Q: 'How do I obtain excellence in a photograph?'
Ans: 'Take a lens and put Xie before it!' (i.e. X-a-lens – or 'excellence').

Alexandra Kitchin had a thin, pale face and her expression, which was sombre, lacked the touch of aristocratic disdain which was so enchanting in Alice Liddell both as a child and as a young woman. (That disdain can be seen in Alice's expression in Carroll's photograph of her as a beggar child and as an older girl under a parasol in a Chinese Mandarin gown). When he dressed his two favourite models in identical costumes eight years apart, Alice's pose stands out for its grace and childish elegance. But, however much Carroll praised Xie as his latest photographic discovery, she could be high-handed and choosy. In a letter to Xie's mother, dated 2 July 1880 when Xie was 16 and he had had enough of her, Carroll wrote:

Dear Mrs Kitchin, Many thanks for all the trouble you have taken about dresses and stockings. The dresses look charming with collars. It is a pity Xie doesn't like them for a photo: but I've found *one* young lady of fifteen who will come and be done in it … .

(See also Albums.*)

Knox, Ronald Arbuthnott (1888–1957)   Ronald Knox made his name at Eton and Balliol College, Oxford as a setter of paradoxes. Having been ordained into the Anglican Church in 1912, he converted to Roman Catholicism during the First World War. He took his vows as a Roman Catholic priest in 1919, being seen at the time as the most distinguished convert to the Roman Catholic faith since Henry Edward Manning* and John

Henry Newman.* He was made Monsignor in 1936 and elected to the Pontifical Academy in 1956. From 1939 to 1955 he worked for the Papal Hierarchy on a new translation of the Bible.

During the 1930s, Knox organized retreats and broadcast as a redoubtable controversialist on the theme of the loss of faith. Evelyn Waugh* wrote his biography and Penelope Fitzgerald memorialized him in a joint biography with his brothers. Knox and Leslie* were friends, fellow-converts and fellow-authors from their schooldays. In 1923, Knox collaborated with Leslie in writing an account of *The Miracles of Henry VI*, which Evelyn Waugh described as 'a handsome memorial to Etonian pietas'. In a very different vein was Knox's *A Book of Acrostics*, acrostics to *The Illustrated Review* and detective stories. He edited *The Best Detective Stories of the Year* in 1928.

Monsignor Knox played a part in the celebration of the centennial of the birth of Lewis Carroll. In informal collaboration with him, Shane Leslie prepared the paper he wrote about a connection between Lewis Carroll's *Alice* and the Oxford Movement, a topic of which Knox and Leslie between them knew more than most commentators of the day of any religious persuasion. Newman and Manning had been barred by the rule of conformity from teaching at Oxford. Knox, two freer, post-Jowett,* generations later, was allowed to. Knox's suggestion, now widely accepted, that Humpty Dumpty* coined the word Impenetrability* as an alias for Papal Infallibility confirmed the wisdom of Leslie's choice of Knox as a sounding-board for his re-examination of *Alice* and the Oxford Movement. In turn, had Knox not felt that Shane Leslie was on to something in his *Alice* investigations, he would never have encouraged Leslie to take the floor at a mainstream Roman Catholic theological conference at Göttingen to air their joint thesis about hidden identities in *Alice* for the first time.

Kraftsohn (alias Dodgson)   This cover-name was given to Lewis Carroll by an undergraduate, John Howe Jenkins (dates unknown), in 1874. Presumably, in Carrollian manner, one part of the pseudonym is 'Krafty', meaning Dodgy and the other part is 'sohn', meaning son. The impertinent Jenkins wrote *Cakeless*, a skit similar to Carroll's skits against the Dean. Jenkins went further, however. He double-bluffed, and attacked Carroll attacking the Dean. Jenkins paid for his satire by being sent down, expelled from the university. He also attacked Alice six years before her marriage. She was still eligible.

The cast of the skit was headed by Dean Liddell in a night cap, playing the part of Apollo – he was an eminent Greek scholar. His socially ambitious wife was Diana. Alice was 'Elicia', one of their marriageable daughters, and she had just hooked her man as the curtain came up. Apollo and Diana's daughters were, in 'Elicia's' words, hunting for 'a Prince, a Peer or else a Member's son'. As all had nearly succeeded, Kraftsohn, alias Dodgson, was angry. As if this were not enough to appal Carroll, Kraftsohn interrupted Elicia's wedding service from time to time, muttering: 'By circles, segments and by radii ...!'

Jenkins' skit shows that it was common knowledge at Christ Church* that the Dean's daughters were intended for suitable matches, and that there was a strong rumour, to date without concrete evidence, that Carroll had been rebuffed by the Dean and his wife as a suitor for Alice. The skit succeeded in making everyone embarrassed. Before Jenkins was sent down, everyone knew that the Liddells had once snubbed Carroll, even if not that it was over marriage, and that he still resented it. The severity of the usually tolerant Dean suggests that Jenkins touched a nerve in that family. The text of *Cakeless* is hard to find, but Anne Clark republished it in the Appendix to her biography of Alice Liddell,* *The Real Alice.*

KIDLINGTON

L is for . . .

'L' In *Looking-Glass*, as soon as Alice entered the wood where things have no names, she found she had forgotten all the names she normally knew. She had forgotten the name for 'wood', the name for 'tree' and even her own name, 'Alice'. Then she ventured: 'L. I *know* it begins with L!' Why 'L'? A method–in–madness runs through these Carroll jokes which shows the layers of thought that went into constructing *Alice*.

'L' was the first letter of Liddell. To all but a chosen few, it was a secret that Alice was based on Alice Liddell. And 'L' was the first letter of 'Lacie', Carroll's anagram for Alice as used by the Dormouse* in *Wonderland*. 'L' was also for Lily, the name of the White Pawn whose place on the chessboard Alice took at the beginning of *Looking-Glass*. At another level, 'L' was the name of a child who might have been the heroine of his story if it had not been Alice Liddell: she was Lily MacDonald* (1852–91). She was the eldest MacDonald, known to Carroll as 'a little mother to them all'. She was a gifted amateur actress, and was photographed with Carroll and members of the MacDonald family. Carroll owed them all a debt for encouraging him to publish *Wonderland* and for offering a warm and creative family circle where his best talents could develop unselfconsciously.

'Lacie' The Dormouse's* anagram for Alice; 'Lacie' was the second of the sisters who lived in the Treacle Well in the Dormouse's story. (See also 'Elsie'* and 'Tillie'.*)

Layout of the *Alice* books   This is a subject that deserves more critical attention. The layout of a book is often left by the author to the publisher or the publisher's designer, although with some children's books the author likes to be involved. Carroll was highly sensitive, perhaps over-sensitive, to issues of layout. His Oxford squibs may have been designed by printers rather than by Carroll himself, but by paying – for an author – unusually close attention to the details of their work, he learned something of the problems of layout. He continued his learning with Thomas Combe* of the University Press in Oxford and Alexander Macmillan* in London. As a result, the two *Alice* books have a crisp visual integrity which is never quite the same when they are repaginated or printed in type sizes or layouts different from the originals. Michael Wace, the editor associated with many *Alice* editions and *Alice*-related books at Macmillan in recent decades, considers 'the most dramatic and effective' of Carroll's ideas about layout to be the back-to-back placement of the two pictures of Alice climbing through the Looking-Glass. Alas, modern publishers lacking Carroll's precision, often leave out this invention. (See also Illustrators,* Looking-Glass and Tenniel.*)

Leslie, (Sir) John Randolph 'Shane' (1885–1971)   Irish patriot, disciple of Tolstoy, author and biographer of Cardinal Manning* (1933). In 1933, Leslie was struck by the resemblance between the Red Queen* in *Looking-Glass* and certain characteristics of the convert to Roman Catholicism (later Cardinal) Henry Edward Manning,* whose biography he had written. He presented, at a theological congress at Göttingen University, a paper entitled 'Lewis Carroll and the Oxford Movement', later published in the *London Mercury*, which proposed that real people in the Oxford religious world lay beneath the surface of the characters in *Alice*. He argued that the Oxford Movement 'gave birth to endless University squibs and parodies' including *Alice*.

> Alice ... may be regarded as the simple Freshman ... who wanders like a sweet and innocent Undergraduate into the Wonderland of a Victorian Oxford when everybody was religious in some way or another.

He reminded his readers that:

> ... the controversies of High, Low and Broad Church ... were uppermost in *every* Oxford man's mind at the time.

Leslie suggested that the Caterpillar* represented Oxford philosophy in the person of Dr Jowett;* the March Hare* and the Hatter* were 'types of Low and High church parsons'; and that the Cheshire Cat,* mad and whispering, was Cardinal Wiseman who, as the first Roman Catholic Archbishop of

Westminster represented an important foothold for the papacy in nineteenth-century England. He identified the Queen of Hearts' executions with Carroll's

> ... memory of the futile legislation against Papal Aggression in 1851, when Parliament passed a Bill to cut off Catholics Bishops from their Titles.

In *Looking-Glass*, Leslie held that the character of Dr Pusey* lay beneath that of the Sheep, and crucially, that of Cardinal Newman* lay beneath that of the White Queen;* the skirmishing between the Red and White Queens in *Alice* reflecting that between the Cardinals. He saw Manning's personality vividly depicted in the staccato speech and hurried actions of the Red Queen. Finally he held that Queen Alice, sitting between two recognizable defectors from the Church of England to the Catholic faith, had become a convert to the Roman Church at the end of the story. Leslie's friend, the Catholic Churchman, Ronald Knox,* contributed his own ideas to this same article, including the idea that Humpty Dumpty's* doctrine of Impenetrability* was a *Looking-Glass* variant of the Victorian Roman Catholic doctrine of Papal Infallibility.

Martin Gardner* in his foreword to *More Annonated Alice* suggested that Leslie's paper was a joke. Morton Cohen* in his biography dismisses Leslie entirely. We believe, like Leslie and Knox and to some extent inspired by them, that there are strong elements of satire in the *Alice* books and that the durability and human qualities of the characters depend on their being drawn from real people, and the attitudes they took in Carroll's, and often Alice's, direct experience.

Shane Leslie's paper was reproduced in full in the section called 'Church and Chess' in Robert Phillips' *Aspects of Alice* (1972). (See also William Empson.*)

Lessons, Alice's   The extent to which Carroll built the *Alice* stories on real experience in Alice's life is striking. The more we read the books, the more we see abstractions of Alice's real experience; a journey through a tunnel-like place where there are marmalade jars on the wall, a seaside with odd creatures, an Oxfordshire landscape that, looked down upon, is like a chessboard. There are many references among these to the schoolroom, whether the lessons be in reeling, writhing, ambition, distraction, drawling, uglification* or nonsense insect names.

The Mock Turtle* separated the art syllabus at The School Under the Sea into drawing (drawling), sketching (stretching – of canvas as well as part of eurhythmics) and oil-painting ('fainting in coils'). The Mock Turtle called history 'mystery', whether it was ancient or modern. Geography* (seaography) included a listing of world capital cities and the concept of latitude and longitude, which Alice aged seven had not really understood. French, German and Italian, for which Alice Liddell had her own tutors were on *Alice*'s list of the subjects with which a well-brought up girl had to be conversant in polite society. So, for the Dean's daughter, were Latin (laughing) and Greek (grief).

The English literary critic Janet Adam Smith pointed out in a review in the *New Statesman* (1973) that Carroll's jokes in *Alice* against lessons learned 'Under the Sea', were directed against the 'instructional and exhortative mode' of earlier Victorian children's books. Twenty years before *Alice* such lessons had been forced on the young Carroll. (See also Books Carroll read as a child* and Governesses.*)

Letters In 1887 Carroll, aged 55, said in a letter to Ellen Terry's* sister, Polly, that 'life seems to go in letter-writing'. He wrote thousands of letters to child*-friends; letters concerned with Common Room business; letters to Macmillan* and to potential collaborators for the stage version of *Alice*; letters to his sisters and brothers; and to admirers, who sometimes had to wait two years to hear from him. Letter-writing brought out the most dutiful and generous sides of Carroll. For 37 years, he kept a register of letters sent and received that had only 1279 entries short of 100,000.

Some of his letters were published in Collingwood's* *The Life and Letters of Lewis Carroll* ... (1898). The next, and more systematic, selection of his letters to be published was that by Evelyn Hatch* in 1933, *A Selection from the Letters of Lewis Carroll to His Child-Friends*, which contained 170 examples. Finally, in 1979, Morton Cohen's* masterful and meticulous two-volume edition, *The Letters of Lewis Carroll*, was published. Cohen first collaborated with Roger Lancelyn Green,* editor of the *Diaries*,* and took over the primary task of tracing the recipients of the letters and their descendants. This task was often made more difficult because many of the young descendants were female and had changed their names on marriage. By both the editing of the letters and the foot-noted descriptions of Carroll's correspondents, Cohen built up a picture of the Carrollian world that is still, arguably, without equal. Possibly he had some blind spots. Of the 4000 letters Green and Cohen found, they chose 1350. They left out mathematical letters of a technical nature and many letters relating to Common Room business. Possibly one blind spot was in failing to emphasize how political an animal Carroll was in Oxford* and Christ Church* matters. Further publication of letters in the next century would reveal more of this aspect of his life and work.

Morton Cohen's edition of the *Letters* did not include letters between Carroll and Macmillan, which were published separately (see the Select

Bibliography). They did include (as had Evelyn Hatch) the text of Carroll's *Eight or Nine Wise Words About Letter-Writing* – a tiny booklet, four inches by three inches, designed to fit into Carroll's *Wonderland Postage-Stamp Case*. On the end-papers the publishers printed a montage of samples of Carroll's direct and pseudonymous signatures, squiggly and straight, grown-up and child-like, including Charles L. Dodgson, C. L. Dodgson, C. L. Dodgson alias Lewis Carroll, Lewis Carroll, 'Pentitentially Yours', 'Your Loving Uncle', 'Yours hydrophobically', 'Thine ever', 'Your sexagenarian lover'.

Carroll's published *Diaries** give a picture of his intensely varied and active life and, sometimes, of his introspection. The *Letters* give a picture of Carroll at his most extrovert and wry. They have, generally, a lightness of touch that he otherwise achieved only in *Alice*.

Lewis Carroll Societies The founders of the Lewis Carroll Society were Anne Clark, who convened the first meeting and was appointed Secretary, and Ellis S. Hillman.* The first meeting of the society was on 15 May 1969 at County Hall, London. Its members were drawn from the staff of the Greater London Council. Other interested outsiders joined, too. They still include Anne Clark, biographer of Carroll and Alice Liddell; Dr Selwyn H. Goodacre (1940–), collector and Carroll scholar; and George Spence, chess master. The Society is responsible for the disappointingly produced but complete and verbatim new edition of the *Diaries* of Lewis Carroll, edited by Edward Wakeling.*

Jabberwocky is the journal of the Society. It is issued quarterly, sometimes in double issues, and is of a high standard, with an average length of 28 pages or so. Its charm is to combine the eccentric with the scholarly. Its fault is an inability to sort out the trivial from more perceptive criticism and comment. There is a separate Lewis Carroll Society (Daresbury*) drawing membership from the north-west of England, founded in 1970. There is also a club for younger members in the north-west and North Wales, the Dodo Club, which publishes its own newsletter. Inter-communicating societies flourish in the USA, Japan, Holland and other countries.

The Lewis Carroll Society of North America was founded in 1974 and an account of its first 20 years was written by its Secretary, Maxine Schaefer in the *Proceedings of the Second International Lewis Carroll Conference* held at Winston-Salem, North Carolina in June 1994. Shortly after its formation it instigated publication of the 'lost' chapter of *Looking-Glass* – 'The Wasp* in A Wig'.* Carroll's proofs of this were in the hands of an American collector. The Society now has nearly 400 members, and its membership is built up from a group of scholars, rare book collectors, authors, publishers, mathematicians and other enthusiasts interested in studying the life, works and times of Carroll. Carroll's works are more energetically collected and annotated in the USA than in England, Japan and the rest of Europe. The Society produces a periodic *Chapbook Series*, a quarterly entitled the *Knight* and a newsletter. It also acts as a clearing house for national and international Carroll conferences. Among Carroll scholars of international standing who are members of the Lewis Carroll Society of North America are Dr Francine Abeles (see Cryptography*), Morton N. Cohen,* Martin Gardner,* Edward Guiliano, Peter L. Heath, U. C. Knoepflmacher, Donald Rackin, David and Maxine Schaefer, the Society's secretaries and themselves authors and filmographers, and Elizabeth Sewell. (See also Critics.*)

Liddell, Alice Pleasance (later Hargreaves, 1852–1934)   This article begins with a description of the life of Alice Liddell, then shows her life arranged in a chronology, and concludes with a digest of the first-hand account she gave of Carroll when she was an old lady.

THE LIFE OF ALICE LIDDELL   Lewis Carroll's fictional Alice was modelled on Alice Liddell. She was born in London, in the Headmaster's house at Westminster School on 4 May 1852. She was the fourth of ten children, two of whom died in infancy. Carroll first saw this pretty child when she was three, at the time that her father, Henry George Liddell,* was appointed Dean of Christ Church.* As a young Student, Carroll worked in an office in the Library at Christ Church. From the window of this room, he had an exclusive view of the private Deanery garden* where the Liddell children chatted and played.

Carroll had just taken up photography. He and another young don, Reginald Southey,* were asked by Alice's mother to take photographs of the Deanery and then of her children. From when she was five until she was eleven, Alice was photographed by Carroll on many occasions. She grew up, and the skill of both subject and photographer developed. Alice for several years was frequently in the young don's company on walks, river trips and other expeditions and returned his affection. All Carroll's letters to Alice were later destroyed by Mrs Liddell, to Alice's distress.

According to Alice, the stories began when Carroll used the technique of spinning tales to keep her, her sisters or her friends in buoyant spirits while photographing them. Thus the pleasure of being photographed, often in fancy dress, was enhanced by the pleasure of these droll and spun-out tales. It is notable that Alice responded well to Carroll's technique for keeping her amused. She possessed a personality that enjoyed projecting itself as well as a delicately-featured face and poise. Carroll's pictures of her, taken while *Alice* was still being gestated and fragmentary, must be among the loveliest of all photographs of children. Carroll caught her in a number of moods and the impact of these is discussed in the article on child*-friends. Two photographs show Alice with partly bare shoulders dressed as a beggar child; others show her sleeping; in Chinese costume; about to eat a luscious cherry. She had a seductive, 'gamine' quality about her. Nimble in her facial expressions and poise, she was also nimble-witted, and laughed frequently at the droll stories which Carroll told her. It was she who became the heroine of the *Alice* stories, rather than Lorina or Edith, her sisters* and constant companions, or others of Carroll's young models. (See also 'Xie' Kitchin.*)

Alice was unique and has gained a unique place in literary history. She was capable of being petulant and snobbish, but the relationship between Carroll and Alice was cordial for eight years. Then in 1864 Carroll reported:

> May 12.(Th). During these last few days I have applied in vain for leave to take the children on the river, i.e. Alice, Edith and Rhoda: but Mrs. Liddell will not let *any* come in future...

(See also Lorina Liddell* for more on Carroll's relationship with Alice's ambitious mother.)

From the little testimony she left it would seem that the real Alice was lively, intelligent, and humorous, as was the fictional Alice. Both were unwilling to suffer people they considered fools, of which there were probably quite a number in the world, given the snobberies of the Deanery. The Deanery set standards of good conversation and of being adventurous which Carroll built on for the way his Alice behaves. The Deanery and the women who ruled the roost there also had strong ideas about who and what opinions were laughable.

Alice Liddell's father did not consider the benefit of a university education when planning Alice's future. Girls could study at colleges on the fringes of the Universities of Oxford and Cambridge by the time she came of age, but they could not then get degrees. (See, for example, Agnes Hull.*) Instead of any schooling, Alice remained with her governess,* Miss Prickett, and her sisters at the Deanery. She was presented at Court. Surprisingly late for a girl of her circle, at the age of 28 she married Reginald Hargreaves,* by no means an intellectual, with whom she lived a rich and comfortable country-house life. Her life was marred by the loss, in the bloom of her youth, of Edith Liddell,* her younger sister, on the eve of her engagement. Two of her three sons lost their lives as army officers fighting for their country on the Western Front in the First World War.

Carroll's relationship with Mrs Liddell virtually ceased from the time she withdrew Alice from his company until the very end of his life. Then she seems to have been flattered by his friendship with Lord Salisbury (see Cecil*), Tory leader and Prime Minister.

Two books have been written about Alice Liddell, one by Anne Clark, the other by Colin Gordon (see Select Bibliography). The article on *Alice's Adventures Under Ground** gives an account of the manuscript that Carroll gave to Alice and which she subsequently sold.

Mary Jean St Clair (1933–) is Alice's only grand-daughter. She was young when her grandmother died in Westerham. Mrs St Clair emphasized in the foreword to a recent edition of the facsimile of *Under Ground* how much Alice Liddell had loved horses. She discussed her childhood interest in natural history, which was encouraged by rides through Bagley Wood and Wytham Park with her father – also, of course, by Carroll.

Mary Jean St Clair inherited a significant collection of material relating to Alice, including the photograph album* given to her by Carroll, papers belonging to her father, scrap books, sketch books, letters and visitors books relating to her married life and a large number of editions of *Alice* in different languages collected by Alice and Caryl Hargreaves. This collection formed the starting point for Colin Gordon's life of Alice, *Beyond the Looking-Glass*. It gives a unique insight into the Deanery milieu during the time that *Alice* was developing into a book. Among the correspondence is a letter from Alice to Caryl Hargreaves in which she signs herself 'Alice in Wonderland'. He annotated the letter to say that it was the only occasion on which she did this.

BRIEF CHRONOLOGY OF ALICE LIDDELL'S LIFE

1852   Born at Westminster School, London where her father was headmaster and a chaplain to the Prince Consort. He was co-author of a Greek Lexicon that became a standard work for British schoolboys and students.

1855   Moved to Christ Church, Oxford when her father was appointed Dean, a clerical and college appointment. Carroll was in residence, working in the library.

1857–62   (aged 5–10) Alice lived in Christ Church, took summer holidays in North Wales at the Liddell's house, Pen Morfa.* Frequently photographed by Lewis Carroll with her elder and younger sisters, taken on river trips, told stories, always in company of Miss Prickett, her governess, or another chaperon friend of Carroll's.

1863 (about)   Alice's mother denied Carroll access to her daughters. Carroll announced with some distaste that Alice's shape was changing awkwardly.

1864   Alice was given a bound volume of *Alice's Adventures Under Ground*.

1865   Alice Liddell became famous as 'Alice' with publication of *Alice's Adventures in Wonderland*. By this time her contact with Carroll had become infrequent and formal.

1865–80   Educated at home, became a competent watercolourist under John Ruskin's* tuition; possibly had romance with Queen Victoria's* younger son, Leopold. (See also the section of Christ Church* dealing with royalty.)

1880   Aged 28, Alice married old Etonian Reginald Hargreaves, previously an undergraduate at Christ Church. Carroll not at wedding and, with a colleague, sent a boring watercolour. Alice went to live at Cuffnells, the Hargreaves' large country house in Hampshire. (See also Servants.*)

1881   Birth of Alice's son, Alan.

1883   Birth of her second son Leopold (after the Prince) Reginald. As a married woman, Alice lived an affluent country life. Her husband shot, fished and played cricket; his income being from his inheritance and landholdings in the north of England.

1885   Alice was approached by Carroll for permission (which she gave) for the publication in facsimile of *Under Ground*. She had been married for five years at this time. She saw Carroll at Christ Church on one or two occasions which she did not record. He spoke of them with poignant nostalgia.

1887   Alice's third son, Caryl, was born.

1898   Death of Carroll. Alice did not attend his funeral. Her father died shortly after Carroll.

1915 & 1916   Death of Alice's two elder sons in World War I, both army officers.

1926   Death of Alice's husband, Reggie Hargreaves. She continued to live at Cuffnells with a number of servants, but found maintenance costs of her lifestyle expensive.

1928   Sale at Sotheby's of the manuscript of *Alice's Adventures Under Groound* with the purpose of defraying expenses. Reached highest price ever paid for a literary manuscript.

1932   Became 'Alice' again briefly when feted in New York at Carroll centenary. (See Dream-Child.*)

1934   Died in Hampshire near to Cuffnells.

1955   Alice's third son, Caryl, died in Scotland. His daughter, Mary Jean St Clair, keeps her archive in Gloucestershire.

ALICE'S ACCOUNT OF LEWIS CARROLL   Of the published documents describing what it was like to be one of Carroll's child-friends, the twelve-page account written by Alice Liddell (Hargreaves) for the 73rd issue of *Cornhill* (1932) is the most intriguing. Following the example of the Arnold* sisters, who had already published a memoir, Alice agreed that her surviving son, Wing Commander Caryl Hargreaves, could interview her about her 'Carrollian Days', and so derive a memoir. Alice was either side of her 80th birthday when this was done, and she vividly brought to light memories of seventy and more years earlier. The recollection reads as a description of the Liddell girls' 'joys and fears' at the Deanery at Christ Church when 'Mr Dodgson' (also 'the mathematical tutor') was allowed to accompany 'Miss Alice' – as Bultitude, the Deanery coachman, called her – on the expeditions that inspired Carroll's *Alice* stories. The recollections have a tone that is as lady-like and patrician as that of Carroll's heroine.

Alice described what Carroll selected in *Alice* from Deanery reality in the early 1860s, such as the cat and her kittens, and the carved panther heads on the bannisters, and what filtered into the stories purely from his imagination. She remembered sitting with her sisters on the sofa in his photographic studio as 'the stories, slowly enumerated in his quiet voice with its curious stutter, were perfected'. She claimed that 'Mr Dodgson told us many, many stories before the famous trip up the river to Godstow' and that 'much of *Through the Looking-Glass* is made up of them, too'. Thus in old age, Alice laid claim in her queenly way to the whole domain of Carroll's imagination at its peak, with one exception. She admitted, of the stories she had inspired, that 'perhaps only a brilliant logician could have written *Alice*'.

Liddell, Edith (1854–76)   Alice's sister, two years younger than she. She died suddenly of peritonitis within a few days of her engagement to Aubrey Harcourt of Nuneham Courtney.* There is a memorial window to her in Christ Church* designed by Edward Burne-Jones.

In *Alice*, she is the Eaglet, perhaps because she was so eager. She was much photographed by Carroll with Alice and Ina, and Carroll's biographer,* Anne Clark, has suggested that she was the child who posed for Carroll's line drawings for the *Under Ground* Alice. In John Ruskin's opinion, the auburn-haired Edith was the loveliest of the Liddell sisters. (See also 'Tillie'.*)

Liddell, Henry George (1811–98)   Dean of Christ Church.* An undergraduate, then Student at Christ Church, he left the college on the occasion of his marriage in 1846 to become Headmaster of Westminster. On the death of Dean Gaisford (1779–1855) Liddell was appointed Dean of Christ

Church to the chagrin of Carroll and others. He remained there from 1855 until his retirement in 1891.

Dean Liddell was, throughout his life, enriched by a steady flow of royalties from the *A Greek-English Lexicon,* and the abridged version of it, which he co-edited with the High Churchman, Dr Robert Scott, Master of Balliol. The Lexicon was an essential book for generations of educated Englishmen. Liddell contrived to be, depending on circumstance, both an entrenched conservative and dynamic Liberal reformer. He added to Christ Church a belfry (see Bats*) tower that fails to fit the architecture of Tom Quad and which was the subject of a satire by Carroll; and Meadow Buildings, which must be among the clumsiest of Victorian additions to Oxford, but which provided essential new accommodation for undergraduates.

Dean Liddell generally favoured the reform of university statutes and the broadening of the curriculum, but he was far from being a radical like Benjamin Jowett.* Carroll appears to have been welcomed by him in early years, the years of friendship with Alice. After this Carroll, together with Thomas Jones Prout,* went to war against what they saw as Liddell's arbitrary use of his powers as Dean. They attacked, in particular, the fact that the Dean turned a blind eye to the corrupt Christ Church Butler and Manciple/steward (see *American Telegrams**). They lamented his changing the time of chapel services. They resented the small rewards and negligible powers given to Students like themselves, with what they felt were exceptionally heavy work-loads. They disliked a reform whereby Students did not always sit at High Table but sometimes mingled with undergraduates in the Hall. In addition, Carroll reviled the Dean's Broad Church tendency, although how strong this was is hard to discern; his arbitrary changes in the mathematical programme for the undergraduates who Carroll taught; and his proconsular social ambition.

Liddell, on the other hand, was tolerant of Carroll's refusal to become an ordained priest, although for 24 hours he gave Carroll what must have been the fright of his life when he in effect threatened him with dismissal for non-compliance with Christ Church's rules in this matter.

In all the recorded photographs and paintings of Dean Liddell, including the one by Carroll, his appearance is haughty. He moved in royal circles and was, with Henry Wentworth Acland,* the obvious protector for the Prince of Wales* when he came to Oxford as an undergraduate. At this time, the Dean antagonized the more decadent of the Christ Church bloods and aristocrats by removing them from the college for rowdy behaviour. Yet the crimes of which they were guilty, tying gunpowder in a kettle to the Deanery door, stealing the busts from the Library, works of art of international importance, and setting fires around them in the Quad, deserved a harsher punishment.

Whereas other heads of colleges, especially Jowett, thought the social make up of the university should be broadened, Liddell thought that he could work with the existing class of undergraduates. That he could not was shown in the college's dismal academic record. Yet in supporting the widening of the university curriculum to include science* and medicine, Liddell was indeed enlightened. Easily bored, skilful at compromise, at meetings he would often doodle. These doodles, showing the skill in drawing which Ruskin praised, can still be seen in the Christ Church library. A couplet about the Dean remembers him as follows:

> I am the Dean and this is Mrs Liddell,
> She plays the first, and I the second fiddle.

Playing second fiddle, vacillating in committee, compromising without explaining his principles over the ordination issue as it affected Carroll, sharing the throne of judgement at the Court of Hearts with his peremptory wife suggested a number of resemblances between the haughty, bored and indecisive King of Hearts and Henry George Liddell. (See also Bread and Butter* and University Reform.*)

Liddell, Lorina Charlotte ('Ina') (1849–1930)   Ina, Alice and Edith were the three Liddell sisters Carroll knew best at the time he wrote *Under Ground*. He photographed them, invented ingenious new games for them, took them out together and went to tea at the Deanery with them. Above all, he told them stories.

Lorina was more of a tomboy than her two younger sisters and went on river expeditions with Carroll and her sisters well past the age when this was respectable. She evidently resented the fact that her age could deny her this pleasure, an objection noted in the mouth of the 'Lory' (a tropical parrot) in *Under Ground*. In 1874 she married William Skene and moved to Scotland, but she remained a staunch support to her mother and father throughout her life.

Liddell, Mrs Lorina, née Reeve (1826–1910)   Alice's mother has not been treated as kindly by history as her eminent husband or noteworthy daughter. She was 15 years younger than her husband and 6 years older than Carroll and looked, and was, strong-minded. Mrs Liddell came from an East Anglian family of landowners. Of her ten children, five were boys of whom two died young.

The role of women married to respected, motivated and highly successful Victorian academics required the qualities of a military adjutant or ADC, particularly in social matters. Such wives were subservient to the rules of behaviour, but creative in their practice. To prepare Alice and her sisters for, say, a royal visit required exact timing as to the ordering of fabric, trimmings, shoes, food, ices in days without refrigerators, tents, musicians, changes of clothes for Church, for a college Ball, and for morning and evening wear.

The marriage of her daughters was a major preoccupation and the undergraduates believed that Mrs Liddell had ambitions for a royal marriage. In fact she and the Dean knew that such a match was most unlikely and discouraged Prince Leopold's fondness for Alice.

Why Mrs Liddell put a stop to Carroll's friendship with Alice, Lorina and Edith may remain a secret. The reasons for speculating that Carroll proposed to Alice are strong, but they are entirely circumstantial. (See also Kraftsohn.*) However much Carroll may have been outraged at Mrs Liddell for withdrawing her children from his company, it should not be forgotten that she had the insight and social flair to accept this eccentric don in the first place, and to make him part of the inner circle of her family – just as she did with Ruskin.* The Dean's wife wanted the best for her daughters. She encouraged the qualities that make 'Alice' so alive in *Wonderland* and *Looking-Glass* by creating an atmosphere – by no means common to such households – in which dance and movement, quick-wittedness, drawing and watercolour painting, literature, languages and mathematics were ingredients that she took seriously on behalf of her daughters. At her most imperious, Carroll may have parodied Lorina Liddell as the Queen of Hearts. Her imperiousness may have been one side to her character: she was also the centre and defining influence on a talented and close family. (See also Dress.*)

Liddon, Henry Parry (1829–90)   Liddon was three years Carroll's senior and a close Christ Church* friend. In 1854 the Bishop of Oxford, Samuel Wilberforce,* appointed Liddon to be the first Vice-Principal of Cuddesdon Theological College,* which was built next to the site of the Bishop's own palace. Cuddesdon was designed to train clergy for the Oxford diocese in Wilberforce's image, that is High Church, and Liddon, as the most talented disciple of Canon Pusey,* was a very suitable candidate. Liddon duly took office, but he was soon suspected of being too High and of leading students to Rome. He left Cuddesdon under a cloud. Meanwhile, he had gained a reputation as one of the most eloquent preachers of the time, having learned to throw his voice by preaching against the roar of waves on the Pembrokeshire coast.

Liddon and Carroll travelled together to Russia in 1867 on a mission to make contact with the Russian Orthodox Church, this being the only occasion on which Carroll left the British Isles.

Liddon could have been Carroll's model for the Mock Turtle* in *Alice*. The Turtle was a 'tortoise' because he 'taught us', not as a schoolmaster but as a theologian. He had a lid on because he was Liddon; and he was in hot water, a weeping *Mock* Turtle because his teaching had been invalidated when he was removed from his job by Bishop Wilberforce.

Lionize   This was a Victorian term for treating a person as a literary or political lion. Carroll's first diary entry for the Oxford Long Vacation of 1855 said that he was going to London with his friend Vere Bayne with plans of lionizing. Carroll's lionizing at this time probably consisted of keeping an eye out for the great in London, perhaps collecting or buying photographs of them or *cartes-de-visite*. Later he used various tactics of acquaintanceship to get into their presence to photograph them. Helmut Gernsheim* listed 46 'distinguished' men and women, artists, literary figures, churchmen, scientists, professors, actresses and politicians whom Carroll successfully approached and photographed.

That list has been extended since Gernsheim wrote – he did not, for example, mention Thomas Henry Huxley.* Most notable among those whom Carroll never succeeded in photographing were the Prince of Wales,* the painter, G. F. Watts (1817–1904), Benjamin Jowett,* Charles Kingsley* and W. M. Thackeray. (See also Faces* and Garden of Live Flowers.*)

Lobster   It is hard to imagine Lewis Carroll eating a lobster, or indeed an oyster – he had difficulty carving mutton – but he loved the seaside* and coastal holidays in Yorkshire, Sussex and Hampshire. He liked to take child*-friends to aquaria like the one in Brighton. Alice, almost certainly, had tasted lobster; at least this is what the fictional 'Alice' said to the Mock Turtle* before realizing the insensitivity of the remark.

Carroll made the speaking Lobster in *Wonderland*, afraid of a Shark. This suggested that the Royal Academy Varnishing Night, with Ruskin* (the critic and Shark) staking out Millais* (the Lobster) in his hostile *Academy Notes* was the basis of the joke. Dante Gabriel Rossetti* knew Carroll and despised Millais by the 1860s. A writer of limericks about his friends, Rossetti wrote to tell Carroll that the nonsense poem, 'Twas the Voice of the Lobster', in *Alice* was the funniest he had ever read.

Logic, Symbolic   Alice Liddell* remembered Carroll respectfully, among her less formal memories of his photography and attire, as a master of logic, as he may have been remembered at the Deanery. Later in life, he constructed, from ideas about syllogisms he had been working on throughout his life as a mathematician, two puzzle books, which Macmillan published in 1887 and 1897. Dover Books reprinted them in 1958. The Dover edition begins with an apology for Carroll's racist examples in his text. The early exercises in the books were intended reading for what he described as 'an intelligent child of (say) twelve or fourteen years of age'. The game is played with red and grey counters on a board made up of four quadrants. (See also Red.*)

Carroll announced the second part of the work on the publication of first and promised further *Curiosa Logica* at this time, having worked up the exercises for publication from 1886 to 1896. He felt his games provided more 'healthy enjoyment' than backgammon, chess or halma. Carroll, at the end of his life, forgot all he had done in the *Alice* stories to arm young girls against 'fallacies' by teaching them to:

> ... tear to pieces the flimsy, illogical arguments, which you will so continually encounter in books, in newspapers, in speeches and even in sermons, and which so easily delude those who have never taken the trouble to master this fascinating Art.

Lacking all the light touch of *Alice*, *Symbolic Logic* is the work of a radical author who cannot get out what he is trying to say without recourse to seriously off-putting pedantry. Sadly, *Symbolic Logic* has the same strangled quality as his difficult 'Oxford Squibs'.

London   Conventionally Carroll is seen as an Oxford* figure. While Oxford provided the background to his social life, London grew more and more of an influence on his artistic development in the early 1860s. Initially Carroll's London visits were to his Uncle Skeffington Lutwidge,* his mother's brother. It was Skeffington who introduced Carroll to photography.* Two years into his photographic career, and with his direct relationship with Alice Liddell at its height, Mrs Acland* introduced him to the London sculptor, Alexander Munro (1825–71). Munro liked Carroll's photographs and offered to use Carroll for copy work in the studio, in return for the right to keep his cumbrous photographic equipment there on what soon became frequent forays to the metropolis.

Munro provided Carroll with a London base at 6 Belgrave Place. It was here that he first caught the imagination of the young Greville MacDonald,* who was posing for Munro's statue for Kensington Gardens, 'Boy With A Dolphin'. Thus connected to Munro and the MacDonalds, Carroll's London circle widened. With the death of his father in 1868 and the loss of the Croft Rectory as a draw to the north-east, Carroll became essentially a southerner, dividing his time between Oxford, short visits to Guildford* (often at Christmas), Eastbourne* (for the summer) and London for friends, theatre, all publishing contacts, photography, child-friends and social life.

Among Carroll's other important London contacts during the period he wrote the *Alice* books were: Tom Taylor,* the lawyer, playwright, contributor to *Punch** and then its editor, the many Terrys,* the Rossetti* family, F. D. Maurice,* the Millais* family, Lord Salisbury (see Cecil*) and Thomas Woolner (1825–92), Munro's rival as sculptor to the great Victorians. Thus there was a point during 1857 or 1858, when Carroll was 35 and 36, when London became more than somewhere to visit from Oxford. The metropolis became the focus of Carroll's literary ambitions, the place where John Tenniel,* the Dalziel Brothers, the engravers, and all his subsequent illustrators could be found, the place where Alexander Macmillan* resided, where *The Times* was printed and where British theatre, of which he was an ardent patron, thrived. London was the place where Carroll's identity could develop, far from the severe clerical eyes of the Dean and Dr Pusey* and the scepticism and cheek of the Christ Church bloods.

The record of Carroll's London visits shows that he had prodigious energy. The diary entries are clipped and compressed, but considerable organization was required to get child-friends and heavy photographic equipment into the right place at the right time before moving the camera back to the station or to Munro's studio. Then he had to organize the children to go to the theatre, to visit tea shops and toy shops, and all that besides visits to toilets which must have been a problem. The chaperoning of children through the crowded streets of a city where beggars and street crime were common – the dark London of Dickens – required care and forethought. Carroll always took his charges to their parents, punctually.

As his fame as the author of *Alice* increased, so did his desire to be anonymous. Still the theatre and visits to child-friends continued to keep him on the train from Oxford to Paddington until the very end of his days. Old Hummums Hotel was often Carroll's base in London. Now a restaurant, it is situated on the south-east corner of the old Covent Garden Market. It was less than two hundred yards from Macmillan's offices at 16 Bedford Street, close to the Fleet Street offices of *Punch* and near the West End theatres. The hotel had been one of a series of Turkish Bath hotels in Covent Gardens, the English place name being an eighteenth-century corruption of the Turkish 'Hammam', a Turkish bath. One of the rooms in 'Old Hummums' was portrayed by Dickens in *Great Expectations* when the hero, Pip, visited the hotel and found himself in a room with a bed so huge that one of its legs sat in the grate. This sounds right for Carroll, who would have wanted somewhere respectable, economical and accessible to theatres, toy shops and places for tea and cakes with child- friends. (See also Sites of interest.*)

Long Vacation   For approximately four months of the year, Oxford city and University virtually closed down. From late June until the early part of October, dons such as Carroll were free to follow their own lives. The University terms only occupied three sessions of eight weeks each. Although Carroll would often work on university business for part of the shorter vacations, a fair estimate would be that he would have about 20 weeks of disposable time or 'vacation' in the year.

Dr Henry Wentworth Acland* wrote, good epidemiologist that he was, of the economic and social effect caused by this periodic closing down of Oxford:

> The long vacation is a great trial to the poor or the improvident. The Cholera occurred towards the close of the vacation. Many families were wholly without work ... I am able to state positively, that the Diarrhoea and Cholera were most rife, speaking generally, in the poorer places, and that in some alleys where meat was given, the Diarrhoea was arrested.

JABBERWOCKY.

'Twas brillig, and the slithy toves
Did gyre and gimble in the wabe;
All mimsy were the borogoves,
And the mome raths outgrabe.

Looking-Glass 'Wonderland' is a rambling sort of place where anything might happen. The idea of an adventure through the looking-glass has a much more formal note to it and is perhaps Carroll's greatest literary concept. It is both a visual idea and one that allows an array of sub-ideas about a world that was in various ways – pictorially, linguistically, logically – back to front.

The mirror is the essential tool in Carroll's hands, like the conjuror's top hat, with which he can play almost endless games once he is given an attentive child. Increasingly mirrors were part of Victorian decor, not so much instruments of vanity, but decorative devices for increasing the size and light in rooms. Hallway mirrors, different to the more delicate ones of a generation

169

before, often came right to the skirting, mantelpiece ones flush with the flat surface above the fire. These were mirrors in which to reflect not just faces, but whole worlds. The Deanery room back-to-front lay beyond the mirror, but what was beyond that? The answer, of course, was not just another familiar room, but a world where a little girl running the gauntlet of a course in backwards and inside-out logic, survived and became Queen. There was no looking-glass in Carroll's study. The looking-glass was in his mind.

Lady Hawarden (1822–65), the photographer whom Carroll admired much more than Julia Margaret Cameron,* often used mirrors to increase the sense of moody reflectiveness in her pictures of women in long dresses and large, Kensington rooms. Carroll took a photograph of his sister Margaret

long before he wrote *Looking-Glass* showing her reflected in profile in a small dressing-table stand mirror. The result is not moody in the way of other photographs of his sisters. It does suggest – its title was 'Reflections' – that his mind was moving in a looking-glass direction. Alice received two mirrors as wedding presents, but neither was from Carroll who shared with another don in giving her a watercolour. (See also Tweedledum.*)

Low Church   Lewis Carroll was a High Church Anglican with one or two dissenting tendencies, which became more marked as his years advanced. Yet his love for simplicity and lack of pomp in church services and his earnest endeavour not to frighten child worshippers with too much incomprehensible ceremony, suggest certain low church tendencies in his deeply pious faith and practice as an Anglican.

Lutwidge, Robert Wilfred Skeffington (1802–73)   'Uncle Skeffington', Carroll's bachelor uncle, was a year older than Carroll's mother, who was his sister. He was an iconoclastic and amusing friend on whom the young Carroll could lean on for advice He lived in London, was a lawyer, and later a Commissioner for Lunacy, and had a fascination for gadgets, which he transmitted intact to his nephew. Skeffington Lutwidge added a mechanical dimension to the young Carroll's view of the world as an odd and interesting place. Aged 21, Carroll wrote to his sister Elizabeth of their uncle:

> He has as usual got a great number of new oddities, including a lathe, telescope stand, crest stamp [a blind stamp, Carroll headed the letter with this], a beautiful little pocket instrument for measuring the distances on a map, refrigerator, etc., etc. We had an observation of the moon and Jupiter last night, and afterwards live animacula in his large microscope ...

On 10 September 1855 Carroll first mentioned going to Richmond with Skeffington 'photographing'. They met again that year at Croft Rectory and in London and in January of the following year he requested that his uncle 'get me a photographic apparatus'. Thereafter Carroll frequently stayed with Skeffington in London, and photographed this portly gentleman wearing a widening waistcoat, a velvet-collared frock coat and heavy watch chain and sitting in a button-backed arm chair with its leather rather worn away.

When Carroll first visited Skeffington from Oxford, his house was off the Tottenham Court Road; later he moved to a large and affluent house in Onslow Square which still stands, less than half a mile from South Kensington tube station. There he was a neighbour of the Raikes family and got to know another Alice, Alice Raikes, the child*-friend on whom Carroll first tested his idea for the looking-glass world in the garden of the Square. (See Dodgson,* the section on first-hand accounts of Carroll.)

In May 1873, while visiting an asylum at Salisbury, Skeffington was attacked by a lunatic. Carroll came down from Oxford immediately and stayed with him for two days, at the end of which Skeffington seemed better. Carroll then returned to his duties in Oxford, but Skeffington died three days later.

Carroll lost a friend who was also a relative, a father-figure who was tolerant and humorous, with whom he had been able to discuss intimate worries. These had almost certainly been unmentionable to his father when he was alive. They were worries over his brother's obsession with young Alice Jane Donkin, and his anxieties about Alice Liddell.

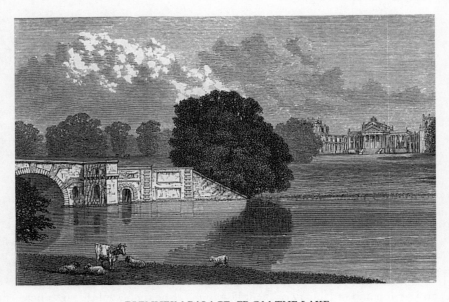

BLENHEIM PALACE, FROM THE LAKE

M is for ...

MacDonald, George (1824–1905)   MacDonald and his wife, Louisa (1822–1902), had a family of 11 children to whom Carroll was devoted. They included 'Lily' (Lilia, 1852–91), Mary (1853–78) and Greville (1856–1944). MacDonald was Scottish born and a writer best known for his children's stories, among them *At the Back of the North Wind*, *The Princess and the Goblin* and *The Princess and Curdie*. At the time of their meeting, MacDonald was having difficulty finding a publisher, although his successful children's story *Phantastes* had already been published in 1858.

According to R. B. Shaberman (*Jabberwocky*, Summer 1976), the MacDonalds first met Carroll in 1857 when they lived in Hastings, with their then five children. The connection is traced through the homeopathic Dr Hale who knew MacDonald and who also knew Dr James Hunt, an authority on stammering whom Carroll visited. Carroll's aunts, the Misses Lutwidge, lived at Hastings. Soon after this, Carroll met Greville and Mary MacDonald, at Alexander Munro's studio in 1858. Carroll was then aged 26, Mary 5 and Greville 2. Munro was using the long-haired Greville as a cupid-like model for 'Boy with a Dolphin', which still stands in Hyde Park, and Carroll argued that the marble head would not have to comb its hair, having in mind the misery he thought Hallam Tennyson, Alfred Tennyson's* son, suffered from this ordeal. That struck a note, although Greville argued back that the marble head would not be able to talk.

Thus began a friendship with Greville and Mary MacDonald, and with their parents that lasted for many years. Carroll's photograph of himself and some of the MacDonalds in their garden in summer suggests that, with them, he really could feel like a member of the family. He stayed with the MacDonalds, went to F. D. Maurice's* church off Oxford Street with them and took their children on expeditions – sometimes shopping for toys.

Greville MacDonald later became an eminent London ear and throat specialist *and* novelist and children's author. He described, in *George MacDonald and His Wife* (1924), how Carroll took them to a toy shop and allowed them to choose, and that he chose a simple wooden toy that he treasured through the years. Such reminiscences of Carroll seen through the eyes of a child*-friend who was a boy are rare.

Undoubtedly the family encouraged Carroll to publish *Wonderland*. Greville's reminiscence is emphatic:

I remember reading [Alice] well, and also my braggart avowal that I wished there were 60,000 volumes of it.

Later, Carroll, needing an illustrator for *Looking-Glass* obtained an introduction from MacDonald to Sir Noel Paton. Paton referred him back to Tenniel.*

George MacDonald had a good deal in common with Carroll. Both were religious. MacDonald was reprimanded by his bishop for heretical views in 1852, and thereafter resigned his status as a priest. Both loved the theatre, both were members of The Ghost Society and both were interested in Spiritual and Psychical* Research. Furthermore, *Phantastes*, a children's story of MacDonald's, was an important influence on *Alice* in terms of structure, transitions, the presence of a white rabbit and a number of looking-glass ideas.

Mary MacDonald died of consumption in 1878, in Italy where her parents were then living. MacDonald called her his 'blackbird' and Carroll's brother, Wilfred, found her so agile that he taught her to box. He called her 'the Kensington Chicken' which implies that he had a sense of humour that was very different from Carroll's. Of all the people pivotal in encouraging the transformation of *Alice* from the adventures *Under Ground* to those in *Wonderland*, the MacDonalds are probably the most important. (See also The Golden Key* and 'L'*)

Macmillan, Alexander (1818–96)   Carroll's publisher, and his senior by 14 years, Alexander Macmillan and his brother, Daniel (who died in 1857) came from the Isle of Arran. Initially they began as booksellers in London, but in 1843 they moved their business to Cambridge. They soon noticed the weakness of Cambridge theological publishing and found themselves to be a meeting place for mainly 'Germanizing'* theologians – those opposed to the Oxford Movement* – that were favoured by Prince Albert and, in particular, the brothers Julius and Augustus Hare.*

Their book *Guesses at the Truth by Two Brothers* was republished by Macmillan in 1866. With funds from the Hares, Macmillan then went on to publish Charles Kingsley* and F. D. Maurice,* making them the most famous Broad Church* authors of their day. Keeping his base in Cambridge, Alexander opened an office in London in 1858, the year after his brother died. They had already published Kingsley's *Westward Ho!* (1855) and Thomas Hughes' *Tom Brown's Schooldays* (1857) by this time.

Carroll first met Macmillan through the Combes* who with the Aclands* − but not the Liddells* − were the two Oxford families who introduced him to his London* connections. This was in 1863, by which time the firm had moved to London. Its original office had been at 23 Henrietta Street; now it moved around the corner to 16 Bedford Street. Both offices were in Covent Garden, within a stone's throw of Old Hummums hotel where Carroll usually stayed.

Carroll was a lucky man; at 31 he had found an exemplary publisher. Alexander Macmillan was now 45 and was shrewd, sensitive to book design, urbane and patient. It was he who suggested the page size of *Wonderland* and the type of cover. It was he who, over a relationship of three decades, put up with, and perhaps benefited from, Carroll's attention to detail.

Morton Cohen* (with Anita Gandolfo) edited Carroll's side of this correspondence in *Lewis Carroll and the House of Macmillan* (1987). The introduction includes some history of the house of Macmillan. Macmillan's own biography by Charles L. Graves, *Life and Letters of Alexander Macmillan* (1910) paints a picture of a stern, commercially astute and wise publisher. It has the briefest mention of Carroll. Alexander Macmillan's description of a walk by moonlight in the Scottish borders, in Walter Scott country, is of such beauty that it makes clear how Macmillan, beneath the mask of the commercial publisher, was able to sense Carroll's lyricism and was patient enough to project it to the public as *Alice*.

Madan, Falconer (1851–1935) Bibliographer, librarian, life-long resident of Oxford from his undergraduate days at Brasenose College, Madan chronicled the University and its strange ways in his charming, forgotten *Oxford Outside the Guide Books* (1923). Madan's recreations were listed by him as walking and chess, most appropriate for Carroll's bibliographer. He was an athlete and won the singles title at Fives in 1874. He was sub-librarian of the Bodleian and compiled many bibliographies. Being a year older than Alice Liddell and 19 years younger than Carroll, Madan was a survivor of nineteenth-century Oxford who lived well into the twentieth − a useful background for collaboration with Sidney Herbert Williams on the first Carroll bibliography,* *A Handbook of the Literature of the Rev. C. L. Dodgson* (1931).

It was subsequently revised by Roger Lancelyn Green* (1962) and then by Denis Crutch (1979). Falconer Madan also edited *The Lewis Carroll Centenary in London 1932*, a catalogue of the Exhibition.

In 1880, Madan caused a stir by mentioning to Carroll that he was to be included in the *Dictionary of the Anonymous and Pseudonymous Literature of Great Britain* which was then in preparation. Carroll objected and at once wrote to the editor: his pseudonym was taken out. In the meantime Carroll rapped Madan on the knuckles for asking him whether he, Carroll, could be included in further editions after he was dead. A piece of extended logic-chopping followed, part of Carroll's unrelenting campaign to preserve his anonymity.*

Magic   Carroll had a life-long interest in conjuring tricks and the art of magic. Many of the events and transitions in the *Alice* stories, particularly in the Sheep's Shop, are reminiscent of what a child witnesses when magic tricks are performed by a conjuror on stage. As a child in Daresbury,* according to Collingwood,* who had the information from Carroll's sisters, he used to perform conjuring tricks and showed considerable 'sleight of hand'. He wore, for these elaborate performances, not the later black and white which were his Oxford uniform, but 'a brown wig and a long white robe'.

John Fisher* published an in-depth account of Carroll's involvement with conjuring and puzzles in *The Magic of Lewis Carroll* in 1973. In 1992, Edward Wakeling* followed up with an investigation of Carroll's mathematical puzzles and games for able children and adults, a lively series of forty-two* *Lewis Carroll's Games and Puzzles*.

Manning, Henry Edward, Cardinal (1808–92)   One of the leaders of the Oxford Movement who became a Roman Catholic in 1851, Manning succeeded in making many converts among well-to-do Anglican families and was elected Cardinal in 1875. He was a constantly discussed figure among members of the Church of England at Carroll's Oxford, whether they were Broad* or High Church. Carroll, as well as his father, would have been privy to significant differences of religious approach between Manning and Newman.* It was the view of Shane Leslie,* who wrote Manning's biography, that Carroll parodied Manning as the Red Queen. (See also Ronald Knox.*)

Manuscript of *Alice*   See *Alice's Adventures Under Ground.**

Maurice, John Frederick Denison (1805–72)   Author, educator and preacher, in his time Maurice was a deeply respected theologian and Christian Socialist. The views of F. D. Maurice, as he was known, on the reform of

Anglican Church doctrine were by and large approved of by Carroll. His political ideas as a Christian Socialist* and educator of working men were not. He believed in the education of women and working men, and called attention to the lot of the poor and underpaid.

We consider that Maurice may be parodied, in spite of the respect in which Carroll held him, as the Dormouse* at the Mad Tea-Party.* All appeared to share, but only the autocratic leader – the Hatter* – had any benefit from the arrangement. The Dormouse meanwhile was in 'hot water', that is in the teapot. Carroll's acquaintance with Maurice coincided with the time when he was adding the Tea-Party scene to the story, which is not in the *Under Ground* version. Mrs Maurice was one of the Hare* family. (See also Kingsley.*)

In 1840, Maurice was appointed Professor of English Literature and History at King's College, London, but was forced to resign – even the High Church Gladstone* could not sustain him – when attacked by Canon Jelf of Christ Church for questioning the Doctrine of Eternal Punishment. (See also Heresy* and Wilberforce.*) So timid and Dormouse-like was Maurice that he stood down as Principal of Queen's College, the pioneering girls' school he founded, fearing that his disgrace was such that he might compromise the institution.

As compensation he was given the Rectorship of St Peter's, Vere Street, which still stands, just north of Oxford Street. He remained active as a teacher at the Working Men's College, of which he was also a founder, throughout these difficulties. In 1862 Carroll stated in his diary that he went to Maurice's church. He liked and admired his preaching.

Carroll photographed Maurice, who looks very bent over and small, and corresponded with him on the issue of Benjamin Jowett. Carroll's own doubts about the doctrine of Eternal Punishment may have been reinforced by his companionship with Maurice. Carroll believed, with Maurice, that children are born innocent in the sight of God. The received view was that a child could not hope for salvation unless baptized into the Anglican Church. 'Child of the clear unclouded brow ...', was thought by Cardinal Newman* to epitomize Carroll's links with Pusey.* It also shows him in a clear light as a disciple of Maurice.

The simplicity with which Carroll willed that his funeral be ordered, and his practical support for Maurice during Holy Communion at Vere Street from 1863 until 1869, also show the influence exerted on Carroll by Maurice's reformed brand of High Anglicanism during the *Alice* years.

There is a personal ode to Maurice by Tennyson,* urging him to take refuge from his London-based detractors on the Isle of Wight* and stay with his infant godson, Tennyson's son Hallam. Tennyson described Maurice in that poem in terms with which Carroll certainly agreed. He called him 'one of the honest few'. Maurice settled in Cambridge and founded 'The Apostles'.

Millais, Sir John Everett (1829–96)   Painter and portraitist, Millais had been a founder member of the Pre-Raphaelite brotherhood together with D. G. Rossetti* and William Morris. His paintings, exhibited annually at the Royal Academy in London, were, in turn, admired and disliked by Carroll on his yearly visits there. To some Millais had, by the time *Wonderland* was published in 1865, sold out; exchanging his medievalism for a more commercial art. It was particularly when he painted children that Carroll admired his work.

Carroll photographed Millais, his wife Effie (previously married to Ruskin*) and their two daughters in a portrait where the photographer is outside a long casement window and the subjects sit on the windowsill. The girls are held and, as it were, framed by their parents. It is as tender a pose of a family group as any in the Victorian era, and avoids the sentimentality of Millais' own pictures of little girls, 'My First Sermon' and 'My Second Sermon' and 'Leisure Hours', for example. For Millais' 'My First Sermon' and its sequel, in which a little girl sleeps in her pew lost to the world as the sermon drones on, the model was one of Millais' little daughters whom Carroll photographed. This painting has long been recognized as the model for Tenniel's illustration of Alice in the railway carriage in *Looking-Glass*.

It is our view that *The Voice of the Lobster* is a spoof against the Pre-Raphaelites and Ruskin; Rossetti relished it. It was based on Carroll's observations on Varnishing Day at the Oxford Union and at the Royal Academy. 'You have baked me too brown' is probably a joke on Ford Maddox Brown (1821–93). On opening night, roving critics, including John Ruskin and Frederick Sandys – portrayed as sharks in Carroll's verse – terrified the preened and dressed-up Millais as a cowardly Lobster. In their early days the Pre-Raphaelites had preferred more Bohemian dress.

Miller, Jonathan Wolfe (1934–)   Actor; director of theatre, opera and film; writer; physician and neuropsychologist, Miller's black and white television film,* *Alice in Wonderland* (BBC, 1966) is one of the most interesting adaptations of *Wonderland* ever made. Miller brought his experience of professional involvement in the theatre and in psychology to the making of the film: it is the work of a polymath with strong interests in human character and the human mind, and an awareness that the book is a portrait of the grown-up world, as Empson* claimed, viewed from the perspective of a child.

Miller cast well-known actors and personalities. The documentary film cameraman, Dick Bush, had no previous experience of drama and this added an informal quality: John Gielgud – great nephew of Carroll's friend

Ellen Terry* and grandson of her talented elder sister Kate – played the Gryphon.* The writer and late convert to Roman Catholicism, editor of *Punch*, Malcolm Muggeridge, played the Mock Turtle* – the first time he had acted. His performance was outstanding. Leo McKern played the Ugly Duchess,* his face bearing a striking resemblance to the original fifteenth-century painting of the Duchess in the National Gallery. Miller cast two comedians, Peter Sellers (1925–80), whom he allowed to ad lib, as the King of Hearts* and Peter Cook as the Hatter.* Michael Redgrave was perhaps too tall to play the Caterpillar, but did it with aplomb. In fact, the casting of the adult characters in *Alice* has not been bettered. The music was composed to film by Ravi Shankar.

Alice was played by a girl of over ten years old, Anne–Marie Mallik. Miller was criticized for casting an actress three years older than the original character (see Age* of Alice) but his pensive, unpert Alice was a tranquil, intelligent foil to the agitation of her turbulent elders. *Alice* is a comic work. It is also a lyrical work. In the hands of Miller, actor and psychiatrist, *Alice* on film has a human scale, philosophical reach and irony that makes other films seem clod-hopping.

Mock Turtle Soup

A very substantial English soup, so called because it has a very gelatinous quality, not unlike turtle.

This is the description of Mock Turtle Soup by Theodora Fitzgibbon in *The Foods of the Western World* (1976). Turtle soup, its original, was one of the gastronomic delights of the best off in Victorian England, but the animals themselves were treated with considerable callousness. Its poor relation, made from a calf's head and shin of beef with Madeira or Marsala added, was a moderately priced substitute. Little wonder that Carroll's Mock Turtle weeps so much. (See also Liddon,* Soup* and Wilberforce.*)

Models   Carroll thought models were essential for drawing. However, Tenniel* refused to use them, saying to Carroll that he no more needed one than Carroll needed multiplication tables 'to work out a mathematical problem'. As a result, Carroll complained later of Tenniel to Gertrude Thomson,* with whom he struggled to photograph and draw nude models:

> He drew several pictures of 'Alice' entirely out of proportion – head decidedly too large and feet decidedly too small ...

History has not been so severe about Tenniel's work. To some extent, however, Carroll is right. Generally in *Wonderland*, Alice's head is rather large and her feet rather small. This is particularly so where she meets the Dodo.* Compare this, for example, with the illustration of Alice where she stands with the Duchess.* Here her head sits more naturally on her small shoulders. Most notably out of proportion are both her head and feet in relation to her body, which seems squashed when she stands between the prancing Gryphon* and the Mock Turtle.* In *Looking-Glass* the same problem of the over-large head is repeated where she stands with the Fawn. Generally in the *Looking-Glass* illustrations, the proportions are more harmonious, as demonstrated by the illustration of 'Wool and Water' where she straightens the White Queen's shawl and hair, or where she sits in the Railway Carriage* opposite the Goat.

While Carroll complained in private, what is extraordinary about the illustrations of Tenniel is the ability they have to convey the idea of Alice as a child who is equal to the combative individuals she meets on her way. She is conveyed as a child only slightly shorter than they are. She stands almost to the height of the Queen of Hearts, the Duchess, and the White Knight.* Only at the Croquet* Ground does she look significantly like a child, standing a good head below the Queen and other courtiers as befits a section of the story in which the King reproaches the Queen: 'Consider my dear, she is only a child!'

Carroll was foolish to irritate Tenniel, whose genius was not in exact modelling, but in the fluid creation of the human models taken from his own imagination and from his work as a political cartoonist which he turned into Carroll's characters.

Morals in *Alice* It is generally agreed that one of the strengths of the *Alice* books is that they are not 'moral tales'. In fact *Wonderland* parodied moralizing, when the Duchess told Alice that:

> "Everything's got a moral, if only you can find it."

Shortly after this, when Alice remarked that the croquet game was 'going on rather better now', the Duchess replied:

> "...and the moral of that is— 'Oh, 'tis love, 'tis love, that makes the world go round!'"

And so the Duchess continued ironically with various morals told in the form of proverbs, about birds of a feather flocking together and the more there is of mine, the less there is of yours. (See also T. H. Huxley.*)

And yet, when the reader comes to the end of *Wonderland*, rather than being a parody of moral tales, it seems supremely moral. W. H. Auden* said that Alice is the person we would all like to be: without losing her clarity, and by developing her perspicacity as her journeys progress, she remains inquisitive, polite and coping, and in that sense moral, in a world full of grotesques. By that view, *Alice* is the most moral of all tales.

Mouse's Tail/Tale   In *Under Ground* the Tail appeared thus:

In *Wonderland* it was changed, thus:

```
        " Fury  said  to
      a  mouse, That
          he   met   in   the
                house, 'Let
                  us  both go
                    to law: I
                    will prose-
                    cute you.—
                    Come,  I'll
                  take no de-
                nial:  We
              must have
            the  trial;
          For really
        this morn-
      ing I've
    nothing
    to  do.'
    Said the
      mouse to
        the  cur,
          'Such a
            trial, dear
              sir, With-
                no  jury
                or judge,
                  would
                  be wast-
                ing our
              breath.'
            'I'll be
          judge,
        I'll be
      jury,'
    said
    cun-
    ning
    old
    Fury:
    'I'll
      try
        the
          whole
          cause,
            and
            con-
          demn
            you to
    death'."
```

The differences between these two tails/tales – difficult pieces of type-
setting – are subtle. In the first tale the story was more specifically about a
cat, a dog and some mice. The second is more of a metaphor: the Mouse
said it was about its hatred of 'C and D'. This appears to be a clear reference
to the Canons and Dean of Christ Church* alias 'The House'. The Mouse
who has to deal, not with an unnamed cat, but with Fury, a cur who was
as arbitrary – 'no jury or judge' – as the D of the House, Dean Liddell.* The
arbitrary creature intends to condemn the poor mouse to death.

An anthology of 15 variants of the Mouse's tale was published by David
and Maxine Schaefer of the Lewis Carroll Society* of North America,

entitled *The Tale of the Mouse's Tail: The Journey of Lewis Carroll's Mouse's Tail Around the World and Through Computers* (1995).

Müller, Friedrich Max (1823–1900)   Oxford professor of linguistics, Müller had a remarkable intelligence and was a crucial figure in the development of Comparative Literature as a modern branch of study. Of all those at Oxford in Carroll's time who were interested in the nature of language, Müller was the most original and stimulating. Writing in *Jabberwocky* for August 1981, August Imholtz, Jr suggested that Müller, whom Carroll met at the Liddells, worked on dreams in Indian literature and that this may have stimulated Carroll's own interest. Carroll photographed Müller, a sign that he was significantly interested in him. Liddell relieved Müller of his teaching duties to do research on Sanskrit texts. In February 1876 Carroll published a squib* with the title *Professorship of Comparative Philology*, which ended his friendship with Müller. It was Max Müller who gave a dachshund to Julia Arnold. The dog attacked Carroll.

MILTON MILL

N is for ...

Nabokov, Vladimir Vladimirovitch (1899–1977)   After taking his degree at Kings College, Cambridge, Nabokov, from a distinguished emigré Russian family, moved to Berlin, where he published an avant-garde translation* of *Alice* in Russian in 1923, a prelude to his subsequent career as a novelist. He used the pseudonym 'Sirin'. After World War II, he was inspired by *Alice* to write the novel, *Lolita*. The epithet, 'nymphet', a reference to an ephemeral stage in the life-cycle of the dragonfly has, since the 1950s, been applied as a Nabokovian metaphor to heroines like Alice.

Natural History Museum (now the University Museum)   This still stands at Oxford,* situated between the older university and the suburbs of north Oxford. The Museum is a monument to the life sciences in the Victorian era and intersects with Carroll's and Alice Liddell's* worlds in a number of ways. It was originally proposed by Dr Henry Acland* with the support of John Ruskin* in May 1849. There was strong opposition from the High Church party and a great deal of debate about a suitable style. Various designs – Gothic, classical and what the magazine *The Builder* called 'Abominations' and 'The Order of Confusion' – were proposed. The one selected was Gothic and designed by the Irish architect, Benjamin Woodward.

In December 1854, the money was given by the University and it has been argued by Acland's biographer, J. B. Atlay, that Pusey* won round much of the opposition, who had considered it sacrilegious to build a science museum in a church style. Carroll certainly had fun with the whole event and, after it was over – the whole process took some ten years – wrote the gentle but

effective satire, the *Examination Statute* (1864) in which each line represents a letter of the alphabet,* followed by a revealing thumb-nail sketch of each of the parties concerned, ending:

> U's University, factiously splitting –
> V's the Vice-Chancellor, ceaselessly sitting.
> W's [Wall], by museum made frantic,
> X the expenditure grown quite gigantic.
> Y are the Young men, whom nobody thought about –
> Z is the Zeal that this victory brought about.

Wall was the University Treasurer, frantic because in the period when the Museum was being built, the overspend became enormous, sharply running down the funds that the University Press's sale of Bibles had put into the University's coffers.

The building is a fantasy of carving in metal and stone and a monument to Ruskin's ideals of handwork; but the carving cost a fortune and the high glass roof gave endless problems. It is our view that the glass roof and green houses and their chimney up which Bill the Lizard* is kicked ('The Rabbit Sends in A Little Bill') parody these problems, and that Acland behaved like the White Rabbit* throughout as he attempted to negotiate them. (See also 'Pat'.*)

We know that Carroll took Alice and other child*-friends to the Museum. The tunny fish skeleton that he photographed for Acland is still there and it was there that the famous British Association meeting between Huxley* and Wilberforce* took place in 1860. The Museum also houses Oxford's valuable claw of the Dodo,* with the extinct owner of which Carroll identified, clumsily 'restored' by Dr Acland.

Newman, Cardinal John Henry (1801–90)   Middle-aged when Carroll was an undergraduate, Newman had been converted to Roman Catholicism in 1845 a few years before Carroll arrived in Oxford.* His conversion, which he described in *Apologia pro Vita Sua* (1864) removed him from the Oxford University scene. He had been a tutor at Oriel College, a stone's throw from the Christ Church* Library and the Deanery garden.* From here he had participated actively in founding the Oxford Movement.*

With the help of both Anglican and Roman Catholic friends, Newman established a Roman Catholic retreat in a modest set of buildings at Littlemore, a village now absorbed into Oxford. This place of retreat and meditation is situated between the University and the Anglican Cuddesdon Theological College.*

The presence of Newman pervaded Carroll's Oxford and in our book, *The Red King's Dream*, we suggest that the White Queen was Carroll's parody of Newman, as seen from his widely-read writings. Throughout the *Alice* period, Newman was often talked about and many established Anglican families had members who were converts, including, most famously, close relatives of the Anglican bishop of Oxford, Samuel Wilberforce* himself.

It has been argued that Carroll's account of the two Queens* in *Looking-Glass* parallels the doctrinal differences between Newman and Manning. If so, it is all the more remarkable, for the book was written when few but Catholic insiders would have known of the clash between these two theologian converts.

It is not known what Newman thought of *Alice* but Carroll knew what Newman thought about 'An Easter Greeting to Every Child who loves *Alice*' and was flattered. He had sent out 20,000 copies of this 'Greeting' as a pamphlet with the 1876 copies of *Snark*. It was, wrote Newman, 'more likely to touch the hearts of old men than those [children] for whom it was intended'. The message was about death, and it inspired Newman to remember his own childhood. (See also John Keble,* Ronald Knox,* Shane Leslie* and F. D. Maurice.*)

Charles Kingsley,* in *Macmillan's Magazine*, accused Newman of not considering truth as a necessary virtue. Newman's *Apologia*, a passionate account of his conversion, was his answer. Oxford also came to the defence of its wayward son: Newman may have been a Catholic and a Cardinal of Rome, but at least he was a gentleman. The disapproval with which Kingsley's attack on this great man was viewed may be reflected in the Hatter's reappearance in *Looking-Glass*. He sits in gaol, with a ball and chain round his ankles. The loquacious Broad Church* Kingsley had gone too far in the press in the eyes of High Church England, as in the eyes of Carroll. Oxford never received nor forgave Charles Kingsley but, by the 1880s, welcomed Newman back as a distinguished visitor.

Newry, Viscount Newry and Morne, Earl of Kilmorey (n.d.)   Newry, one of the few Christ Church 'Tufts' with whom Carroll associated until he was befriended by Lord Salisbury (see Cecil*) shared Carroll's fascination with the theatre and became a playwright. Planning to hold a Ball at Christ Church in term time, Newry found that Dean Liddell* had banned it. Anne Clarke noted in her biography* that at this point Carroll, unlike the aristocratic Newry himself, fell into disfavour with Mrs Liddell* through guilt by association with this and others of Newry's extravagances.

Newry was one of three oarsmen Carroll preferred to invite on the river: the others were Duckworth* and Harcourt. The Dean and Mrs Liddell's rebuff to Newry and Carroll happened two weeks before Carroll first told Alice Liddell* the story on the river at Godstow on 4 July 1862. (See Golden Afternoon* and river Thames.*) By 25 June 1863, all appeared to have been forgiven and forgotten because Newry, Harcourt and Carroll rowed a four-oar boating party up to Nuneham, bearing the Dean, his wife and father and four Liddell girls, including Alice's sister Rhoda, who was allowed to go too. The Deanery party manned the stroke oar in rotation.

After he came down from Oxford, Lord Newry, who owned property near the Liddell's seaside home, Pen Morfa,* worked in the London theatre on occasion. Carroll saw Polly Terry* star in Newry's melodramatic adaptation of Alexander's Dumas' *The Danischeffs* at the Court Theatre in May 1883, in which, in spite of 'much agony and screaming', Carroll noted that Polly acted 'as sweetly as ever'.

Nonsense, Study of See Critics.*

Numbers in *Alice* The *Alice* stories are read by mathematicians, philosophers and logicians, but Carroll wrote *Alice* to amuse child readers. In the course of the stories – under the guise of naivety – he poked fun at the grown-up Victorian passion for fiscal and statistical enumeration. Carroll, a regular delegate to Statistical Section meetings of the British Association for the Advancement of Science, was aware of ways in which commercial and statistical matters were aired in all sectors of public life whether or not their application was logical or their discussion well-bred.

In *Wonderland*, some of the adults Alice met were more cost-conscious than polite. The price 10/6, ten shillings and sixpence, in current money 52.5 pence, was marked on Tenniel's* Hatter's* hat; the price of Father William's* box of ointment was declared by him to be 'five shillings the box' in the *Under Ground* version and one shilling in *Wonderland*.

Alice couldn't help smiling as she took out her memorandum-book, and worked the sum for him :

$$
\begin{array}{r}
3\,6\,5 \\
1 \\
\hline
3\,6\,4
\end{array}
$$

Humpty Dumpty took the book, and looked at it very carefully. " That *seems* to be done right——" he began.

" You're holding it upside down !" Alice interrupted.

In *Looking-Glass*, the numbers Alice happened on were more minute and also much larger than in *Wonderland* and a few *Looking-Glass* characters boast interminably about money. The ticket inspector's time was 'worth a thousand pounds a minute'. The patch of railway* property on which Alice started her ticketless train journey was 'worth a thousand pounds an inch', a reference to the inflated profits made by railway speculators. The Man in the White Paper suit exclaimed: 'Language is worth a thousand pounds a word!' (See Benjamin Disraeli* and Humpty Dumpty.*) If an hour, an inch and a word cost these characters a thousand pounds, how much did they cost on the other side of the Looking-Glass?

Besides disapproving of cupidity in Victorian public life, Carroll also disapproved of over-hearty public behaviour. The 'three cheers' beloved by undergraduates at sporting dinners were amplified to Alice's dismay by thirty times three toasts at her coronation banquet. Those were followed by the even more excessive ninety times nine, the rowdiness of the feast increasing by a square of itself. The last of numerous statistical claims made to Alice, by then a Queen in her own right, was the Red Queen's snub:

"'I'm five times as rich as you are, *and* five times as clever!"

Nuneham Courtney   Augustus George Vernon Harcourt (1834–1919) was a nephew of the owner of the stately home and grounds at Nuneham, William Harcourt, and a scientist friend of Carroll's. The house and the village are down river from Oxford* and Carroll rowed Alice and her sisters there on occasion, most famously on 17 June 1862. Thus Alice wrote:

A pair of sculls was always laid in the boat for us little girls to handle when being taught to row by our indulgent host ... I can remember what hard work it was rowing upstream from Nuneham, but this was nothing if we thought we were learning and getting on.

Vernon Harcourt was two years Carroll's junior and already a brilliant chemist when he rowed with Carroll: he was Lee's Reader in Chemistry at Christ Church* and, in 1863, was elected a Fellow of the Royal Society.

Carroll photographed him with three other scientists examining a fish skeleton at the Oxford Natural History Museum and helped Harcourt's wife set up her own photographic studio. Harcourt seconded Carroll as Curator of the Common Room (see Wine*) after the 'Bread and Butter'* row revealed the short-comings of Dean Liddell's* domestic management at Christ Church.

Nuneham Courtney is a Georgian mansion that sits on a bluff about two hundred yards from the Thames,* facing west and looking across Oxfordshire to the London railway* line, Radley and the Cotswolds. It was perhaps around Nuneham that Carroll set the Pool of Tears scene in *Under Ground*. (See 'Queer-Looking Party'.*)

The whole party moved along the river bank...the Dodo leading the way. After a time, the Dodo became impatient, and, leaving the Duck to bring up the rest of the party, moved on at a quicker pace with Alice, the Lory, and the Eaglet, and soon brought them to a little cottage, and there they sat snugly by the fire, wrapped up in blankets.

The boat-house where they sheltered is still there at Nuneham Courtney. House and grounds are now the Global Retreat Centre for the Brahma Kumar's World Spiritual University, but we had no difficulty getting permission to walk through the meadows to the Vernon Harcourt's pink-washed, disused, Swiss-chalet style boat-house, set back from the river bank.

NUNEHAM BRIDGE

O is for ...

Ordination   Carroll is often described as a 'clergyman'. He was a devout Anglican who was ordained deacon because he had to be. He took services from time to time and gave advice when called upon, but often in the capacity of friend or relative. Oxford undergraduates were compelled, in Carroll's time, to swear obedience to Anglican doctrine by subscribing to the Thirty Nine Articles, as were Oxford dons, who had to be ordained.

Under the Old Foundation of Christ Church,* the rules governing Carroll's tenure when he was made a Student, he should have been ordained Priest; that is be 'fully' ordained. Somehow Carroll sidled out of this. He was reprimanded by Dean Liddell* in October 1862 for not doing so and there was a threat that he could lose his Studentship and therefore his livelihood. It seems that Carroll was in the wrong. Equally it seems that the Dean was tolerant about such issues, more concerned with having able tutors in the college than with the form of their ordination. Carroll was seldom as charitable about the Dean.

Bishop Wilberforce* banned priests from going to the theatre. Had Carroll been a priest this restriction would have greatly altered his life. When he and Liddon* went to London, Carroll attended the theatre, Liddon did not. Carroll sometimes, but not always, wore clerical attire. It is probable that when he attended the theatre he doffed, rather than donned, it.

Owl   Edward Lear read the ballad of *The Owl and The Pussy Cat* in 1867 to J. A. Symond's little daughter, Janet, on the French Riviera resort of Cannes soon after he first wrote it. In a darker vein, Carroll's *Wonderland* equivalent was about an Owl and a Panther, not a pussy-cat. It parodied a poem by Isaac Watts described by Martin Gardner.* In Lear's poem, the Owl and the Pussy Cat were on their honeymoon. Carroll's Panther had a more terminal interest in the Owl.

Carroll's verse began 'I passed by his garden' and he released more lines for this poem from 1871 to 1886. By 1886, it had grown to 16 lines long. Isa Bowman,* his child-friend, recited the long version, under Carroll's tuition, for Henry Savile Clarke's stage version of *Alice*. Carroll had by then extended it so that the last four lines read:

> "When the pie was all finished, the Owl, as a boon,
> Was kindly permitted to pocket the spoon;
> While the Panther received knife and fork with a growl,
> And concluded the banquet by—"

The three ghost words seem to be: 'eating the Owl'!

We have connected the trusting Owl to William Morris and the hungry Panther to D. G. Rossetti,* who relished Carroll's nonsense verse in *Alice* as he read it in his sister, Christina's, presentation copy. Rossetti owed Carroll money for photographs he had commissioned but not paid for. Similarly, Morris and Rossetti's financial and personal relationships were known to Carroll to have been distinctly to Rossetti's advantage.

Oxford   While the colleges dominated the University (see Oxford University below), until the twentieth-century and the coming of the car industry to Oxford, the University dominated the city. This article describes the city, lists a chronology of events in Oxford, then gives an account of the University.

OXFORD CITY   The Oxford monastic settlement, which became St Frideswide's* and then Christ Church,* stood on a piece of raised ground just above marshy land. The first colleges developed in the Middle Ages. By the nineteenth century most employers were there to provide services for the University and by far the largest of them was the semi-autonomous University Press.

T. E. Kebbel in *The National Review* (1887) described his early days at Oxford at the time Carroll matriculated, 1851, as follows:

> We came straight from the woods and the meadows into the heart of the University, and found ourselves at once surrounded by its colleges and churches, without having passed through any intermediate zone of modern brick and mortar.

The painter, J. M. W. Turner (1775–1851) painted watercolours of Oxford which show Christ Church rising from rustic watermeadows. The sense of the remoteness of Oxford University was reinforced by its distance from London,* a long day's coach journey and still the best part of a day even after the railway arrived.

Once the traveller left the quadrangles of Oxford, the landscape, although more enclosed than in the sixteenth century, had changed little since the days when Christ Church was founded by Cardinal Wolsey. This landscape was part of Carroll's and Alice's experience; an idiom which lends character to the *Looking-Glass*, where battles are fought on a chessboard,* the landscape of old England. *Pleasant Spots Around Oxford* by Alfred Rimmer (*c.* 1860) evokes the rural idyll of Oxford in the mid–century. The steel engravings of haywains, of half-timbered mills, of goats grazing in the churchyards of ruined abbeys, of a punt moored by bulrushes, of the glassy river where cows wade, of village ponds and farm animals passing along cobbled village streets suggest how 'countrified' Carroll's Oxford still was when he wrote the *Alice* stories.

MAGDALEN TOWER AND BRIDGE

Gardner's Gazetteer for Oxford in 1852 put at the head of the city hierarchy the Chancellor of the University who was followed by University officers, the Heads and Fellows of the colleges and then, at the lowest rung of the hierarchy, the residents and professions in the city itself. This 'town' was entirely dominated by 'gown'. Oxford town was a city of tailors, brewers and butchers serving the colleges.

As the University grew, so the population of Oxford grew from 11,000 to 50,000 in the course of the nineteenth century. Because of overcrowding and inadequate public sanitation there were three major cholera outbreaks, the first in 1832, the second in 1849 and the third in 1854. During these dire visitations, Carroll was less active in assisting in the remedial measures than the Dean of Christ Church and his physician, Henry Wentworth Acland,* both prominent public health reformers. During outbreaks, most privileged children, like those of the Liddells and Aclands, were despatched to other parts of the country until the cholera had run its course.

A CHRONOLOGY OF SOME MORE IMPORTANT EVENTS IN OXFORD DURING CARROLL'S TIME

1849   Proposals were sought for a new building for the study and teaching of science,* the Natural History Museum.*

1850–2   The first Royal Commission was set up to enquire into the funding of an University Honours School in Natural Science.

1851–4   The University Galleries, which became the Ashmolean, were opened.

1851   Gas lighting was installed in part of the Radcliffe Infirmary.

1852   Birmingham and the north were connected to Oxford by railway.* Carroll came to Oxford as an undergraduate.

1853   Park Town suburb in North Oxford was laid out.

1854   The Oxford Act for the Reform of the University was supported by A. P. Stanley* with the assistance of H. G. Liddell.* The Hebdomadal Board became an elected Hebdomadal Council. Male dissenters were for the first time allowed to matriculate and take degrees. Commissions were set up to oversee reformed College Statutes. A major cholera epidemic struck the city.

1855–60   The Natural History Museum was opened under the aegis of Acland and Ruskin.* There was a crisis over its cost.

1858   The Christ Church Ordinance reviewed the stipends of the Students and increased their number. Salter Brothers was founded to run steamer trips up and down the Thames* and it was from this company that Carroll probably rented his boats for rowing expeditions.

1864　A new workhouse was opened in the Cowley Road, its purpose to cope with an increased number of poor and indigent in the city.

1865　The Oxford School of Art was founded. W. E. Gladstone* lost his seat for Oxford University to a Tory. The Great Western Railway, which ran the Oxford to London railway line, built a carriage works in Oxford. The GWR was the first large-scale industrial employer and rivalled the University Press in the numbers it employed. The plan to build the works was vigorously opposed by the University.

1867　The Christ Church, Oxford, Act re-ordered the distribution of power and emoluments as they had been organized at Christ Church from Tudor times. By extending the qualification for an elector, Disraeli* extended the franchise for the first time since 1832. A children's ward was added to the Radcliffe Infirmary and Bread Riots broke out.

1870　Keble* College was founded for High Church candidates. The Great Library Riot took place at Christ Church.

1871　Dons were allowed to marry and requirements for Ordination were relaxed.

1872　The secret ballot was introduced.

1875　Oxford High School for Girls was founded and supplied some of the students for the new women's halls (later the women's colleges) at Oxford.

1877　Colleges were taxed to provide the income for the Common University Fund.

1882　Death of Dr Pusey,* Carroll and his father's mentor. The end of the clerical majority on the Governing Body of Christ Church.

1884　The Oxford Dramatic Society was founded with encouragement from Benjamin Jowett.* The Franchise Act was extended again and tripled the electorate.

1885　St Hugh's College was founded for women undergraduates.

1890　The Oxford Electric Company began to provide some household and university electricity.

1893　The names of women candidates for degrees were first printed in the Oxford class lists. Death of Dr Jowett.

1898　The death of Carroll, four days before the death of Dean Liddell.

OXFORD UNIVERSITY   Any entry concerned with Oxford University may seem naive to those who know it. The following account is for those with an interest in Carroll who do not know Oxford. Most important, perhaps, is the distinction between the University and its colleges. In Oxford in Carroll's day, it was his college with which an individual identified with rather than with the University as a whole. Carroll was paid by his college, taught within his college and, because Christ Church considered itself paramount at Oxford, it was as a member of 'The House' that Carroll developed his Oxford academic and political identity.

Christ Church was not unique in viewing itself as the most important college in Oxford. Most of the others considered themselves so too, in different ways. The only University appointment Carroll held was the disciplinary role of Proctor. He did, however, from time to time attend the University parliaments (Congregation and Convocation*) and participated once in a debate on the topic of Professor Jowett's salary, attending, voting and press-campaigning, but not speaking, on the vexed question of laboratory vivisection* at Oxford.

These hard-fought issues were side skirmishes in the central debate of the day, that of University Reform, forced on Oxford and Cambridge* by successive Acts of Parliament from 1850 onwards. These effectively altered the balance of power between the colleges and the University. The teaching of science, originally centred on the Museum of Natural History, became a University rather than a college matter. Professorships were University appointments and new ones were created, though administrative appointments continued to be made at college level. Even today, when large central resources are needed for libraries and laboratories, most Oxford dons identify more strongly with their college than with their University.

Oxford Movement   With the end of the Stuart monarchy, Protestantism established itself comfortably in England. The essayist, Christopher Hussey, described the clergy of the eighteenth and early nineteenth centuries as living in 'slightly alcoholic slumber [after which], the Church aroused itself, and at Oxford of all places ...' He was referring to the sermon given by John Keble* in 1833, which claimed that the Church of England was *the* Apostolic Catholic Church, and that succession to the English monarchy was by Divine Right. What became known as the Oxford Movement was dedicated to revitalizing Anglican spiritual life. It tended towards a literal interpretation of the Scriptures and approval of the notion of eternal punishment for all not baptized into its fold. Key place was given to its own precise ritual and church discipline, a formalism known as Puseyism. It opposed the liberalizing tendencies of those, like Dean Liddell,* Dean Stanley* and Benjamin Jowett* at Oxford, who believed in toleration of other Anglican – even non-Anglican – sects or groups, thus opening the way for Roman Catholics, Dissenters and Jews, at the time banned, to attend and teach at the university and be elected to Parliament.

A central debate in the struggle for Christian truth in Carroll's Oxford was whether or not salvation in the life-to-come depended on one's beliefs on earth. While admitting the importance of acts of Christian charity, adherents of the Oxford Movement rejected the primitive socialist* doctrines proposed by Cambridge* reformers such as Charles Kingsley* and F. D. Maurice.* These advocated that the Church should help the poor and disadvantaged in society and that an intolerant High Anglican church would lose social and political credibility. (See also High Church,* Henry Manning,* J. H. Newman,* Edward Pusey* and Samuel Wilberforce.*)

Oysters In Carroll's time oysters were plentiful and comparatively cheap; they would have been consumed at Deanery* dinners, and inevitably Alice would have shown curiosity about whether they were alive. Oysters in Carroll's day were farmed in Whitstable, Rochester, Colchester, Milton, Faversham and Burnham in East Anglia as well as in Anglesey, North Wales, Ireland and Scotland. Substantial quantities of British oysters were also sent to Belgium and France to be fattened and sold. New discoveries of oyster beds – for example at Carroll's holiday haunt, Eastbourne – and new methods of transporting oysters were favourite topics for Victorian food writers.

Are oysters alive when they are eaten?

> 'A loaf of bread,' the Walrus said,
>   'Is what we chiefly need:
> Pepper and vinegar besides
>   Are very good indeed—
> Now, if you're ready, Oysters dear,
>   We can begin to feed.'

The trick played on the Oysters to get them to trot out of the sea for a chat, may be in part a reference to the beguiling, and in Carroll's view un-Christian, ideas of Walter Pater* and John Ruskin.* These aesthetes were beginning to teach Oxford undergraduates, the tempted oysters, the ideal of 'Art for Art's sake'. The oldest, and presumably wisest, Oyster did not want to leave its oyster-bed. But:

> ... four young Oysters hurried up,
>   All eager for a treat:
> Their coats were brushed, their faces washed,
>   Their shoes were clean and neat—
> And this was odd, because, you know,
>   They hadn't any feet.

'I weep for you', the Walrus* said. To no avail: he and the Carpenter* ate all the Oysters. The gullible souls of the undergraduates had been engulfed by the doctrine of hedonism.

P is for ...

Panther   See Owl.*

Parliamentary Representation   This touched Carroll sequentially. 1832, the year of his birth, was the year of the Great Reform Bill which, with the coming of the railways, ushered in the Victorian Age. He was politically active in two more crucial Acts to extend the franchise, that of 1867 and 1884. Among the constitutional anachronisms that remained were the existence of university seats in Parliament, Oxford having three. For these, graduates of the University elected their own MPs. In *The Red King's Dream*,* we have suggested that the *Looking-Glass* story of the Lion and the Unicorn was in part a spoof on the three-way race held at Oxford in 1865. Alice was asked to cut the cake while the Lion and the Unicorn looked on. The Unicorn became petulant when she cut only one third of the plum cake as its share, not enough to allow it to wear the Crown. Carroll's ironical view of the electoral process can also be inferred from the scene where the Dodo* organizes a Caucus-race.

Carroll published a number of pamphlets about voting reform. The one of 1873 suggested how to improve voting procedure at Christ Church. Later his interest moved beyond Oxford to the question of how to apportion votes at general elections. One such pamphlet was entitled *The Principles of Parliamentary Representation*. He published it on Guy Fawkes' Day, 1884 under his own name, but signed another letter from the same period with the pen-name 'Dynamite'. This pamphlet claimed that proportional representation would give fairer results as far as the electorate was concerned than the present 'first past the post' system. (See also Anonymity.*)

'Pat'   This was a Victorian nickname for Irish labourers who came to the north-west of England in search of work. Many landed in Liverpool, only 15 miles from Daresbury,* Carroll's first home. His experience of 'Pats' began when he heard his father preach to them from a floating barge as they worked on the canals near the family parsonage (See Introduction and Charles Lutwidge Dodgson.*)

A character with the name 'Pat' appeared in *Alice* in 'The Rabbit Sends in a Little Bill'. First, the Rabbit mistook Alice for the maid. Then Alice, grown huge, found herself trapped in the Rabbit's little house. The Rabbit ordered 'Pat' to remove her, amid the sound of breaking glass. 'Pat' warned that what was stuck in the window of the Rabbit's House was an arm, which it called, in stage Irish, an 'arrum'.

We have drawn a parallel between this scene and episodes which occured during the building of the Natural History Museum,* which cost the University 'an arm and a leg'. The building was built by Irish stone-masons and designed by Irish craftsmen-architects from Dublin recommended by John Ruskin.* It was the freestyle Gothic carving of the O'Shea brothers and the problems incurred while erecting the steel and glass roof over the vault of the museum that caused a stop to be put to all this artistry. In the interest of science,* Dr Acland* had run up no 'little bill', but a very big one indeed.

Pater, Walter (1839–94)   Pater was an art historian and aesthete, and Carroll's junior by a few years. The popularity of his lectures and his belief in 'Art for Art's sake' marked a trend at Oxford towards a secular world-view. It is our view that the Walrus*-moustache-wearing Pater, who was known to the undergraduates at Brasenose as 'Old Mortality in Cap and Gown', may be parodied in the ballad about the untrustworthy Walrus and the Carpenter* which lured the Oysters,* the undergraduates, into temptation:

> 'O Oysters,' said the Carpenter,
>   'You've had a pleasant run!
> Shall we be trotting home again?'
>   But answer came there none—
> And this was scarcely odd, because
>   They'd eaten every one.

Pen Morfa   This was the name of the North Wales villa built by Dean Liddell* to house his family during the Long Vacation from Oxford. It is an example of the Dean's vanity at its worst. It was built in a fantastic style with jutting-out gable windows and high pinnacles and is inappropriately placed on the shore of a beautiful bay. With no regard for the landscape, it dominates the originally idyllic bay on the inland side of the Great Orme's Head, which juts out into the Irish Sea. On this dramatic grassy promontory, W. E. Gladstone,* in the company of Alice Liddell* and her father, lost his head to vertigo and had to be guided back to terra firma with his eyes shut.

After Carroll no longer called on them, the young portraitist, William Blake Richmond (1842–1921) painted the three Liddell girls sitting together on the Great Orme's Head. Carroll found his rendering of Alice to be 'not quite natural'.

Did Carroll visit Pen Morfa? Welsh Tourist Board enthusiasts have it that the *Alice* stories were written there, and that is the claim on a plaque in front of the house, now further uglified with mock-Tudor extensions. The only evidence that Carroll did visit comes from a print in the album* given to Alice by Carroll, showing unidentified girls in crinolines grouped around the house: it is one of several photographs of North Wales buildings in the album and is probably not a Carroll photograph.

Photographic Society of London   Carroll had four photographs selected for the Society's 1858 exhibition. One of these was 'Little Red Riding Hood' with Agnes Weld, Tennyson's* niece, shown wearing a cape. He used the photograph as his means of introduction to the Tennysons. After this, he did not exhibit publicly again, and took few orders or commissions, with the exception of those he took from Christina Rossetti* and her brother, and the Anglican writer, Charlotte Mary Yonge.* (See also Albums,* Owl* and Photography.*)

Photography   Examples of Carroll's photographs occur in many anthologies of Victorian photography, but a full collection is hard to come by. *Lewis Carroll: Photographs and Letters to Child-Friends* (1975) edited by Guido Almansi is one of the best of these. The notes are by Helmut Gernsheim,* whose *Lewis Carroll: Photographer* is essential reading for anyone interested in the subject. Morton Cohen's* books about Carroll include interesting examples of Carroll's photographs in good offset reproduction.

Carroll bought his first camera in 1856 when he was 24. He had started to take photographs with his uncle, Skeffington Lutwidge.* Carroll's first photographs were of Christ Church* buildings. The prints are lost but it would appear that children were put into these. Initially only outdoor exposures were within Carroll's range of competence and he worked with the help of his friend, Reginald Southey.* Soon improvement in his ability to judge light values, and faster-working chemicals, made it possible for Carroll to take photographs in his rooms, converted to a studio, and with an ever expanding dressing-up and prop box. The Liddell* children became the subjects of which he was fondest and it was Alice of whom he was fondest of all. Even as a child of 5 and 6, she had an ability as a model,* the wit to understand the overall poses and facial (see Faces*) expressions that Carroll wanted from her. Carroll photographed her with her sisters and alone, with a ukulele, holding a bunch of cherries, as a beggar maid, asleep, and sitting in profile. To help his models to hold expressions for a minute or longer, Carroll would tell stories. According to Alice (*Cornhill Magazine* July 1932) he told her many droll and fantastic stories. Some of them later appeared in *Alice*.

Carroll had an ability to use natural light sources to shine into a face and show its humanity so that he became, for all the clutter of costumes and decor that he sometimes used, a very sympathetic portraitist. Carroll's photographs of his sisters in their hooped skirts in the Rectory at Croft,* lit only by an east window, deserve to be placed among the masterpieces of Victorian photographic lighting.

His portraits of adults need to be taken seriously. Where comparisons are made with photographs of the same sitter by other photographers, the compassion and truthfulness of Carroll's portraits are evident. Among great Victorian contemporaries he photographed were Huxley,* Tennyson,* Ruskin,* Bishop Wilberforce,* Dean Stanley,* F. D. Maurice* and George MacDonald.*

One family Carroll courted at the time he was about to publish *Wonderland* was the Rossetti* family. An order Carroll fulfilled was found by Helmut Gernsheim in a letter written in about 1864 to Lewis Carroll by Christina Rossetti, to whom he sent a complimentary copy of *Alice* bound in vellum. The list of 50 Carroll prints which Christina ordered includes some photographed in her brother's garden in Chelsea, 24 copies of photographs of her sister, 9 copies of a close up of her mother, and 2 of Alphonse Legros, the painter and intimate of James McNeill Whistler. She ordered one copy of a portrait of her suitor, Charles B. Cayley and three copies of a photograph of Dante Gabriel Rossetti playing chess with his mother (now missing). Two large ovals of him on his own, holding a wideawake hat show him looking dangerously Panther-like (see Owl*). Carroll's photographs of drawings by Rossetti included three copies of a pastel sketch he made of his late wife, Dr Acland's* Oxford patient, Lizzie Siddal (d. 1862).

In addition to his official photographs of children and adults, from 1867, aged 35, when Alice was 15 and no longer a child-friend, Carroll photographed children in a pose for which he used the French phrase for undressed, '*sans habillement*'. His first child sitter of this kind was Beatrice Latham. Later he approached the illustrator of fairies who drew naked children as models for these. She was Gertrude Thomson.* Miss Thomson's drawings for stories and cards were hardly bundles of fun, but they had about them a cherubic insouciance which he liked. Obligingly her publisher put him in touch with Miss Thomson at Christmas 1878. To her he expressed his views as to the slim ankles of upper class girls and on the merits of back as opposed to front views.

Only four of Carroll's nude studies survive, three so overpainted as to belong more to the genre of Gertrude Thomson's drawings. One is an image of Evelyn Hatch,* lying with her body facing the camera, her hands behind her head. These images are in the Rosenbach Museum in Philadelphia and have been reproduced on several occasions in works of Morton Cohen. Although many have found these images disquieting, it was Evelyn Hatch whom Carroll helped with fees at art school when her father died and it was she who edited Carroll's letters to child*-friends. (See also Albums,* Julia Margaret Cameron,* Collodion* and Spencer-Stanhope.*)

Pig Baby   When Alice visited the Ugly Duchess,* the Duchess was:

> ...singing a sort of lullaby to it...and giving it a violent shake at the end of every line:—
>> "Speak roughly to your little boy,
>>   And beat him when he sneezes;
>> He only does it to annoy,
>>   Because he knows it teases."

At the end of the next verse she gave – or rather flung – the baby to Alice. Alice caught it, nursed it and took it into the open air because, she thought, 'they're sure to kill it in a day or two'. Then she found that it had changed.

> The baby grunted again, and Alice looked very anxiously into its face to see what was the matter with it. There could be no doubt that it had a *very* turn-up nose, much more like a snout than a real nose; also its eyes were getting extremely small for a baby...

William Empson* was the first to note that evolution was shown running backwards until Alice could let the creature run off into the woods to fend for itself.

Frankie Morris, writing in *Jabberwocky* (Autumn 1985) suggested that the item was based on a mock christening of a pig performed by the Duchess of Buckingham to cheer up King James I, an idea that backfired when the king released the animal from its swaddling clothes. It turned out that he hated pigs.

Carroll liked the baby-turned-pig. He had Alice holding it embossed in gold on the red front cover of *Wonderland* and in 'The Wonderland Postage-Stamp Case' in 1888. The case contained twelve pockets for postage stamps of different values and two pictorial 'Surprises' (pictures of Alice from

Wonderland). The price of this item, which included the Pig-Baby, was '1 shilling, post-free 13d' or one shilling and one penny.

Pigeon   Alice's neck was serpentine by the time she met the Pigeon in the tree-top in *Wonderland* and the pigeon feared that she was a serpent in pursuit of eggs.* In trying to explain the difference between a girl and a serpent, she explained that girls liked their eggs boiled, whereas serpents ate them raw. The long-necked Alice was confronted by a key Darwinian species in the tree-top. At just this period, the last breeding pairs of wild Passenger Pigeons vanished, following the Dodo* into extinction.

Poets Laureate   Carroll parodied Tennyson,* the Poet Laureate when he wrote *Alice*. The parodies occurred in 'The Garden of Live Flowers'* and elsewhere. He parodied Wordsworth, who preceded Tennyson as Poet Laureate, in the song of the 'Aged Aged Man',* based on Wordsworth's 'The Leech-gatherer'. He also parodied Robert Southey, who preceded Wordsworth as Poet Laureate. 'Old Father William'* came out 'all wrong' when Alice recited it and was a parody of Southey's original. Carroll did not care whether his sources were recognized. He found the originals hackneyed and lacking in logic. That Carroll should have been given a memorial in Poets' Corner in Westminster Abbey in 1982 (see Sites*) would possibly have flattered him more than any other approbation, except the approval of child*-friends.

Prayers   At the centennial of his birth, one of Carroll's clerical colleagues recalled that he sometimes prayed so intensely that he failed to notice that the Cathedral congregation had dispersed. He recorded his prayers in his Diaries,* writing notes of guilt and self-recrimination which became acute as he saw each New Year in. Henry Parry Liddon* acted as Carroll's personal confessor. The confessional mode was the Puseyite style of prayer. Carroll's self-recriminatory prayers were edited out of the Lancelyn Green edition of the *Diaries*. Morton Cohen's* biography redresses the balance. (See Preaching.*)

Preaching and Sermons   Although he frequently commented on sermons he had heard, the extent to which Carroll himself preached is not entirely clear. Reports of the extent of his speech defect, his stammer,* are inconsistent, as are reports about whether it came more under his control later in life. It would seem that he preached throughout his life, both at the University and away from it, at Croft*, Guildford* and Eastbourne;* but reluctantly. On occasion at Eastbourne he preached to children. At Christ Church,* late in his life, he organized services for the college servants, to whom he otherwise grumbled about the food and drink in Hall (see Bread and Butter* and Diet.*) Selwyn Goodacre, writing in *Jabberwocky* (Summer 1993) noted that Carroll used notes as a prompt, not a written text. Carroll also used his visual imagination to prevent himself from floundering: he would imagine his prompt notes unfurling in his mind's eye as he struggled to complete his sermon. The arguments in a sermon had to be clear and relevant and individuals like Carroll and W. E. Gladstone* might sample and judge up to three sermons by one preacher on a single Sunday.

Carroll, who believed children were 'innocent in the eyes of God', is also known to have told what he called 'sermon stories' to servants and to children in Oxford, Eastbourne and Guildford, as well as in London parishes and in private homes before and after he wrote *Alice*. He felt that such improving stories, printed and taken by a child into church to read, might prevent children from being bored while grown-up sermons were delivered; an unorthodox compromise by the stern standards of the day. Carroll's sermon stories were composed around a single tale. He set out notes for his own reference to such a story in little blocks reading downwards, believing that the momentum of his thoughts as he worked through these would prevent him from stammering. One child-actress whose religious education had been neglected was Florence Ada White (n.d.), 'Florrie', who worked under the stage name of 'Marjorie Chetwynd' and appeared in theatres along the Sussex coast. Her family were enthusiastic to develop her stage career but she had never heard of the Christian parables.

Sermon-stories are concealed in both *Alice* tales. At the end of *Wonderland*, Alice's older sister reflects on her dream and concludes that her children and their descendants will be made happy for ever and ever when they in turn come to hear it. In *Looking-Glass*, Alice embraces the lovely fawn which skips away from her, and holds out her hand for a scented rush which constantly eludes her. The promise of happiness at the end of *Wonderland* has shifted to a *Looking-Glass* regret that happiness is unobtainable. By such tokens the *Alice* stories can be seen as Carroll's best known sermon-stories. (See also Wasp in a Wig.*)

Pre-Raphaelites, The   For Carroll and the Pre-Raphaelites see Critics,* Combe,* Millais* and Rossetti.*

Prickett, Mary   See Governesses.*

The Prince of Wales Albert Edward, 'Bertie', later Edward VII (1841–1910)   For a short time, the Prince of Wales was an undergraduate at Christ Church,* where Queen Victoria placed him in the spiritual and moral care of Acland,* Stanley* and Liddell.* Carroll approved of none of these spiritual guardians. To make things worse, when he applied to photograph the Prince, he failed to penetrate the barriers the Prince erected against him. Carroll lived on in unfulfilled hopes, for on 16 June 1863, on a subsequent royal occasion at Christ Church, Carroll wondered forlornly whether the Prince had not recognized him when he stood near him in a crowd.

Prout, Thomas Jones (1824–1909)   Carroll's fellow Student and fellow conspirator against the Dean at Christ Church.* Prout, unlike Carroll, was a Third-Class, not a First-Class, Man, and a mountaineer. It was Prout who led the Christ Church Students against Dean Liddell* in the struggle for more rights, salaries commensurate with those at other colleges.

Prout had been at Westminster School, where Dean Liddell taught him. Carroll photographed him and backed his every move from behind the scenes in the campaign against the Christ Church Canons and Dean from 1857–67. Many dons shunned Prout because of his daring and his poor scholastic achievement. He and Carroll remained friends long after Prout became

Vicar of Binsey, outside Oxford. Carroll agreed to stand in for him to give a sermon in his absence on 4 June 1881. We proposed in *The Red King's Dream* that the complaints against the Dean and Canons which Prout spearheaded are to be located at every bend of the Mouse's Tail.*

Punch   Also known as *The London Charivari*, *Punch* was the leading comic paper in Britain for nearly a century. Founded in 1841, it was inspired by Philippon's more radical *Charivari* published in Paris. So strong was the impression made by weekly *Punch* cartoons of politicians, bishops, university leaders and royalty, that they established most people's ideas of the Victorians. *Punch* would have been lying on the table in Carroll's room; he cut out his favourite cartoons and pasted them into a scrap book which Alice Liddell* remembered him showing to children who visited his rooms.

Of members of the *Punch* staff whom Carroll met and corresponded with, the most significant was the playwright, Tom Taylor,* contributor and later editor. Carroll photographed Taylor and attended his plays and, most important of all, Taylor introduced Carroll to John Tenniel.* The style of *Punch* cartoons, showing part human, part animal figures (see Zoomorphs*) set its stamp on *Alice*. Carroll made more than one anyonymous contribution to *Punch*, and it may be that there are more to be discovered.

Punctuation in *Alice*   Carroll's nephew and biographer, Stuart Collingwood* noted that Carroll's use of italics was 'a marked feature'. He wrote in the 'Preface' to his biography of Carroll:

> ... it will be noticed that Italics have been somewhat freely employed to represent the words which [my uncle] underlined. The use of Italics was so marked a feature of his literary style, that ... without their aid the rhetorical effect which he always strove to produce, would have been seriously marred.

A glance through *Alice* shows that Carroll used italics on almost every page and often several times on a page. His use of italics is only exceeded by his use of exclamation marks, mainly in dialogue.

All this gives the reader of the book, when reading aloud, a sense of having cue marks, like emphases in a vocal musical score. His use of 'dashes', viz — , of varying lengths was also unusual, although not unique – Laurence Sterne, the eighteenth-century novelist, also employed the device. Sometimes Carroll used them as parentheses, sometimes to show that a speech has been interrupted. In another instance, when Humpty Dumpty* sat on the wall and spoke to *Alice*, dashes show his pauses, not interruptions, as he mused:

> "...Why, if ever I *did* fall off—which there's no chance of—but *if* I did—" Here he pursed up his lips...

"It sounds like a horse," Alice thought to herself. And an extremely small voice, close to her ear, said, "You might make a joke on that——something about 'horse' and 'hoarse,' you know."

Then a very gentle voice in the distance said "She must be labelled 'Lass, with care,' you know——"

And after that other voices went on ("What a number of people there are . in the carriage!" thought Alice), saying "She must go by post, as she's got a head on her——" "She must be **sent** as a message by the telegraph——" "She must draw the train herself the rest of the way——," and so on.

The influence of the punctuation of the Psalms in the Book of Common Prayer was great on many Victorian writers (see also Bible*) and Carroll, so aware of rhetorical effect in *Alice*, probably punctuated more than his contemporaries. When he needed to punctuate a sentence with a stop stronger than a comma but less than a full stop, he used a colon, placing it where most writers today would use a semi-colon. He used brackets to suggest *sotto voce*, as an aside by the reader, or to give an occasional editorial comment. Here Alice struggled with the proportions of the plum-cake she was expected to slice:

"It's very provoking!" she said, in reply to the Lion (she was getting quite used to be called 'the Monster'). "I've cut several slices already, but they always join on again!"

Finally, Carroll employed three lines of asterisks in his own particular way. Rather than using a single line, thus

      ★   ★   ★

to signify a change of pace, he used three lines — in *Wonderland* to signify a change in Alice's state, and in *Looking-Glass* to signify a move to a new part of the chessboard:

Such directions work like a 'fade out' in a film, and serve to show a different pace from a jump cut; another example of Carroll's visual conception of texts.

In July 1990, European and American, but not many English academics gathered in the city of Urbino in Italy to present papers for the conference '*La Linguistica di Alice*'. This then became a book published in English: *Semiotics and Linguistics in Alice's Worlds*. It was in the last cited of these papers, 'Alice's Omissions', by the Turin-based commentator on linguistics, Carla Marello, that the discussion of 'and' in Alice came up. She said that as 'an ellipses hunter I am very sensitive to the use of *and, but, or*'.

These sensitivities exercise all writers, newspaper journalists and book editors. Carla Marello suggested that Carroll used 'and' in part to capture 'children's ways of narrating'. She suggested, too, that an initial 'and' served to negotiate role changes in Carroll's *Alice* because:

> he didn't want to maintain really separated what Alice thinks from what she actually says and sometimes from what Carroll/the narrator thinks of what she says.

For example, Carroll used the initial 'and' to shift voice when the Dodo* explained the Caucus-race to Alice. Here the narrative shifted from the Dodo talking to Alice in her dream, to the narrator, Carroll, whom we, outside the narrative, now know to be the Dodo:

> "Why", said the Dodo, "the best way to explain it is to do it." (*And* [our italics], as you might like to try the thing yourself, some winter day, I will tell you how the Dodo managed it.)

Dr Marello sought out Italian translations* of *Alice* which she considered gave Carroll's 'and' its intended weight. She concluded that no translator should 'try filling what Carroll left empty'.

Another instance of the care which Carroll took over the punctuation marks and pauses in his narrative is his use of the exclamation point. An example is Alice's monologue about falling.*

"Well!" thought Alice to herself, "after such a fall as this, I shall think nothing of tumbling down stairs! How brave they'll all think me at home! Why, I woudn't say anything about it, even if I fell off the top of the house!" [perhaps another reference to Christ Church].

Exclamation marks were used occasionally by Carroll as a stage direction, as if he had in mind children reading the text aloud. (See Recitation.*)

Shortly after the conference in Urbino in 1990, Julian Barnes, who is as at home in France or Italy as in England, suggested that European scholarship had begun to bring new perspectives to *Alice*:

Peut-être est-il [Lewis Carroll] si mêlé à la culture anglo-saxonne qu'il nous est difficile, pour nous Anglais, de le voir avec un oeil neuf. Et il est possible que les traductions révèlent plus clairement les structures et l'étrangeté de l'oeuvre.

[Perhaps (Lewis Carroll's *Alice* text) is so closely intertwined with Anglo-Saxon culture that it is hard for the English to see it with fresh eyes. And it is possible that translations reveal more clearly the structure and strangeness of his work.]

(See also Gattégno.*)

Pusey, Edward Bouverie (1800–82)   Canon of Christ Church,* Pusey was a theologian whose plump, smiling, silver-haired aspect in Carroll's benign studio photograph of him in old age, suggests that he might better have belonged to eighteenth-century Oxford. There is a familiarity in his look which suggests friendship between the photographer and his much senior subject.

Dr Pusey's religious concern about the spread of liberalism in the Church of England had placed him in the forefront of the Oxford Movement.* Finding a place at Oxford depended to some extent on having a sponsor. As a friend of Carroll's father from Christ Church days – they were born in the same year – Dr Pusey found rooms for Carroll in the college. The tendency of the college was to favour the sons of House* men. Further, Carroll's academic ability endeared him to this venerable old theological author of some of the most inspiring Tracts of the Oxford Movement.

The Studentships at Christ Church were in the gift of the Dean and Canons by rotation, and Pusey nominated Carroll on the assumption that he would become a priest, which he did not. This Carroll did not consider a breach of contract. Of all the fighters for High Church* causes in Oxford, Pusey was the most redoubtable. He had been made a Canon of Christ Church and Regius Professor of Hebrew when he was 28, in the year that marked the founding of the Oxford Movement. He was suspended for heresy* when the then Bishop of Oxford considered a sermon of his too strong for the University Church. As though he had not learned his lesson, Pusey in turn became a key figure in the attempt to have Benjamin Jowett* and F. D. Maurice* removed from their academic posts.

The suspension of Pusey led to 18,000 copies of his sermon being sold in pamphlet form. His power was such that when the Prince of Wales* suggested that Charles Kingsley* should be given an Oxford degree, the rumour that Pusey would oppose this was enough to make the Prince step down. Pusey, unlike Queen Victoria* and the Prince, considered scenes in Kingsley's *Hypatia* (1853) blasphemous. He also considered that Oxford should only exist essentially for the training clergy, who should, of course, become High Church clergy. Pusey's connections in the University were the more powerful because his sister was married to Dr Cotton, the Vice Chancellor, one of Jowett's chief persecutors.

Carroll's references to Pusey in his diaries* are cursory, and there are no extant letters between them. Pusey had opposed the appointment of Liddell* to Christ Church, and Carroll followed him to the letter in his antagonism. It would be unfair to say that Carroll was in Pusey's shadow, but he tended to share Pusey's view on most issues, except that where Pusey tended to be certain, Carroll often remained uncertain. Pusey's character and fluffy white hair suggest the woolly old Sheep with her many knitting needles which obliged Alice to row her on the river where the waters were deep and dark and contained, below their surface, many mysteries.

Q is for ...

Quadrille, Lobster   See Dance.*

Queen of England   See Victoria Regina.*

Queens in *Alice*   The three Queens, Red, White and Queen of Hearts, together with the Duchess*, are the only female characters in *Alice* besides the heroine. While there are many irrational characters in the books, the

Queen of Hearts is the most violent, wanting all and sundry beheaded on whim. We have suggested that she may be inspired by the spectacle, familiar to Carroll, of Mrs Liddell* ordering everyone about when preparations were not quite complete for a croquet match. The Queen of Hearts dominated the King, remaining uninterested in the witness' agendas as evidence* was presented in Court.

The *Looking-Glass* Queens also have important roles, one rushing about and imperious, the other befuddled. After subjecting Alice to some royal Looking-Glass lessons,* they 'queen' her. And so the three Queens remain until, in the strangest of all scenes, the White Queen becomes a leg of mutton that drowns in the soup tureen. (See Leslie,* Manning,* Newman* and Religious Doubts.*)

Queen's English It seems appropriate to speculate how *Alice* might have sounded when Carroll spoke or read the stories. English became more homogenized during the nineteenth century and there were fewer and fewer people connected to university life who spoke with regional accents. W. E. Gladstone* was one of them and Edison's short recording of Gladstone's voice still exists. He spoke with a northern accent. Tennyson,* too, had a country accent until his dying day – to modern ears it would sound like Yorkshire but it was from his native Lincolnshire.

By 1865, speaking with a 'received pronunciation' was the norm in a place like Christ Church. This meant speaking with rather a flourish in a manner that would be considered affected today. Prince Albert never mastered this 'upper class' accent, his thinking language being German. Carroll may have mastered it, quickly dropping vestiges of an accent from the north-west during his miserable public school years as a pupil of Rugby. The number of underlined words, emphasized words, in *Alice* and his letters shows the importance he attached to a phonetic component in the way he wrote. (See Punctuation.*) One clue about how Carroll sounded came from the novelist, Aldous Huxley (1894–1963). His recollections of Carrollian Oxford were written in 1945 when he was working for Walt Disney* on a script, for a film project that was never completed, that was to mingle Tenniel's* *Alice* drawings with a real-life account of Carroll's Oxford* life.

Huxley's mother, Julia Arnold* was a favourite model and child*-friend of Carroll. In his interview, Aldous Huxley said, in an accent that by today's standards was drawly, patrician and emphatic in odd ways:

> Unless my ear and memory greatly deceive me, the way I speak is practically identical with the way my mother and her brothers and sisters spoke.

Having declared Carroll's quarrels with Liberal Oxford too obscure to interest people, Huxley explained on the sleeve of a record of his own voice:

> Language is perpetually changing: the cultivated English I listened to as a child is not the same as the cultivated English spoken by young men and women today. But within the general flux, there are islands of linguistic conservatism; and when I listen to myself objectively from outside, I perceive that I am one of these islands. In the Oxford of Jowett and Lewis Carroll, the Oxford in which my mother was brought up, how did people speak the Queen's English? I can answer with a considerable degree of confidence that they spoke almost exactly as I do. These recordings are ... documents from the 'Seventies and 'Eighties of the last century.

Oxford English, like the swans on the River Thames,* belonged to the Queen. The Huxleys and Arnolds were her speech-bearers, and spoke Alice's and *Alice's* English. Recently we met Aldous Huxley's only son, Matthew, outside Washington, DC. He has lived in America for almost all of his life. He spoke with an upper-class English accent which we had not heard since the 1950s. He, too, was 'an island of linguistic conservatism' in a Maryland suburb. It was as if we heard the voice of Lewis Carroll, a 'la-di-da' voice that has snobbish associations, but which is also a musical way of speaking the language, a vestige of the confident and courteous age of the old Queen.

'Queer-Looking Party' Carroll, proper in dress and comportment; an orderly man who liked a meticulous timetable, still managed to cope with some disarray. Anyone fond of walks and expeditions with children in the damp English countryside has to be flexible and it is possible that the rigid side of Carroll's character has been over-emphasized. Taking children on river expeditions meant, inevitably, that they have to pee, probably quarrel over who is to row and who gets which cake, are rained on and stung by insects and nettles.

The wettest 'Party' in *Alice* emerged, led by Alice, from the Pool of Tears at the beginning of Chapter III of *Under Ground* and *Wonderland*. Its members were a Duck, a Dodo,* a Lory, an Eaglet, a Mouse with a Long Tail,* some unnamed animals and various large and small birds. A magpie and her daughter, an old crab and hers, and a canary and her children were described in the text. Not all were illustrated. All except for the Dodo (an extinct flightless bird) were real animals, not heraldic beasts or fantasy creatures.

The creatures in the party were 'dripping wet, cross and uncomfortable'. Alice was Alice Liddell,* behaving like a lady, The Duck was Duckworth,* the Dodo was Dodgson, the Lory (a pretty parrot from the Deanery's natural history book) was Lorina, the Eaglet was little Edith. The pompous Mouse has been thought to be Alice's patient governess,* Miss Prickett, but that may be too obvious an identification given the complexities of Carroll's methods of concealment in satire. However, so near the beginning of *Under Ground* and *Wonderland* is this episode, that it may suggest the way that Carroll's mind was working between fantasy and real worlds; how the handle Carroll used to unlock the window into children's minds and sense of humour was the handle of reality, in this case a parody of creationism. They would not have known the theory, but they would have seen the specimens when he took them to museums.

A monkey and its wife dominated Carroll's *Under Ground* illustrations of this scene; and a single, mournful-looking monkey also found its way into Tenniel's* *Wonderland* illustrations. Tenniel also depicted two crabs, one goose, one seemingly downcast toucan, one pouter pigeon and two guinea pigs, gathered round to listen to the Mouse's long tale and Alice's and the Dodo's interruptions. This assemblage of species is typical of the type of specimens

in Darwin's *Origin of Species* (1859), at the time a best-seller. Domestic dogs, pigeon fanciers' breeds of pigeon, not to mention monkeys, were crucial strands of evidence for Darwin's thesis that life has evolved competitively from simpler beginnings. And the entire story was set in the year in which the *Origin* appeared, as Martin Gardner* realized. (See Age* of Alice).

216

The Party was indeed 'Queer' in the sense that it was suspiciously like a microcosm of the real-life party listening to the story on a real river expedition. If the four people who first heard it – three little girls and a grown up Fellow of an Oxford college – understood the joke when they heard it, or later, the Queerness would have delighted them even more. Because it is so obvious, this parody is an important starting point for wondering, as we and others have done, how far other real people are laced through the *Alice* texts. (See also Empson* and Leslie.*)

Questions   Children of the age* of Alice in the story ask questions. Carroll was child-like enough to ask them too when he was with his child*-friends. He took such questions seriously and so did the Dodo.* It was asked by the 'Queer-Looking Party'* which creature had won the Caucus-race:

> This question the Dodo could not answer without a great deal of thought, and it sat for a long time with one finger pressed upon its forehead [the position in which you usually see Shakespeare, in the pictures of him], while the rest waited in silence.

This interview is the reverse of the situation in a *viva voce* examination at Oxford. In *Wonderland*, the students ask the question and the philosophic don struggles with an answer.

Joyce Carol Oates (see Critics*), the American writer who is also a Carroll commentator, has written of Carroll's dream world:

> The question *Why?* is answered curtly by *Why Not?* – the supreme epigram of the dream world, and it is very likely the supreme epigram of 'our' world.

Alice was questioned by adult characters she encountered, including the Red and White Queens before the banquet at the end of *Looking-Glass*. So gruelling was that last quizzing to which she was subjected that she thought to herself, 'I wish Queens never asked questions'. Alice drew her own conclusion:

> "You can't be a Queen, you know, till you've passed the proper examination. And the sooner we begin it, the better."

The Red Queen led the inquisition and the White Queen followed, checking first whether Alice could add, subtract and divide, as required of a ruler. They did not ask if Alice could multiply. That would have been indecorous. (See also Arithmetic.*)

She could not answer the mathematical questions the Queens set her, so they started to ask if she knew her alphabet. The Red Queen was literate and could calculate, but the White Queen, who could not subtract, also tended to forget letters of the alphabet. She was Queen nevertheless. Alice now made an important social observation on royalty, one that might even apply to British royalty, for she realized that any error she made in sums or reading while the older Queens tested her could not logically be a test for royalty. When the Queens quizzed her on 'useful knowledge' and French, the White Queen confused the issue in a maze of puns before falling asleep on Alice's shoulder. The Red Queen followed suit. Still, Alice questioned what would happen to her as Queen for she knew that: 'there never was more than one Queen at a time'. What would happen to Alice now that there were two White Queens?

R is for ...

Railways and Railway Carriages Croft,* Carroll's later boyhood home, just south of Darlington in Yorkshire, was only four miles from the birthplace of passenger rail travel; the Stockton–Darlington railway opened in 1825. In the Croft* rectory garden, at a very young age, Carroll constructed a railway and invented the following whimsy about railway rules and inconsistencies:

> All passengers when upset are requested to lie still until picked up – as it is requisite that at least three trains should go over them, to entitle them to the attention of the doctor and other assistants.
>
> When a passenger has no money and still wants to go by train, he must stop at whatever station he happens to be at, and earn money – making tea for the Station Master ... and grinding sand for the company (what use they make of it they are not bound to explain).

Before Carroll was 12 he had written an opera called *La Guida di Bragia* for his marionette puppets based on *Bradshaw's Railway Guide*, the bible for the Victorian railway traveller in an age when the new system connected most villages in Britain to one main line or another. He had also built a toy railway station against the wall of the Daresbury* parsonage garden.

In her attempt to get to the third square in *Looking-Glass*, Alice found herself on a train. She had no ticket, and was sitting in a carriage with a gentleman dressed in the white paper of government discussion documents and who looks exactly like Disraeli* in one of Tenniel's* *Punch* cartoons. No text explains this character. Talk of railways suffused Victorian drawing rooms and clubs, and it is not surprising that railways appeared in *Alice*. In the Pool of Tears, Alice thought she had fallen into the sea. The seaside defined itself to her as a place where there are 'row[s] of lodging houses, and behind them a railway station'. It is thought that in the character of Humpty Dumpty* there are shades of George Hudson, the bankrupted railway speculator, whose capital structure was as brittle as an egg and whose girth was prodigious – £78 million was wiped off the Stock Market value of railway shares when his empire fell, as it were, off the wall, and many well-to-do speculators were affected.

The University of Oxford* strongly opposed the building of a railway to the city, fearing it would be a conduit to the flesh pots of London.* However, by the time Carroll came as an undergraduate the march of progress had prevailed. In 1852, Oxford was linked to Birmingham as well as to London. This meant that he could probably travel by rail all the way from Darlington to Oxford. Such was the University's fear of the corrupting influence of the railway that the Proctors (of whom Carroll was one for a time) were allowed by special Act of Parliament to maintain jurisdiction over Oxford station. Carroll complained that his journeys to the London theatre totalled up to the equivalent of several days a year spent on the Great Western Railway.

Reading Habits and Reading Men   Carroll's reading habits were fastidious throughout his life and the catalogue of the sale of his effects at his death has provided a revealing list of the books in his library. As a young man he set himself tasks, systematically dividing the list into subjects and the subjects into specific books. One such list included the Classics, Divinity, History, French, German – Italian was postponed – Poetry, Novels, Etymology, the works of J. S. Mill and a further list of Divinity books required for his ordination.

Undergraduates such as Carroll at Christ Church, if not the exception to the rule, were certainly derided by the fox-hunting and anti-intellectual elite as 'reading men'. A shy undergraduate, Frederick Oakley, on entering Christ Church a few years before Carroll, stated:

> My tutor introduced me to two reading-men ... who were reading so hard that they did not want to be troubled with a new acquaintance, for both of them cut me the day after the introduction.

Recitation   The art of recitation is mocked in *Alice*. Almost all Alice Liddell's* own learning would have been by rote and learning poetry was an important part of this. Jokes about poems coming out 'all wrong' and muddled answers being given to routine questions as a result of rote learning, provide a running joke in both books. Carroll saw the great reciter and actress,

Fanny Kemble, on the stage. Recitations and public readings, notably those by Dickens, were popular entertainments and mothers were keen to develop the abilities of their own children in elocution and the reciting of poems; the children standing with their hands held behind their backs and their toes turned out.

The problem for the children was that they often did not understand what they were reciting. Alice may or may not have learned the original 'Old Father' William* but she would certainly have learned the originals of some of the poems parodied in *Alice*. This makes the idea of them coming out 'all wrong' sympathetic to a child who had to struggle to remember line after line of poetry. (See also Governesses.*)

The Rectory Umbrella This was the title of one of Carroll's early humorous magazines. It shows that his comic writing talent was forming early, as was his talent for feeling out what a book, or booklet, should look like. (See Layout.*) From 1850 until he went up to Oxford in 1852 he edited *The Rectory Umbrella*, wrote prose and poetry for it, illustrated it and dragooned whichever of his sisters he could to contribute to it, sometimes writing their contributions for them. His seven sisters formed his earliest readership. The umbrella in the title of the magazine was the name the family gave to an ancient yew which still stands in the Rectory garden at Croft.*

In the frontispiece, Carroll's drawing showed an umbrella opened out and held up by a jovial old man in a Greek kilt. On its panels were listed the following topics: 'Jokes, Riddles, Fun, Poetry and Tales'. A bevy of seven flying maidens – the precise number of his sisters – poured libations from tiny ink pots into the old man's lap. Their odd little bottles are labelled with the seven virtues he required for his new magazine: 'Taste, Liveliness, Knowledge, Good Humour, Mirth, Content and Cheerfulness'. 'Woe', 'Spite' and so on are written on little rocks, from which the Old Man protects the maidens with their ink-pots. The rocks were aimed at the inspired ones by spidery little male gremlins, banished to the background of the composition.

Red A *bright* red was the colour Carroll chose for the cover of *Alice*. This red is the colour by which many Macmillan editions have become etched in the memories of those who own them. On 11 November 1864, Carroll wrote to his publisher, Alexander Macmillan:

> I have been considering the question of the *colour* of *Alice's Adventures*, and have come to the conclusion that *bright red* will be the best – not the best, perhaps, artistically, but the most attractive to childish eyes. Can this

colour be managed with the same smooth, bright cloth that you have in green?

It was. The green had been used for the first English edition of Charles Kingsley's* *The Water-Babies.*

Beyond black and white, the colour red interested Carroll in several ways. It was used traditionally by typographers setting Red Letter editions of the Bible. Carroll used it for the counters in his difficult *The Game of Logic* (1886). This was played on a board marked out with grids on which the player moved four red counters with which to say 'Yes' and five grey ones with which to say 'No'.

In 1880 Carroll, aged 48, asked his child-friend from Guildford, Dora Abdy (1872–1950) to a matinée of *Much Ado About Nothing.* When she asked him what to wear, Carroll devised an acrostic with the colour red at its core. Turning the familiar letters RSVP written on formal party invitations into its first letters, Carroll dreamed up the following fantasy dress for himself for their meeting: 'Red Scarf: Vest Pink' as far from his actual matinée wear as it is possible to imagine – which is probably why he liked it.

Reed, Herbert Langford (1889–1954)   Reed was a Londoner, a collector of limericks, a journalist and playwright. He published a collection called *Further Nonsense Verse of Lewis Carroll* (1926) and *The Life of Lewis Carroll* (1932). Although light-hearted in his approach to Carroll, Reed did acknowledge the central position of religion in his life. He described Carroll as 'the founder of "Nonsense Literature"'. Reed wrote:

> I do not think that any student of literature, in this country or abroad, will quarrel with me for asserting that neither France nor any other country has produced a writer of nonsense who can be compared with Lewis Carroll, or (I might add) a writer of travesty who can be mentioned in the same breath with W. S. Gilbert.

Reed's biography was one of the first attempts at a life of Carroll after Collingwood* wrote his in 1898. With Walter de la Mare's* book which was published in the same year, 1932, Reed helped to focus attention on a largely forgotten man.

Religious Doubts   Students (Fellows) at Christ Church were expected to become ordained priests in due course, but Carroll lacked the kind of spiritual self-confidence that makes a good priest. He wrestled with God with a continual sense of not being sufficiently good or adequate in His eyes. He knew that logic was his strength, but even this he could not put at God's disposal. He felt inadequate, for example, about a theological argument he had had with his younger brother, Wilfred. This was in 1857, when Carroll was 25. The question was whether obedience to college rules should be a matter of individual conscience, as Wilfred thought. Carroll wrote:

> If I find it so hard to prove a plain duty to one individual, and that one unpractised in argument, how can I ever be ready to face the countless sophisms and ingenious arguments against religion which a clergyman must meet with!

How indeed? Few characters in *Alice* doubted. One of the most dogmatic of all was the Red Queen.* She knew exactly what was right even though

nothing resulted from her decisions. Before she walked away from their first encounter, the Queen gave Alice three queenly rules to see her through:

"Speak in French when you can't think of the English for a thing—turn out your toes as you walk—and remember who you are!"

Reviews of *Alice*   There were over 30 reviews of *Wonderland* when it was first published. Many were ecstatic: 'Few [Christmas books] more attractive to the eye', the *Monthly Packet* said. *Aunt Judy's Magazine* said:

> Forty-two illustrations by Tenniel! Why there needs nothing else to sell this book, one would think. But our young friends may rest assured that the exquisite illustrations only do justice to the exquisitely wild, fantastic, impossible, yet most natural history of 'Alice in Wonderland'.

Several liked the lack of a moral. The *Literary Churchman* said that the story was 'unburdened of any moral'. *The Times* thought it would appeal to adults. *John Bull* said that 'it is quite a work of genius, and a literary study'. The *Pall Mall Gazette* described it as: 'One of the cleverest and most charming books ever composed for a child's reading'. An earlier article had said that it was:

> ... a children's feast and triumph of nonsense; it is nonsense with bonbons and flags ... never inhuman, never inelegant, never tedious.

There was little real critical insight. On the other hand, there were few sour notes. (For denser and more modern views, see Critics.*)

Riddles, Carroll's   Joyce Carol Oates, in her review essay on Carroll (see *English Language Notes* in the Select Bibliography), made the point that in the nonsense world of *Alice* where most people are 'quite content' to be mad:

> Riddles without answers are more pointedly riddles than riddles *with* answers.

Some of the most memorable riddles in *Alice* are unsolved and were intended to remain so by Carroll; in particular the riddle about 'The Raven and the Writing Desk'. Even when they were solved, multiple solutions could hide behind the nonsense rubric.

Many of Carroll's riddles depended on puns. We have chosen two typical ones which were written for girls of Alice's age of about seven. The first is the kind of riddle children like to repeat, and Carroll enjoyed writing.

Q: Why is Agnes [Hull*] like a thermometer?
A: Because she won't rise when it's cold.

The second is a wild flower riddle written for the three Watson sisters, born in the early 1860s, who sat for Carroll's camera in 1869:

Tell me truly, Maidens three,
Where can all these wonders be?
Where tooth of lion, eye of ox [*Dandelion/Ox-eye daisy*]
And foot of cat and tail of fox [*Catsfoot/Fox-tail*]
With ear of mouse and tongue of hound [*Mousear/Hound's tongue*]
And beard of goat, together bound [*Goat's Beard*]
With hair of maiden, strew the ground. [*Maidenhair*]

These eight flowers were to be found in English meadows from May to August, the kind of meadows in which Carroll and the Liddell girls chose to picnic along the river Thames. This flower riddle is reprinted in facsimile in John Fisher's* *The Magic of Lewis Carroll* (1977). Incidentally, Goat's Beard is also called Traveller's Joy. It was the Goat's beard which Alice caught 'in her fright' when the Railway Carriage* in *Looking-Glass* rose 'straight up into the air'. When he set riddles like this, the answers, as with many examples of his word-play, are rooted in reality.

The riddle in *Alice* before Carroll's crucial final question to his readers, 'Who dreamed it?', came in the most vigorous scene in the book, the banquet to celebrate Alice's being crowned Queen. (See also Questions.*) The two Queens* in *Alice* – one bullying and the other placatory – produce 'a lovely riddle' for Alice:

> "'First the fish must be caught.'
> That is easy: a baby, I think, could have caught it.
> 'Next, the fish must be bought.'
> That is easy: a penny, I think, would have bought it ..."

The verse continues with clues about what this fish might be until:

> "For it holds it like glue—
> Holds the lid to the dish, while it lies in the middle:
> Which is easiest to do,
> Un-dish-cover the fish, or dishcover the riddle?"

Unlike some of Carroll's riddles this one had an answer that was quickly discovered, an answer which he never denied. It was a suitably cannibalistic riddle for the last scene of *Looking-Glass*: It was 'an oyster',* a shell-fish that must be prized apart and eaten alive.

Riding and Alice   Mrs Liddell* did not share the popular view among mothers that riding could harm the way in which a girl's shoulders developed. Alice Liddell rode regularly with her father, the Dean, in the woods round Oxford. In her reminiscences of her childhood she described how she fell off her horse on the Abingdon Road and broke her thigh most painfully. She noted that 'during all these weeks Mr Dodgson never came to see me'. Whether or not Carroll disapproved of riding, it is unlikely that he had the physique for it, or the money to stable a horse in Oxford. Certainly he mercilessly lampooned clumsy riders in the White Knight's* adventures. The White Knight fell more often than any rider in fact or fiction. There is also a joke in *Alice* mildly related to riding, about the Rocking-horse-fly; and the one made by the Gnat in the railway carriage:

> ... a hoarse voice spoke next. "Change engines——" it said, and there it choked and was obliged to leave off.
> "It sounds like a horse," Alice thought to herself. And an extremely small voice, close to her ear, said, "You might make a joke on that—something about 'horse' and 'hoarse,' you know."

Alice's love of riding continued when she moved from Oxford to Cuffnells after her marriage. A number of her wedding presents, including a whip from Mr Baldwin, the then Deanery coachman, were of riding-related articles and jewellery. Alice's world was horsy; Carroll's was not. (See also Punctuation.*)

Rossetti, Christina (1830–94) and her brother, Dante Gabriel (1828–82) Christina was a poet, her brother a painter, poet and one of the founders of the Pre-Raphaelite Brotherhood. From 1862 these two were artistic contacts of Carroll's – 'friends' implies more intimacy than existed. At Rossetti's large Chelsea house in Cheyne Walk, Carroll met the poet Algernon Charles Swinburne (1837–1909), photographed some of Rossetti's drawing collection and models, and photographed the Rossetti family on the steps of the garden which doubled as a menagerie.

Carroll liked Rossetti's painting, *Found!*, which portrays a ruined prostitute, in despair in a street, being recognized by a former patron. The theme of ruin and redemption appealed to the Victorians, Carroll included. He carried out a number of commissions for Rossetti, leading on one occasion to an unpleasant quarrel about non-payment. Apart from this, admiration between the three of them seems to have been mutual. Carroll admired Christina Rossetti's *Goblin Market* (1862), a long, allegorical poem for children about two sisters kidnapped by fairies, one of whom never recovers from bewitchment. Christina Rossetti returned the compliment by imitating the dream-like structure of *Alice* in *Speaking Likenesses* (1874), one of many attempts to imitate *Alice*.

Carroll gave Christina Rossetti vellum-bound presentation copies of both *Alice* stories. She liked 'that conversational rabbit, that endearing puppy, that very sparkling dormouse' although she did not like the Hare* or the Hatter*. For a possible satire on the Rossettis and their circle see Owl*.

Rowing   The first Oxford and Cambridge boat race was held in 1829. During Carroll's lifetime a number of educators, including Charles Kingsley* at Cambridge* and Liddell* at Oxford, held that rowing and other competitive sports offered a way of developing character and diverting the energies of young men. When Carroll came to Christ Church* there were probably more hunting dogs in the college than undergraduates. Hunting declined in favour of competitive sports and, by the mid-century, rowing was the most important. Benjamin Jowett* also favoured the extension of sporting activities and facilities for undergraduates. In May 1867 Carroll opposed the proposal that part of the University Parks should be used for cricket and football pitches. However Carroll did attend the Oxford and Cambridge boat race in 1858.

Carroll liked taking exercise, particularly walking,* but he never indulged in rowing as a competitive pursuit. He must have been a competent oar because he rowed in boats with outriggers and knew how to feather, teaching that skill to Alice. Carroll would hire boats from Salter's Boat Yard. These were probably old Thames* wherries, according to W. B. Woodgate.

> [These] contained space for two or more sitters in the stern, and were fitted with two pair of sculls or a pair of oars at option. Their beam on the waterline was reduced to a minimum; but at the same time it was necessary, for mechanical purposes, that the gunwale, at the points where the rowlocks were placed, should be of sufficient width to enable the sculler to obtain the necessary leverage and elevation of his sculls.

Such boats were 22 feet long and narrow enough to make them difficult to steer by an amateur.

Carroll's *Diaries** indicate that he often rowed in the summer months on the river at Oxford. From 1856 to 1863 the Liddell children were his favourite companions on these expeditions. Carroll approved of few other Victorian outdoor games except for croquet.* He abhorred cricket, one of the favourite sports of Dean Liddell and his son. Each of Carroll's three dedicatory poems in the *Alice* books, 'All in the Golden Afternoon', 'Child of the Pure Unclouded Brow' and Alice's acrostic, 'A boat beneath a sunny sky —' are on the river. He described the story of *Alice* in the third verse of 'Child of the Pure Unclouded Brow' as a tale begun as:

> A simple chime, that served to time
> The rhythm of our rowing —

Ruskin, John (1819–1900)   Aesthete, collector, art critic, proponent of artisans and illustrators, lover of nature in art, Ruskin was as famous at the time Carroll wrote *Alice* as Dickens. At the end of the twentieth century he is on the edge of a revival for he was a precursor of green ideas and pacifism. His prophetic eloquence on these themes influenced Leo Tolstoy (1828–1910), Mahatma Gandhi (1869–1948) and Marcel Proust (1871–1922).

Of his views about artistic appreciation, which interested Carroll as a young man in Oxford, only the shadow remains: the two yards of his collected works remain unlooked at in many libraries. Ruskin was a Gentleman Commoner at Christ Church* – thought to be so delicate when he was there that he lodged in Oxford with his mother rather than living in college. He was a close friend of Acland* and Liddell.* He and Acland were the planners of the Natural History Museum* in Oxford,* and the exceptional hand-work and carving there owes much to his influence.

Carroll met Ruskin when he came to stay in Christ Church to vote for Acland as Professor of Medicine. Ambivalent, as he often was with the great – Tennyson* for example – Carroll marked his diary entry for October 1857 with 'a white stone',* but thought Ruskin slight and unimpressive.

It is our view that Carroll parodied him as the Gryphon;* there is a passage of a very mockable nature in *Modern Painters* (1843) where he makes an enormous fuss about whether certain medieval statues of these heraldic beasts were carved in a natural or unnatural way.

Alice was taught drawing by Ruskin, who had also taught her father to draw when they were undergraduates together. In *Wonderland*, 'uglification',* 'beautifying' and 'drawling' appear to parody Ruskin who wanted the world 'beautified' by art and handwork, but was obsessive on the subject.

Carroll broke with Ruskin, as he had with Tennyson, over a mutual insult. Having photographed Ruskin in a large leather arm-chair looking sad and worried (the date was possibly 1871) Carroll asked for the right to distribute the photograph. Ruskin, reasonably, asked for a contribution to a struggling magazine he was editing for working men, *Fors Clavigera*. Carroll refused to buy the magazine and therefore Ruskin refused permission. Though an admirer of Tenniel,* Ruskin never placed *Alice* among the great books of the age. Could he have spotted the aptness of the satire? (For the idea that the Walrus* and the Carpenter* are also a parody of Ruskin and Walter Pater,* see those articles).

S is for ...

Sale of Carroll's Effects   The sale took place in Oxford in May 1898, realized a modest £729 and demonstrated how little standing Carroll had as an author and how he had even less as a photographer. Christ Church* wanted the rooms for another occupant. His relatives were not literary, but no one in the literary world came forward to suggest that his papers and letters be preserved. The hapless relatives burned thousands. Dean Liddell who died a few days after Carroll was given two memorials in the college. Alice's sister Edith Liddell* who had died young has a window in the Cathedral. Until a posthumous portrait by Herkomer* was commissioned, Carroll was not given a memorial.

At the sale, Carroll's photographic albums* were offered among other lots, just after 'two pairs of dumb-bells'. Thirty-two albums were divided into twelve lots of which only one, that with signatures in it, made over £2, at least more than the dumb-bells. The glass negatives have never been recovered and it is uncertain what proportion of the total collection is represented by the albums in the Parrish and Gernsheim* collections in Princeton University and the University of Texas. The next lot was of two pocket flasks, five pocket knives, and six travelling inkpots.

Work on the catalogue of the sale has given important insight into the diverse nature of Carroll's library. John W. Smith noted in *Jabberwocky* (Winter 1984/5) that there were 3000 books on the shelves of Carroll's library when he died; and that a significant number were on medicine and science, even though Carroll had already given a lot of these to his medical student nephew, Stuart Collingwood's* brother. There were 64 books on natural history and 16 on astronomy.

Most indicative of the fact that his papers were not looked at by anyone with a sense of how important *Alice* was – perhaps Carroll's courting anonymity ensured that – the galleys of 'The Wasp in the Wig'* section of *Looking-Glass* went by various hands to an American collector. Mercifully this piece of Carrolliana was not burned.

Science   In Carroll's early days at Oxford the teaching of science was more widespread than is suggested by those who see nineteenth-century Oxford as dominated by theology and classical learning. Before 1850, some colleges had Demonstrators or Readers in chemistry and physics (although it was not called that) and their lectures and slide shows were open to all.

Carroll would have seen demonstrations by Augustus Vernon Harcourt (1834–1919), his friend and fellow-oarsman, a very young Fellow of the Royal Society. Benjamin Brodie was the Professor of Chemistry from 1855 and was to become President of the Royal Society: he and Harcourt were at the cutting edge of modern chemistry. Robert Walker (1801–65) was Reader in Experimental Philosophy. Carroll would have seen the public demonstrations he gave of explosions and of how air guns and magic lanterns worked. Such technological inventions* as photography,* the phonograph and early versions of the automatic calculator were grist to his mill as they had been to his uncle, Skeffington Lutwidge.*

In 1850, just before Carroll matriculated, the University Commissioners established the Honours School of Natural Sciences. This led to the need for a purpose-built Natural History Museum.* Colleges, too, were encouraged to build laboratories. At the time he wrote the *Alice* stories, Carroll photographed Michael Faraday (1791–1867), great but modest inventor, physical chemist and popularizer of science. In 1861, Faraday delivered the first Royal Institution Christmas Lecture for children and their parents as part of his duty as Director of the institution. The lecture was an immediate success. It was published under the title of *The Chemical History of a Candle*. These lectures, given as a Christmas treat, were part of the effort to bring scientific and technological understanding into the general system of education.

Faraday's lectures on the candle provide an example of just what interested Carroll, namely how do the metaphysical and the physical interact? What happens when the candle snuffs? It was the view of William Empson* that Faraday's talk inspired Tweedledum's* warning to Alice that if the Red King woke up, she would be snuffed out.

Carroll was well-informed in the field of biology and followed the moral debate triggered off by Charles Darwin's theory of evolution* with the rest of Oxford. Closer to Carroll than Darwin in his approach to biology was the old fashioned naturalist, William Buckland (1784–1856), Canon of Christ Church with a country living in Hampshire. He was a pioneer in the study of dinosaur fossils. He is said to have cooked and tasted everything in the animal kingdom. In 1845 he became Dean of Westminster in spite of High Church criticism. He wrote about the deluge, which kept his critics happy, in *Reliquae Diluvianae* (1823) and *Geology and Mineralogy Considered with Reference to Natural Theology* (1836). Stories about Buckland abounded in Carroll's Oxford, one being that Canon Pusey thought science could come to an end when he left the college. What came to an end was not modern science but any attempt at a truce between religion and science.

Seaside   Early on in *Wonderland*, when Alice falls into the Pool of Tears, she thinks that she has fallen into the sea.

> Alice had been to the seaside once in her life, and had come to the general conclusion that, wherever you go on the English coast, you find a number of bathing machines in the sea, some children digging in the sand with wooden spades, then a row of lodging houses.

At the time that Carroll wrote *Under Ground*, Alice Liddell's* only visit to the seaside had been in winter to the chilly resort of Lowestoft in 1857 where Dr Acland sent the children to avoid contact with scarlet fever in another Christ Church family.* Later Alice Liddell came to know the seaside well when her family built a house, Pen Morfa,* in North Wales, to which Carroll was not invited. The fictional Alice could swim. In the Pool of Tears, she conversed with the Mouse as she swam, without getting out of breath while

she did so. On the swimming Mouse's suggestion, she also led the animals on shore to get dry.

Carroll first visited the North Wales coast when a boy at Daresbury.* Later such visits became frequent when the Dodgsons and numerous cousins would visit, from Croft,* the east coast fishing port and growing holiday resort of Whitby in County Durham. As a young don he began journeying to the south of the Isle of Wight* after which he developed the habit of holidaying at Eastbourne* every summer.

When Carroll needed bathing dresses for his models, he asked Mrs Kitchin* to obtain them for him as reported by Morton Cohen in his *Lewis Carroll and the Kitchins*. He wrote to her: 'Have pity on my natural timidity'.

Carroll was not alone in getting comic mileage from the sight of people beside the seaside. The Victorians loved the seaside for the fresh air and sense of release it provided, but they also mocked their own enjoyment of it: there is something of this in 'The Mock Turtle's* Story' and 'The Walrus* and the Carpenter'. It is strongly evocative of seaside cartoons in *Punch*,* of men hunting for marine life in frock coats or, like the Walrus and Carpenter, having long and serious conversations about salvation along the shores of an English beach.

Seriousness   A 'serious age' is one way of characterizing the period that was spanned by Carroll's life – from the 1830s, the end of the more frivolous period of the Regency, until the 1890s, the 'gay nineties', when people began to forget Victorian high-mindedness and the idea of the church militant. Carroll's diaries* show his intense self-castigation, particularly at year end, and when the unexpurgated version is produced, more of his self-castigation will be visible.

Each faction of the church developed a new seriousness from the 1830s onwards. The Christian Socialists* were arguing for more conscientiousness about social duties. The Oxford Movement* argued for more attention to the position of the church, its sacraments and to church attendance. When Carroll was writing *Alice*, Lord Palmerston was still alive but the ribaldry and cynicism of the eighteenth century were gone. Science,* notably Darwin's views, had begun to be taken seriously. Dons had always been expected to be celibate and they could not marry. If they broke the rules in the eighteenth century the matter was winked at. If they did so in the later nineteenth century, and Carroll almost certainly did not, then they did so secretly. A new seriousness, lamented by one of Carroll's favourite writers, Catherine Sinclair,* also pervaded the upbringing of children. Alice and Carroll were both products of this serious age and the bite of Carroll's humour seems to reflect that.

Servants   Alice lived in a world in which servants were taken for granted. They cooked, cleaned, lit fires, fetched things, took messages, looked after children; and quasi-servants in the form of governesses* taught girls. In *Wonderland* the White Rabbit* called Alice 'Mary Ann' and expected her to fetch his gloves 'Quick now!' In *Looking-Glass* the White Queen* mistook Alice for the kind of girl who would make a useful servant. Alice acquiesced in the role with amusement. It was an unthinkable one to a little girl raised as a daughter of the Deanery.* Nor did you necessarily understand the details of what the servants did. Boots and shoes were put outside the bedroom at night. How were they cleaned? the Gryphon asked Alice. Tentatively she said: 'They're done with blacking, I believe'.

Later in life Alice was embarrassed when Julia Margaret Cameron* placed her at lunch next to a servant girl whom she felt represented a very earthy type of English beauty. In Mrs Cameron's mind Alice and this rough-handed girl were both models. In Alice's mind they inhabited different planets. It was a planet not to be ignored. The coachmen, cooks, footmen, butlers, housekeepers, gardeners, grooms, house-maids, parlour-maids, laundresses, personal maids and their underlings who had pervaded Alice's life from birth were of course included on the guest list for her wedding.

Here were some of the wedding gifts from these indispensable members of Mrs Liddell's household: the Deanery coachman, Mr Baldwin, successor to 'Bultitude', the coachman when Alice was a child, gave Alice a riding whip; Mr Pigeon, the groom's coachman at Cuffnells gave her a silver napkin ring and Mrs Lloyd gave her a tea cosy. The Cuffnells servants gave her a pair of candlesticks. The Deanery servants gave two brass inkstands, two china figurines and a card-case. The Christ Church* laundress, responsible for the Liddell girls' floating lawn dresses, gave her a silver salver. And Carroll – not a servant, not even a tutor, not even a friend – was not invited. (See also Soles.*)

Sinclair, Catherine (1800–64)   Catherine Sinclair was the author of *Holiday House* (1839), an early Victorian children's book* that was among the liveliest available in Carroll's boyhood. He gave a copy to the Liddell children as a Christmas gift in 1861. He inscribed the copy of the book with the dedication 'L., A., and E. Liddell/ a Christmas Gift/ from C. L. Dodgson'. Written in it were the three verses of the first of the acrostics* he was to compose on the Liddell* sisters' names. The lines encapsulating Lorina's name portray her as a reader, the eldest of his favourite maidens, and begin:

> Little maidens, when you look
> On this little story-book,
> Reading with attentive eye
> Its enticing history,
> Never think that hours of play
> Are your only **HOLIDAY**!'

Catherine Sinclair believed that eighteenth-century children had been lively and individualistic. Carroll approved of this, and perhaps felt nostalgia for the age in which liveliness in children was condoned. In the 'Preface' to *Holiday House*, Catherine Sinclair wrote:

> In these pages, the author had endeavoured to paint that species of noisy, frolicsome, mischievous children, now almost extinct, wishing to preserve a sort of fabulous remembrance of days long past, when young people were like wild horses on the prairies, rather than like broken hacks on the road; and when amidst many faults and eccentricities, there was still some individuality of character and feeling allowed to remain.

Holiday House was the first book Carroll gave to Alice, a preliminary thanks offering. The second was a much more personal gift. It concerned, not a holiday house, but *Alice's Adventures Under Ground.** (See, by contrast, Seriousness.*)

Sisters   Carroll grew up with seven sisters of his own. Carroll's father died leaving some legacy, but it was not substantial and the Dodgson* sisters were, for most of their lives, indebted to their author-brother. None of them was beautiful, though one was mathematically gifted, and only one married. Carroll did much to support her two children, the Collingwood* boys.

When it came to child*-friends, the idea of sisters appealed to Carroll. If he obtained permission to escort one member of the family, permission to escort her sisters followed. Passing from sister to sister saved time: as one sister grew past the witching age of seven or so, another, already used to his games and questions, could take her place. After the Liddells, Carroll pursued a run of sisters from the families of the Arnolds,* the Bowmans,* the Butlers, the Hulls,* the Terrys* and many others. There is no record of the rivalry that Carroll's affection engendered, but perhaps it was implied by the snappish behaviour of some of the flowers Alice passed as she walked through 'The Garden of Live Flowers'.*

Sites of Interest to Carroll Enthusiasts   These are places where a Carrollian atmosphere can still be felt.

DARESBURY*   The parsonage where Carroll was born at Daresbury is gone and there is a plaque where it stood. The church was restored in the nineteenth century, in other words given a Gothic character suitable for the High Church, and contains a stained-glass window with scenes from *Alice*. The only portrait of Carroll in a clerical gown is in that window. The canal where Carroll's father preached to Irish 'navvies' (see 'Pat'*) still runs about a mile away from the Rectory – it can be seen from the M56 and you can walk along its towpath. Nowadays it takes pleasure, rather than commercial, traffic. While new buildings and main roads have come close to Daresbury, to the north and east of the sandstone village, the Cheshire countryside Carroll loved as a boy is still largely unchanged and can be idyllic.

CROFT*   Croft has about it the sense of the isolated north Yorkshire village that it was in Carroll's adolescence. Church, Rectory (in private hands) and the one room schoolhouse where he gave magic lantern shows and demonstrations of magic* still stand.

RUGBY SCHOOL, WARWICKSHIRE   In parts, this is as it was in the nineteenth century.

CHRIST CHURCH*   Access by tourists is strictly controlled. Little visible in the physical structure has changed since the major building programmes of Dean Liddell,* once reviled by Carroll. Tourists, entering from the Meadows, can walk through the college, see the main Quadrangles, notably Tom and Peckwater, where Carroll lived, and visit the Cathedral and the dining hall. Carroll's portrait hangs near the door, not far from W. H. Auden's.* Dean Liddell's is much larger and to the left of high table where he stands, red-robed and expressing an eagle-like hauteur. Standing by the entrance to the cathedral and looking to the opposite corner of Tom Quad, Carroll's rooms occupied the first floor (2nd floor in American terminology) and the one above, the latter hardly visible behind the castellation. If you are confused about directions ask for the Junior Common Room staircase. The rooms were above what is now the Junior Common Room.

Alternatively you can reach Christ Church by walking down St Aldates from Carfax in the centre of Oxford.* When you approach the corner tower of Christ Church on the left, Carroll's rooms are above the elegant emblems of the Cardinal's Hat. The photographic studio he built on the roof is long gone. Going back to the Cathedral entrance as a vantage point, the Senior Common Room suite of rooms is below the Hall on the left-hand side of Tom Quad. Access to the Carroll collections in the Library is strictly limited to serious scholars and an application is necessary. The Deanery* door can be seen and there is a statue of Dean Liddell over the arch across the walkway between Tom and Peckwater Quadrangles. To see it, walk as from Peckwater towards Tom. The Deanery Garden is private, and as invisible as ever to prying eyes. A footpath between the Meadows and Merton Street gives a view of other walled Christ Church gardens of a similar character.

There are memorials in the cathedral to Professor Henry Wentworth Acland;* his wife, Sarah; Bishop Samuel Wilberforce;* a bust of Dr Pusey;* a memorial tablet to Dean Liddell; and a window by Edward Burne-Jones in memory of Edith Liddell,* Alice's sister and Carroll's friend, with a moving epitaph by the Dean himself.

OXFORD BEYOND CHRIST CHURCH The Meadows are much as they were. Most of the elms in the old Broad Walk are gone, but Dean Liddell's new walk to the river, poplar lined, is a dominant and beautiful feature. The river, sometimes called the Isis, as experienced by Carroll and Alice, is described elsewhere (see Thames*). Much of its charm is intact. Port Meadow, where the White Rabbit* probably had his hole, can be approached from Wolvercote in north Oxford. The house and boathouse at Nuneham Courtney,* which was one of Carroll's rowing destinations, are best approached by the path on the Radley side of the river. With the Ordnance Survey map as a guide it is possible to walk – or to row as boats can still be hired from Salter's Boat Yard – the length of Carroll's rowing trips with Alice and her sisters, upstream, and down.

Within Oxford, the Broad where Acland lived is not greatly changed since the nineteenth century, except that it now has few residences and many bookshops. The Natural History Museum* is still a hymn to the mid-Victorian view of nature; to biological science in a less reductionist age. Much of the ground floor is as it was in Carroll's time, dominated by Ruskin's* elaborate schemes for pillars of painted metal and stone. The library on the first floor, the location of the debate between Wilberforce and Huxley,* was above the entrance door but has now been subdivided. All of the door furniture and detailing is still in excellent repair, a witness to Ruskin's concern for craftsmanship. Balliol College, with an entrance on The Broad, today owes much to rebuilding during Jowett's* time, the Gothic parts of which went against Jowett's spirit of reform. Keble College and its extraordinary chapel, which houses 'The Light of the World' by Holman Hunt whom Carroll admired, is still intact, a monument to High Church brick architecture. The Ashmolean, the University's art gallery, houses the Pre-Raphaelite* collection of paintings given by the Combes,* patrons of Carroll as they were of Hunt and Millais.* The murals in the Oxford Union decorated by the Pre-Raphaelites have been recently restored. It is almost certainly here that Carroll came into contact with the Pre-Raphaelites, including William Morris, whose ceiling is the only part of this project lacking in clumsiness.

At the core of the University is the Sheldonian Theatre and, near to it, the throned hall where Convocation and Congregation debated the major issues of nineteenth-century Oxford; science,* heresy* and vivisection* among others. The courtyard in front of the Bodleian Library, with the names of the old schools of learning above its doors, shows how close Carroll's Oxford was to renaissance Oxford. The Natural History Museum is on South Parks Road, opposite Keble College. The Parks are still a large swathe of open ground, some of which retains its Victorian, pre-playing field character.

CUDDESDON THEOLOGICAL COLLEGE   The college (now called Ripon) still stands on the hill south of Oxford and the car factories that have turned Oxford into a small industrial city. Newman's* retreat at Littlemore is still in that village, and still a simple shrine to his memory.

GUILDFORD*   Carroll's home, 'The Chestnuts', and the church where he worshipped, St Mary's, are intact and within reach of the Guildford Muniments Room, the most accessible of all English Carroll collections, and Carroll's grave. While Guildford has grown extensively, much of the Surrey countryside around is as Carroll knew it when he walked there.

HOLIDAY DESTINATIONS   Whitby and the East Coast resorts Carroll visited on family holidays are not known to us. Tent Lodge, in the Lake District above Coniston Water, where he first sought out Tennyson,* is still intact. The article about the Isle of Wight* describes Carroll's haunts there, notably near Freshwater where he visited Tennyson and Julia Margaret Cameron.* Tennyson's house, Farringford, is a hotel that has lost its nineteenth-century atmosphere. Conversely Cameron's 'Dimbola Lodge' is being carefully and imaginatively restored. The hotel where Carroll called on Henry Kingsley* is now absorbed into a fairground.

In Eastbourne* there is a plaque on the house where he stayed in Lushington Road. Christ Church, Eastbourne, still stands on a run-down street among discount and army and navy shops. The resort as a whole has had to struggle with the decline in popularity of the English seaside. However much of the late Regency front is intact and so is the pier. Start Point, where Carroll walked, is still wild and the light of the south coast is still brighter than anywhere else in Britain.

LONDON*   The article of that name describes some of Carroll's haunts. Tudor Lodge, the MacDonalds'* House off Regent's Park, still stands, as does Ellen Terry's* house where Carroll dragged his camera for what was one of the pleasantest weekends of his life.

There is a memorial to Carroll in Poets' Corner in Westminster Abbey which was unveiled just before Christmas 1982, the 150th anniversary of Carroll's birth. The plaque was made by the Welsh sculptor, Ieuan Rees on dark green slate from Moss Rigg in Westmorland. *Charles Lutwidge Dodgson 1832–98* is engraved in the centre circle. *Lewis Carroll* is engraved outside this and in the outer circle of lettering are the words: *Student of Christ Church Oxford/ Buried at Guildford/ 'Is all our life then but a dream?'* (from *Sylvie and Bruno*). Rees, who may not have selected the quotation, said that he had tried to combine the whimsy of Carroll with the seriousness of a mathematician. He seems to have succeeded.

Smiles, Samuel (1812–1904)   A Yorkshireman, radical and author of popular biographies of self-made men, Smiles had witnessed the fall of Henry Hudson, the 'Railway King', believed by Ellis Hillman* to be the original of Carroll's Humpty Dumpty.* Smiles was himself involved in railway finance, was Secretary of the South Eastern Railway Board from 1854 to 1866 and participated in the clean-up after Hudson's fall.

One of Smiles' best-selling books was the volumes of *Lives of the Engineers* (1861–2) which came into prominence when Carroll began writing *Alice*. Smiles showed that many great engineers were self-taught and, like many industrialists, of humble origin. Carroll poked fun at their self-serving style in the Aged Aged Man's* explanations of his own inventions.* Smiles' book *Self-Help* was popular and sold for many years. Such an attitude ran counter to Carroll's Toryism. The Aged Aged Man was deluded into believing himself capable of growing rich by invention. He was portrayed by Carroll as an old codger with no resources, in need of a hand-out. So was the Hatter.* Carroll did not approve of self-made men with pretensions above their station.

Snails   English readers of *Punch** confronted with frogs and snails would at once assume a French connection when they heard the song that accompanied the Lobster* Quadrille. The Whiting* urged the snail on, with the words:

> "There is another shore, you know, upon the other side.
> The further off from England the nearer is to France—
> Then turn not pale, beloved snail, but come
> and join the dance ..."

The French coast is a only few hours sailing from the cliffs at Freshwater Bay on the Isle of Wight* where Carroll spent his summer holidays in the 1860s.

Snails cannot hurry. An edible land snail would no more relish being transported to France, where it might be harvested, than a Mock Turtle might enjoy being made into soup.* Since members of the Anglican clergy like Carroll and Liddon* were not permitted to dance, the Whiting's address to the Snail was nonsense with a very funny purpose.

Socialists, Christian   When Carroll was 16, the revolutions of 1848 broke out across Europe. This radical fervour was an indirect influence on Charles Kingsley* and F. D. Maurice* who sought change in England but in a less violent way. They set out to organize a 'movement' and build colleges to improve working men's education and encourage co-operative forms of economic organization. The Christian Socialist movement was more outspoken than the Charity School Movement. In spite of this its supporters – unlike the Chartists – remained more detached from day-to-day politics.

The form the movement took was best known to Carroll through the works of Charles Kingsley, notably *Alton Locke, Tailor and Poet* (1850), which is a novel about the wretched conditions of garment workers, the Chartist struggle and the relevance of Christianity to this cause. Carroll criticized it for failing to propose definite remedies for changing the 'sweating' system of piece-work, noting in his diary that he felt that Kingsley had nothing to offer as an alternative. He grew closer to Maurice, and Maurice's influential – but iconoclastic to High Church members – *Theological Essays* (1853) was among his books when he died. (See Sale.*) George MacDonald* and Maurice were closely associated and Carroll was frequently in their company in the *Alice* years. The association suggests more concern with social affairs than has been attributed to Carroll.

Soles   Carroll enjoyed fish and fishy jokes,* and references to blacking* and whiting (boot jokes). If a shoe or boot joke could combine together, so much the better:

"Boots and shoes under the sea," the Gryphon went on in a deep voice, "are done with whiting. Now you know."

"And what are they made of?" Alice asked in a tone of great curiosity.

"Soles and eels, of course," the Gryphon replied rather impatiently: "any shrimp could have told you that."

Soup in *Alice*   Of food jokes in *Alice*, the most frequent are ones of a fishy* nature. These are followed by jokes about soup, the *sine qua non* at the head of lengthy Victorian dinner menus. Mock Turtle, Clear Turtle and Thick Turtle – we eat soup in the 1990s, but gone is that sense of its preeminence.

In the words of Victorian commentator, Sir Henry Thompson, author of *Food and Feeding*, its real importance was physiological; the liquid in the stomach ...

> soon enters the blood and rapidly refreshes the hungry man [from whom] in two or three minutes after taking a plate of good warm *consommé*, the feeling of exhaustion disappears.

Gone, too, are the great tureens, the wide-mouthed plates, the mouth-filling spoonfuls of Consommé a la Printanière, a la Jardiniére, Oxtail Soup, Soup Bernoise, Mulligatawny Soup, Hare Soup, Clear Turtle, Mock Turtle* and Thick Turtle. Soup is still soup, but perhaps it is no longer the ...

> "Beautiful Soup, so rich and green,
> Waiting in a hot tureen!
> Who for such dainties would not stoop?
> Soup of the evening, beautiful Soup!"

... as the Mock Turtle sighed.

Southey, Reginald (1835–99)   Long-faced and snub-nosed, of a scientific disposition, Southey was a colleague of Carroll's at Christ Church* and it was with him that Carroll made his first photographs, 'procuring', in Carroll's word, some of the Liddell children as models. Southey was trained in medicine and within a year of Carroll's initial attempts at photography under his tutelage, appears to have been helping Carroll, rather than vice versa. Southey left Christ Church to work at St Bartholomew's Hospital in London and later, as Carroll's uncle, Skeffington Lutwidge* had been, was appointed a Commissioner in Lunacy.

Spencer-Stanhope, John Roddam (1829–1908)   Of his problem with what to do about a sitter's hands* when he was taking three-quarter length likenesses, like one he took of Spencer-Stanhope, Carroll wrote in the *Illustrated Times* on 28 January 1860:

> In single portraits, the chief difficulty to be overcome is the natural placing of the hands; within the narrow limits allowed by the focusing power of the lens, there are not many attitudes into which they naturally fall. If the artist [i.e. the photographer] attempts the arrangement himself, he generally produces the proverbial effect of the bashful young man in society

Spencer-Stanhope was a contemporary of Carroll's at Christ Church.* He was a handsome, bearded man when he sat for Carroll in 1856. He posed casually, leaning forward, his capable hands clasped below his knees. By contrast, the Oxford clerical dons who posed for Carroll were clergymen sitting bolt upright, their collars starched, their hands clasped demurely in front of them.

Spencer-Stanhope was from the family of the Earls of Stanhope who founded the National Portrait Gallery, where Carroll's print of his portrait resides today. He joined the army and then became a painter, spending his apprenticeship in G. F. Watts' studio. When Carroll met him, he had joined Dante Gabriel Rossetti* and William Morris as they painted the Arthurian cycle on the walls of the Oxford Union. From him Carroll would have learned of the comings and goings of the Pre-Raphaelite circle of underfunded artists and undergraduates at work there.

Spiritual and Psychical Research From the age of 13 Carroll was preoccupied with the boundary between real life and Elfland. Spectres, Ghosts, Phantoms, Brownies, Pixies, Fays, Banshees, Fetches, Kelpies, Poltergeists, Doppelgangers, Ghouls, Trolls, Goblins, Sprites, Changelings and Leprechauns crowd the verses of *Phantasmagoria*, which he published between the two *Alice* books.

The other side of the fun he had with poltergeists and banshees was a serious interest in matters paranormal. In the 1880s, Lewis Carroll became a founder member of the Society for Psychical Research. His interest arose from the perturbation he felt about the materialist denial of miracles in the Old and New Testaments, a position argued publicly at the Metaphysical Society by T. H. Huxley.* The Society flourished, and was the experimental taking-off point for the speciality of experimental psychology, as pioneered by William James (1842–1910) of Harvard. Fellow-dabblers in ideas about such matters included John Ruskin,* George Frederick Watts (1817–1904), W. E.

Gladstone,* and Arthur Conan Doyle (1859–1930). Carroll recorded in his diaries instances of thought-reading, trance-like state and telepathic communication, proof of the short-sightedness of the:

> ... scientific sceptics...who always shut their eyes, till the last moment, to any evidence that seems to point beyond materialism.

The story of *Alice* itself is constructed round the tension between dream and reality for a dreaming child. The most ghost-like creature in Alice's dream is the knowing Cheshire Cat, disappearing into a tree above Alice's head, having given her its advice, leaving only its smile behind.

Squib   This is the name of a small firework that might be thrown on the ground by undergraduates in a Commemoration crowd and make a frightening, but minor, bang. Hence, by derivation, a squib at Oxford University* was a parody fired off about a particular controversy or individual, often with the name disguised. For obvious reasons, as some squibs were libellous, their authorship was also disguised.

Carroll wrote a number of squibs as a don at Christ Church.* Their obscurity in the present day should not blind the reader to the strength of the feeling behind them. Carroll's way of having his own propaganda distributed was to see that his squibs were properly typeset (see Layout*) and that the illustrations,* on the occasions these were required, were engraved and the whole printed and distributed throughout the University on Common Room notice-boards. (See *American Telegrams** and Benjamin Jowett.*)

Stage Productions of *Alice*   *Alice On Stage* (1990) by Charles Lovett (see Select Bibliography) is a compilation of Carroll's writings *on* the theatre, *for* the theatre and a record of a number *Alice* plays, ballets and operettas, mainly in Britain and the USA. As a sign of the way that interest in *Alice* is enduring, 150 new productions were performed in the decade 1979–88.

The idea of staging *Alice* was mooted from the time of the publication of the books. Carroll corresponded with various potential collaborators, one being the composer, Arthur Sullivan (1842–1900). Carroll thought Sullivan's fees too high and negotiations ended. Eventually, in 1886 when Carroll was 54, he was approached by an aspiring playwright, Henry Savile Clarke (1841–93). Clarke's credits were not substantial, but his patience in dealing with Carroll was considerable and he was prepared to take great trouble with problems of dramatizing the stories. Carroll responded by writing additional nonsense verse for the play which was something of a compilation of both *Alice* stories. Walter Slaughter was taken on as composer and *Alice in Wonderland, a Dream Play for Children* was first performed in London at the Prince of Wales

Theatre on 23 December 1886. Reviews were generally good and the show made a profit. *Punch** made the point that while the play 'worked' for children, it did not, like the book, have the same appeal to adults.

In 1888 there was a revival under new management. Isa Bowman,* Carroll's child*-friend, played Alice. Unfortunately there was a good deal of acrimony between Carroll, Clarke and the management and on one occasion Carroll threatened to withdraw his name if the Red King persisted in holding his skirts so high. Somehow Carroll managed to argue to himself that it was in good taste for a king to wear a skirt, but not to hold it up. This production closed without profit and there was no revival until after Carroll's death. Meanwhile Clarke had pre-deceased Carroll. Over the next 32 seasons from 1898 to 1930, there were 18 Christmas revivals.

Much of this information comes from Charles Lovett's meticulous record, which includes the script of the Clarke production, bibliographic notes on alterations made to it in various editions and a collection of Carroll's writings on the theatre published at the time in *The Theatre*, often on issues of morality.

Stammer   Do-do*-Dodgson was Dodgson, the extinct bird who stammered his own name. It has been said of Carroll that he could only speak freely in the company of child-friends. Certainly he did stammer, sought treatment for it and did exercises to improve his speech. It was as a result of this that he met, in 1859, one of his most important friends and contacts, the writer George MacDonald.* Carroll's maternal aunts lived at Hastings and he stayed with them when he visited Dr James Hunt, a great authority on stammering and author of *Stammering and Stuttering*. Carroll was still seeing James Hunt at the time of the *Looking-Glass*. Right at the end of his life he said that reading was much more difficult than speaking, even:

> ... a lesson in College Chapel ... I find such a strain on the nerves that I seldom attempt it.

Accounts varied on the issue of Carroll's stammer. He was inclined not to speak unless he felt like it and contemporaries attributed this to his speech impediment, thereby reinforcing the idea that the impediment was the root of some of his odd behaviour. His brother, Skeffington's, eldest child, Amy Irene (later Jacques, 1884–1978) who was 13 when Carroll died, said of the Dodgson brothers and sisters:

> Louisa had [no stammer], Fanny – none remembered, Charles and Wilfred some hesitation, but this has been greatly exaggerated. Caroline, Mary, Lizzie, Etta and Maggie all had particular speech defects each differing from each other.

It is a curious picture, the seven stammering children of the parsonage – four had no noticeable speech defects. Carroll and George MacDonald were two of the great children's authors of the mid-century. Charles Kingsley,* author of *The Water-Babies*, also had a stammer that seems to have been worse than Carroll's although it never prevented him being one of the most notable preachers of his time. Kingsley may have been one of the models for the Hatter* and a stammer joke may be detectable in the Hatter's comment at the Trial of the Knave of Hearts about his inability to control the 'twinkling of the Tea' ('T'). (See also Evidence.*)

Stanley, Arthur Penrhyn (1815–1881)   Stanley came to Christ Church* as a Canon in 1858 soon after H. G. Liddell* was appointed Dean and was, with the Dean, a major figure in the reform of the University from the 1850s. He was a conspicuous supporter – with exalted connections at Court and in Parliament – of more tolerant attitudes to religious dissent. In particular he was a supporter of Benjamin Jowett,* and considered that the autocratic behaviour of the High Church in the matter of Jowett's published Broad Church* views was likely to bring the whole Church of England into disfavour.

Stanley came from the family of the Earls of Derby and was the son of the much-talked-about bishop who considered himself the principal English sponsor of Jenny Lind, 'The Swedish Nightingale'. Wealthy in his own right, he was also an accomplished travel writer. The ease with which Liddell and Stanley – as Dean and Canon – spent money must have grated with Carroll and his impecunious colleagues among the Students. Stanley was the sharpest thorn in the flesh of Dr Pusey* and others of the High Church party in Oxford until his royal connections drew him away to become Dean of Westminster.

The authors consider that Stanley may be a model for the Cheshire Cat,* a character which hovered over the Croquet Ground, had a wide mouth and, metaphorically, sharp teeth; a strong, ghostly presence behind the scenes with an insider's grasp of what went on. Stanley was photographed by Carroll several times. During his residence in Christ Church, Carroll dined with him. He was frequently in the Deanery, and well known to Alice.

Surrealism and Carroll   Carroll's *Alice* and *Snark* were lauded by a group of twentieth-century authors and artists in France and Spain. In ignorance of Carroll's photographs, a component of his work which was not yet well-identified, the Surrealists, Louis Aragon (1897–1982) and André Breton felt an affinity for his writing for children, *Alice* in particular. In European *avant-garde* circles, Carroll stopped being seen as a fusty Victorian. Between 1929 and 1952, he was claimed by the Surrealist Movement as one of their own.

Philip Thody, in *Twentieth Century* (1958), noted how, in 1929, Aragon translated *The Hunting of the Snark* 'without managing to reproduce any of its metre, rhyme or rhythm'. Aragon described Carroll as a don with 'a fair, pointed beard' inventing his appearance to suit a whim of the moment. André Breton, the leading Surrealist, recognized Carroll as 'the first teacher of how to play truant' in the widely acclaimed *Anthologie de L'Humeur Noir* (1940) 'Doubtless', wrote Thody, the Surrealists were:

> delighted at finding a *saboteur* in so strong a citadel of Western culture as Christ Church Common Room and welcomed Carroll quite genuinely as a useful if unconscious ally.

Carroll's subversion of the grown up world through what Empson* called 'the comic primness' of Alice, struck a chord. A similar emphasis on irrationality and disorder characterized the Surrealist movement. Breton and Aragon's co-option of Carroll's text matched the declaration of purpose of their Second Surrealist Manifesto of 1930. This directed its literary and artistic disciples to:

> that point in the imagination where life and death, the real and the imagined, the past and the future, the communicable and the incommunicable, the high and low, cease to be opposed.

Such a geography of the Surrealist imagination overlaps Lewis Carroll's principal preoccupations.

Philip Thody described 1952 as 'the end of the adventurous stage of Carrollian criticism in France'. From that year, interest in Carroll became more academic, but not necessarily more incisive. Carroll could not have crossed the Channel in the 1930s without having been recognized as a literary modernist. The Surrealists were first to acknowledge him. (See also Salvador Dali.*)

T is for ...

Taste in Children's Clothes, Carroll's   Anne Clark suggested in *The Real Alice* (1981) that Mrs Liddell's* choice of dress,* hairstyles and footwear for her daughters showed good taste. Carroll's and Ruskin's* occasionally adverse reactions to what the Liddell sisters wore suggest that the two Oxford dons, who prided themselves on their good taste, felt that Mrs Liddell overstepped the mark in the outfits she chose for her daughters. Their criteria were not the same as hers. The Liddells' outfits are best seen in the assembly of photographs Carroll took of them from 1856 to 1862 as described by Anne Clark:

> Their accessories were always chosen with care: sometimes they wore little tippet hats, at others large-brimmed styles. When muffs were in vogue they carried them ... Their clothes were always charming, the dresses prettily tucked, flounced, spotted or embroidered ... more often than not they wore white, an indication of their social class. There were lots of new dresses in the Deanery.

The trims on the girls' dresses, sometimes identical, involved a good deal of hand work by milliners. Sometimes the dresses featured parallel light silk gussets in contrasting colours, sometimes they were ornamented with tassels and bobbles, sometimes with geometrical Greek motifs in honour of their father's role as co-compiler of the Greek Lexicon. No pinafores such as those worn by Tenniel's* *Alice* are to be seen in Carroll's child photographs, except on servants'* children. Perhaps he asked child sitters to remove them for the camera.

Plain attire and hairstyle was Carroll's preference and he liked girls to wear boys' play-clothes. After the fictional Alice fell down the rabbit-hole, she commented on the straightness of her hair which she also wore short, a style that enhanced the real Alice's elfin looks in all Carroll's photographs:

"I'm sure I'm not Ada,' she said, 'for her hair goes in such long ringlets, and mine doesn't go in ringlets at all."

Straight-haired Alice Liddell* did not wear an 'Alice-band', the tidy band or ribbon which still bears her name. This first became associated with *Alice* in 1872 in the *Looking-Glass* illustrations, along with her striped stockings. Tenniel's fair, long-haired, banded, pinafored Alice protected the identity of Carroll's original model.* Carroll's own drawings of Alice in *Under Ground* show her wearing a simple, apparently diaphanous, tape-trimmed tunic dress tied with a sash. All 26 of his *Under Ground* drawings show how much

he preferred 'natural' dress and hair. He urged Tenniel to keep Alice from looking balloon-skirted and modish, and thereby out of step with his intentions for his heroine.

Carroll confirmed his taste for 'a slight disorder in the dress' when he bought a painting of a young girl from Arthur Hughes (1830–1915), who was also

Tom Hughes' and Christina Rossetti's* favourite illustrator.* That painting, 'Lady with the Lilacs', hung in his room until he died. The young girl, who looks nymph-like, is dressed in a long-sleeved, soft, clinging muslin smock gathered at her waist, and stands dreamily against a heaped bank of lilacs. She is dressed very like Carroll's Alice in the *Under Ground* story.

Older girls' outfits in Caroll's photographs include the elegant silk bridesmaids' attire worn by the Arnold* sisters for their eldest sister, Mrs Humphry Ward's (1845–1926) wedding, and Ellen Terry's* dramatic black imitation Tudor wedding dress, posed after the collapse of her first marriage. None of these dresses were chosen by Carroll. By 1880, his wish to photograph undressed girl-children and to encourage his illustrators to portray fairies naked, replaced his yearning for the clinging, disordered girls' dress and beggar-maid rags that had been to his taste when he first wrote and illustrated *Alice*. (See also Albums.*)

Taylor, Alexander L. (1909–)   Alexander Taylor taught English in Ayrshire, Scotland and Oregon, USA. His biography, *The White Knight: a study of C. L. Dodgson (Lewis Carroll)* was published in 1952. Taylor said that he had written about Carroll because of the extreme reaction he had against claims by Shane Leslie* and Ronald Knox* – amplified by claims by other externalist commentators like Empson* – that controversial issues and characters of Carroll's day such as the Oxford Movement* and John Henry Newman's* conversion to Rome were identifiable in the *Looking-Glass* world.

Disturbed by the idea of a satirical element in a nonsense adventure, Taylor nevertheless admitted that Carroll's 'New Method' squib placed Carroll's High Church patron, Edward Bouverie Pusey* on a geometrical curve characterized by 'many multiple points'. In this Taylor himself, whilst denying Leslie, identified Pusey as the Sheep at the Mill busying itself as Alice rowed it, with 14 different pairs of knitting needles. Taylor also agreed with Ronald Knox that Humpty Dumpty's* term 'Impenetrability'* mocked Roman Catholic claims as to the Pope's 'Infallibility'.

Taylor, Tom (1817–80)   Simultaneously a lawyer, playwright and a contributor to *Punch*,* Taylor was one of those whose career Carroll watched and whose company he had succeeded in cultivating by 1863, at the time he got to know the MacDonalds* and the sculptor, Alexander Munro (1825–71). Munro introduced Carroll to Taylor who introduced Carroll to Tenniel.*

Carroll attended the first nights of many of Taylor's light-hearted plays. Taylor posed for Carroll in London wearing, oddly, an American Civil War uniform (see *American Telegrams**). Carroll photographed his little son as a tiny

Henry VIII in Royal Tudor costume. He endeared himself further by finding some mistaken arithmetic in the script of Taylor's play, 'The Ticket-of-Leave Man', which Taylor corrected. In 1863, Taylor took Carroll to Wandsworth to call on his favourite painter, Arthur Hughes (1832–1915) to see his pictures and to meet his four little children. It was here he heard that Taylor could grant him a personal introduction to the Terry sisters; as indeed he did.

As *Alice* matured as a project, Carroll above all needed to contact Tenniel; he also needed to enhance his own sense of worldliness, and to become a literary Carroll whose preoccupations went beyond the clerical and mathematical. Tom Taylor, like Sarah Acland* and Alexander Munro, put Carroll in touch with the metropolitan world. (See also London.*)

Taylor, Una (1857–1922) Una Taylor wrote *Guests and Memories: Annals of A Seaside Villa* for Oxford University Press in 1924. She was the youngest daughter of the Victorian writer, Sir Henry Taylor (1800–86) and in her book described Julia Margaret Cameron's* and Emily Tennyson's distaste for Carroll and his portrait photographs. She reported that Cameron had said to her father that Carroll's photograph of him made him look like 'a sea monster fed upon milk'. Carroll only photographed Taylor because he met him through Cameron. Una Taylor reported this and other derisory remarks made by the Tennysons* about Carroll.

In fact – this was forgotten in her memoir – Una Taylor had sat for Carroll as a little girl. She posed curled up reading a book and was photographed both at Freshwater, Isle of Wight* and in London.* By that time, all she remembered was that Cameron had told her father, apropos of one of Carroll's family photographs of the Tennysons:

> The Tennysons *abhor* that photograph ... It has printed so ill – come out so white and feeble and grotesque ... I am going to order no copies of it.

Carroll's memory was that Una had an Alice-like sophistication very young. He had no recollection of what a tittle-tattle tell-tale she was. He wrote to his sister, Mary, of her in 1862:

> The youngest, Una (about 5) [he was correct] has quite learnt the rule of 'speak when you're spoken too', and indeed gives long explanations with her answer.

(See also Child*-Friends.)

Tea-Party The Mad Tea-Party is perhaps the most powerful *mis-en-scène* in either *Alice* story – probably the scene most often remembered. Alice

Liddell,* by then Mrs Hargreaves, said in her recollections in *The Cornhill Magazine* in 1932, that tea, afternoon tea, was not yet taken in the 1860s. This may be part of the joke about a tea-party where wine is offered but not available and where the teapot is used for acts of barbarity against the wretched and sleepy Dormouse* – like 'dunking' the Dormouse – rather than as a pot for tea. (See also Stammer.*) We have suggested that the Mad Tea-Party was in part Carroll's parody of Christian Socialism,* with the Hatter* expressing the ideal of sharing, everyone moving around, and no one getting anything except the Hatter.

Tears, Alice's Alice wept copious tears in *Wonderland* out of loneliness and frustration. When she could not remember her lessons,* she cried so much that she filled the Pool of Tears. In *Looking-Glass* she wept twice, the first time being when she was bullied by Tweedledum* and Tweedledee.* They threatened to wake the Red King and suggested that she would vanish if they did. She was not real, they said, she was only part of his dream.* Alice shed a tear on a second occasion when she was dressing the White Queen,* who screamed that her finger would be pricked. The Queen said she wished she:

> "...could manage to be glad...Only I never can remember the rule. You must be very happy, living in this wood, and being glad whenever you like!"
>
> "Only it is so *very* lonely here!" Alice said in a melancholy voice; and at the thought of her loneliness two large tears came rolling down her cheeks.

Alice forgot her loneliness. The White Queen joked her out of it, but little girls who cried may have been Carroll's worst nightmare, so close was he to their despair and fears himself.

Henry Parry Liddon* recalled that Carroll himself wept like a child on their voyage to Moscow together. In July 1867, Carroll, overcome by the beauty of the Gothic Choir of Cologne Cathedral, was thrown into floods of tears by the harsh voice of the verger 'in the presence of so much beauty'. Liddon reported:

> I found him leaning against the rails of the Choir and sobbing like a child.

Temper in *Alice* There are no records of Carroll's child*-friends bursting into tears because they hurt a finger or were separated from their mothers. There is equally little record of their losing their tempers. Sanitized, sweetened as the record has been, there are suggestions that Alice Liddell* had a strong and wilful personality. *Wonderland* starts with Alice being bored by a book without pictures. It ends with Alice standing up to the Queen:

"Who cares for you?" said Alice..."You're nothing but a pack of cards!"

Alice then behaved in a precise parable of a Victorian adult's view of child behaviour, one of those 'if you do this, then that will happen' situations. The cards rose up against Alice and the story ended.

The world's temper is slower but more erosive than a child's. At the end of the first story, Alice was no longer in Wonderland. She woke up on the bank where she had fallen asleep. and her musing older sister imagined her repeating the story of her dream to a new generation, her own loving children.

Tenniel, Sir John (1820–1914)   A cartoonist and illustrator of *Alice*.

INTRODUCTION   Tenniel was a decade older than Carroll. He was 44 when they first met in 1864, and Carroll was 32. A significant fact, often missed but admitted in Tenniel's reminiscences, is that both author and illustrator were Tories, though Tenniel tried not to let this influence his satirical work for *Punch*, and W. E. Gladstone* overlooked it when he knighted him.

Tenniel was an enthusiastic ham actor, and performed in benefits for the widows of artists and engravers, provided the Terry sisters took the female lead. He was a keen oarsman as well.

Information about Tenniel's relationship with Carroll is sparse. It is known that the collaboration was painful to both of them most of the time. Carroll badly wanted Tenniel as his illustrator at a time when Tenniel's reputation as a political cartoonist was high and Carroll's work was unknown. In 1864, when Carroll approached him, Tenniel had just been promoted to the role of chief cartoonist of *Punch*, which made him responsible for the 'Big Cuts', the whole page cartoons that were the most important critique of national events in the national press. *Punch* had the knack of showing up political, royal, academic and ecclesiastical pretension.

Tenniel's cartoons were biting and incisive, eagerly awaited by those who feared the damage they would do and by those who relished it. Carroll was a regular reader and Alice Liddell* remembered that he collected his favourites in a scrap book. Often the mechanism of the satire was to use animal heads on recognizable human bodies or vice versa, as Grandville* had done with such effect in the pages of the Parisian satirical journal, *Charivari*. (See also Zoomorphs.*) This view of humans as grotesque animals and animals as grotesque humans, Carroll emulated in his illustrations for *Under Ground*, and Tenniel did in *Alice*.

In one case, an actual portrait is known to have suggested a Tenniel grotesque. It is the canvas of the hideously ugly Duchess of Carinthia (1318–69), Margaret, who married John Henry, Prince of Bohemia in 1330 at the age of 12, discarded him in favour of Louis, heir to the Emperor until he abdicated to give way to the founder of the Austro-Hungarian Habsburg dynasty. Tenniel used her portrait by Quentin Metsys at the National Gallery in London as one of the models for Carroll's Ugly Duchess.* (See also T. H. Huxley.*)

Tenniel's zest as a cartoonist may have been one of the reasons why Carroll wanted him as the illustrator* of *Alice* in preference to other illustrators with more experience in children's books and less of a workload. By Harry Furniss' (1854–1925) account, Carroll later complained that only one of the *Alice* illustrations by Tenniel pleased him – the full-length picture of Alice looking up at Humpty Dumpty* high on the wall. (See also Charles Lutwidge Dodgson;* first hand accounts and Models.*)

Among the adjectives applied to Tenniel by his biographer, Rodney Engen, are 'courteous', 'reserved', 'elusive', 'enigmatic' and 'private'. Tenniel was, as Carroll was well aware, a master of line, of brilliantly comic juxtaposition. A perfectionist, used to organizing deadlines and production schedules, this large, moustachioed man loved riding, dancing, observing large animals and fencing. He left posterity little evidence about himself apart from his remarkable penmanship, which Ruskin,* the most demanding of critics, praised.

According to Engen, Tenniel's method for creating the *Alice* pictures was the same as the method he used for *Punch*, namely preliminary pencil drawings, further drawings in 'ink and Chinese white' to simulate the wood engraver's line, then transference to the wood-block by the use of tracing paper. Then the drawings were painstakingly engraved to the highest standards; by the Dalziel Brothers in this instance. The final stage in the reproduction process was to make electrotype plates from the wood-engravings, using them as masters. It was the electrotype plates that were used for the actual printing. In 1981, the original wood-blocks were discovered in a bank vault where they had been deposited by the publisher. They are now at the British Library. Engen noted that the engravers endured 'numerous expensive changes ordered by Dodgson, as well as Tenniel's short proof notes'. For a full history of the *Alice* blocks and engravings see *Tenniel's Wood-Engraved Illustrations to the* Alice *Books* introduced by Leo de Freitas (1986) and *Tenniel's Alice* (1978).

By the time the *Looking-Glass* illustrations were completed, Tenniel himself had encroached sufficiently on Carroll's territory as a writer as to have persuaded Carroll to cut the entire incident about the Wasp* from his second story. Tenniel commented: 'A *wasp* in a *wig* is altogether beyond the appliances of Art'. The galleys, proofs of the text of the wasp incident were in Carroll's rooms at Christ Church when he died and have since been reprinted with a fresh series of Steadman illustrations. (See Sale of Carroll's Effects.*)

When the first print run of 2000 copies of *Wonderland* appeared, Tenniel objected to the 'disgraceful printing'. Some of these copies had already been given away and the balance of the edition went to an American publisher. Tenniel in part objected to some rather poor presswork of the first 20 pages, printed by the Clarendon Press in Oxford. A second – and satisfactory – edition was produced by Richard Clay, the printers, and this became the first British edition of the book.

TENNIEL AND *WONDERLAND*: A CHRONOLOGY

25 January 1864   Carroll asked Tenniel to illustrate *Wonderland*.

5 April 1864   Tenniel consented. The fee agreed was £138.

2 May 1864   Carroll 'sent Tenniel the first piece of slip set up for *Alice's Adventures*'.

12 October 1864   Tenniel's first 'drawing on wood' of the White Rabbit scurrying away from Alice was inspected by Carroll and 34 illustrations were agreed.

28 October 1864   The Dalziel Brothers showed Carroll proofs of several of Tenniel's pictures including the four for Father William.* The cost for the engraving of Tenniel's plates by the Dalziels was £142 for 42 plates, a little more than for the drawings.

26 November 1864   Carroll gave the Deanery Manuscript to Alice for Christmas.

c. May 1865   Carroll sent the galley proofs for all the text to Tenniel so he could complete the illustrations. Forty-two illustrations were completed.

June 1865   The Clarendon Press, Oxford, printed 2000 copies of *Alice* at a cost of £131.

20 July 1865   Tenniel objected to the quality of this first printing and Carroll rejected it.

November 1865   Richard Clay, the new printers, achieved an edition which satisfied Tenniel and Carroll. Carroll proposed to employ them again if he wrote a second *Alice* story.

TENNIEL AND *LOOKING-GLASS*: A CHRONOLOGY

8 April 1868   Carroll reported Tenniel's warning that there was 'no chance of his being able to do pictures for me until the year after next, if then. I must now try Noel Paton'.

19 May 1868   Noel Paton, Kingsley's* illustrator, urged Carroll to persist with Tenniel. So did Ruskin.* Carroll, in desperation, offered to pay *Punch* for his time 'for the next five months' to free him to illustrate the second *Alice*.

18 June 1868   Tenniel made what Carroll described as a 'kind offer to do the pictures (at such spare time as he can find)'. Tenniel hoped the illustrations would be ready by Christmas 1869.

12 January 1869   Carroll sent the first chapter of *Looking-Glass* to Alexander Macmillan.*

20 January 1870   Carroll saw, a year later than he had anticipated, the first ten Tenniel sketches for the pictures of *Looking-Glass*.

12 March 1870   Carroll and Tenniel met for two hours in London to set out the plans for 30 more pictures, having already sent three to the Dalziel Brothers, George and Edward, at Camden Press for 'cutting'.

4 January 1871   Carroll 'finished the MS of *Looking-Glass*'. This manuscript has never come to light.

16 January 1871   Carroll sent the completed galleys, including the Wasp incident, to Tenniel for pasting up and illustrating.

March 1871   Concerned that children might be frightened by the picture of the Jabberwock,* Carroll consulted some mothers. As a result of their advice, he moved the picture to the text pages and substituted Tenniel's White Knight,* wearing his own moustaches, as the frontispiece.

25 April 1871   Carroll was still waiting, having received only 27 pictures to that date. Tenniel now hoped to complete by July, two years later than his original estimate.

21 November 1871   Carroll sent authorization to Clay by telegraph to electrotype: 'all the rest of the *Looking-Glass*. I afterwards sent two corrections by post. So ends *my* part of the work'.

30 November 1871 Macmillan advised Carroll that they already had orders for 7500 copies: 9000 were to be printed and a further 6000 were ordered.

6 December 1871 Carroll received the first copy of *Looking-Glass*.

15 December 1871 Carroll sent the Dalziel Brothers a cheque for £203.16 for the engraving.

27 January 1872 15,000 copies of Carroll's *Looking-Glass* story had been sold by his fortieth birthday.

By 1885 Carroll was able to write to Alice to tell her that, including the People's Edition and the first translations* into foreign tongues, 120,000 copies of *Wonderland* had sold.

1890 Tenniel agreed to supervise the colouring of 20 illustrations for *The Nursery Alice*. The book was colour-printed by Edward Evans and the sentimental cover was drawn by Carroll's friend and life-drawing teacher, E. Gertrude Thomson.* Although Carroll thought the first page 'far too bright and gaudy – [They] vulgarize the whole thing', children liked the book. Tenniel seems to have lost the correspondence between himself and Carroll and never worked with Carroll again.

Tennyson, Alfred Lord, (1809–92) In 1850 Tennyson became Poet Laureate* and was ennobled by Queen Victoria.* He was her favourite poet because he had identified her late husband, Prince Albert, with King Arthur in his *Morte D'Arthur* poems. Carroll was raised on Tennyson's verse and, as a young man, hurried to buy each new collection Tennyson published. He sought out Tennyson with his camera. At the same time he could not resist parodying Tennyson's poetry and it was the view of Charles Tennyson, the poet's grandson and biographer, that Tennyson knew about this. By getting close to Tennyson, Carroll was close to literary fortune in mid-nineteenth century England. In 1864, the relationship ended with an uncomfortable quarrel between the two when Carroll asked Tennyson for permission to circulate a song lyric he had written, which was unpublished, among his friends. No permission was given. Each forthwith accused the other of not being a gentleman.

Carroll first stalked Tennyson in the Lake District where the Tennysons were holidaying, and Carroll made out he was holidaying, in September 1857. Carroll was 25. He had already photographed Agnes Weld, whose mother was Emily Tennyson's sister. Using this as a means of entry, he photographed the Tennyson boys, Hallam and Lionel, looking sulky and lounging in velvet suits. He talked with Tennyson late into the night and seemed to enjoy

Tennyson's derogatory remarks about John Ruskin.* In 1859 Carroll went on holiday to the Isle of Wight.* Here Tennyson had rented, and later purchased, the rambling house, Farringford, near the pretty Freshwater Bay where Julia Margaret Cameron* lived. (See also Una Taylor.*)

Tennyson loved to work at clearing the woods around the house and scything the lawn as well as walking along the chalk cliffs. Cameron's entourage were similarly outdoor-minded, casual dressing and Bohemian. The two 'sets' included a number of Liberals whom Carroll parodied, F. D. Maurice,* Edward Fitzgerald (see Caterpillar*), Benjamin Jowett* and even Charles Darwin. Black-suited and, in the summer, with a straw boater, Carroll must have appeared a stiff figure among them. As with Carroll's photograph of T. H. Huxley,* his picture of Tennyson, sitting and slightly nervous, is a compassionate and human view of an individual usually shown in a more heroic light.

The relationship did not flourish. Carroll caused a battle between Hallam and Lionel by giving one a pen-knife and the other a telescope. The correspondence over the circulation of the unpublished song by Tennyson ended the unequal friendship. Carroll had in all earnestness produced, with his sisters, an index to *In Memoriam*, published anonymously by Tennyson's own publishers. It was flattering to the poet. He also published *The Two Voices*, a parody of Tennyson's *The Three Voices*. In Charles Tennyson's view, Carroll was as incisive as any critic about the fact that Tennyson's poetry was past its prime at the time that Alice was being written. In 1855, Carroll read *Maud* and referred to it in his diary. Martin Gardner* said of 'The Garden of Live Flowers'* in *The Annotated Alice*:

> The entire episode is a parody on the talking flowers in Section 22 of Tennyson's poem *Maud*.

Tennyson, he noted, used a passion flower but Carroll:

> ... changed it to a tiger-lily when he learned that the name had reference not to human passions but to the Passion of Christ on the Cross.

It is our view that there are shades of Hallam and Lionel – originally to Carroll 'the most beautiful boys of their age I ever saw' – in Tweedledum* and Tweedledee.* They were not twins but for a time Emily Tennyson did what she could to dress them alike, which could have been caused by her desire to make them a decorative appendage to the poet's household. The White Knight may also be inspired by the Knight of Wight that Tennyson was, the medievalist living on the Isle of Wight. The Knight, before reciting, said to Alice:

"It's long...but it's very, *very* beautiful. Everybody that hears me sing it—
either it brings the *tears* into their eyes, or else—"

"Or else what?" said Alice, for the Knight had made a sudden pause.

"Or else it doesn't, you know..."

It did not.

In the decade of the deterioration of their relationship, Carroll sent
Tennyson, described as 'his idol' by Morton Cohen, vellum-bound
presentation copies of *Wonderland* and *Looking-Glass*. In private he noted these
gifts as 'a peace offering'. Receipt was acknowledged from Farringford, but
no reactions to the stories by Tennyson, Emily or the boys survive. While
the White Knight's song, 'The Aged, Aged Man'* may parody several other
works, the fact that it brought no tears to Alice's eyes is a reminder of a famous
line of the Laureate's from *The Princess: A Medley*, published in 1847: 'Tears,
idle tears, I know not what they mean!'

The White Knight's recitation has a great deal in common with Tennyson's,
whose recitals of his own poems Rossetti* found intolerably protracted – his
listeners never knew whether they would ever end – and Carroll himself may
have been subjected to them at Farringford. Rossetti and Carroll's preference
was for concision. Compare Carroll's petulant Rose in 'The Garden of
Live Flowers' too, with the description of her equivalent in *The Princess*:

> A rosebud set with little wilful thorns,
> And sweet as English air could make her, she.

By the time his sovereign ennobled him in 1884, Tennyson's writing was
thought by his friends, including Edward Lear and Edward Fitzgerald, to be
in further decline. Carroll mimicked its style and content for the delight of
his nursery readers, whether or not his spoofs were noticed by their elders
and betters – or by future readers of *Alice* inured to Tennyson but not to
Carroll.

Terry, Dame Alice Ellen (1847–1928) Ellen Terry was the greatest
actress of her day. As an example of his capacity for talent-spotting, Carroll
noted her talent on the very first West End theatrical appearance she made.
This was in a boy's part when she played Mamillius in a production of
Shakespeare's *The Winter's Tale* at the Princess's Theatre in June 1856. Ellen
was nine. He described her at that age as 'a beautiful little creature who played
with remarkable ease and spirit'. In Ellen's memoir of her own life, she recalled
the period when Carroll first became aware of her talent. As Mamillius, she
remembered playing in 103 performances of the play for 15 shillings a
week. Ellen was the third of 11 children of the talented Terry family. Apart

from a brief period when her common-law children, Edith and Gordon Craig, were infants, she never retired from the stage.

Carroll's personal and lasting contact with the Terrys, which Anne Clark was the first to discuss, started when Ellen was 17 and continued throughout his life. He photographed Ellen and her sisters, and perhaps his most moving portrait of a young girl is of the brooding Ellen, aged 17, in her theatrical black Tudor-style wedding dress after she had been scandalously abandoned by her husband, the painter G. F. Watts (1817–90) whom she had married in January 1864. A separation was arranged against her will in June 1865, in which Julia Margaret Cameron's* sisters played a mischievous part. It is our view that the Tiger-lily* parodied the passionate Ellen on stage in one of her dramatic roles 'waving gracefully about in the wind'. Alice asks her:

"...And can *all* the flowers talk?"
"As well as *you* can," said the Tiger-lily. "And a good deal louder."

Ellen Terry's enunciation and emotional range had always been remarkable, even when she was a young actress working extraordinary hours. In her memoirs she wrote:

Rehearsals lasted all day, Sundays included, and when there was no play running at night, they lasted until 4 or 5 the next morning ... Sometimes I could hardly keep my eyes open when I was on the stage.

The Tiger-lily criticized all the other flowers:

"Silence, every one of you!" cried the Tiger-lily, waving itself passionately from side to side, and trembling with excitement.

The relationship between Carroll and Terry lasted 42 years, from 1854 until his death. It was one of deep mutual respect but lacked the initimacy or informality of true friendship. Certainly Carroll was ambiguous about her when she lived in secret with the architect, E. W. Godwin (1833–86), a member of Whistler's Bohemian circle, which she joined at that time. Carroll felt, although with regret, that his clerical status meant that the friendship had to be suspended for a while. Once she remarried he allowed himself to take it up again.

Ellen Terry, in turn, always took great trouble to find seats for her performances for Carroll and his child*-friends. Ellen relished being the friend of the author of *Alice*. Unlike his friendship with the Liddells* and Tennyson,* Carroll's friendship with Ellen and the Terrys survived a stinging set-back when Carroll complained that she was 'indelicate' in the way she partly undressed playing Margaret in *Faust*. Terry said that this was an insult that 'blighted her'. Carroll remained her 'dear Mr Dodgson' nevertheless. 'Dear

Mr Dodgson' could, however, be accused of having his cake *and* eating it. On one occasion he contrasted the clumsy slowness of her woman's body with the enchanting body-movements of her smaller sisters, 'Polly' and 'Flo', as they darted about the stage, typecast as Ellen had been in the role of Puck aged nine – nymphet roles. Carroll blamed girls of whom he was fond when the course of nature changed them into women. In 1879, he found Ellen's Ophelia 'simply perfect', but in comparison with her little sisters, Carroll noted that Ellen's maturity marred her appearance. She was at this time at the height of her beauty. Of another performance, he noted:

> The gush of animal spirits of a light–hearted girl is beyond her now, poor thing! She can give a very clever imitation of it but that is all.

Carroll used his friendship with Ellen Terry, as he used word games, to impress child-friends. In 1883, he took Ethel Arnold* from Oxford* on a jaunt to London* to show her he could gain entry to the Terry sisters' homes. He gate-crashed a Terry children's party after intercepting Polly Terry against her will as she left a performance at the Court Theatre. In a camp flurry of a letter, Carroll gossiped about his and Ethel's adventures to another child-friend, Agnes Hull (see Riddles*) who had seen them together:

> I want to tell you what a Terryble time I have had of it for the last few days.

He was trying to show how absent-minded Ellen Terry had become as she helped her children to act leads at the family party. Carroll introduced Ethel to Ellen three times, the cause of the 'Terryble' time. First he introduced her at the cloakroom, then during the play, when Ellen sat next to Ethel and fidgeted nervously with Ethel's necklace, by Carroll's account. Finally Carroll introduced Ethel again when they were in the hallway as the *invited* guests departed. Each time, Ellen forgot her. On the third occasion, Ethel presented a bouquet of violets and Ellen explained that she had not realized she was being introduced to the same girl every time. Seeing Ethel with her hat on and without it had made her think Mr Dodgson had brought with him more than one child-friend. Ellen had a point. This was not the first time Carroll pursued her uninvited to one of the Terry sisters' private children's parties with a child-friend in tow.

Thackeray, William Makepeace (1811–1863)   Novelist, humourist and one of the founder contributors to *Punch*.* Carroll tried to arrange a photographic session with Thackeray, but failed. Thackeray was a close friend of the Liddells,* and went riding with them in Hyde Park when they lived at the Headmaster's House at Westminster. With Edward Lear, he created the Victorian fashion for loose, comfortable and humorous line drawings, at which he excelled. This style influenced Carroll's *Under Ground* drawings, which lack Thackeray's and Lear's fluency. Thackeray's face, with its flat, broken nose, which Tenniel had watched again and again during editorial meetings at *Punch*, can be discerned in the visage of Tenniel's* White Queen,* and that of her ineffectual husband, the White King.

Thames, River   The river at Oxford* is called either the Isis or the Thames. The word Isis is used by Oxonians for the Thames above Oxford. Above and below this the river is the Thames. When Carroll and Alice rowed in 1857 and subsequent years, the Isis/Thames was channelled away from the drifting shallow streams of the Middle Ages when the priory had first been founded on the site of Christ Church* Cathedral. By 1857, the entire river was navigable. Much of the charm of days on the river derived from the contrast between the wilder reaches, overhung with willow and alder, where kingfishers and coots secreted themselves and the mechanically-ordered channels of locks and weirs. Going through the locks in itself must have been a thrilling experience for the Liddell children, with opportunities for face-pulling as the waters lowered themselves and the slimy walls became visible. Barge traffic still carried coal and building materials to Oxford. Connected by canal to Birmingham, Oxford was an important junction on Britain's most important river, busy with commerce and pleasure.

From the formal regattas at Eton, Henley and Oxford, to the inspired idleness of summer punting and paddling – the 'messing about in boats' of Kenneth Grahame (1859–1932) – the Thames was a constant source of pleasure. Between June and September, boating offers the experience of sweet moods and history, of old abbeys and Roman fords, fit subjects for English poetry and painting. 'Alice was beginning to get very tired of sitting by her sister on the bank' established the warm air currents and slow flowing water of the 'golden afternoon'* in July that Carroll dreamed about. In contrast, in Chapter V of *Looking-Glass*:

> the boat was left to drift down the stream as it would, till it glided gently in among the waving rushes ...

This sequence, set in November, established a darker, more fearful mood where, as in J. E. Millais'* paintings, girls like Ophelia, and even innocent babies in their wicker cradles, could be dragged down into deep and mysterious waters. In winter, the Thames could flood violently and drownings were not unknown, particularly close to weirs.

Carroll's journeys on the river started with the girls walking hand in hand across Christ Church Meadow, Carroll in a straw hat carrying the picnic basket. From the Meadow they would cross the old bridge that carries St Aldates Street, the one that ran in front of Tom Tower and Carroll's rooms, out of Oxford to the south. Salter's Boat Yard, still in business, was across the river beyond the strange Folly Bridge house, a castellated building sitting on an island.

The boat Carroll hired was probably a clinker–built gig rigged as a double sculler, revarnished each winter and fitted out with velvet cushions in the coxswain's seat. Such boats, while heavy, had an elegant line to them and could achieve some speed, being used for coaching and training college oarsmen. The girls would take the tiller (see 'Tillie'*) or sit in the bows trying to steer the long craft and being distracted by ducks on the water and the pleasures of draping a small arm in the water. Carroll probably hired sculls for them rather than oars, which would have been too heavy for little girls. There is reference to the girls being allowed to take the sculls and learn to 'feather'. This means to turn the oar flat as the body swings forward between the rowing strokes. Alice had difficulty understanding the word when she was rowing the old Sheep in *Looking-Glass*.

When Carroll and his party went upstream, they followed the curl of the river through the poorer parts of Oxford. Here it was probably polluted with the effluent from the city drains, which were the principal cause of cholera and excited the interest of Alice's father and Dr Acland* who courageously inspected the pollution in this underground world and advocated remedial measures.

Leaving the town behind, the party made their way under the railway* bridge that took Carroll north to Birmingham, on to Croft,* through the lock at Osney, and then through a narrow section where the river splits in two. Here they would enter a dark, rather mysterious wood, reminiscent of the 'Wood Where Things Have No Name' where Alice met the Fawn (see Preaching and Sermons* and Prayers*). Above the divide in the river, the countryside opens out, with willows and alders overgrowing the river on the west bank, and Port Meadow where cattle came down to cool themselves on the east. *Under Ground* and *Wonderland* almost certainly start here on a large stretch of unenclosed land where it was possible to beach the boat. A little further on was the weir at Godstow, as picturesque as anywhere on the Thames, and close to this was the papermill at Wolvercote where Carroll took the girls to see Thomas Combe,* printer to the University.

Downstream to Nuneham* was altogether a longer expedition. To the middle of Port Meadow is about two and a half miles from Folly Bridge, to Godstow, three. To Nuneham is almost five miles, but it is a journey along one of those overgrown parts of the Thames that still give the sense of being in deep countryside. The reaches are lined with billowing trees, with the pretty, rustic Sandford Lock as a bonus. A particular delight is the view of the Oxford spires from Port Meadow. The view, with the exception of Nuffield College, is little changed from the view that Carroll would have shown Alice.

It is still possible to explore Carroll's journeys on the river. On the upstream journey there is more housing along the river before the lock near Osney, but after this the wooded section, Port Meadow and Godstow, are little changed. Cattle still graze on unenclosed farm land on Port Meadow. On the downstream journey, the College Barges, old London livery barges towed there with the beginning of competitive rowing, are now gone and replaced by modern college boat houses. In the next mile or so there is more embanking of the river and the Oxford bypass is new. Beyond that, over the next three-and-a-half mile stretch to Nuneham, where a shower of rain surprised Carroll's boating party into taking shelter, little, including the weather, has changed.

Theatre   From his nursery days, Lewis Carroll loved the theatre. His adult journals recount every production he ever attended (see for example Ellen Terry*), and are unmatched sources for the theatre historian. Sometimes he went to several performances in one evening. If his clerical companions felt obliged by their vows to cut short a visit or avoid one all together, as Liddon* always did, Carroll hardly ever followed suit. He was stage-struck, and well able to give an informed amateur's account of the Victorian theatre world. Most unusually, however, Carroll watched – above all – for child acting talent, of which he was a fair judge. In addition, he kept a sharp eye and ear open for moral lapses on stage; if they did occur, he would follow them up with vigour.

Alice herself, with her clear enunciation and movement across the sets of the stories he created for her, is the leading actress in *Alice*. Carroll's over-romantic late article, 'Alice on the Stage' showed how he relished dramatic presentations of *Alice*, particularly if he had been able to ensure that there was a child-friend in the leading role. (See Isa Bowman.*)

Marionettes were another of his passions. In his childhood in Daresbury,* the village carpenter built a little wooden stage for him which he designed. It was 18 inches high, 23 wide and 27 deep. In the wings of his wooden stage, he set an inverted tray fitted with pegs to hold the scenery and wings. The stage was lit with candles which served as footlights. His nephew, Stuart Collingwood* recalled his Dodgson aunts remembering that:

> he was very clever at manipulating the innumerable strings by which the movements of his puppets were regulated.

One of his first plays, which he wrote, dressed, and voiced himself, was *The Tragedy of King John*. Carroll's wooden nursery stage survived, together with 11 of the cardboard characters he made to go with it, although three of them were headless by that time. These were among the personal memorabilia that went on sale in New York in 1937. (See also *Alice* on Stage.*)

Thimble   Commentators on *Alice* and *The Hunting of the Snark* are intrigued by the number of conjurors' props Carroll introduced into his stories. These included top hats, white rabbits, gloves, thimbles and fans. They lace the story and lend mystery to the everyday. His fascination with such props was matched only by that with marionettes. (See Magic* and Theatre.*)

The Mouse with the Long Tail* asked the Dodo* to present Alice with a prize for herself after the Caucus-race. The Dodo proposed: 'We beg your acceptance of this elegant thimble'. In Grandville's* original version of this scene, a Guillemot priest, not a Dodo, hands a nymph who is older than Alice, a wedding ring, not a thimble. Awareness of this source, pointed out by Marie Mespoulet (see Illustrators*) intensifies the impact of the priest-like Dodo's gift in Tenniel's* plate.

Thirty Nine Articles of Religion   These were agreed upon in 1571 and 'set out the Anglican position on Reformation controversies'. All Anglican clergy were – and still are – required to consent to them, as were undergraduates until 1854. Particularly pertinent in Carroll's time was the article declaring eternal punishment for all those Anglicans or other Christians, who did not accept this article. F. D. Maurice* and Carroll were among the devout reformist Anglicans who chose to dissent from this doctrine.

Thistle

> ...Alice dodged behind a great thistle to keep herself from being run over...

When the Puppy, perhaps a 'Beagle' puppy, rushes at Alice, who is protected by a Thistle in *Wonderland*, it is possible that a parody of Darwin is involved. The only Thistle who was a biologist at Christ Church* was William Turner Thistleton Dyer, a Member of the Senior Common Room with Carroll. A Christ Church scientist, he was not a Darwinian and became Director of the Royal Gardens at Kew.

There is a remarkable overlap between Tenniel's* puppy face and that of the young Darwin drawn by George Richmond (1809–96), friend of Liddell* and Ruskin.* Seekers of anagrams* in *Alice* may also find in Alice's encounter with the lumbering Puppy hidden references to the impact of Charles Darwin's (1809–82) ideas on High Church* Oxford, in particular to Darwin's best-selling books; *Journal of Researches into the ... Natural History of the Various Countries visited by H.M.S. 'Beagle'*, the editions of 1839, 1845 and 1860 having appeared by the time *Wonderland* was published; and *On the Origin of Species by Means of Natural Selection, or the Preservation of Favoured Races in the Struggle for Life* (1859). According to Darwin's editor and son, Francis Darwin, Darwin was more hurt and offended by an unspecified reference to himself as a 'Dog', than by any of the thousands of attacks on his person in the form of an Ape by opponents of his theory that appeared after *Origin* was published.

Perhaps, like Ruskin and Tennyson* this great man had been alerted to the possible parodies of Darwinism in *Alice* in his publicity-conscious circle. (See also William Empson,* T. H. Huxley* and Science.*)

Thomson, Emily Gertrude (1850–1929)

Thomson, Emily Gertrude (1850–1929)   A graphic artist who made her living with sentimental illustrations for the growing market for gift stationery, Christmas and birthday cards and other paper keepsakes. Her speciality was children, whom she drew from life, often in the role of fairies. Carroll gave her the commission for the cover of *The Nursery Alice*, in spite of John Ruskin's* indication that he found the samples of her work mechanical and cloying. (See also Models.*)

An adolescent living in Lancashire when the *Alice* books were first published, Miss Thomson gained Carroll's confidence and shared sketching sessions with him, including sessions using nude child models. He seems to have found her sympathetic: they agreed about which children were suitable models and she acted as chaperon. She did, however, let him down with publishers' deadlines, as Tenniel* had. Miss Thomson seems to have been an unthreatening, valued late associate of Carroll's; a spinster, she may have been hopeful of more than encouragement as a children's artist from Carroll, but there is no evidence that he was interested in her other than as a facilitator of drawing sessions he sought in her company, with dressed, fancy-dressed or, very occasionally, nude children. (See Albums.*)

Tiger-lily Passion flowers hung over the gate in Tennyson's* 'Maud'. In Victorian books called the 'language of flowers' passion flowers were likened to the instruments of Christ's Passion, because the scourge and a crown of thorns seem discernible in the flower. For this reason, Carroll switched his parody *Looking-Glass* flower to an erect, swaying, theologically-neutral plant.

The fashion for Chinese and Japanese prints, porcelain, costume and decor accorded with the taste of the James McNeill Whistler circle, which the young actress, Ellen Terry* joined during the most Bohemian phase of her eventful personal life.

'Tillie' This was the Dormouse's* name for Edith, the third Liddell* sister, also named Tertia by Carroll. She was eight when the tale was first told. Her sudden death on the eve of her engagement to Aubrey Harcourt, and before Alice's marriage, was one of the Liddell family's most tragic losses. She was in John Ruskin's* estimation, though not in Carroll's, the most beautiful of the three older Liddell girls.

Two explanations have been proposed for Edith's pet-name 'Tillie' in the story the Dormouse told of the sisters in the Treacle Well. One was that the name was Edith's lisping way of pronouncing 'Little E'. The most likely explanation, however, was that little and persistent E was very occasionally allowed to take the tiller on river picnics. In any event, each name the Dormouse chose, 'Elsie',* 'Lacie'* and 'Tillie', ended with 'ie'. In each name, also, 'L' for Liddell was prominent. Edith's nickname is the only one with a 'T' in it. All are bisyllabic, all are in sequence and all are as lively as the Liddell girls in their accustomed high spirits.

Time Lewis Carroll was wittiest and most urbane in his nonsense, on the grounds of which he was surest as a mathematical thinker. His interest in time as a physical concept, rather than a metaphysical one, drew on his scientific expertise. He participated in the Victorian effort to fix an International Date Line, a venture launched by the Royal Society of London. Carroll's paper on this subject was published in the Macmillan journal *Nature*, still the principal journal for key new scientific papers.

His humorous handling of the concept of time included the scene where Alice witnessed the Hatter's* watch being dunked in the March Hare's* teacup at the Mad Tea-Party;* the 'Jam tomorrow — jam yesterday' comments made by the White Queen* in *Looking-Glass*, and the Red Queen* and Humpty Dumpty's* flat refusal to accept that time passes. Manic jokes about time were the other side of the coin to occasional depressing references to Death in *Alice*,* in particular, the Tweedle* brothers comment that Alice would snuff out like a candle if the Red King woke up.

Alice, as Carroll's Dream Child, was exempt from all this. She could not age or be snuffed out, but lives on in dream time. (See also Spiritual and Psychical Research.*)

Tory Carroll, like his father, and unlike the Liddells* at the time of the *Alice* presentation, was a Tory. He took a keen interest in debates in the House of Commons, which he attended in the Strangers' Gallery with the enthusiasm he devoted to the theatre.* He campaigned in 1865 against William Ewart Gladstone,* the sitting Liberal Member for one of the University of Oxford* seats. By the 1870s, Carroll was sufficiently respected as a children's writer, mathematician and photographer for the Marquess of Salisbury (see Cecil*), Carroll's kind of Tory, to enjoy a post-prandial saunter with him in the grounds of Hatfield House.

Translations of *Alice* Part of the success of *Alice* is that, while so difficult to translate into each new language, *Alice* herself remains English, yet the events around her seem to take on a believable new national character in every good translation. Thus the sense and sounds of the essentially English *Alice* intermingle across the globe.

THE FIRST TWO TRANSLATIONS OF *ALICE* The first published translator of *Alice* was Antonie Zimmermann who worked with Carroll's help to produce a German edition, which was published in Leipzig and London in 1869. Carroll was generally pleased.

The first French translation was initiated before the German one but completed after it. Almost as soon as *Wonderland* was published, Carroll's mind had turned to translation. French seemed the obvious language with which to start. The first translator was Henri Bué, son of an Oxford French tutor,

Jules Bué. French was, as in the Mock Turtle's School Under the Sea, still an 'extra' at the university. Bué, with the help of his father, spent the months of April and May 1867 working on the text, which readers declared 'delicious'. Carroll took two years before pronouncing the translation ready. It was published in August 1869.

There were problems common to all translations: how to deal with rhymes, portmanteau words, puns, nonsense words and traditional verse and rhymes in other languages than English. When the spoofing and punning of the original English did not translate, Bué interpolated recognizable French children's sources. Disappointingly, Bué's version of 'Will you walk a little faster...?' uses only three verses of the four in the original version. His translation missed out the eminently translatable:

> There is another shore you know, upon the other side.
> The further off from England the nearer is to France—

Nevertheless, Bué succeeded in incorporating a French classic into an English nonsense song to Carroll's satisfaction.

Carroll supervised these two original translations – Zimmermann's German *Alice* of February 1869, and Bué's French one of August, 1869 – in person, before *Looking-Glass* was published.

REFERENCE BOOKS ABOUT TRANSLATIONS OF *ALICE*   Besides German and French, 40 of the many languages into which *Alice* has been translated several times are Afrikaans, Albanian, Armenian, Bulgarian, Chinese, Croatian, Czech, Danish, Dutch, Farsi, Finnish, Frisian, Gaelic, Georgian, Greek, Hebrew, Hindi, Hungarian, Italian, Japanese, Korean, Latin, Lithuanian, Marathi, Pitjantjatjara (the language of an Australian aborigine nation), Polish, Portuguese, Rumanian, Russian, Serbian, Slovenian, Spanish, Swahili, Swedish, Tamil, Thai, Turkish, Urdu, Ukrainian and Welsh.

One country where *Alice* does not need translating, namely the USA, took the lead in classifying translations and delineating problems. Warren Weaver was the first to write a clear chronology of translations and index it thoroughly. His book was called *Alice in Many Tongues: the Translations of 'Alice in Wonderland'* (1964) published in Madison by the University of Wisconsin Press. This book was a milestone in the branch of *Alice* studies which concerns itself with the problem of rights and wrongs of versions of *Alice* in languages other than English. For further non–English translations of *Alice*, a useful source is Edward Guiliano's *Lewis Carroll: An Annotated International Bibliography, 1960–1977*. Pages 226–7 in this bibliography give a series of references to translations by language of origin.

DUTCH TRANSLATIONS OF *ALICE*   Many editions of *Alice* have appeared in Holland since 1945. An account of the standard of these translations in *Jabberwocky* is sub-titled, 'A Dutch Mystery'. Few texts that are true to the original story had appeared in Dutch by the end of the Second World War, in contrast with the situation in Germany, France and Italy. The co-founder of the Dutch Lewis Carroll Society is Caspar Schuckink Kool and its magazine is *Wauwelwock*; the Dutch variant of Jabberwock.

However, four good Dutch translations of *Alice* are currently on sale in Holland, of which the best is the most recent. Dr Hans Moolenburgh of Haarlem has examined these, starting with a post-war, 1947, translation of *Alice* by A. Kossman and C. Reedijk, and a later one by Eelke de Jong in 1981. They did not convey Carroll's magic, but did well with the word-games in the Lobster Quadrille.

The 1970s edition of *Alice* in Dutch illustrated by Arthur Rackham's original plates (see Illustrators*) was translated by Gonne Andriesse in 1976. She arrived at a number of elegant solutions to puns and rhymes but her version of the Mock Turtle's syllabus of Lessons Under the Sea, a translator's nightmare, 'was not a thundering success' according to our discerning informant, Dr Moolenburgh.

In 1989, the ninth Dutch translator of *Alice* overcame many problems of honesty to the original. His name is Nicolaas Matsier and the edition is published by Van Goor and illustrated by Anthony Browne. The author's foreword claims: 'This translation is complete' and Dr Moolenburgh confirms that this is the case.

RUSSIAN TRANSLATIONS OF *ALICE*   The Russian love of chess, as well as Carroll's own voyage to Imperial Russia in 1867 as an Anglican delegate with Liddon,* recommended *Alice* to the Russian-speaking world. It was in Berlin in 1923 that the first avant garde literary translation appeared (See Nabokov.*)

FRENCH TRANSLATIONS OF *ALICE*   Since the *Alice* stories were first read in France in 1869, *Alice* and Carroll have had an independent following of artists, illustrators, philosophers, logicians and literary critics in the French-speaking world; a rare accolade for a foreign poet or his muse. (See Jean-Pierre Gattégno.*) Henri Parisot is one of several distinguished French translators of the *Alice* stories and his translations include *Alice Racontée aux Petits Enfants* (*The Nursery Alice*) and *The Hunting of the Snark*. His first translation was published in 1940. He edited *Lewis Carroll* (1971), an important collection of essays. (See also Marie Laurençin, and Marguerite Mespoulet in Illustrators*.)

GERMAN TRANSLATIONS OF *ALICE*   Carroll commended the work of his chosen translator, Miss Zimmermann, in generous terms in a paragraph designed to be set opposite the Table of Contents of the first Leipzig edition. This edition was also noteworthy for its fine printing of Tenniel's original illustrations as preserved in the fine 1974 Dover facsimile. Carroll travelled through Germany in 1867 and his able woman translator may have been recommended by the Oxford philologist, Professor Friedrich Max Müller.* Carroll evidently left Zimmermann free to incorporate German kinderlieder in her translation. In the first German Dormouse's* Tale, the Dormouse, in German, 'Das Murmelthier', named words beginning with 'M' even if they were different from those cited by the English Dormouse: 'Wie Mausefallen, den Mond, Mangel, und manches Mal...' The resonance of the songs in *Alice* is preserved in 'Beautiful Soup, so rich and green' well-translated as 'Schöne Zuppe, so schwer und so grun'. In this way, *Alice* was read early in translation in German states already rich in imaginative children's literature.

Drittes Kapitel.

Caucus-Rennen und was daraus wird.

˙˙˙˙˙˙˙˙

Es war in der That eine wunderliche Gesellschaft, die sich am Strande versammelte — die Vögel mit triefenden Federn, die übrigen Thiere mit fest anliegendem Fell, Alle durch und durch naß, verstimmt und unbehaglich. —

ITALIAN TRANSLATIONS OF *ALICE*   At the age of 23, Carroll stated that he had begun reading Italian at Christ Church,* and Alice herself from a young age had an Italian, French and German tutor in addition to her governess. The first Italian translation of *Alice* was made by a cousin of Dante Gabriel and Christina Rossetti,* Teodorico Pietrocola-Rossetti, whom Carroll met at Dante Gabriel's house in Cheyne Walk. *Alice* studies flourish in Italy. The Italian language accommodates easily to the pace and emotion of Carroll's *Alice* stories. (See the latter part of Punctuation.*)

A recent Italian translation of *Alice*, *La Meravigliosa Alice*, was published in Milan in 1962. The translator was Marina Valente. Alessandro Schiaffonati translated *Through the Looking-Glass* in 1976 with the title, *Attraverso lo*

Specchio. Other applauded recent translators include Milli Graffi, Masolino d'Amico and Tomasso Giglio.

JAPANESE TRANSLATIONS OF *ALICE* Like several Victorian English children's books, in particular those of Beatrix Potter and Kate Greenaway, Carroll's *Alice* stories have a strong following in Japan. The readership is among girls and in the university community. There is a Lewis Carroll Society* of Japan, of which the Secretary is Katsuko Kasai of Bunkyo University. The President is Professor Yasunari Takahashi. The Founder Member was Yoshikyki Momma.

Alice's name in Japanese is pronounced 'Arisu'. The first *Alice* book to be translated into Japanese was *Looking-Glass*. It was translated by Tenkei Hasegawa in Tokyo as *The Looking-Glass World* in *Boy's World*. The publisher was Hakubunkan. The translation was serialized from 15 April to December 1898 to coincide with world-wide tributes to Carroll in the year after his death. The first two serializations were entitled: 'The Looking-Glass House' and 'The Garden'. *Wonderland* was translated into Japanese and serialized nine years later by Sumako.

A good translation of *Alice* into Japanese appeared in Tokyo in 1920. This was by Masao Kosuyama, and another in 1955 was by Toshio Tanaka. Masayoshi Edagawa, Shoko Ema, Yukio Tsuchiya, Akira Honda and others have devoted their literary skills to the same task and Japan shares with the USA and the UK the reputation as a zealous *Alice* reading nation, with its own Lewis Carroll Society and scholarly, artistic following.

LATIN TRANSLATIONS OF *ALICE* Latin translations of *Alice* have been among the most ingenious. One of many early Latin *Alice* versions was the Cambridge scholar, Augustus Vansittart's 1881 translation of the *Jabberwocky** poem into Latin, which Macmillan,* the publisher, admired sufficiently to publish on its own, as it has later Latin versions.

The translation of Clive Harcourt Carruthers, which has been reprinted, is notable. *Alicia in Terra Mirabili* appeared in 1964 and two years later, Carruthers' *Aliciae per Speculum Transitus* was published by Macmillan. In Carruthers' version, 'The Pool of Tears' became 'Stagnum Lacrimarum'; 'Pig and Pepper' became the euphonic 'Porcus et Piper'; and 'The Cheshire Cat' became a 'Feles Cestriana', using the original founding language for the Roman city of Chester, the capital of the county in which Daresbury* was and is the sleepy rural village of Carroll's childhood. In Latin, 'The Shriek of the Gryphon' echoes in the memory of Alice's elder sister as a resonating 'Ululatus Grypis'. As with other tongues, the translation of *Alice* into Latin since 1867 has provided some great challenges and great rewards.

Tweedledee   Alice emerged from the Wood Where Things Have No Name and began to see double. She followed two signs which led her in the same direction. The first sign read 'TO TWEEDLEDUM'S HOUSE' and the second 'TO THE HOUSE OF TWEEDLEDEE'. She realized that, although the signposts were separate, the house she was calling on was one and the same. (See, for a similar odd experience in Alice's analysis of her own sense of direction, 'Wabe' in *Jabberwocky** words.) Alice's exploration of the principle of equal and opposite made her familiar with a *Looking-Glass** theme. (See also under C. L. Dodgson,* the first-hand account of Alice Raikes.)

Alice helped the equally fat, cowardly Tweedle brothers prepare for battle. (See also Boys.*) She paid attention as they threatened that when the Red King woke from his dream* she would be 'nowhere' because she was 'only a sort of thing in his dream'. Nevertheless Alice, calling out: 'First Boy!' and 'Next Boy!' took control. Although they taunted her, she could rise above it. She really was on her way to becoming a Queen. (See also Wasp.*)

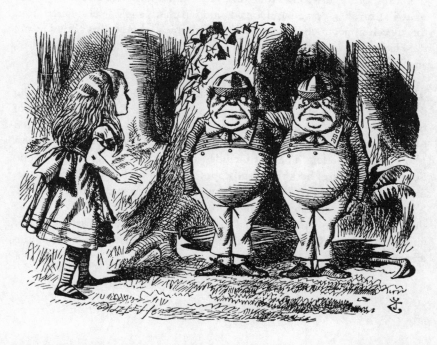

Tweedledum   Alice remarked that everything about the Tweedle brother with DEE sewn on to his collar was 'contrariwise', his word, to the one whose collar read DUM. Martin Gardner* noted that John Tenniel* had engraved the names on the twins' collars in parallel, not as mirror-images as he should have done. He was surprised that Carroll had not required Tenniel to correct the illustration. On the other hand, as wood-engravings register in verso when printed off, it is perhaps forgivable that Tenniel erred and Carroll, desperate about the late delivery of the plates, desisted from protest.

Two spoilt brothers who were interested in battles and whom Carroll knew on the Isle of Wight* were Lionel and Hallam Tennyson.* Carroll befriended their tutors, exchanged poems and gifts and photographed them. They lived in splendid isolation and were known from time to time to behave like holy terrors.

Twinkle   In *Wonderland*, the King of Hearts pointed out in court that twinkling begins not with an 'I' (pun on 'eye') but with a 'T'. At tea with the Hatter,* the Hare* and the Dormouse,* bats twinkle; cups-of-tea twinkle; 'most things twinkle'. Could the twinkle jokes in *Wonderland* hint that the Hatter stammered? As he nervously gave evidence about the twinkling of tea in Court, the King interrupted him: 'You're a *very* poor *speaker*'. Carroll, George MacDonald* and Charles Kingsley* all suffered from this speech impediment in varying degrees, which suggests that Kingsley and the Hatter had more than one characteristic in common. (See also Stammer* and Tea-Party*.)

Twiss, Quintin F. (n.d.)   Carroll kept the dressing-up cupboard in his studio for the use of child*-friends like Alice, her sisters and Xie Kitchin,* two of his best early child models.* One early exception was his Christ Church undergraduate friend and contemporary, Quintin Twiss, one of his earliest photographic models. The rest included members of his family, his friend Southey,* buildings he knew, landscapes with which he was familiar, girls and museum skeletons. Twiss dressed up as a jolly mariner and as Dickens' 'Artful Dodger'. He later became a professional actor but could only have dreamed of success when he posed for Carroll's camera at Christ Church as an undergraduate. Carroll saw Twiss in a number of West End productions after 1867.

U and V are for ...

Uglification This was on the syllabus of the Mock Turtle's* School under the Sea, but Alice learned different subjects, which made the Mock Turtle sceptical about her lessons:

> "I never heard of 'Uglification,'" Alice ventured to say. "What is it?"
> The Gryphon lifted up both its paws in surprise. "Never heard of uglifying!" it exclaimed. "You know what to beautify is, I suppose?"

Uglification was a portmanteau of 'multiplication', known to Alice as a maths topic, and the act of uglifying, an aesthetic term. John Ruskin* and William Morris (1834–96) taught that the mass replication of ornament down-graded the quality of life in Victorian England, especially as industrial cities spread into suburbs on their edges and along railway lines.

Carroll, on the other hand, viewed the multiplication of mechanically-produced objects with equanimity. He was a gadgeteer, loved inventions* and had few qualms about how many of his stamp cases or Nyctographs (tablets for taking notes in the dark, when in bed) went into production. He regarded replication by machine as one of the wonders of the world. When he met the Prince of Wales* at Christ Church* in 1860 he told him about 'the new American process for taking 12,000 photographs in an hour'. When it came to aesthetic improvements of which he disapproved, like H. G. Liddell's additions to Christ Church in 1873, he pamphleteered with ferocity against such uglification. He noted in his diary:*

> The new West Entrance to the Cathedral almost rivals the [new] Belfry [see Bats*] in Ugliness. At night began a manuscript on the subject.

Unicorn   Identifying mythical beasts on heraldic crests was a favourite amusement for the Liddell sisters.* The envelopes containing correspondence for the Deanery* from other colleges, the family, friends, or royalty would often have embossed shields or coloured seals on their flaps. The children cut these out, and collected and studied them and, with Carroll's help when he was visiting, put them in an album.

Carroll turned such beasts into characters. In his stories heraldic beasts became live creatures which made remarks, danced and sang and argued like children and dons. The Gryphon,* the Cheshire Cat*, the Lion and the Unicorn* were all heraldic characters. The Lion and Unicorn bear the Royal Arms over the motto 'Honi Soit Qui Mal Y Pense'. Humpty Dumpty's* pride in the cravat the King and Queen gave him to wear also sounds heraldic. Alice could not be sure whether it was a belt or a cravat but perhaps it was closer to an Order of the Garter.

As for the Liddells' nursery crest-collecting, Mavis Batey pointed out in her book, *The Adventures of Alice* (1991), that the Liddell crest, a Yorkshire heraldic one, was biased to the cat family. On the crest was a black Lion Rampant crowned with an Eastern Crown. The coat of arms bore three Leopards' faces wearing crowns as collars. They hovered in the air as the Cheshire Cat* did at the Queen's Croquet Match.

University Reform   Between the time that Carroll arrived at Oxford*
as an undergraduate in 1851, and 1871 when *Looking-Glass* was completed,
the rules that governed Oxford University changed. Eighteenth-century
Oxford lacked innovation, and the numbers of undergraduates, many of whom
never took examinations, had declined. The main purpose of the University
seemed to be to train clergy, many of whom were beneficiaries of livings that
the colleges controlled. This sleepy environment suited many dons, who
looked on the University as a place to live out their lives as bachelors, while
being looked after as to creature comforts and free to worship God and do
a little teaching.

Dean Liddell,* Dean Stanley,* W. E. Gladstone* and Benjamin Jowett*
knew that the University had to modernize. Their views were not identical
but between them they led a movement that abolished religious tests for
undergraduates and, for the first time since the Cromwellian period, Jews,
dissenters and Roman Catholics could attend the University. Furthermore,
science* and other new schools were consolidated and the central position
of classics declined. The social basis of the University intake gradually
widened, and has continued to do so. Finally, in 1871, the requirement that
dons be celibate was removed and the idea that women might enrol began
to take hold with the foundation of the first women's colleges.

Carroll either disliked or was uncertain about most of these changes and
satirized them. He particularly bemoaned the decline of the classics. As a
bachelor don who did no teaching during his last two decades, he lived all
his life in college. Although not among those who thought undergraduates
superfluous to the smooth running of Oxford, Carroll certainly did not see
the teaching of undergraduates as its purpose. By the 1860s he had begun
to parody himself as an extinct bird, a Dodo.*

Victoria Regina (1819–1901)   Queen of the United Kingdom of Great
Britain and Ireland and Empress of India. Her name and character are
stamped on the age in which Carroll wrote. Carroll was four when Victoria
and her future consort, Albert, met at Kensington Palace in 1836. She came
to the throne in 1837 and married Albert in 1840, before Carroll left
Daresbury* Parsonage. Of her nine surviving children, four were sons.
Among these were Albert Edward, the Prince of Wales,* whom Carroll met
at Christ Church* and to whom he gave 12 photographs; and her youngest
son, Leopold, who was tutored by Carroll's friend, Robinson Duckworth*
and photographed by Carroll as an Oxford undergraduate. A. P. Stanley,*
the Broad Church* Canon of Christ Church, served as tutor and travelling
companion to the Prince of Wales, accompanied him to the Holy Land and
assisted him in his betrothal arrangements with the Danish Princess, Alexandra.

Carroll and the Pusey* party at Christ Church feared this charming, subtle reformer, who was in a position of considerable influence in court circles.

During the *Alice* years, Carroll was in the presence of the Queen twice when she visited Christ Church, of which she was the Visitor (a role like that of an honorary chairman, but with spiritual implications). Later she chanced to spot Carroll striding alone on the carriageway in Windsor Park and he fancied that she acknowledged him with a movement of her head. Thereafter, on two further occasions, his attempts to contact her were fielded by her efficient lady-in-waiting, the Lady Augusta Stanley, wife of A. P. Stanley who was by now, and by Royal appointment, Dean of Westminster.

Unlike Stanley, Acland,* Liddell* or Tennyson,* Carroll never had a private audience with his Queen. It is not altogether clear that Carroll wanted this privilege. Prince Albert's Low Church sympathies had been a strong influence on the Queen and Carroll was wary of a number of the clerical appointments she had endorsed as Head of the Church. Carroll did not send his books for children to the Queen, but he did send a presentation copy of *Wonderland* to the Queen's youngest daughter, Princess Beatrice, and of *Looking-Glass* to her grand-daughter, later Princess Alice of Athlone. Princess Alice left a record of her meetings with Carroll, whom she found odd. Carroll said of her that she had 'rather unruly high spirits'. When she was older, he entertained her and her brother Charles:

> I taught them to fold paper pistols, to blot their names in creased paper and showed them a machine which by rapidly spinning, turns the edging of a cup into a filmy solid.

Carroll surprised a child*-friend one day by faking the Queen's handwriting for an invitation to a garden party. At this time the Queen was 16,000 signatures in arrears for the commissions she was supposed to issue personally to officers in the armed forces, so Carroll, with his talent for inventing copying machines, might have been useful to her. The Queen did not honour Carroll. Falling Knights, weak-willed Kings, demanding Queens and child-friendships may have been viewed with suspicion by some of her most trusted subjects.

Queen Victoria adulated domesticity and turned it into a cult, as she had her widowhood. She wrote in the year of Alice's birth:

> We women are not *made* for governing – and if we are to be good women ... *feminine and amiable and domestic*, are not fitted to reign.

Yet she reigned, and she reigned alone. The Alice of the *Alice* stories, Carroll's logical, defiant heroine, does not fit her mould.

Vivisection   Later in life, Carroll became an ardent anti-vivisectionist and was befriended by Frances Power Cobbe (1822–1904), co-secretary of the National Anti-Vivisection Society. His articles on the subject were so strongly worded that he had unusual difficulty in getting them published. His passion was fuelled by the fact that animal experimentation was becoming more and more important as a biological issue at Oxford. To add to the irony, Dean Liddell* supported Professor Acland* as a leading proponent of the vivisection of experimental animals.

In *Alice*, Carroll's attitude to animals has some ambiguities. Alice herself tells attendant animals about the skill of her cat in catching mice. Yet the Mock Turtle weeps at the idea that there is a possibility of its becoming soup. The Mutton took similar umbrage when it was introduced to Alice. Perhaps, even in the *Alice* years, Carroll's sensitivities were moved by the plight of the animals on the table.

W is for ...

Wakeling, Edward (n.d.)   Chronicler and devotee of Carroll, editor of a new, unexpurgated edition of Carroll's diaries* and Inspector of Schools. Since 1975, Edward Wakeling has been closely involved with the Lewis Carroll Society.* He has devised books for a popular readership based on his own rendition of intriguing puzzles, ciphers and games invented by Carroll. These have included *The Logic of Lewis Carroll* (1978), *The Cipher Alice* (1990), *Lewis Carroll's Games and Puzzles* (1992), *Rediscovered Lewis Carroll Puzzles* (1995–6) and *Alice in Wonderland Puzzle and Game Book* (1995). In 1989, he organized the First International Lewis Carroll Conference at Christ Church* and his definitive collection of modern illustrations* inspired by Carroll's *Alice* is a highlight of a touring exhibition organized for the centennial celebrations of Carroll's death.

In 1992, Wakeling published a study of Lewis Carroll's clergyman brother Skeffington, named after his uncle, Skettington Lutwidge,* *Skeffington Hume Dodgson, Brother of Lewis Carroll, Vicar of Vowchurch (1895–1910): a Brief Biography*.

Walking   Besides praying and considering the lot of mankind, walking was *the* archetypal activity of the Victorian clergyman. Wordsworth and the Romantics had made walking respectable, so that it ceased to be associated with vagabondage as in the eighteenth century. The countryside and the beach appear frequently in *Wonderland* and *Looking-Glass*. Not surprisingly, the journeys Alice takes, when not travelling by train* or swimming or rowing, are on foot. Like many of his contemporaries, Carroll walked extensively, although he did not walk to chalk up records in the overly energetic way of the Christian Socialists, Charles Kingsley* or Thomas Hughes (1822–96).

Carroll was stronger and fitter than certain aspects of his image suggest and at the age of 51 he recorded a 22-mile walk. He walked for exercise and for contemplation, for the opportunity to absorb the sights and sounds of country lanes, to talk or think about God while taking exercise and, when possible, added to these comforts that of having a child*-friend in hand. To most Victorian mothers, walking, after the well-brought-up child had left the pram, was beneficial and healthy. Carroll had both the time and the inclination to oblige. (See also Rowing.*)

Walrus The Walrus and the Carpenter* were a greedy, knowing, vaudeville pair, given to tearfulness and false emotion, the central characters in the brilliant 18-stanza poem recited to Alice by Tweedledee.* Carroll could not stop himself mocking the metre or substance of much that was most accepted by the Victorians. In this case, as Martin Gardner* pointed out, it was the metre of a poem by Thomas Hood (1799–1845) that he used. Alice was worried about the length, the worry she showed when the White Knight* recited his long poem. Poor Alice! Girls like her had to recite, or listen to, large chunks of poetry with meanings and emotions that were beyond them. She tried to brush Tweedledee aside but failed:

> Tweedledee smiled gently, and began again:

> > "The sun was shining on the sea,
> >   Shining with all his might:
> > He did his very best to make
> >   The billows smooth and bright—
> > And this was odd, because it was
> >   The middle of the night.

> > The moon was shining sulkily,
> >   Because she thought the sun
> > Had got no business to be there
> >   After the day was done—"

At one point the Walrus said that 'what we chiefly need' was 'a loaf of bread' – a possible reference to Edward Fitzgerald's popular *The Rubáiyát of Omar Khayyam*:

> > Here with a Loaf of Bread beneath the Bough,
> > A Flask of Wine, a Book of Verse – and Thou
> > Beside me singing in the Wilderness!

What the Walrus expected was not 'Thou' but 'pepper and vinegar beside'.
The Walrus and Carpenter liked seafood, swimming and shoreline visiting,
as did the Gryphon* and the Mock Turtle* in *Wonderland*. (See Caterpillar,*
Pater,* Poets Laureate,* Ruskin* and Tennyson.*)

Washing   It was almost inevitable that Alice should have been educated
at home. It was equally inevitable that her brothers should have been
educated away from home. In trying to put Alice down, the Mock Turtle*
claimed that it:

"had the best of educations—in fact, we went to school every day—".

To which Alice retorted that she too had been to day-school.

"With extras?" asked the Mock Turtle, a little anxiously.
"Yes," said Alice, "we learned French and music."
"And washing?" said the Mock Turtle.
"Certainly not!" said Alice indignantly.

'Extras' were the bane of the middle-class Victorian parent, for they were
added to the school bill. They included subjects such as modern languages
and music; but also laundry, thus 'washing'. Alice, educated at home, learned
subjects over and above those Miss Prickett taught her, but of course washing
would never have been among them. She put down the Mock Turtle by

saying he could not have had much need of washing, 'living' as he did 'at the bottom of the sea'. (See also Governesses* and Lessons.*)

Wasp in a Wig, The   This is an episode in *Looking-Glass* which was hidden from *Alice* readers from 1870 until 1974 (See Sale of Carroll's Effects.*) Carroll set the Wasp *Looking-Glass* episode in early November, a month when insects which fail to hibernate weaken and die. Alice met it as she waited by the brook. She was hoping to cross to the eighth square. It was 'something like a very old man (only that his face was more like a wasp)'. The wasp was the most fully characterized of the *Looking-Glass* insects.*

She listened kindly to its complaints, and though wary of the threat of each and every gesture, for wasps sting, cheered it by reading to it from an old newspaper with which it had littered the ground. Then she helped it to a sheltered place. The Wasp was wearing a bright yellow wig tied on with a yellow bandanna and she read to it about raiding parties, wigs and mouth-parts. It warned her of the perils of conceit, a failing it had not heeded in its own younger life. The episode includes a recitation by the Wasp: 'When I was young, my ringlets waved', jokes about human versus insect mouth-parts and a skit on the vogue for oriental porcelain led by James McNeill Whistler (1834–1903). (See also Terry.*)

When Carroll's library went up for sale on his death, the manuscript of *Alice's Adventures Under Ground** was safe in Alice Liddell's* (Hargreaves) hands, but the original manuscript, or manuscripts, of *Wonderland* and *Looking-Glass* were not preserved. However, Stuart Dodgson Collingwood,* Carroll's literary executor, knew of a reference by Tenniel* to a missing chapter in the story. In 1974, it re-surfaced at Sotheby's and was purchased by a rare book dealer from New York for Norman Armour Jr. Edited by Edward Guiliano with a foreword by Martin Gardner,* the episode, *The Wasp in a Wig: a 'Suppressed' Episode of Through the Looking-Glass and What Alice Found there*, was published in deluxe and trade editions for the Lewis Carroll Society* of North America in 1977 by Macmillan.

The entire set of *Looking-Glass* galley slips numbered 64–67 and portions of those numbered 63 and 68, recalling Alice's kindness to a selfish old Wasp before she was crowned Queen, were preserved by Carroll and had survived among his effects after all. Carroll corrected these galleys during the summer of 1870 in black ink. The Wasp episode was subsequently 'suppressed' on the way to press on Carroll's instruction, added in purple ink. His instruction is on slip 63 and reads: 'omit to middle of Slip 68'. The initiative for the 'suppression' came, not from Carroll, who after all took it to galley stage, but from John Tenniel, advising suppression for length reasons. He said he was 'in an agony of haste', behind with *Alice* and had a *Punch** deadline looming. He observed:

> Don't think me brutal, but I am bound to say that the 'wasp' character doesn't interest me in the least, & I can't see my way to a picture. If you want to shorten the book, I can't help thinking – with all submission – that there is your opportunity.

Carroll capitulated. The Wasp episode is popular with Carroll enthusiasts, although some belittle it. It was later illustrated in colour by Ralph Steadman, one of Carroll's innovative twentieth-century illustrators.* Arguably what Ralph Steadman relished, and what was traditional subject-matter to J. J. Grandville* – a decrepit insect zoomorph* meeting a lovely young girl – was not beyond the bounds of Tenniel's art. This led Martin Gardner to suggest that it was the Wasp's criticism of Alice's eyes which impelled one-eyed Tenniel into non-cooperation. The Wasp commented, as did the Flowers in the Garden* and the Unicorn,* on the proportions of Alice's human face:

> "Then your eyes—they're too much in front, no doubt. One would have one as well as two, if you *must* have them so close—"

In the world of Carroll collecting, the discovery of the episode is perhaps the most important missing piece of Carrolliana to come to light since his photographs* were found and his diaries* published. Curiosity value, and speculation over why Tenniel dismissed the section, should not detract from how important the episode is in the scheme of *Looking-Glass*. In the printed version Alice goes from the White Knight,* to whom she is kind, to be crowned. The Wasp episode, however, gives her the opportunity to show herself as a truly Christian and charitable girl. Without fear of this dangerous creature, setting aside her ambition to be crowned queen, good samaritan-like, she goes to the aid of the Wasp. Arguably the plot of *Looking-Glass* is less rambling than appears. Alice's final act of contrition can be seen as an essential step to her being spiritually prepared to be a true Christian Queen. Carroll, stung by Tenniel, acted as a Christian should, turned the other cheek, but did not destroy this vivid episode. (See Anatomy.*)

Waugh, Evelyn (1903–66) Waugh wrote only briefly on Carroll, but with perception. This was in the *Spectator* (October 1939). He wrote a review of the Nonesuch Edition of Carroll's works which he considered confusing. Without explanation, it mixed Carroll's, Dodgson's and anonymous works. The criticism is pertinent but he made a further point. Waugh, a practising Catholic like his contemporaries and fellow *Alice* commentators, Shane Leslie,* and Ronald Knox* speculated that 'one explanation that occurred to one reader' was that Carroll was 'tortured by religious scepticism'. (See also Critics.*) Waugh believed that the prattle of Bruno in *Sylvie and Bruno* was a narrative device that reflected 'some psychological peculiarity of [Carroll's]'. Waugh's point relates to *Alice* for he believed that Carroll was an author so afraid of the direction in which rational analysis of God would lead him that he escaped into writing fantasy for children.

White Knight   This is a kindly character who beats off the Red Knight in a battle that satirized Pre-Raphaelite ideas of knightly chivalry, with Alice as the maiden. We think that the medievalism is also based on that of Tennyson,* the Knight from the Isle of Wight,* even though the face of the White Knight as Tenniel* drew him may have been based on the less famous long-moustachioed Tenniel himself.

Alice was patient with the incompetent White Knight. In the original narrative, she then met the older and even more decrepit Wasp.* It was Martin Gardner's* view that Alice's patient progress in dealing with these ancient buffers was a metaphor for what he called:

the chasm [of age] that separated Alice Liddell from the middle-aged teller of the story.

Alice's reward for being so patient and decent was to be crowned Queen* of this essentially moral tale which might (see Wasp*), have been more moral still without a missing beat.

White Pawn   In *Wonderland* Alice was just herself. In the framing of *Looking-Glass* she was both Alice and a White Pawn on the *Looking-Glass* chessboard. Carroll's apology for the game as it was played in the *Looking-Glass* story was published in time for Christmas, 1896. Carroll noted that the 'White Pawn (Alice)' set out 'to play and win in eleven moves'. He devoted 12 chapters to her attempt, one of which was very long indeed and one of which can be read in just a few words. (See also Chess* in *Alice*.)

White Queen   Martin Gardner noted that both Carroll's *Looking-Glass* Queens* ran a great deal, reflecting the liberality of movement the Queen has on the chessboard. The White Queen has none of the authority of Carroll's stronger-minded *Alice* characters, the other Queens,* the Hatter,* Humpty Dumpty,* Tweedledee,* Tweedledum* or the Ugly Duchess.* However, apart from the problems with her shawl and perhaps with her sex (is she really a woman?) and with her humanity (she turns into a shop-keeper Sheep), her presence pervades the *Looking-Glass*. There were exciting suggestions from Ronald Knox* and Shane Leslie* that she was as significant to Alice's experience through the Looking-Glass as was the debate over Roman Catholicism in Carroll's time. (See also Cardinals Manning* and Newman*.)

White Rabbit   The White Rabbit which led Alice into *Wonderland* was the master of ceremonies at the court of the King of Hearts. It controlled court proceedings and produced key evidence at the trial of the Knave. At least, its evidence seemed important to the King, though not to Alice. The busy, hurrying White Rabbit, who was also the King's Herald, is often a favourite of readers of *Alice*.

In the *Under Ground* story, Carroll described the Rabbit carrying a fan and a nosegay. In the *Wonderland* story, it mislaid its gloves. The Rabbit had human hands and a fob watch. In spite of this, it was unpunctual. The workmen outside its house disobeyed it. So did Alice, especially when she became lodged inside its house, grown into a large girl. This scene, where Alice is trapped in the White Rabbit's house, can be seen as a skit on the person who was responsible for the construction of the Natural History Museum,* Dr Henry Wentworth Acland,* Professor of Medicine and doctor to the Liddell*

family. The Museum, a new science centre in the University, was being built when Carroll wrote *Alice*.

   Acland was in charge of the building of the Museum, with Ruskin* as his architectural adviser. Carroll photographed Acland's specimens for the museum and took portraits of his children. The view that there are elements of a parody of Acland in the character of the White Rabbit is reinforced by the Rabbit's dress, the way he hurried, and the dark chamber of strange bottles and poisons which Alice found down the Rabbit-hole – Acland's huge study at his house on Broad Street, was full of books, biological specimens and master drawings.

   Carroll may have been inspired to animate a White Rabbit by a White Rabbit in one of George MacDonald's* early tales.

White Stone   'I mark this day with a White Stone' at the end of Carroll's diary* entries was as demonstrative as Carroll ever became. Meetings with Ruskin* and Tennyson* were marked such, as were high points in Carroll's life with Alice Liddell.* The *Oxford English Dictionary* explains that the phrase is a Biblical one expressing joy and pleasure, a piece of 'provincial phraseology'. With no intimate companion, Carroll's diary was one form in which he could express a modicum of emotion. The 'White Stone' is the epitome of Victorian formality and self-restraint.

Whiting The whiting is a common fish. So are the sole and the eel – and they all suggested shoe jokes.

> "Thank you," said Alice, "it's very interesting. I never knew so much about a whiting before."
> "I can tell you more than that," said the Gryphon. "Do you know why it's called a whiting?"
> "I never thought about it," said Alice. "Why?"
> "*It does the boots and shoes*", the Gryphon replied very solemnly.

Carroll chose a common fish for the first speaker in "Will you walk a little faster?" only because 'walk' and 'whiting' share a 'w'. A whiting cannot walk. It has to ripple and glide. It was foil for the Gryphon and Mock Turtle's dialogue about boot-blacking under the sea.

Carroll's boots and shoes were always black, even on summer river expeditions such as those with the Liddell girls. For these, in Alice Liddell's words in retrospect, he 'replaced his black top hat by a hard white straw hat' ... but 'of course retained his black boots'. (See also Fish and Fishy Jokes.*)

Wight, Isle of Carroll's holidays there were important to him in widening his circle of acquaintance beyond Oxford. With the development of seaside* resorts after the Regency period, the island became popular, particularly when Tennyson* and Julia Margaret Cameron* settled there. These two lived on the south-western shore of the island, near Freshwater Bay.

The Isle of Wight was discovered as a holiday retreat – in Tennyson's case a year-round retreat – in the 1850s and 1860s. Carroll first went there on holiday with his walking companion, the Rev J. M. Collyns (1827–1912) in 1859, the year in which *Alice* was set. He returned there in 1862 and 1864 and stayed in Freshwater Bay at Plumblys Hotel, an imposing structure on the chalk cliffs that was within two hundred yards of 'Dimbola Lodge', two fishermen's houses converted by Julia Margaret Cameron into a home and studio, half a mile from Tennyson's imposing house, Farringford.

Carroll hoped to have access to Tennyson there by attaching himself to the periphery of Mrs Cameron's wide and frolicking circle of friends and their children, which included Benjamin Jowett* and the young Ellen Terry.* Carroll's uneasy relations with Tennyson and Cameron are described under those entries.

Today the local historian and librarian, Brian Hinton, has done much to revive interest in the famous Victorians who made their homes as well as their holiday retreats at this end of the island. (See Bibliography.) Plumblys Hotel where Carroll stayed still stands as a youth holiday centre overlooking Freshwater Bay where Carroll met several new child*-friends.

On the shoulder of the huge, windswept, wild-flower strewn Tennyson Down that towers over the English Channel, Carroll walked to blow away his troubles, until they caught up with him and he stopped visiting the island. It was on the Isle of Wight that Carroll first met Henry Kingsley,* brother of Charles, who admired his children's writing. Osborne, the Royal summer residence, was at the other end of the island. Tennyson was invited there, as were the Aclands* and Liddells,* the latter selling their house in North Wales, Pen Morfa* in order to holiday in closer proximity to Queen Victoria.*

It was during one of Alice Liddell's* holidays on the island, after Carroll had stopped coming there, that Cameron photographed Alice as Shakespeare's King Lear's daughter, Cordelia and as a severe-looking Roman goddess of the harvest, Pomona. Thus Alice Liddell became a preferred model to two of the great amateur photographers of the age. Cameron's photographs were as much of a monument to Alice's beauty as a young débutante as Carroll's were to her charm as a little girl.

Carroll and Alice were long separated by the time Carroll returned to the island in 1873, the first of a number of visits to the resort of Sandown. According to Brian Hinton, Tennyson managed to prevent the railway reaching Freshwater. Not so, Sandown: the branch line from Ryde made it convenient for Carroll to reach it by train before it was developed with the worst of late nineteenth- and early twentieth-century seaside residences and small hotels. Then only a cluster of these attracted the families of clergy and others to play and walk and look out on a particularly nice sandy beach and bay.

After 1876 Eastbourne* became Carroll's chosen place for summer visits and holidays. Sandown, usually visited later in the year in September after a stay at Eastbourne, also had its charms in terms of encounters with child-friends. It was on one of his visits to Sandown that Carroll made the acquaintance of Gertrude Chataway.* It was also a place where Carroll could discharge his family duties. He came to Sandown with those he called 'the sisters'. (See also Sites of Interest.*)

Wilberforce, Samuel, Bishop of Oxford (1805–73) Samuel Wilberforce was Bishop of Oxford, son of William Wilberforce (1759–1833) the slave emancipator, and known as 'Soapy Sam'. In spite of his fame, he never achieved the Anglican Church's highest offices. He had been too controversial a bishop for too long. Six years older than Dean Liddell* and a generation older than Carroll, Wilberforce consecrated Carroll as a deacon in the

Anglican Church and was responsible for setting up Cuddesdon Theological College* south of Oxford.*

Cuddesdon commands a view of the spired city that Wilberforce thought contained within its teaching body the seeds of heresy – correctly, as it turned out. Wilberforce was already a clergyman when Newman* left the Oxford Movement and defected to Rome, taking with him most of Wilberforce's siblings. At this time, Dr Pusey* was banned from preaching in Oxford. The Bishop's intention at Cuddesdon was to train High Church* clergy for the Oxford diocese – as long as they were not too high.

Newman's retreat at Littlemore was built just down the hill, between Cuddesdon and Oxford proper. Wilberforce's spies, other dons who were self-appointed guardians of the Truth, would watch the retreat from the bushes to see which undergraduates and theological students were paying visits to the great Papist.

A fox-hunting man, physically energetic in the manner of Gladstone,* whose Liberalism he always shared, Wilberforce frequently spoke in the House of Lords. His opinions were hard to tie down – hence the sobriquet, 'Soapy', but he was aggressive and personal in his attacks. It was he who incautiously jeered at Huxley* at the Natural History Museum.* This was at the debate sponsored by the British Association over Darwin's Theory of Evolution by Natural Selection. Wilberforce mocked Huxley for believing himself to have been descended from an ape, only to have the jibe backfire.

It was he who went on the attack against Broad Church Benjamin Jowett,* and attempted to revive the power of the Church Court, the Court of Arches, in order to try for heresy those Anglicans with whom he disagreed. Carroll was privy to the details of the row with Henry Parry Liddon,* his friend and mentor, whom Wilberforce dismissed as Vice-Principal of Cuddesdon.

It was the contention of Shane Leslie* that the Ugly Duchess is a parody of Wilberforce – 'who represents Episcopacy' – at his most imperious. The Duchess' emphasis on the moral of this and the moral of that, is particularly like Wilberforce, as is the Duchess' cruelty to her infant child. Wilberforce's culpable neglect of undergraduates who had religious doubts, to whom Liddon was willing to listen, was the talk of Oxford.

Wilberforce was contentious and difficult but had a finger on the pulse of the issues that drove mid-century society. However, he had little patience with their resolution. Because he pulled rank, he was unable to gain the support of able intellectuals with other points of view like Liddon, Huxley, Carroll and even Gladstone.

Carroll photographed Wilberforce in gaiters and frock-coat, jaw thrust out as if at the prow of a spiritual ship under sail. The photograph sits in the album* that Carroll gave to Alice, a few pages away from Carroll's portrait of

Huxley. Alice met the Bishop at Deanery functions and at Pen Morfa,* where he was a summer visitor.

Wilson, Edmund (1895–1972) An American literary critic who commented on Carroll in 1931 at the time of the celebration of the centennial of Lewis Carroll's birth. He compared the framing device Lewis Carroll used in *Alice*, her dream-state, with the device James Joyce used in his experimental novel, *Finnegan's Wake*, which contains a number of references to *Alice*. Wilson pointed out Joyce's satisfaction with Sigmund Freud's (1856–1939) suggestion that people invent 'portmanteau words' (a preoccupation of Carroll's) when they dream.

He suggested that Joyce exploited this by making such words the language in which he couched his least comprehensible novel; but that in this case, the device lacked an anchor in everyday English. Wilson noted that when dreaming, the mind uses language:

> ... more like the looking-glass language of Jabberwocky than anything resembling ordinary speech. Joyce's attempts to write the language of dreams have a good deal in common with those of Lewis Carroll; but the difference between this new novel (*Finnegan's Wake*) and the 'Alice' books is that, whereas in the 'Alice' books it is the author who is supposed to be telling in straight English the adventures which his heroine thinks she is having, and the literary language peculiar to dreams appears only in a poem which she reads, in Joyce's book he is plunging us directly into the consciousness of the dreamer itself, which is presented ... entirely in the *Jabberwocky* language.

Mysteriously, Alice felt that she almost understood when she thought about the meaning of Jabberwocky* words as she dreamt. Lewis Carroll's experimental writing in *Alice* remained, for Wilson, the touchstone of English literary innovation.

Wine Curator, Christ Church Carroll drank sherry at lunch, or what he considered lunch – usually no more than a dry biscuit. The only wine joke in *Alice* occurred when the Hare* offered her wine that did not exist at the Mad Tea-Party,* a party full of 'bread-and-butter'* jokes. It was as a result of the Bread-and-Butter Row at Christ Church* that the Fellows of the Senior Common Room were put in charge of their own cellar, an elected office which Carroll held from 8 December 1882 to 4 March 1892, in spite of two serious warnings that he was about to resign.

Carroll's records as Curator of Common Room, held in the Christ Church archives, include his wine lists and show the enviable quantities of

Chateau Margaux and vintage Champagne the Fellows put away. What he lacked in interest in the mystiques of wine-tasting, Carroll made up for in meticulous attention to cellaring, in the purchase of thermometers, and in a system of pricing that was scrupulous in the fairness of the minute rebates he awarded his fellow dons each time he made a mistake.

Woolf, Virginia (1882–1941) As an author, Virginia Woolf possibly owed a large debt to Lewis Carroll's literary ideas. Her father was Leslie Stephen (1832–1904) who, unlike Carroll, rejected the cloth entirely and gave up his Cambridge* career because of the necessity of ordination. Leslie Stephen freed his daughters from the constraints of the clerical morality that Carroll espoused. Carroll, however, freed them in another way. It has been argued by Juliet Dusinberre in *Alice to the Lighthouse: Children's Books and Radical Experiments in Art* (1987) that:

> Lewis Carroll had little inkling of the irreverent generation which the 'Alice' books would usher in for reasons which reached far beyond, but in which their overturning authority was central.

The title of the relevant chapter is 'Virginia Woolf and the Irreverent Generation' and her argument about the liberating influence of Carroll is cogent. (See also Critics.*)

Woolf herself, through her mother, a relative of Julia Margaret Cameron,* recorded Cameron taking a milk cow in the hold of the ship when she went back to India. She, like Evelyn Waugh,* reviewed the Nonesuch edition of Carroll's collected works during the centennial of his birth. The piece was short but insightful. Woolf's view was that 'reading Carroll, you become a child again' because he had never ceased to be one. For reasons that are not understood, Woolf suggested that Carroll's childhood 'lodged in him whole and entire. He could not disperse it'. This is how, in her view, he was able to identify so closely with Alice's perception of the world about her, and to enable adults to do so as well.

X, Y and Z are for ...

X-penditure   Carroll believed that the reforming Dean of Christ Church,* Alice's father, should release part of his archaic powers as financial manager of Christ Church because he was unequal to the task. He published a squib on the subject, called *Examination Statute*, in which each new line starts with a fresh letter of the alphabet*. 'X' is for 'X-penditure', at Oxford in 1864 said by Carroll to have 'grown quite gigantic' due to the overspend on the Natural History Museum.* This was eroding the surpluses built up from the University Press's best-sellers, *The Bible*, and Clarendon's *History of the [English] Rebellion*.

Carroll was as economical about 'X-penditure' as it was possible for a don whose pastimes were photography and the theatre to be, having been brought up by his father in such a tradition (see also Charles Lutwidge Dodgson*). In 1855, as a young don on the Bachelor's Table in Christ Church Hall, Carroll noted a box of letters:

> The box belonging to the Bachelors' table was brought to me as 'caterer'. I shall have to manage the accounts and order the dinners henceforward; the books go back as far as 1812, and I find a long period in my father's hand.

So began Carroll's involvement with catering and catering reform at Christ Church, which culminated in the post of the Curator of the Common Room (see also Wine Curator*). His commitments to the college buttery from a young age are reflected in numerous sparkling catering jokes in *Alice*.

Yonge, Charlotte Mary (1823–1901)   Yonge spent her life in Otterbourne, Hampshire, where she is buried and where her father, William, was a churchwarden. She was a plain woman with a receding chin and a prominent Adam's apple; she did not marry. She was a prolific author of fiction for adults and children and wrote some 160 titles in all. Carroll met her once at a luncheon given for her by Professor Bartholomew Price, the mathematics professor nicknamed 'The Bat'.* On the day after they met, 4 May 1866 Alice's birthday), he took three photographs of her in his rooms at Christ Church.* She was delighted with the photographs and ordered three dozen copies. She was chaperoned, because Carroll was an unattached bachelor, by her mother, as was Christina Rossetti* when he called on her. Carroll was impressed by her books and had honoured her by sending her an inscribed copy of the 1866 edition of *Alice*.

Yonge was a follower of John Keble,* and from 1851 to 1898 edited *The Monthly Packet*. This girls' magazine was a lifeline to readers shut away in the country as the Dodgson* sisters were when Carroll edited *The Rectory Umbrella** for them. In spite of the occasional coal-mining disaster — of which topic Carroll did not approve — her serializations in *The Monthly Packet* provided such girls with acceptable reading matter. Carroll contributed word-games, the 'Knots' he collected in *A Tangled Tale* (1885), and through the correspondence that followed made a host of new 'young-lady-friends'.

Carroll sent Yonge reissues of *Mischmasch*, the magazine he put together with his family, and also sent her the complicated game of 'Lanrick'. He drew her attention to new methods of learning French and German and tried to persuade her to draw up a standard Shakespeare edition (Bowdlerized) on which girls could be examined to a high standard.

Carroll's gave Yonge's first book, *Scenes and Characters*, to Alice Liddell as a birthday present in 1863, together with his 'Croquet Castles'. It appears that Carroll could be contrary and clever at a safe distance from this benevolent and able Anglican lady author.

Zincography   On 22 December 1885, having re-lettered the end of the manuscript of *Under Ground* with the words – 'and the happy summer days' – and cut Alice Liddell's photograph out to preserve her anonymity, Lewis Carroll published 5000 copies of the facsimile of the Deanery manuscript of *Alice's Adventures Under Ground*.* He now sought a wider public for the *Alice* story as he originally wrote and illustrated it.

So that the manuscript could be reproduced, Alice Liddell,* by now Hargreaves, sent it to Carroll. Ninety-two pages were to be originated by the new reproductive process known as zincography, which involved photographing each page. This venture into a process new to him led to a series of misadventures which the professionalism of John Tenniel,* and of the Dalziels as wood engravers had spared him during work on *Wonderland* and *Looking-Glass*.

Carroll would not work with the first zincographer because he refused to let Carroll supervise the turning of the pages while the manuscript was being photographed. Another man was found, Mr Noad, who was willing to let Carroll turn the pages in his former photographic studio at Christ Church,* but as he was in a small way of business, he required to be paid in advance for *all* the zinc blocks.

Mr Noad produced a 'first rate set of negatives' in July 1885 and some 72 of the 92 pages of the blocks were delivered. In the meantime, on 18 October, Carroll returned the manuscript by registered post to Mrs Liddell at the Deanery, for Alice's sisters to return to her on their next visit to Hampshire. Alice forgot to acknowledge that she had the precious manuscript back, but there were far more serious worries ahead.

Mr Noad was in financial difficulties and went into hiding from his creditors, who included Lewis Carroll. However in April, he delivered eight more blocks of the zincographs to Macmillan,* and then once more disappeared.

Carroll took advice and was told by a solicitor, who managed to locate the elusive Mr Noad, that he would have to take out a summons, which he did. It was only the threat of arrest which finally persuaded Mr Noad to produce the missing negatives – the blocks had not been made but Carroll quickly arranged for that and all was well. Carroll wrote to Alice that he had as many problems 'above ground' as she had had below it. She did not respond.

Zoomorph   Representations of people as animals are zoomorphs. John Tenniel* turned politicians, kings and emperors into cavorting ungulates and snarling carnivores, and Disraeli* from an Ape to an Angel. It must in part have been Tenniel's zoomorphs which led Carroll to become so dependent on him for the *Alice* illustrations. Tenniel's zoomorphs include the egg-eccentric Humpty Dumpty,* self-satisfied high on his wall; the toothy, untidy Jabberwock;* the Sheep Shop-keeper and the Frog Footmen. All are endowed with an animal vitality that Ruskin* admired – the energy that springs out of Tenniel's weekly *Punch** 'big-cuts' which he continued to deliver punctually as he worked on *Alice*.

Certain of Tenniel's political cartoons are recognizable in *Alice*, notably the full face and profile of William Makepeace Thackeray* in the profile and full face of the White King* and Queen; of Cardinal Manning* in the face, form and manner of the Red Queen;* of the younger Disraeli* up a slippery pole, in this case the White Rabbit's chimney vent, as Bill the Lizard* and, later, in the railway carriage* wearing a strange hat; and of Tenniel's histrionic, handsome self as the White Knight.*

Tenniel's zoomorphs were close to what Carroll had in mind when he created his characters. From the White Rabbit* with a pocket watch which opens *Wonderland* to the Red Queen-Black Kitten at the end of *Looking-Glass*, zoomorphs most truly characterize *Alice* as a work of satire.

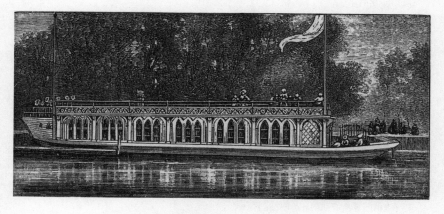

THE UNIVERSITY BARGE

Select Bibliography

Abbott, Evelyn and Campbell, Lewis, *The Life and Letters of Benjamin Jowett, MA, Master of Balliol College, Oxford*, 2 volumes, E. P. Dutton, New York, 1897.

Acland, H. W., *Memoir of the Cholera at Oxford in the year 1854 ...* London, 1856.

Acland, H. W., *Notes on Drainage with especial reference to the Sewers and Swamps of the Upper Thames*, London, 1857.

Almansi, Guido, ed., *Le Bambini di Carroll* which was a limited edition containing comments by, among others, Helmut Gernsheim. It was issued in Italian, French and English, 3000 copies of each, published in Parma by Franco Maria Ricci n.d.

Atlay, J. B., *Sir Henry Wentworth Acland, Bart. KCB, FRS, Regius Professor of Medicine in the University of Oxford: A Memoir*, Smith, Elder & Co, London, 1903.

Batey, Mavis, *Alice's Adventures in Oxford*, Pitkin Pictorial, 1980.

Batey, Mavis, *The Adventures of Alice: the Story behind the Stories Lewis Carroll told*, Macmillan, London 1991.

Bill, E. G. W. and Mason, J. F. A., *Christ Church and Reform, 1850–67*, Clarendon Press, Oxford, 1970.

Blake, Kathleen, *Play, Games and Sport: The Literary Works of Lewis Carroll*, Cornell University Press, London and Ithaca, New York, 1974.

Blake, Robert, *Disraeli*, St Martin's Press, New York, 1966.

Bowman, Isa (and others), *The Story of Lewis Carroll Told for Young People*, J. M. Dent, London, 1899.

Burd, Van Akin, *Winnington Letters: John Ruskin's Correspondence with Margaret Alexis Bell and the Children at Winnington Hall*, edited by Van Akin Burd, Belknap Press, Harvard, 1969.

Burd, Van Akin, *John Ruskin and Rose La Touche: Her unpublished diaries of 1861 and 1867*, Clarendon Press, Oxford, 1979.

Burne-Jones, Georgiana, *Memorials of Edward Burne-Jones*, 2 volumes, Macmillan, New York, 1904.

Caine, Hal, *Recollections of Rossetti*, Cassell, London 1928, reissued with an introduction by Jan Marsh, Century, 1990.

Carpenter, Humphrey and Pritchard, Marie, *The Oxford Companion to Children's Literature*, Oxford University Press, 1984.

Carpenter, Humphrey, *Secret Gardens: A Study of the Golden Age of Children's Literature*, Allen & Unwin, London, 1985.

Carroll, Cross-References:

Criticism   see Gray; Kincaid and Guiliano; Parisot; Phillips.

Diaries   see Green; McDermott; Wakeling.

Letters   see Cohen; Hatch.

Pamphlets   see Dodgson & Wakeling.

Papers   *Jabberwocky: The Journal of the Lewis Carroll Society*, edited by Selwyn Goodacre and others. Ongoing papers about Lewis Carroll's life and works.

Photographs   see Cohen; Gernsheim; Guiliano.

Carroll, Works: *The Complete Works of Lewis Carroll*, Nonesuch Press, introduction by Alexander Woollcott (1939–) not complete, but extensive. The Nonesuch edition of Carroll's works was originally published in 1939 by Random House in the USA and the Nonesuch Press in England. It was based on *The Complete Works of Lewis Carroll* published by the Modern Library in New York in 1936. Various reprints and reissues have been made.

Carroll, Works: *The Wasp in A Wig*, intro by Martin Gardner, Clarkson Potter, New York 1977.

Carruthers, Clive Harcourt, trans., *Alicia in Terra Mirabili*, Macmillan, London, 1964.

Cassell's Book of Indoor Amusements, Card Games, and Fireside Fun, Cassell, London, originally published in 1881, facsimile edition 1973.

Cecil, Lady Gwendolyn, *The Life of Robert, Marquis of Salisbury*, 2 volumes, 1921.

Chadwick, Owen, 'Newman', in *Past Masters*, Oxford University Press, 1984.

Chitty, Lady Susan, *The Beast and the Monk: A Life of Charles Kingsley*, Mason Charter, New York, 1974.

Clark, Anne, *The Real Alice*, Michael Joseph, London & Schocken, New York, 1981.

Clark, Anne, *Lewis Carroll: A Biography*, Dent, London & Schocken, New York, 1979.

Clark, Ronald W., *The Huxleys*, Heinemann, London, 1968.

Cohen, Morton N., *Lewis Carroll at Christ Church*, introductory note by Morton M. Cohen, reproduces some of the Christ Church Album photographs, National Portrait Gallery, 1974.

Cohen, Morton N., *Lewis Carroll, Photographer of Children: Four Nude Studies*, pamphlet, Clarkson Potter, New York, 1978.

Cohen, Morton N., ed., *The Letters of Lewis Carroll*, 2 volumes, Oxford University Press, 1979.

Cohen, Morton N. and Gandolfo, Anita, eds, *Lewis Carroll and the House of Macmillan,* Cambridge University Press, 1987.

Cohen, Morton N. *Lewis Carroll: a Biography*, Macmillan, London & Knopf, New York, 1995.

Cohen, Morton N. ed., *The Russian Journal II: a Record Kept by Henry Parry Liddon of a Tour Taken with C. L. Dodgson in the Summer of 1867*, 1979.

Collingwood, Stuart Dodgson, *The Life and Letters of Lewis Carroll (Rev. C. L. Dodgson)*, T. Fisher Unwin, London, 1898.

Columbia University, *Catalogue of an Exhibition to Commemorate the One Hundredth Anniversary of the Birth of Lewis Carroll*, Columbia University Press, 1932.

Colvin, Howard, *Unbuilt Oxford*, Yale, 1983.

Curtin, Michael, *Propriety and Position: A Study in Victorian Manners*, Garland, London & New York, 1987.

Darwin, Charles, *Journal of Researches into the Geology and Natural History of the Various Countries Visited by HMS Beagle*, and with Fitzroy, Captain Robert, *Narrative of the Surveying Voyages of HMS Adventure and Beagle and the Beagle's Circumnavigation of the Globe*, Henry Colburn, London, 1839.

Davies, Rev J. Llewellyn, ed., *The Working Men's College, 1854–1904*, Macmillan, London, 1904.

de la Mare, Walter, *Lewis Carroll*, Faber, London, 1932. Reprinted and revised from *The Eighteen-Eighties* which was edited by Walter de la Mare, Cambridge, 1930.

de Maré, Eric, *The Victorian Woodblock Illustrators*, Gordon Fraser, London, 1980.

Desmond, Adrian and Moore, James, *Darwin*, Michael Joseph, London, 1991.

Dodgson, C. L., *The Principles of Parliamentary Representation*, London: Harrison and Sons, 1885.

Dusinberre, Juliet, *Alice to the Lighthouse; Children's Books and Radical Experiments in Art*, Macmillan, 1987.

Ellis, S. M., *Henry Kingsley: Towards a Vindication, 1830–1876*, Grant Richards, London, 1931.

Elwyn Jones, J. and Gladstone J. F., *The Red King's Dream*, Cape, London, 1995.

Empson, William, 'The Child as Swain' in *Some Versions of the Pastoral*, Chatto and Windus, London, 1935.

Engen, Rodney, *Sir John Tenniel: Alice's White Knight*, Scolar Press, Aldershot, 1991.

English Language Notes. This journal produced by the University of Colorado devoted its December 1982 edition to Carroll on the 150th anniversary of his birth. The edition includes articles by Nina Auerbach, Edward Guiliano, James R. Kincaid and Joyce Carol Oates (see Kincaid, J. R. below).

Faber, Geoffrey, *Jowett: A Portrait with a Background*, Faber, London, 1957.

Feiling, Keith, *In Christ Church Hall*, Macmillan, London, 1960. Includes essays on Pusey and Ruskin.

Fisher, John, *The Magic of Lewis Carroll*, Penguin, London, 1973.

FitzGerald, Edward, *Letters of Edward FitzGerald*, edited by J. M. Cohen, Illinois University Press, 1960.

Fordyce, Rachael, *Lewis Carroll: A Reference Guide*, published by Hall & Co with Macmillan in Boston and London, 1992.

Fordyce, Rachael and Marello, Carla, *Semiotics and Linguistics in Alice's Words*, Proceedings of a Workshop entitled 'La Linguistica di Alice' organized in Urbino in July 1990. The book was published by de Gruyer, Berlin & New York in 1994 as part of the series *Research in Text Theory*. The participants were American and European. Two bibliographical studies are included, one by Fordyce, the other (of mainly European items) by Maurizio del Ninno.

Fuller, Hester Thackeray, *Three Freshwater Friends*, 1933, pamphlet, reprinted by Hunnyhill Publications, Isle of Wight, 1992 for Cameron, Tennyson and Watts on the Isle of Wight.

Furniss, Harry, *Confessions of a Caricaturist,* 2 volumes, 1901.

Gardner, Martin, *The Annotated Alice: Alice's Adventures in Wonderland & Through the Looking-Glass*, Clarkson Potter, New York, 1960.

Gardner, Martin, *More Annotated Alice*, Random House, New York, 1990.

Gardner, Martin, *The Universe in a Handkerchief*, St Martin's Press, New York, 1996.

Gattégno, Jean, *Lewis Carroll: Une Vie*, Editions de Seuil, Paris, 1974. Translated by Rosemary Sneed as *Lewis Carroll: Fragments of a Looking-Glass*, published by Crowell, New York, 1976.

Gernsheim, Helmut, *Lewis Carroll: Photographer*, originally published in 1949 by Max Parrish, London, expanded in 1969, Dover Books, New York.

Gernsheim, Helmut, *Julia Margaret Cameron: Her Life and Photographic Art*, Aperture Press, New York, 1987.

Gordon, Colin, *Beyond The Looking-Glass*, Hodder & Stoughton, London, 1982 (on the Liddell and Hargreaves families).

Grandville, J. J., *Scènes de la Vie Privée et Publique des Animaux*, 2 volumes, J. Hertzel et Paulin, Paris, 1842.

Grant Duff, Right Hon Sir Mountstuart E., *Out of the Past: Some Biographical Essays*, 2 volumes, John Murray, 1903.

Graves, Charles L., *Life and Letters of Alexander Macmillan*, Macmillan, London, 1910.

Gray, Donald J., ed., *Alice in Wonderland: Lewis Carroll/ Alice's Adventures in Wonderland, Through the Looking Glass, The Hunting of the Snark: Backgrounds, Essays in Criticism*, Norton Critical Edition series, 1971. (Note: these include the hard-to-find articles by William Empson, Shane Leslie and Alice herself, together with essays or sections of essays by Virginia Woolf, W. H. Auden, Walter de la Mare and others.)

Green, Roger Lancelyn, *Tellers of Tales*, Ward, Leicester, England, 1946.

Green, Roger Lancelyn, ed., *The Diaries of Lewis Carroll*, 2 volumes, Cassell, London, 1953, reprinted by the Greenwood Press, Westport, Connecticut, in 1971.

Green, Roger Lancelyn, *The Story of Lewis Carroll*, The Bodley Head, London, 1949.

Greenacre, Phyllis, *Swift and Carroll; a Psychoanalytic Study of Two Lives*, International Universities Press, New York, 1995.

Guiliano, Edward, ed., *Lewis Carroll Observed: A Collection of Unpublished Photographs, Drawings, Poetry and New Essays*, Clarkson Potter, New York, 1976.

Guiliano, Edward: *Lewis Carroll: An Annotated International Bibliography, 1960–1977*, Harvester Press, Sussex, 1981 and University Press of Virginia, 1980.

Hancher, Michael, *The Tenniel Illustrations to the 'Alice' Books*, Macmillan, 1986.

Hare, A. J. C., *Memorials of A Quiet Life*, Strahan, New York, 1873.

Hare, Augustus and Julius C., *Guesses at the Truth by Two Brothers*, Ticknor & Field, Boston, 1865 edition.

Hargreaves, Alice, edited by Caryl Hargreaves, ... *Recollections of Carrollian Days* ..., Cornhill Magazine, July 1932. (See also Gray, Donald J.)

Hatch, Evelyn M., ed., *A Selection from the Letters of Lewis Carroll to His Child Friends*, Macmillan, London, 1933, reprinted by Folcroft Library Editions, Pennsylvania in 1973.

Heath, Peter, ed., *The Philosopher's Alice: Alice's Adventures in Wonderland and Through the Looking-Glass*, St Martin's Press, New York & Academy Press, London, 1974.

Hinton, Brian, *Immortal Faces: Julia Margaret Cameron on the Isle of Wight*, Isle of Wight County Press, 1992.

Hiscock, W. G., *A Christ Church Miscellany*, 1946 (Quartercentenary of Christ Church's foundation by Henry VIII), printed for the author by the Oxford University Press, Oxford.

Hodnett, Edward, *Image and Text: Studies in the Illustration of English Literature*, Scolar Press, London, 1982.

Hudson, Derek, *Lewis Carroll*, Constable, London, 1954. An illustrated 2nd edition was published by Constable in 1976.

Huxley, T. H., *Man's Place in Nature and Other Anthropological Essays*, Macmillan, London, 1894.

Huxley, Francis, *The Raven and the Writing Desk*, Harper & Row, New York, 1976.

Jowett, Benjamin, ed., *Essays and Reviews: Recent Inquiries in Theology by Eminent English Churchmen*, Longman, London, 1860.

Ker, Ian, *John Henry Newman: A Biography*, Oxford University Press, 1988.

Kincaid, J. R. and Guiliano, E., eds, *Soaring with the Dodo: Essays on Lewis Carroll's Life and Art*, English Language Notes, December 1982.

Kincaid, James R., *Child-loving; the Erotic Child and Victorian Culture*, Routledge, London, 1992.

Kingsley, *Charles Kingsley: His Letters and Memories of His Life* 'edited by his wife', viz by Fanny Kingsley, 2 volumes, Kegan Paul, London, 1877.

Kingsley, Charles, *Cheap Clothes and Nasty*, 1850, reprinted in *Prose Masterpieces from Modern Essayists*, Putnam, New York, 1893.

Kingsley, Charles, *The Water-Babies*, Macmillan, 1863.

Kingsley, Henry, *Tales of Old Travel Re-Narrated* ..., 5th edition, Macmillan, London, 1876.

Kitchin, G. W., *Ruskin in Oxford and Other Studies*, John Murray, 1904.

Knox, Ronald A., *Let Don's Delight, being Variations on a theme in an Oxford Common-Room*, Sheed & Ward, London, 1939.

Knox, Ronald A., *Literary Distractions*, Sheed & Ward, London and New York, 1958.

Laurençin, Marie, illustrator, and Marchesseau, Daniel, *Marie Laurençin: Catalogue Raisonné de l'Oeuvre Gravé*, with collaboration Tatsuji Ohmori, Kyuryudo, Japan, 1981.

Lehmann, John F., *Lewis Carroll and the Spirit of Nonsense*, Nottingham University Press, 1972.

Lennon, Florence Becker, *Victoria Through the Looking-Glass; the Life of Lewis Carroll*, Simon Schuster, New York, 1945.

Leslie, Shane, *Henry Edward Manning: His Life and Labours*, London, 1921.

Leslie, Sir Shane, 'Lewis Carroll and the Oxford Movement', in *The London Mercury*, vol 28, 1934. (See also Phillips, Roger.)

Liddon, H. P., *Life and Letters of Henry Parry Liddon DD, DCL, LLD, Canon of St. Paul's Cathedral, and Sometime Ireland Professor of Exegesis in the University of Oxford*, by John Octavius Johnson, MA, Longmans, London, 1904.

Lovett, Charles C., *Alice on Stage: A History of Early Theatrical Productions of 'Alice in Wonderland' Together with A Checklist of Dramatic Adaptations of Charles Dodgson's Works*, Meckler, Westport, Connecticut, and London, 1990.

Lovett, Charles C., ed., *Proceedings of the Second International Lewis Carroll Conference, Winston Salem, North Carolina*, published by the Lewis Carroll Society of North America, New York, 1994.

McDermott, John Francis, ed., *The Russian Journal and Other Selections from the Works of Lewis Carroll*, E. P. Dutton, New York, 1935.

MacDonald, Greville, *George MacDonald and His Wife*, George Allen and Unwin, London, 1924.

Madan, Falconer, *Oxford Outside the Guide Books*, Blackwell, Oxford, 1923.

Madan, Falconer, ed., *The Lewis Carroll Centenary in London including a Catalogue of the Exhibition with Notes; an Essay on Dodgson's Illustrators by Harold Hartley ...*, Bumpus, London, 1932.

Magnall, Richmall, *Historical and Miscellaneous Questions for the Use of Young People with a Selection of British and General Biography*, 'A New Edition', London, 1824.

Magnus, Sir Philip, *King Edward VII*, John Murray, London, 1964.

Manning, Henry Edward, *The Unity of the Church*, 2nd edition, John Murray, 1845.

Maurice, Frederick, ed., *The Life and Correspondence of Frederick Denison Maurice*, 2 volumes, Scribners, New York, 1884.

Mespoulet, Marguerite, *Creators of Wonderland*, Rydall Press, Santa Fé, New Mexico, 1935. (Gifted to Pierpoint Morgan library in 1938, subsequent to publication.)

Mitford, Nancy, ed., *The Stanleys of Alderly: Their Letters between the Years 1851–1865*, Hamish Hamilton, re-issued 1968.

Moser, Barry, illustrator, *Alice's Adventures in Wonderland and Through the Looking-Glass and What Alice Saw There*, Preface by James R. Kincaid, Pennyroyal Press, Northampton, Massachusetts, 1982.

Norman, Edward, *The Victorian Christian Socialists*, Cambridge University Press, 1987.

Oman, Sir Charles, *Memories of Victorian Oxford*, Methuen, London, 1941.

Ovenden, Graham, *The Illustrators of Alice in Wonderland and Through the Looking-Glass* (with an Introduction by John Davis), Academy Editions, London, 1972.

Owen, Rev Richard, *The Life of Richard Owen by his Grandson*, 2 volumes, John Murray, 1894.

Papy, Jacques, trans. *Alice au Pays des Merveilles*, Jean-Jacques Pauvert, Paris, 1961.

Parisot, Henri, ed., *Lewis Carroll*, an important selection of essays about Carroll's work, both French, and English translated into French, together with some Carroll fragments that are very hard to find in French, Éditions de l'Herne, 1971.

Peters, Cuthbert, *Thackeray's Universe: Shifting Worlds of Imagination and Reality*, Oxford University Press, New York, 1987.

Phillips, Robert, ed., *Aspects of Alice: Lewis Carroll's Dreamchild as seen through the Critics' Looking-Glasses, 1865–1971*, Vanguard Press, New York, 1971; Gollancz, London, 1972. (Contains many important papers.)

Prest, John, ed., *The Illustrated History of Oxford University*, Oxford University Press, Oxford & New York, 1993. In particular chapters on 'The University's Contribution to Religion' by Geoffry Rowell and 'The University's Contribution to the Life Sciences and Medicine' by Paul Weindling.

Prothero, R. E. (Lord Ernle), *Life and Letters of Dean Stanley*, John Murray, 1894.

Pudney, John, *Lewis Carroll and his World*, London: Thames & Hudson, 1976.

Pusey, E. B., *First Letter to the Very Rev. J. H. Newman in Explanation chiefly in regard to the Reverential Love due to the Ever-Blessed Theotokos and the Doctrine of Her Immaculate Conception*, by the Rev E. B. Pusey, Rivingtons, London, 1869.

Pusey, E. B., *Selections from the Writings of Edward Bouverie Pusey, D.D.*, Rivingtons, London, 1883.

Raeper, William, *George MacDonald*, Lion Publishing, Tring, England, & Batavia, Illinois, 1987.

Raven, Charles E., *Christian Socialism, 1848–1854*, Macmillan, London, 1920.

Reed, (Herbert) Langford, *The Life of Lewis Carroll*, London: W. & G. Foyle Ltd, 1932.

Rimmer, Alfred, *Pleasant Spots Around Oxford*, Cassell, Petter & Galpin, London, *c.* 1860.

Ruskin, *The Works of John Ruskin*, Library Edition, 39 Volumes, edited by E. T. Cook and Alexander Wedderburn, George Allen, London, 1903–12.

Schaefer, David and Maxine, *The Tale of the Mouse's Tail*, Mica, 1995, Silver Spring, Maryland.

Sinclair, Catherine, *Holiday House*, London, 1839, 1885, 1908 (retold by Olive Allen).

Steadman, Ralph, illustrator, *The Complete Alice and The Hunting of the Snark*, Jonathan Cape, London, 1986.

Stern, Jeffry, ed., *Lewis Carroll's Library: A facsimile edition of the catalogue of the auction sale following C. L. Dodgson's death in 1898, with facsimiles of three subsequent booksellers' catalogues offering books from Dodgson's library*, published by the Lewis Carroll Society of North America, distributed by the University of Virginia Press, Carroll Studies no. 5, 1981.

Strachey, Lytton, *Queen Victoria*, Harcourt Brace, London, 1921.

Strachey, Lytton, *Eminent Victorians* (includes essays on Manning and Dr Arnold of Rugby), re-issued by Chatto and Windus, London, 1966.

Taylor, Alexander, *The White Knight*, Oliver & Boyd, Edinburgh, 1952.

Taylor, Una, *Guests and Memories: Annals of a Seaside Villa*, Oxford University Press, 1924.

Tenniel's Alice: Drawings by Sir John Tenniel for Alice's Adventures in Wonderland and Through the Looking-Glass, pamphlet, Harvard/ Metropolitan Museum of Art, 1978.

Tennyson, Hallam, *Alfred Lord Tennyson: A Memoir by His Son*, 2 volumes, Macmillan, London, 1897.

Tennyson, *The Farringford Journal of Emily Tennyson, 1853–1864* edited by Richard J. Hutchings and Brian Hinton, Isle of Wight County Press, 1986.

Terry, Ellen, *Ellen Terry's Memoirs with Preface, Note and Additional Biographical Chapters by Edith Craig and Christoper St John*, Gollancz, London, 1933. Originally published in 1908 as *The Story of My Life*.

Thackeray, *The Letters of William Makepeace Thackeray* edited by Gordon N. Ray, Harvard University Press, 1946.

Thoiron, Philippe, and Pavé, Alain, *Index et Concordance pour 'Alice's Adventures in Wonderland' de Lewis Carroll*, Champion-Slatkine, Paris and Geneva, 1989.

Thompson, Rev Henry L., *Henry George Liddell, D.D.: A Memoir*, John Murray, 1899.

Tuckwell, Rev W., *Reminiscences of Oxford*, Smith and Elder, London, 1907.

Vance, Norman, *The Sinews of the Spirit: The Ideal of Christian Manliness in Victorian Life and Thought*, Cambridge University Press, 1985.

Victoria Regina, *Letters of Queen Victoria.*, edited by Arthur C. Benson and Viscount Esher, 3 volumes, John Murray, 1907.

Vidler, Alec, *F. D. Maurice and Company: Nineteenth Century Studies*, SCM Press, London, 1966.

Wakeling, Edward, ed., *Lewis Carroll's Games and Puzzles*, Dover, New York, 1992.

Wakeling, Edward, ed., *The Pamphlets of Lewis Carroll*: Volume I, The Oxford Pamphlets, University of Virginia Press, 1993.

Wakeling, Edward, ed., *The Private Journals of Charles Lutwidge Dodgson*, Volume I, 1993; Volume II, 1994; Volume III, 1995; other volumes in progress. This publication by the Lewis Carroll Society marks the beginning of the project to make available in printed form an unexpurgated version of the manuscript diaries.

Waugh, Evelyn, *The Life of the Right Reverend Ronald Knox, Fellow of Trinity College, Oxford and pronotary Apostolic to His Holiness Pope Pius XII, compiled from original sources*, Chapman and Hall, 1959.

Wilberforce, *Life of the Right Reverend Samuel Wilberforce, DD ... with Selections from His Diaries and Correspondence*, by A. R. Ashwell, 3 volumes, John Murray, 1880.

Williams, S. H. and Madan, Falconer, *A Handbook of the Literature of the Rev C. L. Dodgson (Lewis Carroll)*, London, 1931.

Williams, S. H., *A Bibliography of the Writings of Lewis Carroll*, London, 1924.

Williams, S. H., Madan, Falconer, and Green, Roger Lancelyn, *The Lewis Carroll Handbook*, London, 1979.

Williams, S. H., Madan, Falconer, Green, Roger Lancelyn and Crutch, Denis, *The Lewis Carroll Handbook*, London, 1962.

Wilson, Edmund, *The Shores of Light: A Literary Chronicle of the Twenties and Thirties*, W. H. Allen, London, 1952.

Wimperley, Arthur, *Lewis Carroll and Cheshire*, pamphlet, Overcoat Publications, Cheshire, 1991.

Woolf, Edwin, and Fleming, John F., *Rosenbach*, World Publishing Company, Cleveland, Ohio & New York, 1960.

Zimmermann, Antonie, trans. *Alice's Abenteuer im Wunderland*, by Lewis Carroll, Leipzig: Johann Friedrich Hartknoch, 1869.

Index of Article Titles

Index of Names

Page numbers in **bold** refer to article titles. 'Alice' the character and Lewis Carroll are not included in this index as they are mentioned on almost every page. However Alice Liddell and Rev C. L. Dodgson are included wherever this name is used.